FRAGILE TRUTHS

TWENTY-FIVE YEARS OF SOCIOLOGY AND ANTHROPOLOGY IN CANADA

FRAGILE TRUTHS

TWENTY-FIVE YEARS OF SOCIOLOGY AND ANTHROPOLOGY IN CANADA

Edited by

William K. Carroll
University of Victoria

Linda Christiansen-Ruffman
Saint Mary's University

Raymond F. Currie
The University of Manitoba

Deborah Harrison
Brock University

Carleton University Press
Ottawa, Canada
1992

ISBN 0-88629-169-0 (paperback)
ISBN 0-88629-168-2 (casebound)

Printed and bound in Canada

Canadian Cataloguing in Publication Data
Main entry under title:
Fragile Truths

(Carleton library series ; 173)
Includes bibliographical references.
ISBN 0-88629-168-2 (bound) - ISBN 0-88629-169-0 (pbk.)

  1. Sociology--Canada.   2. Anthropology--Canada.
I. Carroll, William K.   II. Series.

HM22.C3F72 1992   301'.0971   C92-090140-9
               73274

Distributed by: Oxford University Press Canada
                    70 Wynford Drive
                    Don Mills, Ontario
                    Canada. M3C 1J9
                    (416) 441-2941

Cover design: Y Graphic Design

Acknowledgements

Carleton University Press gratefully acknowledges the support extended
to its publishing programme by the Canada Council and the Ontario
Arts Council.

This book has been published with the help of a grant from the Faculty
of Arts and Social Sciences of Carleton University.

CONTENTS

Part Three
The Academic Milieu

Part Four
Sociology, Anthropology and Social Change

Part Five
Selected Bibliography

Part Six

ACKNOWLEDGEMENTS

We wish to thank *Society/Société* for permission to reprint part of "The Evolution of the CSAA" by Frank Jones, and "The Two Solitudes between Canadian Sociologists" by Guy Rocher (which originally appeared as "Les deux solitudes chez les sociologues canadiens").

We are grateful to the following administrators, who provided funds to assist with publication costs: Susan Clark, Vice-President (Academic), and Lewis Soroka, former Dean of Social Sciences, at Brock University; Marion Vaisey-Genser, former Associate Vice-President (Research) at the University of Manitoba; Michael J. Larsen, Dean of Arts, Saint Mary's University; and Samuel Scully, Vice-President Academic at the University of Victoria.

Michael Gnarowski, Steven Uriarte, and Anne Winship of Carleton University Press, Stephen Richer, C.U. Press's sociology editor, Janet Shorten, who copyedited the manuscript, and JoAnne McFarlan, who formatted the text, deserve our appreciation for their interest and encouragement, and for making the publication of this book a notably smooth and enjoyable process.

For assistance in preparing the manuscript, we wish to thank Larry Hurtado, Director, Institute for the Humanities, at the University of Manitoba, and his Assistant, Helga Dyck, who prepared the references, cleaned up the files, and put the whole package together.

We will always remember our contributors for their patience, their good humour and, last but not least, their tolerance of a final product that will inevitably be less than perfect. We are especially grateful to Alan Pomfret and Gary Rush, for pitching in at the last minute with information on, respectively, the Ontario Association of Sociology and Anthropology and the events at Simon Fraser University, which assisted us in completing our introduction.

Finally, we four would like to thank each other for a working relationship—forged across great distances mainly by electronic mail—that has been productive, efficient, and delightfully amiable.

William K. Carroll   Linda Christiansen-Ruffman
Raymond F. Currie   Deborah Harrison

INTRODUCTION

This volume arose out of our planning for the 25th annual meetings of the Canadian Sociology and Anthropology Association (CSAA), held at the University of Victoria in May 1990. As co-organizers, we wanted to provide an occasion for critical reflection upon the past twenty-five years of sociology and anthropology in Canada and for contemplation of the insights and achievements of our disciplines. As co-editors, we felt it important to capture a number of the general issues that have been preoccupying Canadian sociologists and anthropologists, recognizing that we were operating within the specific context of the early 1990s. Some of the papers chosen for this book were presented at four special sessions that formed the centrepiece of the 1990 meetings; others, delivered in regular sessions of the same meetings, touched on the issues that, for us, appeared to be most appropriate for inclusion in a general overview of the first twenty-five years of Canadian sociology and anthropology. Because almost all the papers were prepared specially for the 1990 meetings, and the authors supported the promise of this collection, we are pleased to note that virtually none of them has been published elsewhere, and that several have been written by younger members of the profession. These considerations give us cause to hope that this collection offers a glimpse into the preoccupations not only of our past and present, but also, perhaps, of our immediate future.

At their best—that is, when refined through careful social analysis—the themes of this book might be said to have attained the status of fragile truths. The truths that our disciplines offer are not fast-frozen and absolute; they are historical, interpretive, and contingent—as are the social and cultural realities of which our disciplines speak.

One of us remembers her ambivalence in 1963, as she encountered the reality of the stone-carved message over one of the doors to Victoria College at the University of Toronto: *The truth shall make you free.* A sociology undergraduate at the time, she wasn't sure that she wanted to endure the painful process that necessarily accompanies the shattering of one's reality when one achieves such freedoms. Yet she had also felt the intellectual excitement that comes with understanding the world anew, and had been challenged by "the sociological imagination."

What enabled our co-editor to really "see" those words was a course by Rex Lucas at the University of Toronto. Lucas was using Robert Merton's *Social Theory and Social Structure* as a text and a model of sociological analysis, and was helping his students to understand the socially organized nature of the world and the concepts of unanticipated consequences, functions, and structures. Lucas used the dominant sociological paradigm of the time to call into question the taken-for-granted realities of our everyday worlds. In the context of the day, the sociological truth he was teaching did not seem fragile, but profoundly powerful, even universal. Not only did Merton's text and Lucas's reading of it seem unshakeable, but in the eyes of an undergraduate the institutional setting itself—the departments of sociology and of anthropology at the University of Toronto—seemed solid and impermeable. One had no idea at the time that these disciplines were not yet established in Canada. One did not focus on the fact that sociology had only just achieved independent departmental status at the University of Toronto. It is only in retrospect, with an historical and comparative perspective, that we can fully recognize the fragility of truths and the multiple nature of realities. In the eyes of an undergraduate just beginning to analyze Canadian society, sociological truths and social structures in Canada seemed not to be fragile but to have incredible power; indeed, they possessed the quality of absoluteness.

It did not take long for the truth of structural functionalism to be challenged by and then supplanted by the truths of ethnomethodological and neo-Marxist perspectives and by the gradually evolving truths of feminist studies. It was not only that Lucas had used Merton as a role model. What had been profoundly powerful insights two years previously seemed tired, irrelevant, and hackneyed through the eyes of a Columbia University graduate student in the politically charged mid-1960s. But perhaps it has been most particularly in the post-positivist 1990s that we have been continually forced to recognize both the rhetorical power of sociological and anthropological discourses and the fragility of their truths.

There is another sense in which our truths—and all other truths—are fragile. In every field of human endeavour there is a continual process by which truth becomes reconstructed as people make history. The CSAA's decision to celebrate its twenty-fifth anniversary was itself part of an ongoing reconstructive process. That process was highlighted in the conference theme, "Taking Stock, Looking Ahead" and also in the plenary session on "The Role of the CSAA in the Development of Sociology and Anthropology," which was followed by a reception in honour of fourteen scholars whose outstanding contributions have shaped the development of our disciplines and our truths.[1] This book, too, is part of that celebration and critical reflection, and each of its co-editors played a major role in the CSAA 25th Anniversary meeting:

- Deborah Harrison organized three theme sessions on "Aspects of the Development of the Disciplines of Sociology and Anthropology," "Sociology and Social Policy," and "Forgotten Constituencies in the CSAA," at which several chapters in this volume were first presented;
- Raymond Currie served as Programme Chair for the conference and organized the plenary session mentioned above;
- Linda Christiansen-Ruffman served as CSAA President in 1989-90

and was thus centrally involved in conference preparations, in chairing the 25th Annual Business Meeting and award celebrations, and in co-editing with Raymond Currie a special 25th Anniversary issue of *Society/Société*;

• William Carroll was Chief Co-ordinator and Sociology Co-ordinator for the conference and constructed its programme.

A celebration of Canadian sociology and anthropology was essential because the sociological/anthropological community has to some extent been fractured by a legacy of controversies in its founding decades. There has been a need to rethink and reconstruct our pasts collectively, to recognize both the contributions to truth-making of those who have gone before us and the fragility of the truths that we have (re)constructed. The twenty-fifth anniversary of the CSAA was an occasion for this reflection. Yet, as Frank Jones's article on the early activities of sociologists and anthropologists within the Canadian Political Science Association (CPSA) indicates, a lot of work and a great deal of history preceded the founding of the CSAA, a history that has only begun to be adequately conceptualized and appreciated.

There was, in this sense, an arbitrariness to the way we titled our celebration. In retrospect, the "25th anniversary" could have been celebrated equally well as the 35th anniversary since the founding of the Anthropology and Sociology Chapter of the CPSA, or the 67th anniversary of the founding of Canada's first autonomous department of sociology at McGill. As some of us know from work with, on, and about feminist organizations, the really hard work is at the initiation, founding, creating, and organizing stages and is virtually never recognized. In our bureaucratically structured societies, such activities often fail to be acknowledged by contemporary definitions of historical truth and/or historical reality.

It is not surprising that in placing the CSAA's first twenty-five years at the centre we have unintentionally marginalized other highly relevant histories, such as that of *L'Association canadienne de sociologues et anthropologues de langue française*, whose 700 members form a community centred in Quebec with distinctive approaches to their disciplines.[2] Another part of the history of sociology and anthropology in Canada that is not adequately reflected in the chapters that follow is the history of the regional networks and associations. For example, the Western Anthropology and Sociology Association was founded in 1962, three years before the CSAA, and continues to hold annual meetings in western Canada and the north-western border states of the U.S.A. The Atlantic Association of Sociologists and Anthropologists has been meeting on an annual basis since 1966 (Christiansen-Ruffman, 1990). The Ontario Association of Sociology and Anthropology was founded in 1978. As Alan Pomfret tells us, at its inception the OASA had a broad vision that included not only the promotion of research and teaching but the professional recognition of sociologists and anthropologists who are employed outside academic institutions, and the application of sociological and anthropological knowledge to societal problems.[3] Thus, the national association has not been the only centre of community for sociologists and anthropologists nor, for some, even the most important one.

In honour of the 1990 twenty-fifth anniversary, and notwithstanding our various caveats, the group of essays in Part One of this book ("The Development of Sociology and Anthropology in Canada") reflects upon the development of our disciplines from the vantage point offered by the CSAA as a focal organization. The history is an unavoidably political one, traversed by issues that since the 1960s have been salient not only within the CSAA but throughout Canadian society—such as the questions of nation and gender.

The essays by John Hofley and Guy Rocher address the national question in two of the three predominant forms in which it has been posed since the 1970s in Canadian sociology.[4] Hofley discusses the Canadianization issue from the unique perspective of having been president of the Association through a particularly heated period, by reviewing how the issue has been dealt with in recent sociological literature, and by assessing how far we still have to go. Rocher describes with regret the process through which Québécois sociologists decided to go their separate ways in forming their own association.

In different ways, the essays by Margrit Eichler and Eleanor Maticka-Tyndale and Janice Drakich consider barriers that have marginalized women within the CSAA and the progress made toward greater gender justice within the disciplines. Eichler charts the uneven pattern of women's participation in CSAA offices, in annual conferences, and in the Association's official journals; she also considers the role that sociology and anthropology have played as disciplinary sites for the development of feminist thought. Maticka-Tyndale and Drakich recount the history of women's struggles within the CSAA to achieve a distinctive political voice in the Association, through formation of a Women's Caucus and the designation of a "Status of Women" spot on the Executive. Both these analyses emphasize the great amount of individual and collective effort that was needed to bring about a recognition of women and women's perspectives within Canadian sociology, but they also offer relatively hopeful diagnoses of the prospects for women and feminists in the CSAA to continue to enlarge the space within which their voices will carry.

Finally, Gordon Inglis provides a slightly whimsical account of the concerns that particularly occupied Canadian anthropologists in the early 1970s, and that culminated in the formation of the Canadian Ethnology Society (now the Canadian Anthropology Society) in 1973. Like Jones, Inglis makes reference in his reminiscences to the firing of eight social science faculty members at Simon Fraser University in 1969, a pivotal event in the history of the CSAA, which led the Association to take collective political action in the form of a seventeen-year boycott. As Gary Rush recalls in the appendix to this Introduction, the SFU case was "rife with contradiction, paradox, and irony"; it attests to the complex and unavoidable relationship between apparently learned issues and political struggle.

Taken together, these essays affirm that the fragility of social-scientific truth has its source not only in the epistemological and ontological problems that underlie paradigmatic differences, but also in the fragility of social relations themselves—those that are constitutive of disciplines and those that are constitutive of societies. This proposition seems to apply with particular force to the case of Canada. In the past twenty-five years, a number of dichotomies have become politicized sites for struggle around issues of autonomy, resource allocation, and the very nature of sociological/anthropological discourse. The most important ones have been:

- anglophone/francophone
- sociology/anthropology
- American/Canadian
- male/female

The essays by Rocher, Inglis, Hofley, Eichler, and Maticka-Tyndale and Drakich intimate that the first twenty-five years were marked by a fracturing of the unitary truths and hegemonic social relations around which our disciplines were initially formed. The dominant voices within the CSAA of 1965 were those of anglophone, male, American-trained sociologists, as they still may be today.

In the interim, however, the formation of separate associations by francophones and by anthropologists dissolved the hegemony of anglophones and sociologists as majority groups within a single association. In the process, the social relations embodied in the first two dichotomies were profoundly reorganized. With the new associations came a more dispersed pluralism and the lament (primarily by anglophone sociologists) for a more integrated community of scholars. The same fault lines can be traced in the composition of this book as a whole, which has little to offer from anthropologists and French-Canadian sociologists and, incidentally, nothing to offer from non-academics. These silences largely reflect the composition of CSAA meetings, which are dominated by anglophone Canadian sociologists who live out their careers within universities. There is no way in which these omissions can be justified, but we hope that their absence will speak eloquently to the reader about the current hegemonies within our organization.

The story behind the second pair of dichotomies—American/Canadian and male/female—has revolved less around the search for autonomy outside the CSAA than around the internal transformation of Canadian sociology and of the CSAA since the mid-1960s. Twenty-five years ago, the pre-eminence and universality of American positivism in sociological theory and methods was taken for granted among most Canadian sociologists, as was the appropriateness of recruiting American sociologists to staff the rapidly expanding programmes of that era. At the same time, the male voice and gaze were also deemed to have universal validity within Canadian sociology.

By this reference point, the sociology and anthropology of the 1990s are barely recognizable as the same disciplines. Feminist analyses, for example, are present in every section of this volume. Similarly, countless discussions in this book bear witness to the enormous influence of the Canadianization movement—the attempt to ground Canadian sociology and anthropology in the historical reality of Canada in order to counter the intellectual dominance of American sociology/anthropology that mirrors the American control of Canada in other spheres.

In pointing to this profound reorganization of the disciplines and reconstruction of their truths we do not mean to suggest that some kind of Procrustean unity has been (re)produced. Indeed, precisely because its truths have been so radically reconstructed, Canadian social science may be to some degree in a unique position—more able to recognize the fragility of sociological knowledge, and less prone to ethnocentrism and universalistic pretensions. One of the most significant daily practices of Canadian social science may be the continual realization that truths are always fragile because their construction as "truths" depends on contingent relationships of economic, political, cultural, racial, and gendered power—that every constructed "truth" has become so by virtue of concealing one or more layers of reality beneath it.

Canadian social scientists, in other words, seem to be special experts on relationships that are fragile for reasons of power, likely because of Canada's own fragile economic, political, and intellectual relationship with the United States. In the last twenty-five years, Canadian sociology, for example, has become especially noted for: (1) Political Economy, the relationship between power and property (cf. Marchak, 1985), initially (as in Harold Innis's work) applied to metropolis/hinterland relationships involving Canada as a whole and various regions of Canada, subsequently applied to a range of phenomena in Canadian society, including the mass media, education systems, domestic labour, paid labour, and race relations; (2) Feminist Studies, especially in political economy and Dorothy Smith's institutional ethnography methodology, which attempts to rescue the "real" experiences of subjects from their colonization by various "relations of ruling"; (3) Ethnic and Race Relations, Immigration, and Underdevelopment, as evidenced most recently in the work of Sedef Arat-Koc, Wenona

Giles, Winnie Lem, Roxana Ng, and Charlene Gannage; and (4) Aboriginal Peoples, the profound colonization of whose experience we are only beginning to unravel.

Perhaps only a Canadian sociology/anthropology book celebrating an important anniversary would call the "truths" it celebrated "fragile." But it is this sense of fragility that has motivated the best Canadian work to continually excavate further, in order to lay bare new layers. Clearly, we can no longer say that social science in this country is exclusively characterized by middle-class Anglo-Saxon males proclaiming their experience of the world and being satisfied to obliterate everyone else's. Many of the formerly submerged layers of experience have been exposed in recent years in Canadian sociology and anthropology, even if they have not yet become ascendant.

As editors, we have found that we do not necessarily agree with each other on every point, nor with each of the contributing authors, and have sometimes been startled to read accounts of our experience framed in ways that seemed to have little to do with the times but yet might be part of a more complex sociological picture. This points to another aspect of our truths' fragility: the multiple ways in which any social experience can be read, and thus the essentially contested character of sociological interpretation. For example, all of us are uncomfortable with the dichotomous interpretive framework that Frank Jones employed in arguing that the CSAA has evolved from a learned society to a professional association; we also question Jones's dismissal of what we have experienced as important features of a Canadian (in contrast to an American) sociology.

In a different vein, one of the editors is startled by the conceptual frame of the 1990s that Maticka-Tyndale and Drakich apply retrospectively to what they term "the initiation of grassroots, disengaged activism in the mid 1970s." Their account of this phase of feminist activism points to "special interest groups such as Indian women, black women, lesbian women and farm women," to "the 'politically correct' strategy," to "the discourse of women in the Association," to "engaging in disengaged activism," and to "the critical mass of feminists in the Association committed to the improvement of women's status." These signifiers—part of the political and intellectual agenda of the 1990s—reconstruct the past in a way that renders it intelligible to contemporary readers, and in doing so they construct a certain "truth." Yet the same terminology estranges the earlier participants from their own actions by imposing a conceptualization of events that is foreign to that lived reality.

Such re-visioning is to some extent inevitable in any social analysis, which by nature requires abstraction, but it is even more pronounced in historical descriptions. The upshot is that "the truth" as we knew it and as we lived it—or as others knew it and lived it— becomes appropriated by contemporary sociological and historical analysis and woven into the fabric of narratives that express the preoccupations of the present. This is yet another dimension of the fragility of truths, and of their transformation as history is made. The need we have for collective histories that enable us to connect present preoccupations with our collective past is one reason why we decided to edit a collection of articles that would specifically reflect upon the first twenty-five years of the CSAA in Canadian sociology and anthropology.

The essays in Part 2 of this volume ("The Constitution of Knowledge") most closely reflect the book's title, as each contributor exemplifies in his or her own way how the "truths" that inform the work we do are truly fragile ones, which cannot be easily separated from the various (and usually hierarchical) social structures in which they are embedded.

The articles in this section are focused on a pair of dangers that threaten the veracity of social analyses: on the one hand, the colonization of experience and, on the other, the reification of fragile truths into canonical certainties. Sylvia Hale analyzes Robert Hagedorn's introductory sociology text as an example of how the "debate" amongst major paradigms is often only a pseudo-debate, as other paradigms remain submerged beneath the taken-for-granted assumptions of Kuhnian "normal" sociology—structural-functionalism and societal consensus. Hale's paper implies that, if we are to avoid inculcating in our students this same false complacency about the nature of our social formation, we must initiate them early into a social constructionist way of thinking and doing sociology; that is, we must constantly draw their attention to the documentary and other practices of reification that some sociologists use to present consensus, liberal democracy, et cetera, as if they were actual characteristics of our social reality, instead of idealized concepts. David Nock similarly considers the footnoting practices of Canadian sociologists, showing how the citations in Robert Brym and Bonnie Fox's book, *From Culture to Power*, reflect the intellectual domination of certain regions of the country at the expense of sociologists who work elsewhere, and also reflect the personal networks and graduate training experiences of the book's two authors. David Howes tries to excavate what he terms "Canadi>n" anthropology out from under the ways it has been colonized in the past, and to make a case for what he considers to be its unique features and characteristics, especially relative to American anthropology.

Finally, Dorothy Smith and Janet Burns treat the theme of experience, gender, and power, each from a different vantage point. Burns provides an insightful narrative of how power relations intruded into her attempt, as a woman, to conduct an ethnographic study of Pacific coast fishermen. Smith discusses how the Canadianization movement gave her some of the intellectual tools she needed to help her discover how "malestream" North

American sociology (cf. O'Brien, 1981) had similarly colonized her experience as a woman and mother. The account she provides of her early attempts at UBC to break away from this mould serves as a case study in the relationships between knowledge, power, and identity. Smith's critical and reconstructive efforts in the 1970s were part of a broader intellectual and political movement, to which we have already referred. Canadian sociologists learned a tremendous amount about the colonization of experience from the confrontation of their own society and history with American paradigms, and from the recognition that they didn't fit. As Smith notes, this same kind of confrontation kindled the growth of feminist sociology. On both counts, the result has been a style of sociological analysis that views human practices and social relations in their historical context, and that resists the reification of those practices and relations into ahistorical or transhistorical laws.

The essays in Part Three ("The Academic Milieu") interrogate the specific institutional arrangements within which sociology, anthropology, and other academic disciplines are embedded, and the influence that the changing academic milieu has had on the development of our disciplines. Here again, the connection between relations of power and the production of knowledge figures prominently.

In an essay originally given as the Harry Hawthorne memorial lecture, Dorothy Smith takes a long view of the historical and philosophical roots of modern academe. She sees in it a male-centred regime of rationality built upon a deep contradiction between claims to universality and practices of gender exclusivity. Beginning from the concrete instance of Marc Lépine, Smith discerns the contemporary grounding of male rage in the anomalies created with women's entry into the male domain of objective knowledge. Yet she sounds a hopeful note in pointing to an emerging terrain—formed in great part through women's political agency—on which women and men can press for the realization of an Enlightenment project whose original promises of reason and equality continue to be worth striving for. Certainly, the feminist presence within the CSAA comprises an important part of that favourable terrain.

The essays by Newson, Cassin and Morgan, and Polster also take up the power/knowledge nexus within academe, but they focus upon contemporary class relations, in particular the growing influence of corporate capital within higher education. Newson's essay extends the incisive analysis she presented (with Howard Buchbinder) in *The University Means Business* (1988). She suggests that the decline of faculty influence on Canadian campuses is rooted in complex social changes that are closely interwoven with efforts to forge new links between the university and the corporate sector. The trend towards the "market-driven university" has ominous implications for the organization and content of academic work, and for the kinds of truths that disciplines such as sociology and anthropology are likely to bear in the future. Cassin's and Morgan's chapter can be read as a companion to Newson's. Using as a critical case their own campus—Dalhousie—Cassin and Morgan explore how, through the implementation of textually mediated forms of control, the administrative assumptions and methods predominant in the corporate world are being incorporated into the academy.[5] Finally, in Claire Polster's essay the focal point shifts from a critique of the corporate agenda in academe to a critique and reconstruction of the project of radical education with which many Canadian sociologists and anthropologists have identified themselves. In view of the gravity of the changes underway in Canadian academe, Polster argues that academics committed to liberatory education must do more than resist the incursion of the corporate agenda into the spaces they have won; they must pursue a broader strategy in concert with other groups to transform the university in the direction of greater autonomy and democracy.

These essays reveal another aspect of the fragile basis upon which the truths of our disciplines rest. The penetration of academe by corporate capital is by now itself an established reality. It is evident in the proliferation of direct institutional ties between business and universities, in the neo-liberal state's shifting priorities for funding higher education, and in the new discourses and practices of corporate-style efficiency and productivity. "Value-for-money," "cost-effectiveness," and "accountability" are criteria central to the "truth" of the marketplace. Whether they come to be more centrally inscribed in the work of Canadian sociologists and anthropologists and to influence the content of social-scientific discourse is the focus of considerable struggle and anguish amongst the practitioners of these disciplines.

The essays in Part 4 ("Sociology, Anthropology, and Social Change") provide a range of sometimes conflicting assessments of the relation between our disciplines and processes of social change. Indeed, there is probably no section of the book where the authors disagree as much with each other as to how relevant or irrelevant our disciplines have been to social policy and other arenas of change.

Is social policy research nothing but fluff, an afterthought, or is it at the heart of sociological and anthropological investigations? What role should sociology and anthropology play *vis-à-vis* other social sciences and social policy? In addition to addressing this question directly (Harding), the papers look at several aspects of the issue. McFarlane cites with convincing confidence the various royal commissions to which sociologists and anthropologists have contributed. Whyte and Harding, in different ways, express scepticism about our collective influence on social policy. Neis offers a case study of the admirable record of sociologists and anthropologists at Memorial University in conducting research that is relevant to social policy and that is typically grounded in the realities of human communities; yet she expresses doubts that contributions to social policy *per se* can be made within the parameters of a "successful" academic career. Reiter, whose research involved interviews with a number of trade union activists, agrees with them that the social scientists who attempt to become advocates for unions neither understand nor assist them to any significant extent. Armstrong and Armstrong present a similar analysis of recent feminist scholarship in Canadian sociology. The motto that they have incorporated into the title of their essay "Better Irreverent than Irrelevant" offers good advice to sociologists and anthropologists in all applied fields.

A key insight, shared by several of these papers, is that the political relevancy of a particular social-scientific work is typically itself no more than a fragile accomplishment that can be fairly easily subverted. When sociologists and anthropologists address the state, their work becomes subject to the whims of governments, which sometimes do not want to hear the message (as Neis's chapter illustrates) and at other times quickly dismiss it when their agenda changes (as Whyte's essay suggests). The capacity to "be relevant" is very often beyond the control of the disciplines themselves. In the circumstances, it is sometimes necessary to be irreverent towards existing centres of power if we are to make our analyses socially relevant.

When sociologists and anthropologists address themselves to movements for change, such as the women's and labour movements, their own professional detachment can present a formidable barrier to making their ideas relevant. It may be that such relevance can only be achieved if a discipline comes to include among its ranks intellectuals who are also active in the movement, and who are thus imbued with the appropriate political sensibilities and experiences. Certainly, the strong presence that feminists have achieved within the CSAA has enabled them to combine theory and practice in ways that have contributed to social change both in Canadian society and within the disciplines. But alongside this example is the alternative case, illuminated by Reiter's constructive criticisms of academics who despite their good intentions are unable to connect their work to the agenda of the labour movement. Reiter's essay invites us to consider carefully the practices through which we can make our truths relevant to a range of subordinate groups without reproducing the hegemonic relations that designate our expertise as a privileged discourse.

Lastly, we must underscore Harding's call for an ecological sociology that would address the global environmental crisis with the same interdisciplinary vigour with which the classical sociologists tackled the great epochal transformations of their times. At the 1990 CSAA meetings only 5 of 167 paper sessions featured the environment as a thematic. An understanding of the complex relationships between environment, culture, and society is of crucial import if sociology and anthropology are to have relevance to the social and environmental challenges of the last years of this century.

We thought, finally, that no volume of this kind would be complete without a selected bibliography of the development of our disciplines. We are fortunate that Dr. Gale Moore, Book Selector at the University of Toronto Robarts Library, was able to prepare this bibliography for us.

What, then, can we say in conclusion about the first twenty-five formative years of sociology and anthropology in the Canadian context? "The truth" certainly has not made us free, as the sign above the door to Victoria College advised one of us years ago. Indeed, the post-modernist sensibilities evident in our disciplines today and in several of the chapters in this book have questioned the philosophical basis for any immediate relation between knowledge and emancipation. Moreover, the truths we are able to produce within sociology and anthropology are, as we have emphasized, fragile and provisional. Yet sociology and anthropology are richer disciplines in Canada than they were twenty-five years ago, and in various ways sociologists and anthropologists have contributed to social changes that have enriched the possibilities for a humane world. Despite the many limitations that we have emphasized in this Introduction, we remain hopeful that in the future the corpus of the work we achieve will continue to build in collaborative ways upon the differences that remain amongst segments of us, that we will take up the intellectual challenges that confront us through comparative research, and that the contributions we make to social policy debates will be even more relevant and irreverent than they appear to be today.

NOTES

[1] The recipients of the Outstanding Contributions Awards were Bernard R. Blishen, Raymond Breton, Jean Burnet, S.D. Clark, Hubert Guindon, Oswald Hall, Gordon Inglis, John D. Jackson, M. Patricia Marchak, Bruce A. McFarlane, Guy Rocher, Aileen D. Ross, Dorothy E. Smith, and Marc-Adelard Tremblay. See the special issue of *Society/Société* (Vol. 14, No. 3, May 1990) for details.

[2] For an overview of the state of the art of francophone Quebecois sociology, see Juteau and Maheu (1989b).

[3] Alan Pomfret continues:

Since its inception the organizers for most of the Association's annual conferences have attempted to reflect the Association's objective by including sessions on teaching the disciplines, new and emerging directions in the disciplines, policy or applied issues, and the nature of employment for anthropologists and sociologists in the non-academic settings.... Still, during the first decade the Association's activities tended to emphasize the scholarly rather than the professional component of its mandate. Discussions continue concerning the appropriate relationship between academic and professional concerns and how best to achieve and maintain a desired balance. In addition, there are ongoing challenges associated with maintaining an effective link between anthropologists and sociologists when one discipline is numerically dominant. More recently, attention has shifted to the professional component of the mandate, especially how to involve anthropologists in related university departments and in non-university settings such as community colleges, government and private employment, and secondary schools. In pursuit of these objectives the Association is considering a number of structural and procedural changes designed to connect with previously under-involved constituencies (personal communication, October 1991).

[4] We must note that the issue of Native self-government—a third dimension of the national question that is foundational to Canada as a European settler society and that is clearly central to contemporary politics—constitutes another lamentable silence in the present collection.

[5] We leave it to the reader to judge how closely Cassin's and Morgan's account of the case of Dalhousie compares with their own academic milieu, but at least one of us questions their tendency to equate administrative concerns for accountability with the adoption of market-oriented managerial criteria.

Appendix

Reflections on the SFU CASE

Gary B. Rush

As mentioned in the Introduction, an important set of issues in the development of the CSAA was crystallized in the events surrounding and following the firing of several social science faculty members at Simon Fraser University in 1969. The role of the CSAA in the Simon Fraser University case is discussed in the two essays by Frank Jones and Gordon Inglis respectively. We have invited Gary Rush to provide an additional commentary on that period of the history of the Association.

Possibly by virtue of having been a charter member of faculty of Simon Fraser University, I was requested by the editors of this volume to contribute a brief comment on the issue that locked the CSAA into a seventeen-year boycott of that institution. Reflecting upon Gordon Inglis's account of the role of animals in the fall from grace (infra), I was inclined to let sleeping dogs lie. However, since apparently sleeping dogs may also be road kill, I have accepted the task with certain caveats.

The first is to inform the reader that I support, then as now, the principles of departmental autonomy upheld by the eight faculty members who were fired ("not renewed" or "dismissed" in other versions). Our eventual parting was over tactics. Second, this is neither the time nor the place to analyze and debate the Simon Fraser issue. Perhaps the publication of this volume will be an incentive to that undertaking, which many of us have discussed over the years. Finally, I shall confine my remarks to the question raised by both Gordon Inglis and Frank Jones: the CSAA—learned society or professional/political organization?

The issue between the Administration of Simon Fraser University (SFU) and the then PSA (Politics, Sociology and Anthropology) Department was unquestionably political. Imprecations from the Board of Governors about the "radical" nature of the Department began shortly after the University opened in 1964, and prompted the resignation of the Department's founding head, T.B. Bottomore, in 1967. By May of 1968, Administration/Departmental relations had deteriorated to the point where, following a dispute over hiring (notably of Andre Gunder Frank), the first CAUT censure was imposed. The Administration hastened to install procedures for tenure, promotion, and hiring, and the censure was lifted in November of the same year. Perhaps emboldened by this reprieve, the Administration resumed its harassment of the PSA Department. By 1969, other members of faculty, and the Faculty Association itself, were beginning to take alarm. In this climate of escalation, and in the face of a potential broadening of the issue, the ultimate confrontation of strike and dismissal was perhaps inevitable.

Considering the position taken by the CAUT in the preceding year, it is hardly surprising that its censure was reimposed. When the CSAA joined the issue in 1971, its response was equally political, adding boycott to censure as tactics towards the goal of reinstatement of the dismissed faculty. The history that followed is perhaps better known to the reader than the precipitating events, and does not bear repeating here.

In the course of setting down these recollections, I reflected on the distinction posed between the CSAA as learned society and as professional organization. Ponder as I may, I cannot separate these roles. Perhaps what is being set for us here is an academic version of the Irish question: Ah now, that works very well in practice, but how does it work in theory? By the same token, might it not be that we seek to avoid facing the contradiction and paradox of the practical world by concentrating on the theoretical?

The SFU case was rife with contradiction, paradox, and irony. Although initially attempting to remain neutral, the CSAA eventually acted as a political agent, adding its boycott to the CAUT censure. This position was sustainable for six years, until the CAUT censure, evidently getting nowhere, was lifted. This left the CSAA with a hot potato that was rapidly growing cold, and fuel was added to the fire by the irony of censuring the CAUT. From then on, at every AGM, we went through the agonizing political process as to whether or not the censure/boycott (which no one seemed able to define) should be upheld. A personal paradox of this situation was that, as a continuing faculty member at SFU, my membership in the CSAA was politically rescinded, but I still could, and did, present papers at the annual meetings on the basis of the learned ideal of the freedom to disseminate knowledge. To add irony to paradox, I was delegated, in 1985, as part of the three-member Task Force to negotiate the lifting of the censure/boycott. In the spring of 1986, I returned to SFU as a lone, tentatively exploring innocent from abroad, to be confronted by a team of University negotiators armed and loaded for bear. It took at least twenty minutes, and eventual intercession by the Dean of Arts, to convince them that I did not carry a list of demands.

As this final anecdote attests, it is a political world, in which our actions and inactions have consequences. In the case of Simon Fraser, had the Association maintained the neutrality of a learned society, and not responded, would this not have been an equally political statement? Although history is difficult enough as it is without making it hypothetical, it may well be that the Association would not have survived unless it responded to the concerns of its membership, and been pro-active on matters, for example, of the status of women, social policy, and professional ethics. Moreover, having served the Association in many capacities, I can assure you that apparently learned issues also contain political dimensions: editorial policy, sociology/anthropology representation, and anglophone/francophone scholarship being a few cases in point. In the final analysis, we must return to an admonition contained in Gordon Inglis's account of charter myths. There are things moving around out there: if they look like ducks, walk like ducks, and squawk like ducks, they well may be ducks.

Part One
The Development of Sociology and Anthropology in Canada

THE EVOLUTION OF THE CSAA
Frank E. Jones

Steps towards Autonomy

The Setting in the 1940s and 1950s

Sociology was a thin patch in Canada until late in the 1950s. Clark (1979) describes how, within the universities, sociology was lowest in the pecking order of disciplines, behind all the natural sciences, the humanities, and the other social sciences. Clark (1979), Brym (Brym and Fox, 1989), and Hiller (1982) observe that the few appointments of sociologists that were made were to departments housing other disciplines, typically, as at the University of Toronto, in a department of political economy. The McGill Department of Sociology, established in 1922[2] jointly with Social Work, became, when its formal connection with Social Work was severed in 1925, the only department in Canada with an exclusive focus on sociology (Ostow, 1984:12).[3] Outside the universities, sociology was largely ignored. As late as the 1940s, references to Weber, Durkheim, and Simmel were rare at best in publications, such as *The Canadian Forum* and the *New Statesman*, which focused on social issues. References in the press to sociology or to sociological research or perspectives did not occur as frequently as they have since the late 1950s, when words such as "charismatic," "serendipity," or phrases such as "self-fulfilling prophecy" became common coin for columnists and editorial writers.

When I began undergraduate study in 1946, the McGill Department consisted of C.A. Dawson, Forrest Laviolette, Oswald Hall, and Aileen Ross, with Eva Younge holding a part-time appointment and Nathan Keyfitz coming down from Ottawa one day a week to teach statistics (Ross, 1984:4-5).[4] The few appointments and the low standing of sociology did not discourage the small band of Honours and Master's students in sociology,[5] who, must have shared some confidence that sociology would eventually be recognized as a valuable discipline. The faculty's enthusiasm for sociology helped to keep up our spirits and to maintain our motivation to stay in the Honours course and go on to graduate work. Even in 1954, after I had left Harvard for the federal civil service in Ottawa, academic appointments in sociology were scarce in Canada. The situation improved dramatically within a few years when universities were encouraged "to tool up" in advance of the anticipated arrival of large numbers of undergraduates.

No separate organization of anthropologists or sociologists existed in those days. Members of these disciplines, as well as economists, were accepted as members of the Canadian Political Science Association (CPSA).

The Association, which was founded in 1913, "foundered in 1914" and was re-established in 1929 (Bladen, 1960), provided a forum for social scientists to voice common scholarly concerns. Its journal, *The Canadian Journal of Economics and Political Science (CJEPS)*, was established in 1935 and was open to submissions from all social scientists. Most important, the CPSA took responsibility for organizing an Annual Meeting as part of the Learned Societies Conference. When I joined in 1950, the total individual membership, including ordinary, joint, life, and student members, for all disciplines, was 1,421.[6]

The meetings, in those days, were quite different from the current Learneds. Most people stayed in university campus accommodation rather than in hotels, and there was considerable interaction among those from different disciplines whose meeting dates overlapped. The CPSA Minutes do not record the numbers attending its annual meetings, but it is my recollection that many of those attending would know each other. Moreover, there was more interaction among members of different disciplines, both formal and informal, than I think occurs now.

CPSA sessions typically consisted of one or two papers and were organized to meet the specialized interests of members. Thus, sessions focused on economics, political science, anthropology, and sociology. The result of deliberate policy,[7] there were also sessions, sometimes held jointly with another learned society, that appealed to a wide range of social science interests and attracted a broad representation of social science disciplines. A paper given by Everett Hughes was guaranteed to attract such a mixed audience. In 1960, when Hubert Guindon gave his critique of Philippe Garigue's perspective on Quebec as well as Garigue's rejection of "the Chicago School's view of French Canada" (Guindon, 1960), a very large room was required to accommodate all those interested in attending this further round in a conflict of perspectives that had begun with Garigue's rejection of the view of Quebec presented by earlier scholars, including Gérin, Miner, and Hughes (Garigue, 1956).

There were advantages to these small meetings. The programme did not overwhelm the latent functions of the meetings: the opportunity for informal discussion of professional interests and for meeting friends from across the country. Moreover, the session format allowed for a depth of discussion and gave the presenter an opportunity to develop ideas or to present findings in a degree of detail not possible under today's format.

There were benefits for anthropologists and sociologists as members of the CPSA. Although outnumbered by economists and political scientists, anthropologists and sociologists were fairly treated. The programme provided sessions for these disciplines and I do not recall any collective dissatisfaction with our allotment of time. For example, the 1955 meeting provided for one anthropology session and three sociology sessions among the thirteen listed, exclusive of an evening general session and a joint evening session of presidential addresses (CPSA and the Canadian Historical Association). In most if not all years (at least from 1950), there was representation of anthropology and/or sociology on the CPSA Executive Council which, among other responsibilities, served as the Programme Committee. There was similar representation on the Editorial Advisory Committee of the CJEPS and at times on its Board of Editors. S.D. Clark served as co-managing Editor in 1953-54. Although the 1955 minutes[9] report that Volume 20 of the Journal contained 17 articles on economics and economic history, 12 in political science and 3 in sociology and anthropology, its report on manuscripts received indicates that the 8 manuscripts submitted by anthropologists and sociologists enjoyed a higher acceptance rate (62.5 per cent) than those submitted by economists and political scientists (45 per cent). In addition, anthropologists and sociologists had access to the CPSA's travel fund which was used to assist members to attend annual meetings. Still, as pleasant as the CPSA meetings and our relations with other social scientists were, there was a developing opinion early in the 1950s that there was a need to establish a clearer, more positive identity of the discipline and for some form of association exclusive to sociologists.[10]

The Anthropological and Sociological Chapter

In 1955, according to the CPSA Annual Meeting Minutes,

The President reported that the Executive Council, at its meeting two days previously, had had representations from Mr. S.D. Clark, as Chairman of a Committee of Canadian sociologists, seeking the Council's attitude toward some proposals which the committee intended to put before the larger group of sociologists the following day. The committee's action, and indeed its formation, had arisen from a desire of the Canadian sociologists represented by it for a more cohesive and effective form of organization than they felt was at present provided with the CPSA. The committee's tentative proposals were 1) that the title of the Journal be changed to "The Canadian Journal of Economics, Political Science, and Sociology" and 2) that the formation of a Sociological Chapter of the CPSA be authorized. The Executive Council had indicated that it was not opposed in principle to such proposals, and had expressed hope that suitable arrangements could be made to give the sociologists a more effective place within the Association, in view of the high value it put on the contribution of sociology and on the unity of the social sciences in Canada. Mr. Clark then reported that, after the Executive Council meeting, the meeting of the larger group of sociologists had rejected the committee's proposals and that a new committee had been set up (CJEPS 1955:374).

Although this was the first formal mention of the move to change the form of representation of sociologists in the CPSA, an interest in such a change had begun a year or so earlier. In my view, the interest in some degree of separation was driven basically by a shared concern or objective of sociologists to generate a much clearer identity of the discipline than could be realized in an organization that, despite its name, was a general social science association. This form of association had served well prior to the war and in the immediate post-war period, but as numbers in all the social science disciplines began to grow, it was seen, earlier by some, later by others, that specialized associations would replace the CPSA. Indeed, in 1965, when the anthropologists and sociologists voted to establish the CSAA, the economists decided to separate and to establish the Canadian Economics Association, leaving the political scientists to inherit the CPSA but with a more narrowly defined membership.[11]

Anthropologists and sociologists, individually and collectively, may have thought and talked about a more distinctive organization prior to 1953, but I think the context for a growing consensus supporting some measure of autonomy was provided by some annual meetings, dubbed the Ontario/Quebec Sociology Conference, that began in 1955.[12] These meetings held early in the spring, grew out of some sessions internal to the University of Toronto organized under the leadership of S.D. Clark. Clark extended an invitation to these sessions to anthropologists and sociologists who held appointments in universities or who were elsewhere employed in Ontario and Quebec. These meetings, included a session or two given by a visiting speaker, such as Kingsley Davis, C. Wright Mills or Talcott Parsons, and one or more by Quebec/Ontario anthropologists and/or sociologists. They were well attended and, in due course, were hosted by other universities. I believe that the satisfying experience of participating in meetings limited to sociologists and a few anthropologists contributed to the development of a consensus towards the establishment of a distinctive association. What kind of an association it would be and what would be its relationship to the CPSA were questions yet to be answered.

The solution, of course, was to establish a committee—in fact, as it turned out, to establish a series of committees. As I have not be able to find copies of reports or minutes of any of the committees that made recommendations concerning the organization for anthropologists and sociologists, I cannot claim accuracy for any dates I attach to their recommendations or to the action resulting from them, but I think they are in proper sequence. The first committee was chaired by S.D. Clark and reported as described in the excerpt from the CPSA Minutes (CJEPS, 1955:374) quoted above. The second committee, also mentioned in the excerpt, I believe, was one I chaired whose report Bruce McFarlane describes (1965) as leading eventually to the formation of the Anthropology and Sociology Chapter of the CPSA. Its members were Jean-Charles Falardeau, Jim Giffen, Kaspar Naegele, and David Solomon.

The idea of a chapter as part of the CPSA had been accepted in 1954 when the Ottawa Chapter was formed as a regional unit of the CPSA. The Ottawa Chapter, however, welcomed all members of the social science disciplines included by the parent organization.[13] Although the Ottawa Chapter held two or three general meetings a year, it was also organized into six study groups which were representative of the different disciplines—for example, Problems in Economic Theories—or of special interests that crossed discipline boundaries, for example, Industrial Relations. In our case, the study group was labelled—Projects and Problems in Sociology; in its first year it was chaired by Nathan Keyfitz. On the basis of hindsight, I suggest that the Ottawa Chapter established a precedent that facilitated acceptance of the Anthropology and Sociology Chapter. It provided an acceptable compromise for anthropologists and sociologists who were not of one mind about separation: for those favouring no change, for those who wanted a measure of autonomy without surrendering membership in the CPSA, and for those who saw it as a step towards complete separation.

Sometime between June 1955 and June 1956, the anthropology and sociology members of the CPSA endorsed the Jones Committee proposal that an Anthropology and Sociology Chapter be established. The Executive Council of the CPSA welcomed the proposal (CJEPS, 1956:385) and in June 1957, David Solomon reported to the Annual Meeting of the CPSA that the "Chapter had adopted a constitution and was now fully formed" (CJEPS, 1957:441), with anthropologist Harry Hawthorn as President and sociologist Kaspar Naegele as Secretary-Treasurer. The CPSA Treasurer's Report for 1958 notes that the Chapter's principal concern is "the enhancement of research and instruction in anthropology and sociology" (CJEPS, 1958:412). In pursuit of these objectives, the Chapter established a Committee on Publications, to be responsible for reviewing manuscripts submitted by anthropologists and sociologists for publication and for the preparation of a directory of anthropologists and sociologists in Canada. This committee, presumably, was also responsible for proposing the publication of a newsletter. The first issue of the Bulletin, with Sy Yasin as Editor, was published in April 1960.

After its formation, the Chapter organized its own sessions at the CPSA's Annual Meetings. From 1962 until the CSAA was formed, the Minutes of the Annual Meeting reported the details of these Chapter sessions in its first paragraph. This practice directed attention, not necessarily intentional, to the separate activities of the Chapter, but anthropologists and sociologists continued to participate in CPSA sessions and to hold office in the CPSA. S.D. Clark and Jean-Charles Falardeau, for example, served as CPSA President, respectively, in 1958-59 and 1964-65. Jean Burnet served as Managing Editor of the CJEPS in 1961-62 while John Dales, an economist, was on leave; and others, at least up to and including 1965, served on the CPSA Executive Council or on the Editorial Board of the CJEPS.

The Move towards Autonomy

Nonetheless, discussion of the possibility of an organization separate from the CPSA continued among anthropologists and sociologists. The Western Anthropology and Sociology Association (WASA) was formed in 1962 and the Ontario/Quebec anthropologists and sociologists, referred to as the Eastern members of the Chapter, continued their mid-winter meetings. In due course, a committee, chaired by Aileen Ross, with Bill Dunning, Bob James, John Meisel, Kaspar Naegele, and Guy Rocher as members, was appointed to report on "the advantages and disadvantages of an association separate from the CPSA and to recommend on the establishment of a separate journal" (McFarlane, 1965:1).

Plans went ahead, with strong support from WASA, to establish a scholarly journal. In due course, with financial aid from the University of Calgary, the *Canadian Review of Sociology and Anthropology*, with Jean Burnet as Editor and Henry Zentner as Managing Editor, published its first issue in February 1964 as the official journal of the Anthropology and Sociology Chapter of the CPSA. Dr. Burnet has reported that the most difficult problem she faced, in the initial years, was a scarcity of acceptable manuscripts. As a consequence, the *Review* could not maintain a regular schedule of publication. Not until the early 1970s would the Review Editor have a sufficient number of accepted manuscripts to meet printing deadlines, which would guarantee the scheduled publication dates.

With the *Review* underway, and with the membership growing steadily from 50 to 189, confidence in the prospect of a viable separate organization increased over the period from 1957 to 1965. However, the small number of anthropologists and sociologists in Canada at that time was a major constraint on the formation of a separate association. David Solomon reported to the 1957 CPSA Annual Meeting that membership in the Chapter had grown to 50 from an estimated 12 anthropologists and sociologists who were CPSA members in 1955 when discussion of a chapter began.[18] As there were 69 sociologists employed in Canada in 1955-56, with 42 of these holding university appointments (Jones, 1977:160), it does appear that the Chapter's partial independence led to an increased interest among anthropologists and sociologists in membership in the CPSA. On the reasonable assumption that a fully independent association would attract an even greater number of anthropologists and sociologists, a committee, chaired by Bruce McFarlane, was established to investigate the feasibility, based on detailed estimates of costs and revenues, of a separate association.

In 1965, the McFarlane Committee presented its report to the Tenth Annual Meeting of the Chapter. Instead of recommending either the continuation of the Chapter or the establishment of a separate association, the Committee asked for an extension of time to allow it to poll the membership concerning its preferred course of action. Apparently, however, even anthropologists and sociologists can have enough of committees, for the fifty or so members attending the annual meeting that year refused the request of the McFarlane Committee. Instead, S.D. Clark moved, seconded by Frank Vallee, that "the meeting go on record as favouring the establishment of a separate Anthropology and Sociology Association." This motion, as amended on a motion by William Westley, seconded by Marc-Adélard Tremblay, was "carried overwhelmingly." It required the incoming Executive to poll the membership and, if the poll showed a majority of members in favour, empowered the Executive to proceed with the formation of a separate association.

As a majority of the members voted for a separate organization,[19] the Executive Committee of the Chapter, chaired by Marc-Adélard Tremblay,[20] along with representatives of the Editorial Board of the *Review* met in Montreal in October as a provisional CSAA Executive to draft a constitution, prepare a budget, and begin organization of the Annual Meeting to be held at the University of Sherbrooke in June 1966. The CSAA came into existence when, with about 50 members attending,[21] the constitution was approved, sub-committees were established and the first CSAA Executive was elected.[22]

The CSAA

This section will continue to focus on evolution but, as 1968-73 were my years of most active involvement in the CSAA, I rely much more on the minutes of AGMs, the Executive Committee, and its sub-committees and task forces, and other documents than on personal recollection to trace developments in CSAA activities and concerns from its establishment to 1990. This being so, my earlier caution to readers to treat my conclusions as hypotheses bears repetition.

The main aim of this section is to describe developments in the CSAA's activities and concerns over its first twenty-five years. However, I thought it would be useful to attempt this within a perspective in the sociology of organizations that gives prominence, among its components, to organizational objectives. Accordingly, I use three categories of objectives (the terms *objectives* and *orientations* are used interchangeably in the discussion) to capture differences in CSAA's activities and concerns as I perceived them. These are defined as follows:

> Learned Society—in which the organization's chief concern is to realize the values underlying scholarly activities: the search for knowledge as an intrinsic good, impartiality in analysis and in reporting findings, and an open exchange of ideas and research findings. Action supportive of these values would include encouraging research, facilitating the exchange, publication, and communication of scholarly work, and encouraging excellence in teaching.

Professional—in which the main objective is to achieve and maintain proper conditions of employment for its members. In the academic case, such conditions include freedom of expression, participation in institutional governance, employment equity, and an appropriate salary structure.

Political Action—which places emphasis on intervention in public affairs to support either conservation or change in economic, political, or social policies.

A study of organizational objectives will not, of course, tell all there is to tell about an organization. However, thinking about objectives leads, at least as applied in the sociology of organizations and social systems analysis generally, to questions about the sources of objectives, success or failure in their realization, and various other consequences to the organization. For example, it is common knowledge that multiple-objective organizations, such as the CSAA, experience tensions in the degree that objectives are inconsistent or conflict. Familiar examples are those psychiatric hospitals and prisons that embrace both custodial and rehabilitative objectives. Other possible sources of tension include inconsistencies in values that underlie different objectives and therefore inconsistencies in determining priorities in allocating resources to achieve them. Moreover, competing organizations that are components of an organization's environment and that threaten its survival can create tensions within the organization.

This analysis may be regarded as a first step in understanding CSAA's development. To pursue these ideas in depth would have required documentation and time beyond the scope of the present project. Even so, some evidence has been provided of uneasiness as new interests and activities wrestled for place with those legitimated by the learned society orientation adopted when the CSAA began and reaffirmed as its highest priority by the results of the 1989 Referendum.

CSAA Objectives

The CSAA adopted as its objectives those defined by the Chapter: the encouragement of research and teaching of sociology and anthropology. As reflected by Executive Committee and Annual General Meeting Minutes,[23] the CSAA's concerns were those of a learned society: the communication of ideas and research findings through scholarly meetings and publications, the promotion and funding of research, and, of course, the promotion of the two disciplines it represented. The sub-committees[24] established in 1966 reflected these interests and concerns—Programme, Research, and Selection (responsible for allocating travel grants)—into the 1970s. As well, sub-committees were established to find ways and means for increasing and retaining members (membership) and with responsibility for the overall management of the Association's scarce funds (finance). Although sub-committees were added, such as those on the future of the two disciplines and on student participation in the Association, these seemed consistent with the activities and concerns of a learned society.

Organizations, however, are subject to internal and external pressures that may generate change in their objectives, concerns, and activities. As the CSAA entered the 1970s, events in the larger society as well as in the universities would impact on the CSAA's activities and its concerns. During this period, professional ethics, the status of women, social policy, nationalism with respect to faculty appointments as well as to the focus of the disciplines, the Simon Fraser University dispute, and other employment-related issues all claimed considerable attention from the Executive Committee and the AGMs.

Even with the important changes to come in its orientation during the 1970s, attention continued to be given to scholarly concerns. The programmes of the Annual Meeting, the nurturing of support for research and publication outlets,[25] and relations with funding agencies[26] and with other learned-societies continued to occupy the attention of Executive Committees and AGMs. Moreover, in June 1969, the Executive established a Future of the Disciplines Sub-committee with a mandate to determine the requirements for the growth and development of the two disciplines in Canada as these related to their present strengths and weaknesses and to the needs of Canadian society. Although the mandate of this sub-committee had a clearly learned-society orientation, the reference to the "needs of Canadian society" foreshadowed a concern with social issues and applied research that would also be adopted by the CSAA. Even if its learned society responsibilities were not neglected, it is apparent that new concerns, identified above and discussed below, would bring change to the CSAA's orientations.

Professional Ethics

The question of establishing an Ethics sub-committee was first raised at the 1967 AGM and referred to the Executive. The response at the AGM, subsequently supported by the Executive, was that such a committee was not appropriate for a learned society, although it was for a professional association. It was also agreed that any ethical problems that did arise could be dealt with by the Executive. In 1970, however, the Executive Committee decided to establish an Ad Hoc Committee on Professional Ethics and by 1971, the AGM approved an Executive motion to convert it to a Professional Ethics Sub-Committee. While it is not clear what specific ethical issues concerned the members at that time, it is reasonable to assume that among growing anthropology and sociology departments, norms of conduct with colleagues and with students might not have been firmly established and that such a situation could generate uncertainty about acceptable conduct.[28] A standing committee, charged with developing a code of ethics and with hearing complaints about unethical conduct, would be a reasonable response to such concerns.

This sub-committee continued its work throughout the 1980s and its responsibilities were extended to include employment-related complaints and issues.[29] The volume of ethics complaints appears to have been small from the time the Committee was established and throughout the 1970s and 1980s. Nonetheless, the sub-committee was kept busy by its task of developing a Code of Ethics, and afterward by revising it. The extent of the Association's responsibilities for employment-related cases was a recurring topic of discussion for the Executive from the time of the Association's involvement in the Simon Fraser dispute and as it addressed other individual complaints. Although there seems to have been a general view that the CAUT was the appropriate association to respond to such complaints, there remained an uneasiness about the CSAA's responsibilities. In 1980, the Ethics sub-committee was asked to review and make recommendations on the relations between CSAA and CAUT. At the 1983 AGM, two recommendations were approved which, essentially, recognized the CAUT as the appropriate body, without CSAA involvement, to deal with routine cases, but required the CSAA to be involved in cases that concerned "issues of substantial significance," such as academic freedom, ethnic or gender discrimination, or violation of Canadianization employment policies. The trend for the 1980s, then, was for the CSAA to continue to act as a professional association.

Social Policy

The period beginning in 1968 and lasting well into the 1970s was a time of considerable social unrest in many countries. In particular, the period was marked by protests against the U.S. war in Vietnam as well as protests, often violent, against existing authority. Canada was no exception. Although protest against authority was mostly centred in Quebec, these events likely led to a further change in the Association's orientation. This change is reflected by concerns with public matters on which members wanted the Association to express a collective opinion and thus to intervene in public debate. The explicit involvement of the CSAA in social issues and policy probably began when the Executive, at its December 1970 meeting, discussed the consequences of the imposition of the War Measures Act[30] by the federal government in response to events in Quebec that had been marked by bombings and, in particular, by the kidnapping of the U.K. Trade Commissioner and by the kidnapping and murder of Pierre Laporte, a member of the Cabinet of the Quebec government. Although the Executive did not adopt any motions concerning these events, at its meeting in May 1971 it had received a report from a Panel on the War Measures Act, and decided that the report should be made available to members and that a copy should be sent to the Prime Minister. The report and the Executive's action were approved by the 1971 AGM.

The formation of a Social Policy Sub-Committee was approved, "after much discussion," by the Executive at its December 1970 meeting. At the 1971 AGM, in the discussion of the sub-committee's first report, concern was expressed about the nature of the Association's involvement in other than professional issues and a motion authorizing the CSAA to become involved in general social policy issues was referred, on a close vote, to the Executive Committee. The discussion continued and broadened to include not only the terms of reference of the Social Policy Sub-Committee but other politically oriented motions generated in the AGMs. The Executive, noting that the CSAA membership was ideologically and politically heterogeneous, expressed concern that such motions as well as policy generated by the sub-committee could be divisive. However, the sub-committee was firmly established and the intervention concerning the War Measures Act was followed by others throughout the 1970s. These included motions concerning the "critical situations of aboriginal peoples in many countries" (1972-73 Exec), Canadian aid to Vietnam (1975 AGM), United States policy on the readmission of Vietnam resisters to the U.S. (1975 AGM), on the Canadian government's Green Paper on Immigration (1975 AGM), and in support of the Berger Commission Report on the Environmental Impact of Pipeline Construction in the Northwest Territories (1977 AGM).[31] This interest in political involvement went further than reaction to specific policies or events. In fact, at its December 1970 meeting, the Executive approved a proposal to "invite both theoretical and position papers on social issues, especially regarding civil liberties and the sociological input possible on a number of pressing Canadian problems," as submissions to the programme of the Annual Meeting. Further, when the Social Policy Sub-Committee was established by the Executive, its responsibilities included generating discussion of the role of anthropologists and sociologists in policy formation, providing opportunities for the study of social issues, developing means of communicating criticism and policy recommendations to government agencies, and advising the Executive and the membership on social policy issues on which the Association might wish to make recommendations.[32] Clearly, the initiative of the 1970 Executive and the actions of the Social Policy Sub-Committee through the 1970s support the view that Canadian anthropologists and sociologists had a responsibility to conduct research on social problems and on matters of social policy. The work of the sub-committee, presumably with Executive Committee support, increased in the 1980s. The President's report for 1983 to the Executive and to the AGM, noting the important role of the Social Policy sub-Committee, emphasized the capacity of the CSAA to impact on Canadian society. His successor reported that social policy issues represented one of the two activities that had most occupied his attention during his term of office. Although the sub-committee's concerns, such as the government's decision to cancel the 1986 Census, were in part scholarly, most of the issues it addressed were not. These included motions on welfare funding, medicare, old age security, the Canadian Intelligence Service, nuclear weapons, gay rights and native rights. While it might be claimed that these actions implied a scholarly interest, they clearly involved the CSAA in an interventionist role in the affairs of Canadian society. In that respect, they may have provided some comfort for those anthropologists and sociologists who perceived their disciplines to be instruments of social change.

As the decade neared its end, the sub-committee appeared to become less active, perhaps as a consequence of an internal discussion of CSAA priorities.

Status of Women

Although feminist concerns had been voiced in Canada and elsewhere long before the 1970s, these concerns became far stronger following the publication of The Second Sex (de Beauvoir, 1954).[33] While it is unlikely that women anthropologists and sociologists were unaware or uncritical of male domination of their disciplines, organized action in the CSAA did not begin until May 1970, when the Executive Committee established an Ad Hoc Committee on the Status of Women, consisting of Katie Cooke, Lynn MacDonald (Chair), and Gillian Sankoff. This committee reported to the 1971 AGM, which passed several motions relating to gender discrimination. The committee was converted into a standing committee by action of the Executive Committee following the AGM, in May 1971, with Katie Cooke as its first Chair. The concerns relating to the status of women, as expressed in a series of motions passed in the 1970s by the Executive or AGMs, emphasized professional objectives. Almost without exception these motions concerned hiring, firing, tenure, pay equity, and other conditions of employment (see, for example, AGM 1976 Minutes, pp. 7-9). These concerns continued to be expressed in the late 1970s and 1980s, likely influenced by the formation of a Women's Caucus as a separate grouping within the CSAA.[34] A motion, carried in the 1970s, requiring admission quotas for women applicants to anthropology and sociology graduate programmes, and motions passed in the 1980s (for example, AGM 1982 Minutes, p.19; AGM 1988 Minutes, p.10) may imply a learned-society orientation. None-theless, the view enunciated by women anthropologists and sociologists that is clearly consistent with a learned-society orientation—that women could bring different perspectives, through different concepts and methods, to the study of human beings—received little emphasis in CSAA committees responsible for its women members or in AGMs throughout the 1970s and 1980s.[35]

Canadianization and Canadian Studies

The Canadianization movement, as it is referred to by Brym (Brym and Fox, 1989: 19-24) and by Hiller (1982:33-39) had its roots in a general concern, raised in 1968 by Mathews and Steele (1969) at Carleton University, about the numbers of non-Canadians holding faculty appointments in Canadian universities. For anthropologists and sociologists, it concerned both matters of employment, the hiring of Canadians to teach anthropology and sociology in Canadian universities, and the content of curricula and the conceptualization of research problems in Canadian terms. Organizationally, these issues, the one professional, the other scholarly, were treated separately. The December 1971 Minutes of the 1971-72 Executive contain the first reference to concerns about the hiring of non-Canadians: the hiring and contracting practices of the National Museum and other museums that were seen to favour non-Canadian anthropologists. At the same meeting, the question of employment opportunities for graduate students of anthropology and sociology programmes offered by Canadian universities was raised. The 1972 AGM approved an Executive proposal to establish sub-committees on Canadianization and on Canadian Studies. Both sub-committees were unusually large.[36] The Canadianization Sub-committee was to concern itself primarily with employment issues, specifically, with priority in favour of Canadian citizens in hiring and tenure, and in the appointment of departmental headships. The Canadian Studies Sub-Committee's concerns were to promote studies relevant to Canadian society and to encourage the development of relevant materials.[38] Hence, the Canadianization Sub-Committee pursued professional objectives, while the Canadian Studies Sub-Committee's interests were more in keeping with a learned society perspective.

In 1974, however, as part of a reorganization of the CSAA's committee structure (See Bulletin, 1974), the Canadianization Sub-Committee was disbanded and a "responsable"[39] was appointed. The status of the Canadian Studies Sub-Committee is less clear. The reorganization proposal recommended that this sub-committee continue to be active throughout 1974-75 but required that a report of its three-years' activity be made to the Executive Committee in 1975. At that time, the sub-committee was also to recommend whether it should continue to be active. References in the Executive Minutes for August 1974, however, indicate that Dennis Magill had been appointed as "responsable" for Canadian Studies, which would suggest that this sub-committee was also disbanded. Moreover, except for a reference in the November 1974 Executive Committee Minutes to a letter from Dennis Magill, included under "Reports from Responsables," no other references to Canadian Studies, appeared in the Executive Committee or AGM Minutes until 1981.

In 1975 the AGM approved[40] the establishment of a twelve-member Task Force on Canadianization with responsibilities similar to those of the disbanded Canadianization Sub-Committee. Although not included in a formal statement, the responsibilities of the Canadian Studies Sub-Committee may also have been taken over by the Task Force. In any case, Dennis Magill, who had been a member of the Canadian Studies Sub-Committee and, as noted above, "responsable" for Canadian Studies, was appointed to the Task Force on Canadianization. He and John Lee reported on its activities and those of "related sub-Committees since 1972" to the 1975 AGM.

These various bodies appeared to be more active in the first than in the second half of the decade. Only brief reports or none from this Task Force appeared in Executive Committee or AGM Minutes after 1976. Even so, it is likely that the Task Force continued to monitor the effects of motions on Canadianization passed at earlier AGMs. Moreover, Dennis Magill and Paul Grayson were working, in the latter period, on the state of Canadianization in Canadian Anthropology and Sociology departments as an update of the relevant section of the 1975 Symons Report (Grayson and Magill, 1981; Magill, 1981). However, in June 1979, the Executive (1-3 June, p. 8) moved adoption of a report authored by Patricia Marchak that stated that there was no longer an immediate need to maintain a full committee on Canadianization although an Executive member should be appointed as a "watchdog" on Canadianization concerns.

Nonetheless, interest in Canadianization issues persisted. In 1981, the AGM passed nine motions, based on the Magill-Grayson Report of the Task Force on Canadianization. These essentially demanded that appointments in sociology and anthropology be restricted to Canadian citizens, with preference given to women, that universities be urged to further the development of Canadian Studies, and that the CSAA encourage publication of textbooks focused on Canada. The Canadianization Committee was charged with monitoring the implementation of the motions. By action of the 1984-85 Executive Committee, however, the Task Force was disbanded and its responsibilities transferred to the Social Policy Sub-Committee.

Simon Fraser University

In 1969, a strike in the Department of Political Science, Sociology and Anthropology, Simon Fraser University, led to the dismissal of seven faculty members (Berland, 1970). Although those dismissed included anthropologists and sociologists, the CSAA was cautious in its initial response to these events. At the December 1969 Executive Committee meeting, Richard Salisbury, CSAA President, reported on a letter he had written to the President of SFU expressing concern about the dismissals and indicating support for the Canadian University Teachers Association as the appropriate investigating organization. Moreover, when one of the dismissed SFU faculty members asked the CSAA to intervene, the Executive instructed the President to respond by stating that the request should be directed to the CAUT. The SFU case, however, was to involve the CSAA increasingly throughout the 1970s and its involvement would not end until 1986. Although the 1969-70 Executive, consistent with the learned society perspective of the CSAA, took the view, supported by the 1970 AGM, that the CAUT was the appropriate body to respond to professional concerns and issues, including relations between faculty members and the university administration, as time passed the CSAA became more and more involved and acted more and more like a professional association. Thus, the 1971 AGM not only confirmed its support for the CAUT censure of SFU but added a CSAA boycott of the university. Eventually, when in May 1977 the CAUT lifted its censure, the CSAA not only decided to continue its boycott[42] but moved to censure the CAUT for "failure to conduct the SFU dispute in a victorious manner." This progressive involvement of the CSAA in the SFU dispute provides further evidence that professional interests had become a major concern of the Association. Even so, there is evidence to suggest that the Association was becoming weary of the SFU boycott. In 1981, the Executive decided that no attempt to negotiate the SFU dispute would be taken unless the seven dismissed faculty members changed their positions "significantly" (Executive, 31 May 1981, p.6). By 1985, the Executive, acting on a request from CSAA members in British Columbia "and elsewhere," to review the boycott, appointed a Task Force for this purpose. The latter submitted its report and recommendations to the 1986 AGM (Minutes, p.10), which passed a motion to lift the boycott. After 17 years, the SFU affair was over.

Signs of Change

During the early 1980s, ethics, social policy, status of women, Canadianization, and the SFU dispute continued to be prominent among the CSAA's concerns. In the President's remarks to the Executive and to the 1983 AGM, he referred to the "old litany of issues: Canadianization, SFU, AF&T matters, and new editorial appointments," but assessed the CSAA as more mature and more able to impact on Canadian society. This emphasis on social policy was continued by his successors—in 1985, the President reported that he had given high priority to lobbying governments on matters concerning the recession, high unemployment, and cutbacks in social programmes. However, change was in the offing. As early as 1980, the Executive expressed concern over the quality of sessions at the annual meetings. As a remedy they looked for ways of attracting "more senior members" of the Association to participate. In November 1986, the President reminded his Executive that the *Canadian Review of Sociology and Anthropology* and the Annual Meetings were "the core of the Association" and that each activity of the CSAA should be examined in the light of these priorities. The President-Elect presented a paper to the 1987 AGM that recommended changes in emphasis in CSAA orientations, and as a consequence of the ensuing discussion, the Executive established a Task Force to Review CSAA Objectives and Performance.[43] Its mandate was to recommend ways and means to improve the academic aspects and intellectual events of the Association and to explore the idea of limiting the roles of COPEEC (Committee on Professional Ethics and Employment-Related Cases) and the Social Policy Sub-Committee. The draft and final reports of this Task Force were a major concern of the Association in the last two years of the decade. In the main, its recommendations[44] are consistent with its mandate: to give priority to the learned society activities of the CSAA, focusing on the Annual Meetings and the *Canadian Review of Sociology and Anthropology*. This did not mean a complete return to the CSAA of 1966, since the Task Force recommended that some activities and concerns that have evolved over the years should be retained although with a more limited scope. Thus, it recommended that the Social Policy Committee be replaced by a Professional Issues Sub-Committee with the promotion and representation of the professional concerns of anthropologists and sociologists as its main responsibility (Marchak et al., 1988, Recommendations 5.1., 5.2) It also recommended that COPEEC, renamed as the Committee on Professional Ethics (COPE) (Marchak et al., 1988, Recommendation 2.2), should no longer deal with individual complaints concerning ethics but limit its interest in ethical issues to maintaining the Code and to educational activities relating to ethical issues (Marchak et al., 1988, Recommendations 6.1, 6.2). A further recommendation (Marchak et al., 1988, 5.2) was to transfer responsibility for employment-related issues from COPEEC to the proposed Professional Issues Sub-Committee. These and other recommendations were modified by discussion in the AGM and by the Executive. For example, as a result of the so-called "Looker amendment," the new name of COPE was accepted but not the total restriction on handling situations of individuals. A mailed ballot was circulated to the membership. Those who returned the ballot strongly supported priority for scholarly activities, especially the Annual Meetings and the *Canadian Review of Sociology and Anthropology*, and for a reduced role for COPEEC, but also strongly supported retention of the Social Policy Committee with an increased emphasis on professional employment issues and trends and on research policy.

Concluding Comments

The evolution of the CSAA from a learned society to an association that combined such interests with those of a professional association and with those relating to political action resulted, in part, in response to the widespread social unrest that developed towards the end of the 1960s and continued into the 1970s. In particular, the imposition of the War Measures Act generated support for political intervention, which was sustained in ensuing years by a wide variety of events that invited political action. In part, the rapid growth of the disciplines probably increased the heterogeneity of perspectives among anthropologists and sociologists. As a discipline, sociology, which has many mansions, was in considerable ferment. Interest increased in critical sociology and social policy, which are both consistent with a sociological perspective that neither takes social institutions for granted nor treats them as sacred. Value-free sociology was out, value-laden was in. A strong emphasis on the study of Canadian society, including a call for uniquely Canadian theory, emerged. Events in the universities, especially those directed towards achieving more collegial relations between academic administrators and faculty and towards less authoritarian relations with students, supported a strong interest in employment-related issues, as reflected by the CSAA's involvement in the SFU dispute and other individual cases, and hiring as it affected Canadian citizens, especially women.

However, the interest in reaffirming a priority for its learned society activities was also influenced by conditions both internal and external to the CSAA. In the years following the CSAA's involvement in the SFU dispute, there were improvements, for example, in the organizational resources for dealing with employment-related problems. Both faculty unionization and a strengthening of faculty associations led to improved procedures for regulating relations between faculty members and their university administrations and to greater experience with collective bargaining on the part of those involved. In the face of such developments, the CSAA, with its more limited experience and scarce material and human resources, could be more effective by restricting its involvement to monitoring relevant disputes. In the arena of political intervention, the CSAA found itself competing with a variety of organizations that focused on specific issues, such as those concerned with civil liberties, the environment, poverty, and seniors, rather than on the wide range of issues that had evoked responses from the CSAA. The trend in such action organizations was to use paid staff and selected volunteers and to emphasize their expertise in dealing with the issues which concerned them. In the face of these developments, it was difficult for the CSAA, even if it reduced the scope of its concerns, to be effective.[46]

The acceptance of the recommendations of the Task Force Report suggests that the evolution of the CSAA with respect to its objectives and concerns is not necessarily linear. Even though a renewed emphasis on the objectives and concerns of a learned society provides continuity, the CSAA of the 1990s will not be the same organization it was in earlier decades. Since change is the most probable consequence for any organization as necessity requires response to external and internal pressures, it cannot be otherwise.

NOTES

1   In the first section of this article, I shall describe the events that led to the establishment of the Canadian Sociology and Anthropology Association (CSAA); in the second section, I shall discuss the major concerns that have occupied the CSAA over the past twenty-five years. The article is based on my direct involvement in the pre-CSAA events that led to organizational autonomy as well as on my experience on various CSAA committees, including a five-year term on the Executive Committee and the Editorial and Publication boards during my tenure (1968-73) as Editor, *CRSA*. In addition to a largely personal view of the events and actions I describe, I have read or reread the minutes of the Annual Meetings and the reports of the Secretary-Treasurer of the Canadian Political Science Association, minutes of the CSAA Executive Committee and Annual General Meetings (AGMs), issues of the *Bulletin*, of *Society/Société*, and articles, books, and other material cited under "References." However, as time did not permit as careful a checking of these materials as I would have wished, it may be prudent to treat my conclusions as hypotheses. Although my comments will be mostly limited to matters concerning sociology and sociologists, I am, nonetheless, very much aware of the contributions made to the CSAA by Marc-Adélard Tremblay, Dick Salisbury, Gillian Sankoff, Frank Vallee, and other anthropologists.

I thank Linda Christiansen-Ruffman, Jim Giffen, Deborah Harrison, Ted Hewitt, Bob James, Dennis Magill, Bruce McFarlane, Bill Reimer, and Fran Shaver who responded promptly to my requests for help in finding documents and other references. Pete Pineo, my long-time colleague at McMaster, volunteered suggestions and reminded me of relevant events. Raymond Currie, who persuaded me to take on this task, gave invaluable assistance, sending copies of his own materials as well as arranging for materials to be sent from the CSAA office.

2   Shore (1987:25) states that "a separate Department of Sociology was established in 1922," but later (p. 122) states that in 1925 the Department of Social Science was renamed the Department of Sociology. Ross (1984:4) refers to 1933 as the year Sociology and Social Work were separated.

3   Brym (1989:15) inaccurately states that this situation persisted until 1961. For example, McMaster established its department in 1958, and Bruce McFarlane reports that Carleton established its department in 1950.

[4] Over the years as I completed the B.A. Honours Sociology programme and an M.A. in sociology, Bernard Meltzer was appointed to teach social psychology, and William Kelly came as McGill's first appointment in anthropology, to be replaced eventually by Fred Voget.

[5] Among those whose names I recall are Jacques Brazeau, Bernard Blishen, Tom Bishop, Rex Lucas, Reuben Sircus, and Leo Zakuta.

[6] As a comparison, the CSAA had 908 individual members in 1989.

[7] The Minutes of the 1954 Annual Meeting include the following: Mr. Anglin asked if it would be possible to have, in future programmes, four sessions in political science, including one in international relations; Mr. Bladen urged that there not be a full complement of sessions for each of the branches of knowledge with which the Association was concerned, since much of the value of the meetings on the present plan was in the opportunity they gave for learning of developments in other than one's own field.

[8] Hughes' well-known paper "Mistakes at Work" was presented, initially, to a CPSA session in 1951.

[9] The Reports of the CPSA Annual Meeting and of its Secretary-Treasurer appear in the August issue of CJEPS. They are not listed in the references.

[10] Although relations between anthropologists and sociologists were cordial— and members of both disciplines participated in the same session—I think that the preference of most members of each discipline was for separate organizations. While social anthropologists and sociologists shared theoretical and research interests, anthropologists in other sub-fields had no more reason to join forces with sociologists than with those of other disciplines. If anthropologists and sociologists ended up together organizationally, it was, as in the case of joint departments, a matter of expediency.

[11] Joint memberships were available in the three associations for those who wished to maintain interdisciplinary contacts.

[12] I thought the meetings began in 1954, but Hiller (1982:20), who presumably had access to the records, gives 1955 as the starting date.

[13] The Ottawa Chapter elected an Executive Committee to guide its activities. In its first year, neither anthropology nor sociology was represented on it, but John Porter was elected as an Executive Member in 1955.

[14] The CPSA Annual Meeting Minutes refer to the Sociology and Social Anthropology Chapter but I believe that to be an error and that the CPSA's Secretary-Treasurer's Report for 1958 is correct in referring to the Anthropological and Sociological Chapter. There is a similar confusion in the reference to the title "President" in the Annual Meeting 1957 Minutes and the CPSA Secretary-Treasurer's 1958 Report which refers to the same post as "Chairman."

[15] Both were members of the Department of Anthropology and Sociology of the University of British Columbia.

[16] Presumably in the CJEPS.

[17] I wish I could list or at least mention some of the information included in that first issue, but I have only had access, thanks to Raymond Currie and Bruce McFarlane, to a few issues published in the 1960s and 1970s. If writing this essay accomplishes anything, it should be the establishment of an archiving function, including the responsibility to find missing materials relating to the CSAA and the Chapter. A fire in the CSAA office destroyed much of this historical record.

18   If the estimate is accurate, the representation of anthropologists and sociologists in meetings, in publications, and on committees of the CPSA was remarkably high.

19   I was unable to obtain the issue of the *Bulletin* in which the results were published.

20   Other Executive Committee members were: David Solomon (Past Chairman), Vice-Chairman Bill Dunning, Secretary-Treasurer Rex Lucas, and Members-at-Large Reg Robson, Charles Hobart, Richard Salisbury, Desmond Connor, and Jean Burnet. Henry Zentner, Managing Editor of the *Review*, and Jacques Brazeau attended as representatives of the Editorial Board. Brazeau was actively engaged in translating the drafts of the constitution, written by Reg Robson, from English to French.

21   The membership at that time was 189.

22   President, Marc-Adélard Tremblay; Vice-President, R.W. Dunning; Secretary-Treasurer, Céline St. Pierre; Members: Desmond Connor, Reg Robson, Father Lazure, Charles Hobart, Richard Salisbury, John Kantner, Rod Crook, Douglas Rennie, and Martin Meissner.

23   As was the case with *CJEPS* Minutes, where I cite CSAA documents, I have not, in most instances, included them in the References. Although AGMs and reports of the sub-committees were published in the *Bulletin* and *Society/Société*, I used, for most years, the typed reports prepared by the Montreal office.

24   CSAA's Standing Committees were called "Sub-Committees," i.e., sub-committees of the Executive. More recently, they have been called committees.

25   Mainly in the form of CSAA publications.

26   Such as the Social Science Research Council (SSRC) and, when it was established, the Canada Council.

27   This Sub-Committee was further subdivided in terms of discipline.

28   My editors suggest that a "rising consciousness about the rights of research subjects" could also have been a reason for establishing the sub-committee.

29   It was renamed the Committee on Professional Ethics and Employment-Related Cases (COPEEC).

30   This was a CSAA panel, chaired, I believe, by Hubert Guindon, but I found no reference to its appointment.

31   Other interventions include: a motion urging Université de Laval not to co-operate with Chile (1976 AGM); a motion demanding that Argentina release two political prisoners, presumably academics (1976 AGM); a motion concerning the civil rights of CSAA members but which included a clause concerning the actions of the police in a raid to the office of a periodical not associated with the CSAA (1978 AGM); a motion calling on Canadian universities to divest their holdings in companies involved in South Africa (1978 AGM); a letter to the Prime Minister from CSAA President regarding the violation of human rights in Argentina (1978-79 Exec).

32   Approved by the 1971 AGM.

33   First published as *Le Deuxième Sexe* in 1949.

34   There was a move in 1984 (AGM 1984 Minutes, p. 9; Executive Committee Minutes, 23 November, 1985, p. 13) to convert the Women's Caucus to a Sub-Committee on the Status of Women but subsequent discussion showed that the Caucus preferred to remain independent but maintain informal contacts

within the Sub-Committee. Although I found no reference to the dissolution of the 1971 Sub-Committee, I assume it was disbanded during the 1970s. There is a reference (Executive Minutes, 9-10 June 1977, p. 11, 11-12 November 1978, p. 15) to its responsibilities being assigned to the Social Policy Sub-Committee and to the Equal Rights Review Committee established in 1978 (the latter being "phased out" in 1978 [Executive Minutes 1 June 1978]). The Social Policy Sub-Committee reported on women's issues until 1985 when the AGM (Minutes, p. 6) passed a motion to establish a Status of Women Sub-Committee.

[35] My readings of the Minutes and Maticka-Tyndale and Drakich's (this volume) detailed account of the struggle to advance the interests of women anthropologists and sociologists support this conclusion. The contention that women's perspectives brought new directions to anthropology and sociology was certainly voiced by individuals and in the Women's Caucus. (See, for example, Smith [this volume] and Eichler [this volume]).

[36] The Canadianization Sub-Committee consisted of 9 members and 17 Resource Persons; the Canadian studies Sub-Committee, of 10 members and 13 Resource Persons. The Resource Person category was abolished for both sub-Committees by Executive action at its May 1973 meeting.

[37] A motion at the 1975 AGM to substitute "resident" for "citizen" was defeated.

[38] Concern about "relevant Canadian materials" was active long before the 1970s. My wife Jean reminds me that, on a drive from Toronto to Ottawa in 1955, Kaspar Naegele, John Porter, and I discussed at length the problem of providing students with accessible references on Canada relating to our lectures. In the course of the discussion, we decided to collaborate on a textbook that would help to overcome the problem. Later, we invited Bernard Blishen to join us. The result was the publication of *Canadian Society* in 1961, and of three revised editions, the last in 1971. It is reasonable to think that other sociologists held similar concerns at that time.

[39] The term was adopted to refer to a person, usually an Executive Member-at-Large with relevant expertise, given a "Task Appointment."

[40] The November 1974 Executive Committee passed a motion to strike such a Task Force.

[41] *Committee* was used in the AGM Minutes but it should have been *Task Force*.

[42] Despite the long discussions in Executive meetings and at the AGMs, the CSAA did not attempt to define the different conditions implied by the terms, disapproval, censure, and boycott until 1978 when it asked the Professional Ethics Sub-Committee to do so.

[43] Its members: Patrick Marchak (Chair), Raymond Breton, Gordon Inglis, and Suzanne Peters. (Executive, 1 June 1987, p. 7; Executive 6 June 1987, pp. 1-2).

[44] The sources of the information reported here are the CSAA Task Force Report on Priorities and Reform (Revised Version, 1988) and the results of the 1989 Referendum on the Task Force recommendations.

[45] Response was low (22%).

[46] See Marchak et al. (1988:16) for further comments on the financial, operational, and membership constraints that limited the effectiveness of the Social Policy Committee.

Striking a Balance
Women Organizing for Change in the CSAA

Eleanor Maticka-Tyndale
Janice Drakich

In 1966, the newly formed Canadian Association of Sociologists and Anthropologists was predominantly an association of men. Women, relative to men, were invisible in numbers, positions of office, and in the Association's minutes, newsletters, and concerns. Between 1970 and 1990, women organized to improve their position in the profession and in the CSAA. As illustrated in Margrit Eichler's paper, elsewhere in this volume, women moved from a position of relative obscurity in the CSAA to occupy a prominent role in the Association. This paper addresses the context of these changes and the processes that contributed to them.

Our review of the minutes and newsletters of the Association, its committees, and the women's groups within the Association (Drakich and Maticka-Tyndale, 1991) suggests that women's activism has followed the two lines discussed by Adamson, Briskin, and McPhail in their book on feminist organizing (1988:176): mainstream and disengaged activism. The perspectives of mainstreaming and disengagement provide the framework for our description of the process of women's changing status within the CSAA and the disciplines of sociology and anthropology. The chronicle extends only to the limits permitted by the documentation and the memories of participants. Gaps in the story and weaknesses in the analysis occur at some points as a result of absence of empirical data.

Mainstreaming and Disengagement

Adamson, Briskin, and McPhail portray mainstreaming and disengagement as politics of feminist organizing that are in opposition in both their location and content. With mainstreaming, the content of activism is directed at redressing concrete experiences of inequality and oppression. The locus of activism is within the established structures of existing institutions. Coalitions between members (men and women) and institutional resources are used to effect change, with strategies of change focused predominently on eliminating barriers to women's access to existing positions. The weakness of this form of activism is that women and their concerns are easily co-opted by the organization. Moreover, women's agenda is merely one of many, and is subject to cutbacks, redefinition, and subversion in favour of concerns that are considered more important in the organization (Adamson, Briskin, and McPhail, 1988:176-86).

In disengagement, the locus of feminist activism is most often outside existing institutions. If within them, it takes place outside the established institutional structures. Separate, distinctly feminist associations are created by women coming together at the grassroots level. Released from the need to negotiate and comply with institutional requirements, these groups apply all their energies to the development of unapologetically feminist analyses that may go beyond institutional boundaries to expose and address the foundations of women's oppression in the larger social fabric. The weakness of disengagement is the potential for marginalization of feminist concerns, critiques, actions, and of women themselves. Such marginalization impedes access to institutional resources and separates disengaged women from women who remain within the mainstream institutions.

In reality, the separation between mainstream and disengaged action is rarely as distinct, rigid, or wide as portrayed here. According to Adamson, Briskin, and McPhail, the key to social change is to bring the two together, not to see them as conflicting, opposing forces, but to develop "a feminist practice that is finely balanced between abstract vision and concrete reality" (Adamson, Briskin, and McPhail, 1988:186-87). Women's activism in the CSAA between 1970 and 1990 illustrates a process of fine-tuning the balance and developing a creative tension between mainstream activism within the structures of the Association, and disengaged activism both within and outside the Association.

The History of Women's Organizing in the CSAA

The history of women's organizing in the CSAA can be separated into five phases.[1] In the first phase, 1970-74, feminist activism utilized a primarily mainstream politic in both its locus and content. The second phase, 1974-77, saw the addition of the first clear steps towards disengaged activism. Spontaneous, grassroots organizations of women added a more far-ranging feminist critique to the continued mainstream praxis within the Association. Eventually, in the third phase, 1977-79, many activist women disengaged from the Association itself. The disengagement was so complete that some feared women's issues might disappear entirely from the agenda of the CSAA. During the fourth phase, 1979-85, activism within the Association was revived and the balance between mainstream and disengaged action was further developed. The fifth, and current, phase began with the institutionalization of a Committee on the Status of Women within the Executive structures of the Association in 1985 and the decision of the women of the Association to continue the grassroots, disengaged Women's Caucus.

Phase One: Beginnings of Activism

In the earliest years of the CSAA's existence, 1966-70, there is no mention in Association minutes or bulletins of concerns surrounding the entry of women into academia, the position of women academics in the Association, the exclusion of women from sociological and anthropological scholarship, or of concerns for the status of women in society in general. It was not until 1970, when the Report of the Royal Commission on the Status of Women exposed women's second-class status in the academy, that there is any record in the official documents of the CSAA of women's activism on their own behalf. From 1970 to 1974, activism was initiated by women on the Executive of the Association and addressed concerns regarding employment of women in the academy, remaining mainstream in both its locus and content.

In May 1970, an *ad hoc* Committee on the Status of Women was formed in response to a request from Lynn McDonald, a member of the Association's Executive Committee. From 1970 to 1973, the issues addressed by the Committee arose from women's experience as academics, and included: the effects of nepotism rules on women's access to employment, recruitment policies that discriminated against women as students and professionals, and the ghettoization of women in the lowest paid, least secure positions. The strategies for change included study and documentation of the status of women, passage of motions, and referral of those motions for action to committees within the Association and related institutions—university departments, deans, department heads, the Canadian Association of University Teachers (CAUT), and the Canadian Labour Congress. Motions focused on expanding access to full-time positions, tenure and regular salary scales, and catch-up wages, all within the mainstream pursuits of an academic association.[2] When no action occurred, the Association prodded departments with letters and formed a Manpower Committee (later renamed the Professional Registry Committee) to monitor new academic placements and compile lists of available sociologists and anthropologists. Despite these actions, little change was evidenced in women's access to academic positions during this period.

Women's activism did, however, effect a visible improvement in their position within the Association during this first phase. In response to resolutions passed by the AGM and the pro-active stance of the *ad hoc* Status of Women Committee, women's representation on the Ethics and Social Policy Committees improved. In addition, the first session on women, "Current Research on Women in Canada," appeared on the programme of the Annual Meetings in 1972. Finally, in 1974, Gillian Sankoff, active in the early inquiries into the status of women, became the first woman elected President of the Association. It is during Sankoff's presidency that the key weakness of mainstream activism, co-optation, became clearly visible. Sankoff began her tenure as President with an unwieldy organizational structure of 15 committees regularly reporting to the Executive and the Annual Meeting. To streamline this structure, all committees were eliminated and replaced by "task appointments" or "les responsables." "Responsables" had the task of (1) monitoring and reporting on all developments relevant to their areas; and (2) ensuring that workshops on pertinent research topics occurred at the Annual Meetings (*The Canadian Sociology and Anthropology Association Bulletin*, July 1974:7). This had a two-fold effect on women's actions. First, since action on motions had been directed to committees, the dissolution of all committees eliminated the very bodies mandated to act on the status of women motions. Second, the Status of Women Committee itself had been dissolved. There was no longer an institutional locus where women studied, discussed, formulated motions, or planned actions. All these were now left to one member of the Executive. The motions relevant to women and women's mainstream actions had been co-opted to the larger good of the Association: its need for more efficient, streamlined structures.

Phase Two: The Initiation of Grassroots, Disengaged Activism

The dissolution of policy committees within the Association together with at least four additional events both inside and outside the CSAA were influential in stirring women to disengaged activism. First, women across Canada were organizing in their communities. They were taking the women's movement outside of unions, political parties, and academe to reach special interest groups such as Indian women, black women, lesbian women, and farm women. They were establishing women-centred services such as rape crisis centres, transition houses for battered women, consciousness-raising groups, and women's centres. Activism outside existing institutional structures was fast becoming the "politically correct" strategy. Second, along with this diversification came the development of theory and articulation of differing feminist politics. This discourse, developed by feminists organizing outside of academe, became part of the discourse of women in the Association. Third, women in the CSAA had the example of women in other professional associations (e.g., the American Sociology Association's Sociologists for Women in Society and women's caucuses in other professional associations) who were engaging in disengaged activism. Finally, a factor that not only stimulated the initiation of disengaged action but sustained it, was, and still is, the critical mass of feminists in the Association committed to the improvement of women's status. These four factors, together with the absence of a Status of Women Committee, prompted interested members to act on their own behalf.

At the 1974 Annual General Meeting, a grassroots association of women faculty, graduate students, and others, called Women in Canadian Sociology and Anthropology, was formed. The group was disengaged from the established structures of the Association and took on characteristics common to other feminist grassroots organizations. Joined by the common experience of gender, membership cut across faculty/student lines to bring women together as equal, participating members who shunned formal structures for leadership and decision-making. Women in Canadian Sociology and Anthropology provided a forum for critical inquiry, analysis, and dialogue about the status of women, reaching beyond the women on the Executive and attending the Annual Meetings with the publication of *The Bulletin for Women in Canadian Sociology and Anthropology*. The tone of the intellectual debates are reflected in the first issues of the *Bulletin*. Kathryn Kopinak and Deborah Sheppard (Tannenbaum) argued the case for disengaged activism (Kopinak and Tannenbaum, 1975), while Anne-Marie Ambert (Henshel), presented the position that mainstream activism should not be abandoned (Ambert (Henshel), 1975). Dorothy Smith, the Executive "Responsable" for women, made the case for the impotence of the Association in implementing its own motions, pointing out that the CSAA had neither mechanisms nor power to enforce motions that called on bodies outside the Association (e.g., universities, government offices, etc.) to take action. On the empirical level, Gladys Symons Hitchman documented the continued absence of change in her review of the status of women sociologists and anthropologists in Canadian universities, published in the Association's newsletter (1974). Though all the Status of Women motions had passed with near unanimous assent, sociologists and anthropologists sitting on the university committees which would implement these motions had not acted to redress inequities.

During this phase, women's activism was predominantly disengaged in its organization and analysis, but mainstream in its strategies. Motions founded on feminist analyses were brought to the Association's Annual Meeting in 1974. These motions went beyond the mainstream issues of equal access to existing structures. Instead, they addressed the concerns of women outside as well as inside the professions of sociology and anthropology, and challenged the existing valuation of work and research. The 1974 motions called for equal pay for work of equal value, for catch-up wages for women support and clerical staff in universities, and for provincial and federal governments to establish special funds for research on women during 1975, International Women's Year.[3]

Coincident with and supportive of the activism within the CSAA, a distinct feminist scholarship was developing. By 1975, the first two academic books on women in Canada, Marylee Stephenson's *Women in Canada* and Anne-Marie (Ambert) Henshel's *Sex Structure* had been published. *The Canadian Newsletter of Research on Women*, edited by Margrit Eichler and

Marylee Stephenson, had been publishing for three years. These publications helped to initiate and maintain relationships between scholars doing feminist research, to encourage a sense of community among feminist scholars and to foster a continued analysis. The analyses developed in disengagement were introduced into the scholarship and teaching of mainstream sociology and anthropology. This growth in feminist scholarship was recognized with the publication of a special International Women's Year volume of the Association's journal, *Canadian Review of Sociology and Anthropology (CRSA)*, in 1975: *Women in the Canadian Social Structure.*

At the 1975 International Women's Year meeting of Women in Canadian sociology and anthropology, the dual approach of study and formulation of motions was again taken. This time women's attention turned to the incorporation of feminist scholarship into sociology and anthropology curricula. In-depth studies on the status of women's studies in departments of sociology and anthropology were launched. The resulting "Report on Women's Studies in Graduate Departments of Anthropology and Sociology," by Anne-Marie Ambert (Ambert (Henshel), 1976:3-5), documented an absence of graduate options in Women's Studies, a scarcity of women faculty who could direct graduate work on women's issues, and a marginalization and isolation of the women who did hold faculty positions. The continuing restriction of women's access to positions in departments of sociology and anthropology hampered the development of feminist scholarship and women's studies within the discipline. Activism and motions now shifted to promoting women's studies and educational equity. Two sets of motions were proposed at the 1976 AGM. The first, proposed by Peta (Tancred) Sheriff and Marylee Stephenson, called for 50 per cent women in M.A. programmes and 20 per cent women on faculty by 1979, and for hiring of women equal to their proportion of new Ph.D.s by 1981. Rather than leave implementation to the goodwill of Association members, however, a Standing Committee on Equal Rights Review, a Professional Registry Committee, and the Executive Committee's "Responsable" for Social Policy were mandated to take specific actions to monitor and facilitate the implementation of the motions. The second set of motions addressed the workings of the Association itself. The Publications Board and the Executive were to eliminate sexist language from the Association's publications, Constitution, and By-Laws, and the Programme Committee was to ensure that child care was available at annual meetings and that regular sessions on women appeared on the agenda. The motions again passed unanimously.

Women's activism during the years 1974-77 demonstrated the strength and power of the interweave of mainstream and disengaged action. Each contributed in a unique way to women's organizing. Disengagement provided the context for the development of feminist critiques that led to proposals for action. In contrast to proposals for equitable treatment and access, these asked that the roots of inequality within the practice of sociology and anthropology as disciplines be addressed and that affirmative action in the form of hiring and admission quotas to redress historical imbalances be implemented. Mainstream activism in the passage of motions and mandating of committees enshrined, in the very structures of the Association, the actions demanded by the disengaged critique, and ultimately changed the Association itself.

Towards the close of this phase, three women of the Association, Susan Clark, Lynn McDonald, and Linda Christiansen-Ruffman took action for recognition of feminist scholarship outside the CSAA. In response to an absence of federal support for women's research and publication, they organized the first Canadian conference on women's research, held in November 1976. Just as these women worked outside the regular structures, in the next phase of activism women moved their activism outside the Association.

Phase Three: Increased Activism Outside the Association

From 1977 to 1979, little action took place addressing women's concerns. That which did was situated predominantly in the mainstream committees of the CSAA. Disengaged, grassroots women's associations met only haphazardly, often lacking a chair and/or attendees. The women's newsletter disappeared. During this period, women's issues nearly disappeared entirely from the agenda of the Association. In 1977 and 1978 Susan Clark, the Status of Women "Responsable," frequently had no report at Executive Committee meetings. Both watchdog committees, the Equal Rights Review Committee and the Professional Registry Committee, disappeared. In 1978, the Equal Rights Review Committee reported its inability to carry out its mandate, and recommended that the committee be phased out with its responsibilities assigned to the Ethics Committee. The Professional Registry Committee stopped reporting to the Executive, and in its last report questioned the feasibility and even the desirability of fulfilling its mandate. Without continued, disengaged feminist analysis and strategizing, the mainstream committees dropped their feminist agenda when fulfilling it became problematic.

Feminist activism within the Association was on the wane. The Association's records do not provide an explanation. The advantage of hindsight and recent experiences, however, offer some suggestions. The latter part of the 1970s was a dismal employment period for young academics, and particularly for women. It was also a period of shifting professional standards, with community service devalued and greater emphasis placed on publication in specific journals and with specific publishing houses. Academic institutions were "chilly climates" for women, with the road to promotion or tenure paved with malestream (non-feminist) expectations. Women fortunate enough to obtain full-time employment were reluctant to engage in feminist activism. They had witnessed or heard of the consequences of feminist scholarship and activism for career progress. Such scholarship, and the grassroots community activism so vital to its maintenance, were not valued by mainstream academicians. Women activists, while not a rarity, were labelled "radical women." The effect of the "chilly climate" in a virtually closed employment market served to constrain the activism of junior women academics. The increasing emphasis on publication records forced many women to withdraw their service activities. The constraints on women had consequences for the maintenance of grassroots activism, then and now.

Many women recognized that change in their academic status could not be realized through the CSAA alone with its limited power and influence on academic structures and departments. In response, women's activism turned to establishing alternative forums that would provide them with arenas for their research and publications and with a place to develop their collective voice and feminist analysis. The latter part of the 1970s saw the burgeoning of unapologetically feminist groups with women sociologists and anthropologists focal to their organization.

The Canadian Research Institute for the Advancement of Women (CRIAW) was formed to foster new research specific to the needs and concerns of women. Its roots may be situated in the first Canadian conference on women's research held in November 1976. CRIAW has continued to be an alternate support for feminist research with an annual conference, grants for new researchers, activism to promote the recognition of researchers who do not have a university affiliation, and publication of research with policy implications. Alternative educational experiences established by women in community centres, Ys, and women's centres fostered and facilitated teaching and research into issues of direct and immediate concern to women in communities, and brought academics together with non-academic women activists. *Atlantis*, Canada's first feminist journal, began publishing in 1976. The Women's Press of Toronto (established in 1972), and women's presses forming in other cities became increasingly active as publishing houses for work by and about women. These publications moved into mainstream book stores and university courses. Women sociologists and anthropologists were active in these publishing endeavours as authors, editors, reviewers, and contributors. They were active, as well, in the various organizations forming across the country to address women's concerns. This activism was completely disengaged from existing institutions and often crossed traditional barriers between academic women and the community.

These external, disengaged activities indirectly contributed to women's struggle within the CSAA and the academy. The position and demands of women in the CSAA were strengthened by the increased visibility and legitimacy of women's scholarship that identified and elaborated the systemic barriers to women's full participation in the profession.

Phase Four: A Return to Grassroots Activism within the CSAA

Women's activism within the CSAA was revived in 1979 when Linda Christiansen- Ruffman, Chair of the Social Policy Committee, resurrected that Committee's mandate to address the status of women and implement the motions of the early 1970s. Christiansen-Ruffman called for women to caucus at the 1979 Learned Societies meetings. After reviewing the lack of progress on earlier motions, the Caucus prepared a new set of motions for the 1979 AGM. The motions revived issues that had been addressed but not acted on: the representation of women's scholarship at society meetings and the lack of child care. In addition, the CAUT's disbanding of its Status of Women Committee was addressed. Rather than turning to Association committees to "watch over" and implement these motions, the Women's Caucus took on the task of maintaining its own watching brief on the status of women sociologists and anthropologists in academe and the progress on the CSAA motions. Regularly scheduled meetings of the Women's Caucus during these years facilitated the co-ordination of women's concerns and actions. Reports on the progress of departments in implementing motions of the CSAA related to employment, women's studies courses and programmes, and sexist language were published in Society/Société (Christiansen-Ruffman, 1979, 1981; Maxwell, 1981; (Maticka) Tyndale, 1981). Besides its monitoring work, new avenues of action were initiated. Roxana Ng's survey of the number of Social Science and Humanities Research Council of Canada (SSHRC) applications and successful awards for leave fellowships, doctoral fellowships, and research grants led to motions protesting the low priority given women and women's scholarship in SSHRC funding.[4] An Association-initiated review of its Professional Code of Ethics included a Caucus recommendation that sexual harassment be addressed in the Code. In response to concerns about access to Canadian feminist resources, the Caucus initiated a project to develop a bibliography on the Sociology of Women.

This era illustrates the melding of grassroots and formal institutional action, with the Caucus (a disengaged group of women) setting priorities, and taking action within the mandate and framework of the (mainstream) Social Policy Committee. These co-ordinated efforts ensured that women's concerns were included in the Association's agenda. The moratorium on hiring non-Canadians called for in the Ethics Committee's Report on "Canadianization" (Society/Société, October 1983) recommended first preference in hiring be given to Canadian women. University chairpersons and presidents received letters from Elliot Leyton (1984), CSAA President, urging them to honour the resolutions relating to affirmative action in the hiring of women. A Women's Caucus session on "Women and Violence" was funded with $100 from the Social Policy Committee. Stewart Crysdale (*Society/Société*, 1985) gave recognition to sociologists and anthropologists who had made an impact on social policy through advocacy research in the area of the rights and responsibilities of women.

While women's activism in the CSAA was energized during this period, women continued to be involved outside the Association. The increasing number of women's studies courses, minors, and programmes led to the formation of the Canadian Women's Studies Association (CWSA), an interdisciplinary association including many sociologists and anthropologists. The Canadian Congress of Learning Opportunities for Women (CCLOW) was formed in 1981 to address women's access to non-traditional and traditional education, and teaching with a view to meeting the specific needs of women. The Ontario Coalition of Faculty Associations (OCUFA) in 1984 established a Status of Women Committee with three of the five positions occupied by sociologists—Peta Tancred-Sheriff (chair), Alena Heitlinger, and Helen Breslauer.

This phase illustrates a full integration and balance between disengaged and mainstream activism and the accomplishments such a balance makes possible. Despite the successes of women's grassroots activism, however, the Caucus recognized the limitations of volunteer energies and the absence of a permanent voice on the Executive of the CSAA. The creative tension between mainstreaming and disengagement had been instrumental in the initiation and realization of women's objectives. Women were eager to establish a permanent institutional structure to empower their mainstream activism and to provide disengaged activism with access to the power of the CSAA. At the 1984 meetings, Suzanne Peters, Chair of the Women's Caucus, proposed that a Status of Women Committee be a formal committee of the CSAA with the chair to be a member of the CSAA Executive. The mandate of this committee would be to develop, survey, monitor, and report on the implementation of policy resolutions on the status of women. At the 1985 AGM, this motion, as with all others, was carried with virtually no opposition. Suzanne Peters became the first chair of the Status of Women Committee with Roxana Ng and Sheva Medjuck as the first committee members.

Phase Five: Maturation of Creative Tension

With the establishment of the Status of Women Committee, the first decisions facing the women of the CSAA were the continuation of the Caucus, and its relationship with the Status of Women Committee. The debates around mainstream and disengaged activism were raised once again. A Status of Women Committee had been established; was there need to continue the Caucus? Those recognizing the potential for co-optation in exclusively mainstream activism, argued for the continuation of the CSAA Women's Caucus, stressing that the creative tension between the two strategies had served the women of the Association well. The relationship between Caucus and Committee was articulated in *Society/Société*: the role of the Women's Caucus was to advise the Status of Women Committee of the concerns and priorities of the women of the Association and to monitor the activities of the Committee and the Association (Maticka-Tyndale, 1987:29).

The years from 1985 to the present reflect, for the most part, a positive working relationship between mainstream and disengaged action. Regularly scheduled annual meetings of the Caucus have been well attended and a great deal has been accomplished in its annual two-hour "time-slot." Together, the Caucus and the Committee produced the women's studies bibliography initiated years earlier, and have regularly brought motions and proposals to the Executive. For example, the Caucus developed questions for candidates running for office in the Association, asking them to address their use of feminist scholarship in teaching and their support of women's actions to redress inequalities within the Association and their universities. The questions were taken by the Status of Women Committee to the Executive and the Association as a whole.

Separately, the Caucus produces a newsletter to keep the women of the Association informed, and co-ordinates the yearly mounting of sessions on women and women's scholarship for the Learneds. The Status of Women Committee, on the other hand, responds, on behalf of women, to issues raised in the Executive and the profession. As a member of the Social Science Federation of Canada, Women's Network Committee, The Status of Women Committee participates in research funding and publishing inquiries and decisions that concern women in the profession. The Committee has also conducted research on the distribution of women faculty in sociology and anthropology departments.

Overview

Women's mainstream and disengaged activism in the CSAA has produced research and put motions in place that have advanced the status of women in the profession. The successes for women were accomplished by the efforts of the women on the Executive and committees of the Association, and in the grassroots lobbying and organizing of women in the Association. Equally as important as the work inside was the work outside the Association. The innovative work of women outside of the Association provided women scholars with alternative forums for feminist research and publication and legitimized feminist scholarship.

In twenty years of documented activism, women have established a firm foothold within the Association, its activities, and the practice of sociology and anthropology in Canada. Margrit Eichler's (1986) review of feminist scholarship in the CRSA's special issue on the state of the art, and the 25th anniversary edition of the *Review*, edited by Pat Armstrong and Roberta Hamilton, focusing on feminist theory, clearly illustrate the entrenchment of feminist scholarship in the discipline. Women have not fared as well in academic positions, however. Though their representation in departments of sociology and anthropology has increased, it has not yet met the proportions called for in the motions passed unanimously in the 1970s. For many departments, redressing disparities in gender representation is given mere lip-service, with policies grounded in systemic discrimination often guiding hiring and promotion decisions.

We have reconstructed this history for both personal and analytical reasons. As women of the Association who have benefitted from this history, we wanted to share it with all the women of the Association, to record the progress of women's activism, and to show our appreciation for the work that women did, often at the expense of their own careers and family. Analytically, we wanted to show that the creative tension between mainstream and disengaged activism produced a variety of responses, strategies, and alliances in addressing the status of women, strengthened the voice of women, and advanced the women of the Association.

NOTES

[1]   In an earlier analysis (Drakich and Maticka-Tyndale, 1991) we addressed four phases, with the second phase consisting of two periods, referred to here as the second and third phases. We have chosen to address these as distinct phases rather than periods within a phase for purposes of simplification.

[2]   Motion moved by L. McDonald and seconded by J. Porter, June 8, 1971:
(1) that the CSAA go on record as actively opposing discrimination on the basis of sex, age or marital status in the...;
2) that the association encourage university departments to recruit women as graduate students and faculty on an equal basis with men;
(3) that the association encourage university departments to eliminate any discrepancies between the sexes in fellowships, salaries, promotion and tenure;
(4) that the association encourage universities to adopt more flexible policies concerning career patterns; for example, holders of part-time academic positions should be eligible for tenure and should be paid at regular salary rates. (*Bulletin*, November, 1971:8)

[3] Motion 1: We recommend that incumbents of part-time positions shall become entitled to all customary benefits of university positions. These should include entitlement to life and health insurance, suitable office space, access to administrative facilities, retirement benefits, sabbatical leaves, and such.

Motion 2: We further recommend that incumbents of part-time academic positions shall be eligible for university research grants, travel assistance, and research assistants.

Motion 3: We further recommend that all incumbents of part-time academic positions shall be eligible for tenure and that each academic year of part-time teaching count as one full year toward tenure in the part-time position.

Motion 4: We further recommend that when a full-time position opens, the incumbents of part-time positions must be, if they so wish, considered for the position before any outside applicants. The full-time appointment need not imply full tenure, but refusal of full-time tenure shall not annul the part-time tenure already worked.

Motion 5: We further recommend that the motions just passed be communicated by the executive, through the CSAA, CAUT and AUCC Bulletins to: (a) Presidents of Canadian universities; (b) Deans of relevant faculties; (c) Heads or chairmen of departments and directors of institutes hiring sociologists and anthropologists.

[4] Motion 8: The CSAA protests the low priority given to women in the economy by SSHRC as manifested in the Strategic Grants Programme by (a) the funding for women and work area which is the lowest level for all the other areas and which discourages applications for comprehensive research; and (b) the limited time between publication of guidelines and the deadlines for applications.

We demand that (a) the amount of money available for women and work be raised to at least the average for all Strategic Grants areas; (b) the deadline for submissions be extended to September 30, 1983; (c) the grants be allocated by the regular December decision date.

Motion 9: Given that women have in the past been inadequately represented on peer review committees of SSHRC for sociology and anthropology research grants, be it resolved that all such committees have at least one-third representation of women and/or provincial representation of the number of scholars in the discipline, whichever is greater.

REFLECTIONS ON NOT BEING SUED
Gordon Inglis

At the first meeting of the CSAA Executive that I ever attended, in the spring of 1971, one of the first items to be discussed was the necessity of getting the Association legally incorporated. I had come late to academic life, and it was all new to me. I could not understand the note of urgency that I detected in the discussion, even when it was pointed out that if the unincorporated Association were to go bankrupt or be sued for large sums of money, its officers could be held personally liable: the possibility of such a thing happening to a respectable organization of scholars seemed so remote as to be hardly worth considering. It was not very long, however, before I became as avid a proponent of incorporation as any of them.

The meeting approved a motion directing that a CSAA censure and boycott of Simon Fraser University be publicized in Britain and the United States as well as in Canada. It dealt with a resolution from the Annual General Meeting that urged that the Association express its views on important questions of social policy, and listed several examples, mostly involving Quebec. The work of no less than fifteen sub-committees was reviewed, and the Sub-Committee on the Status of Women was raised in status from *ad hoc* to standing. Letters to the federal government commenting critically on several matters were approved. The chair of the Sub-Committee on Professional Ethics reported on progress towards a Code of Ethics and plans for adjudicating individual complaints, and it was suggested that an opportunity be provided to air grievances at the AGM.

Not surprisingly, perhaps, it was decided to increase the time allotted for Executive and committee meetings, and to extend Annual General Meetings to two sessions. A theme for the next year's meetings was suggested: "Canadian Identity and Social Change."

A few years later, with heated debate raging over a dozen issues, the extended time allotment for business meetings was stretched even farther. Executive and administrative sub-committee meetings could each fill a couple of twelve- to fourteen-hour days twice a year, and other sub-committees met as intensely. Some members had resigned in protest over one or another of the controversies, and Annual General Meetings were lengthy and heated, full of emergency resolutions, challenges to the chair, amendments to amendments, and quorum calls. The Association had not gone bankrupt or been sued, but if either had happened—or both together—the event would have occasioned no great surprise among most of its members, and some sociologists and anthropologists, both members and non-members, would have greeted the news with considerable satisfaction.

I recall one animated discussion in a corridor of a Quebec university, in the aftermath of a particularly rancorous AGM, that stopped just short of physical assault when one of the participants was dragged away by his supporters, still shouting final arguments and imprecations over his shoulder. A small group of *Québécois* students had been observing the exchange with interest, and one of them came over and asked me, as one of the survivors, what it had been about. When I explained he said, "I didn't know English Canadians could get so excited about debates!" There was wonderment and even a hint of respect in his voice.

Still, this was surely not the sort of thing the founders had in mind when they established, first a chapter of the Canadian Political Science Association, and later an independent Learned Society dedicated to "the encouragement of research and publication in, and teaching and general development of, Sociology and Anthropology."

We seemed to be re-enacting a sequence of events that is familiar from origin myths of societies all over the world. Typically, in such stories the original condition of the society is depicted as a paradisiacal age of peace and harmony; so it seemed to be with the CSAA. Programmes of early annual meetings present us with a glimpse of Eden, where the lion lay down with the lamb, the sociologist—well, at least *sat* down—with the anthropologist; where anglophone and francophone, phenomenologist and structural functionalist were as sister and brother; where one session could be chaired by a Jacques Parizeau and another by a Eugene Forsey (Annual Meeting Programme, 1965); a time when, as Eliade (1984:149) says of the Aranda myth, "the ancestors were free from the multitude of inhibitions and frustrations that...obstruct all human beings who are living together in organized communities."

Inevitably, however, there comes an end to innocence, and from then on the society must live with conflict, disagreement, and contention. In most mythical traditions, the Fall from Grace is attributed to a single quite specific event, usually either a mistake or a malicious act by a particular being or class of beings. In the Judaeo-Christian narrative it is blamed on the only available woman, who causes humanity's downfall with some assistance from a representative of one of the least popular animal species. The Ekoi of Nigeria, according to Frazer (1918:58), say that it was caused by "the gross misconduct of a duck."

There are sectarian versions of this story, too, in the CSAA mythology, with various events cited and various candidates for the role of Eve. Or snake. Or duck, for that matter. Like other origin myths, of course, these stories are primarily symbolic rather than historical. Readers will be relieved to find that I do not intend to repeat them, but merely to present some reflections on the period to which they refer.

To begin with, it is necessary to remind ourselves of some demographic facts (all figures from von Zur Meulen 1982:48).[1] In 1956, when the Sociology/Anthropology Chapter of the CPSA was formed, there were 4,973 full-time teachers in Canadian universities, of whom nine were anthropologists and 32 sociologists. By the time the CSAA was founded, nine years later, there were 51 anthropologists and 195 sociologists out of a total of 12,084 university teachers. When I attended my first Executive meeting in 1971, the Canadian professorate had grown to 24,603, including 195 anthropologists and 702 sociologists. By 1980 the score was anthropology 403 and sociology 962, out of a total of 32,803. That is to say, in twenty-four years the Canadian professorate had grown by about 660 per cent, the sociology portion of it by about 3,000 per cent, and the anthropology portion by about 4,475 per cent. Taken together, sociologists and anthropologists had risen from slightly less than one per cent of all university teachers to slightly more than four per cent. A considerable number of people from both disciplines had also found positions in non-university settings.

That this exploding population of sociologists and anthropologists had general scholarly interests in common could be taken for granted, but the specifics of those interests and the communication of them would take time to work out. In the meantime, and more immediately, most of them had in common their position as faculty members in rapidly expanding universities, many of which were new institutions. They also, as students of society and culture, could be expected to have opinions—though not necessarily the same opinions—about the social and political events that were unfolding around them. And the CSAA was the only national forum where they could come together. (Not all of them, I hasten to add—it was frequently a matter of concern within the Association that many chose not to belong—but it was nonetheless the only real national meeting ground.)

In such circumstances it was inevitable that professional and social policy matters would begin to occupy an increasing amount of attention when sociologists and anthropologists came together. However, for many of them in the late 1960s the notion of social science as "objective" and "value free" was still an article of faith, and they were uneasy at the thought of the Association involving itself in matters other than those they defined as purely scholarly. The CSAA's elected officers were feeling their way, working out the organization's role as they went along, and the process might have been more gradual and peaceful had it not been for some dramatic events that forced themselves onto centre stage.

In October of 1969, the Canadian academic community was shaken by the dismissal of eight faculty members in the social sciences from Simon Fraser University. A year later, the whole country was shaken by events in Quebec and the imposition of the War Measures Act. In both cases the CSAA Executive took rapid action that was followed up by resolutions at the Annual General Meeting. Without having had the time to work out in any detail how it was going to do it, the CSAA had become an organization that took actions and made public comment on professional and political issues. And once that was established, there was no lack of material to occupy its attention.

For the next dozen years, those long business meetings grappled with questions and cases relating to academic freedom, language policy, employment, international affairs, professional ethics, and on and on. Typically for an organization with an annually changing executive, there were inconsistencies and variations in position and emphasis. The actions of one executive or incumbent were repudiated or modified by another, and heatedly supported or opposed by the membership at the AGM. The issues overlapped and interconnected, and through them all the political, professional, and scholarly dimensions were hopelessly intertwined. To illustrate the point, I shall trace out briefly one set of connections with which I had some partisan involvement. I do not intend to re-argue the issues, but merely to demonstrate some of the complexity.

The American Anthropological Association (AAA) was scheduled to meet in Toronto in the fall of 1972, on the strength of an invitation that had been issued in the mid-1960s by the University of Toronto Department of Anthropology. As the date approached, some Canadian anthropologists began to question the appropriateness of the meeting. They were not, however, all motivated by the same considerations.

At the time, there was a general public upsurge of the perennial Canadian concern that growing American influences threatened Canada's economic, political, and cultural independence. Many academics who shared this concern felt that the rapid influx of professors, most of whom came from the United States, was having the effect of skewing the style and content of university teaching and research too heavily toward American models. Some sociologists and anthropologists felt that these concerns were of particular significance in their disciplines, which had been growing more rapidly than almost any of the others and which, even without the influx of newcomers, were in any case already largely staffed by people trained in the United States. These people saw the universities and scholarly organizations not solely as foci of international scholarship but also as important national cultural institutions. Why, they asked, should an American organization hold its meetings in a Canadian city, hosted by a Canadian university? For them, the Toronto meeting of the AAA was symbolic of both Canadian anthropology's and Canada's position vis-à-vis the U.S.A.

Others who questioned the appropriateness of the meeting started from a very different perspective. As members of the American Anthropological Association, they had become alarmed by what they perceived as an inappropriate "politicization" of that organization. They disapproved of the fact that the AAA had, at meetings in the late 1960s, passed resolutions concerning American government policies, both foreign and domestic. They opposed the idea of any scholarly organization concerning itself with matters that they defined as lying outside the academic realm, and they opposed the Toronto AAA meetings as an expression of this.

Various expedients were proposed: that the University of Toronto should withdraw its invitation; that the meetings should be a joint CSAA/AAA enterprise; that the CSAA should be the official host rather than the University of Toronto. It was even suggested that the AAA's scholarly sessions could be held in Toronto but that the business meetings should be held across the border in Buffalo. However, the Department of Anthropology at Toronto decided by majority vote not to withdraw or modify the invitation, and the Executive Committee of the CSAA was unwilling to intervene. As a result, some anthropologists began to promote the idea of an independent Canadian anthropology association that would take its own stance with respect to the AAA.

Although the meetings had been planned for some time, opposition to them began to be articulated rather hurriedly only a year or so before the projected date, and in the flurry of correspondence on the subject it was not immediately apparent to some of those raising the objections that there was such a wide divergence of reasons for doing so. The idea of an independent Canadian anthropology association was supported by people from both of the opinion categories described above.

While this was going on, two *ad hoc* committees of the CSAA were at work preparing a brief to an AUCC commission on what was termed the "rationalization" of university research in Canada. Their combined brief generated a storm of controversy by stating bluntly that the central problem of anthropology and sociology in Canada was that "Both...are...strongly dominated (some would say `colonized') by the academic and cultural traditions of a single country, that of the United States of America." It went on to argue

> ...that for anthropology and sociology to play constructive roles in the development of an *independent* Canadian society these disciplines must now become more Canadianized in content, orientation, and personnel. This means it will be necessary to change the trend of hiring, to restructure our curriculum, emphasize scientific perspectives more germane to our conditions and needs, and to respond to the problems of *this* country rather than to the problems posed by the academic traditions of other countries.
>
> In a word, then, the rationalization of research in our two disciplines means, first of all, the Canadianization of the disciplines. (CSAA n.d. Emphases and parentheses in original)

This brief was discussed and given qualified approval at a meeting of Toronto-area anthropologists, and was the basis of a lengthy and acrimonious plenary session at the 1972 annual meeting of the CSAA in Montreal (cf. CSAA *Bulletin*, October 1972). Two sub-committees concerned with Canadianization were created, and the Executive sent letters to university departments and museums across the country making recommendations on hiring, promotion, and a number of other matters. These actions were applauded by some and vigorously denounced by others. Not surprisingly, among the latter were some who had opposed the Toronto AAA meetings because of what they perceived as the "politicization" of that organization, and among the former some who had done so as an expression of Canadian nationalist sentiments. The letters to museums and university departments were particularly controversial: the framers of the motions had intended that the recommendations be accompanied by an explanation of the rationale for the suggested policies, but the letters sent out presented merely the text of the motions, which made the recommendations seem peremptory and perhaps presumptuous.

Meanwhile, the movement for an independent or partially independent anthropology association was growing, fuelled by a number of concerns. Since the 1950s at least, anthropologists had been fewer in number than sociologists in Canada, and because of the nature of the discipline were probably even more diverse in their scholarly interests. Many who came to Canada in the 1950s and 1960s maintained their AAA or RAI (Royal Anthropological Institute) memberships but did not join the CSAA, and those specializing in archaeology and physical anthropology had formed their own Canadian associations. By the early 1970s anthropologists were outnumbered by three or four to one in the CSAA, even though they had near-parity in most of its structures. Those who favoured splitting the CSAA into two independent associations argued that it did not provide an adequate forum for scholarly exchange among anthropologists: the meetings had too few anthropology sessions, partly because of their timing, and the *Review* did not carry enough anthropology articles (cf. Weaver 1972). Some anthropologists, both members and non-members of the Association, had been disturbed by the controversy over the AAA meetings and by the emerging Canadianization debate, and felt that the CSAA was coming to be too much concerned with matters they considered to be outside the scholarly mandate. Among some Quebec anthropologists there was a feeling that the CSAA had not served either anthropology or francophone scholarship very well, and that a smaller, independent anthropology association might better facilitate exchanges between the two linguistic groups.

Those who favoured remaining with the CSAA were mostly social anthropologists whose research interests were closer to those of the sociologists, and those who felt that the larger association could better represent the two disciplines in relations with government and granting agencies and other bodies. On the whole, they were more comfortable with the CSAA's stance on Canadianization and other controversial issues. They argued that the problems of scholarly communication could be addressed within the CSAA structure (cf. Inglis 1972).

Arguments for and against splitting the Association were presented at a CSAA-sponsored Anthropology Caucus in Montreal in 1973, to which were invited representatives from all university anthropology departments and museums, and from existing sub-disciplinary associations. As we know, the Association did not split, but a group of anthropologists established the Canadian Ethnology Society, which was intended to be "a small, informal association to further communication among ethnologists in Canada," complementary to rather than in competition with the CSAA (*Bricoleur*, 1973, No. 2:3). The CES is now, as of 1989, the Canadian Anthropology Society and is flourishing, and the CSAA, in spite of having several times debated the advisability of deleting "anthropology" from its title, continues at the time of writing to retain its name and small but loyal membership of social anthropologists. Both organizations have contributed to the support and encouragement of a substantial body of work on Canadian society and culture.

After a quarter of a century as a Learned Society the CSAA, with its customs and conflicts, myths and practices, is like any other society a product of its history. Its contribution to scholarship and to the larger society has been made not only in the scholarly sessions and the pages of the *Review*, but also in those seemingly endless meetings devoted to "business." I have recounted this compressed and truncated fragment of our past— whether as history or as myth will be up to the reader to judge—to illustrate a simple and perhaps obvious point: that our scholarly activity and the institutional arrangements within which we carry it on are both part and product of the social and cultural forces that are our object of study: that scholarship does not exist in a box of its own, sealed off from the context within which it is pursued. If that sounds trite in the 1990s, then so much the better; but it is worth remembering that twenty-five years ago it was not a cliché at all, but a somewhat radical idea.

NOTES

[1] These figures, all from Statistics Canada, may not agree exactly with sources that arrived at their figures by different methods. They do not quite agree, for example, with figures cited by Frank Jones in this volume. The disagreements are minor, however, and do not detract from the point I am making about rapid increase.

THE TWO SOLITUDES
BETWEEN CANADIAN SOCIOLOGISTS

Guy Rocher[1]

It is an honour to be associated with the celebrations and publications marking the 25th anniversary of our Association. At the beginning of the 1960s, while active in the Sociology and Anthropology Chapter, I was involved in the discussions we had to decide whether we should create a distinct Association or remain within the Canadian Association of Political Science which was then sheltering us. The opinions were divided; some feared that a new Association would isolate us from sister disciplines, while others saw in this move the essential step to face the coming changes. Today we can conclude from twenty-five years of experience that both points of view were accurate: our Association has facilitated the development of our two disciplines, but we are also much more distant from other social sciences. The two roads were probably inevitable. It seems clear that the decision of twenty-five years ago indeed has accelerated the development of sociology and anthropology, and it is likely that the distance from the other social sciences would have occurred in any case. Even housed within the same Association, sociology and anthropology have gone their separate ways with little interaction. By way of illustration of that very point, I will address only the sociology of sociologists.

While reminiscing about past memories, permit me to recall a very personal one. When I began my career as a young assistant professor at Laval in 1952, Professor Jean-Charles Falardeau—one of the pioneers of Canadian sociology, recently deceased—who had taught me from 1947 to 1950 was then becoming my colleague. He had established strong links with colleagues from other provinces, particularly in Ontario and British Columbia, and was very active in the Canadian Political Science Association. This was at the time when we did not have separate social science associations; it was even before the existence of chapters within the Canadian Political Science Association, which was the origin of distinct associations. Jean-Charles Falardeau strongly advised me to take part in the ACSP/CPSA meetings which were about to take place in June of 1953 at London, Ontario. I was only beginning to teach and I had to prepare new classes all year. Therefore I had no paper to present. The only reason for my trip was to meet colleagues from other provinces. This was my first plunge into the Canadian social sciences and Canadian sociology. I retain a very vivid memory of this experience.

Three years later, in 1956, with Yves de Jocas I presented the results of my first research project to my Canadian colleagues gathered this time at the Université de Montréal. Once again I was encouraged to do this by Jean-

Charles Falardeau, who even corrected the English version of my text. It was a study of inter-generational mobility, comparing francophone and anglophone Quebecers, based on a sample of marriage certificates. I remember that I was in awe as I appeared before about thirty of my colleagues in a classroom, and it seems to me even today that I did not answer the questions very well.

I recall these personal memories for a more general reason. I want to illustrate the fact that in the 1950s, among most of my Quebec francophone colleagues, there was the sense of belonging to a Canadian sociology and the desire to establish ties and active relationships with anglophone colleagues in other provinces. We felt the need to share with them the fruits of our research and our endeavours.

Then came the creation of the Sociology and Anthropology Chapter; the first grouping of our disciplines; the first gesture of distancing from the Canadian Political Science Association in this genesis of our Society which came about in 1965. Francophone Quebecers continued to be present and active in the Chapter in the early 1960s. I was one of the presidents; if my memory serves me well it was 1962 or 1963. The programme of the last meeting of the Chapter, in 1965, provides evidence of the significant participation of francophones. Jean-Charles Falardeau was President of the Canadian Political Science Association. In addition, in spite of the distance to British Columbia where the meetings were held, I can recall the names of at least 15 Quebec francophones out of 75 participants. That is one-fifth, a proportion that we have never again achieved to this day.

In fact, the creation of our Association that same year marked a rupture in the tradition I have just recalled. The reasons for the discontinuity need to be explored. Since 1966, French-speaking sociologists have attended our annual meetings so rarely that those who come are virtually invisible. I have examined the programs for each of the 25 meetings; they reveal an extremely weak pattern of participation by francophones. One has to turn many pages to gather a few names. For example, beginning with the meetings of 1967, of the 90 names of participants, I discovered only 1 colleague from Laval, even though the meetings were held at Carleton, at the very borders of Quebec. So also in 1968; I found only 1 francophone sociologist from McGill among the 60 participants, at the same time that nearly a third of the active participants that year were American colleagues. Beginning in 1971 the Annual Meetings became quite large, attracting more and more colleagues. Let us consider 1972 because the meetings were held at McGill in Montreal. I could count only 13 Quebec francophones out of 340 active participants, less than 4 per cent. The meetings of 1976 mark the reappearance of francophones because the conference was at Laval in Quebec City. That year, a little more than 50 out of 370 participants were francophones from Quebec, Ontario, and New Brunswick: about 14 per cent. But their participation fell to almost zero the next year, at the meetings held at the University of New Brunswick. There were a few more at the 1980 meetings held at the Université du Québec à Montreal, but insignificant given the location of the meetings. Let us finish this review by looking at the 1989 conference at Laval. We can find 40 francophone participants out of 337, a meagre representation given the Quebec location.

It is futile to continue with this; the evidence is clear, all the meetings offer the same spectacle. One could speak of a presence less than nominal, or more precisely, of an absence more than simply uncommon. Reading these programmes one might conclude that Quebec sociology was almost suppressed after 1965, when in fact it was in a period of full expansion. This under-representation of francophone Quebec sociologists is an indication of a profound rupture. A canyon was carved out between francophone sociologists, particularly those from Quebec, and Canadian anglophone sociologists. A wall of silence has arisen between us, which seems stronger and more lasting than the Berlin wall. There was no separatism, but an effective separation, a remoteness, a removal. All that without a referendum!

What has happened? How can this be explained? Let us attempt a sociological explanation; we have known for a long time that our disciplines are influenced by the social, cultural, and political milieu in which we live. It is therefore not surprising that sociology has felt the effects of the questioning of the Quebec and Canadian identity that has gone on for the last three decades in Canada. To a certain degree and in its own way, sociology has reflected, been a mirror, of the societal crisis that Canada has passed through and is still passing through.

Let us try to observe how these things have come to pass in this history. Quebec francophone sociologists have been absorbed by the major changes that were occurring in Quebec, both in order to understand them and to intervene. Quebec sociography was extremely active; there is not another province, another region of Canada that was studied, analyzed, dissected as much as Quebec. At the same time, sociologists were energetically involved, again more than elsewhere, as agents and actors in the transformation of Quebec. This focus on Quebec as a privileged field of study and action created among Quebec sociologists a common ground of intellectual exchange. If it contributed on the one hand to limit the horizons, on the other hand it created a wonderful homogeneity. Without doubt this explains why Quebec francophone sociologists felt the need to get together on the margins of the CSAA. This began in a grouping with social psychologists, which in 1969 gave rise to the Association canadienne des sociologues et anthropologues de langue française (ACSALF), attached to L'ACFAS (Association canadienne-française pour l'avancement des sciences) which has played a role parallel to that of the Royal Society in Canada. L'ACSALF was an active group, well aware of the issues in Quebec; it was there, among other places, that sociologists began to exchange among themselves the fruits of their work.

Nevertheless it is important to add that Quebec francophone sociologists actively sought to widen the audience of their conversations to include the international francophone community. Numerous contacts were established with sociologists in France, Belgium, Switzerland, North Africa, and francophone Africa, as well as with those from Latin America and the United States. Young Quebec francophone sociologists—as well as those not so young—rather than turn towards their Canadian colleagues, which they had done in the 1950s, addressed other audiences. Quebec sociologists had the feeling they were being read and understood more outside than within Canada.

From its standpoint, the CSAA appeared as a unilingual anglophone group. The very weak francophone participation at the annual meetings caused French to disappear from the programmes, which further convinced francophone sociologists that that was not their place. We were thus victims of a vicious circle, impossible to break into. Quebec sociologists quickly acquired a conviction that if they came to the CSAA meetings, they would have to speak English if they wished to be understood and have some reaction to their papers. One need only rapidly glance through the programmes to see the almost exclusive domination of the English language.

Let us look at an indicator that is closely related to the very organization of the annual meetings: the language used in the titles of the different sessions. The CSAA has been inconsistent on this matter, and in general, inhospitable to the French language. Here are the results of my chronological search:

- from 1967 to 1971 inclusive, the titles were in English only
- in 1972, 1973, and 1974 they were bilingual
- they were unilingual English in 1975
- from 1976 to 1981 they once again became bilingual
- from 1982 to 1988 they were unilingual
- they were bilingual in 1989
- they became unilingual in the preliminary programme of 1990

One can see the absence of a coherent policy on this matter, with a resulting lack of continuity. When programmes were bilingual, it was usually because the meetings were held in Quebec: McGill in 1972, Laval in 1976 and 1989. Even under these conditions there is no continuity: the 1985 meetings at the Université de Montréal were unilingual English.

Nevertheless, the CSAA made some efforts to interest francophone sociologists. They were always invited to sit on various committees, and bilingualism was maintained in the Association publications. The CSAA has sought to establish and maintain contacts with ACSALF, although in a somewhat sporadic manner. But one can note that francophone sociologists made no effort to be represented on the Executive Committee, where their absence since 1982 stands out. No francophone has been elected President of our Association in more than fifteen years.

In spite of these efforts, which should not be minimized, I believe there is reason to address three criticisms of the CSAA and more broadly of Canadian sociology. The CSAA could have been the key meeting place of Canadian sociologists, francophone and anglophone. Beyond political conflicts, constitutional or otherwise, it could have contributed to preserving a conversation between us, as academics and as researchers. That would have been completely logical given that our main field of study is our very own country! But it was not so. The CSAA has been divided by the same grand canyon that has also divided the rest of Canadian society; it has undergone the same societal crisis as the Canadian people.

Second, through exchanges between francophones and anglophones, the CSAA could have played another role that it seems to me it has neglected. It could have encouraged, and even initiated, comparative research between our two linguistic and cultural communities and thus contributed to the progress of comparative sociology, which is gravely neglected both theoretically and empirically. Canada offers sociologists a rich laboratory where two great cultural and linguistic, groups cohabit, as well as both Aboriginals and Inuits, the first occupants of the land. In addition, a large number of other ethnic, linguistic and cultural communities have been added and have multiplied, especially since World War II. We have neglected an extraordinary opportunity to deepen and extend our knowledge of Canadian society, as well as to make a completely unique contribution to the advancement of our discipline. Throughout the world contemporary sociology suffers terribly from the lack of comparative research. This could have been the trademark by which Canadian sociology could have been distinguished, and which would have given it an exceptional identity.

Finally, Canadian sociology, in my judgement, has not contributed as much as it should to theoretical and basic research. While the distinction between basic and applied research comes to us above all from physics and the natural sciences, it is a distinction that makes sense in the social sciences. Canadian sociology has been rich in empirical studies, but poor in the theoretical reflection and analysis that one would consider fundamental. I believe that stems from the neglect of comparative studies. Max Weber demonstrated it very well; comparative studies are the essential route to take if we wish to make generalizations, in the framework of an active and productive preoccupation with theoretical issues.

An anniversary, such as we celebrate in this volume, is the occasion to congratulate ourselves for the distance travelled. It is also a moment to cast a critical glance on what we have done and what we have neglected to do;

that is what I have wished to do—not in order to beat ourselves or humiliate ourselves, but to better see how we might modify the course ahead. I believe in the voluntarism of history; I believe in the scope of liberty and uncertainty from which one can derive profit for human behaviour. Would it display an exaggerated optimism to hope that we might undertake the means to sew new seams between academics and researchers that go beyond political contingencies, false constitutional accords, and partisan opportunism?

NOTES

1　Translation by Raymond F. Currie, with permission.

THE UNFINISHED TRANSFORMATION: WOMEN AND FEMINIST APPROACHES IN SOCIOLOGY AND ANTHROPOLOGY[1]

Margrit Eichler

Sociologist: "It would be interesting if your survey shows...that sociology is probably one of the most significant areas in the history of the development of feminism and women's studies..."

Anthropologist: "The interesting...theoretical material came from anthropology."

Introduction

When the organizers for the 25th anniversary conference asked me to be one of four panellists who would critically assess some aspect of the role of the CSAA in its twenty-five years of existence, I realized, for the first time, that I had personally experienced twenty out of these twenty-five years as a participant in the CSAA. Until I was challenged to reflect about the Association, I had taken its form and shape as given, rather than as socially created. Examining the role of women and feminist scholarship in the CSAA brought home the fact that the Association has been an important vehicle for promoting ties among sociologists. Personally, I came to know many other sociologists—and some anthropologists—in my various roles as paper presenter, discussant, session organizer, committee member, and lately president. As a group, female sociologists and anthropologists contributed in important ways to shaping the Association into its present form.

Trying to assess how the CSAA has treated women (and, by implication, men) in the first quarter century of its existence is not easy. Minimally, it involves two aspects: one, the role of women as women within the Association, and secondly, the manner in which anthropology and sociology have dealt with that portion of scholarship that looks at women as being equally worthy of consideration as are men: feminist scholarship.

I will first examine the role of women in the Association, and then turn to the issue of feminist scholarship.

The Role of Women in the Canadian Sociology and Anthropology Association 1965-1989

The Role of Women in the CSAA Annual Meetings

In 1965, the first handful of anthropologists and sociologists met as the Anthropological and Sociological Chapter of the Canadian Political Science

Association. By the standards of later years, it was a small meeting, with 22 sessions, which decreased to 4 sessions in 1966, the year of the first Annual Meeting of the Canadian Sociology and Anthropology Association—a modest start indeed. The annual conferences took off in the early 1970s, and have tended to have around 70-90 sessions per conference since that time.

If we look at the role women have played in these meetings, we find a steady increase. In order to measure the participation of women in the sessions, we looked at every programme from 1965 to 1989, and identified the participants by first name as male or female.[2] Those we could not identify (5 per cent) we listed as "sex unknown" and ignored in the computation of percentages.[3] I first measured the participation of women and men in the various annual conferences by role played.[4] The following figures, then, do not tell us how many women and men participated in the various annual conferences; they tell us instead the proportion of female to male participation in the sessions.

While there is some difference in female participation by role, looking at the picture as a whole the differences do not appear to be striking. Women were a bit more likely to present papers[5] (31.4 per cent female participation over the twenty-five year period) than to chair sessions (29 per cent) or to serve as discussants (27.8 per cent),[6] but overall the differences are not notable.

Given that yearly fluctuations cannot be assigned the same importance as trends over many years, and given that due to the manner in which the data are organized a few particularly active individuals might have an effect on the overall sex distribution in any given year, I aggregated the data, by adding up all forms of participation and looking at five-year periods. The results are presented in Table 1.

Overall, two things are clear: the meetings clearly allow for female participation, and the participation has been steadily increasing from around 11 per cent in the first five years (1965-69) to around 42 per cent in the last five years (1985-89).

Sessions in the CSAA are generally pretty open for participation by anybody who wishes to participate. That is not to imply that every paper submitted or session proposed is actually accepted—such is not the case—but it is not too difficult for young scholars (for instance, students or beginning lecturers or assistant professors) to present papers or to organize sessions. Usually, only a notice to the conference organizer(s) is needed with a session title and description in order to be included in the official call for papers, and papers are accepted or rejected on the basis of an abstract and its relationship to the session title. When there are particularly numerous paper submissions for one particular session, organizers will often try to set up a second or even a third session on the same topic, to accommodate the expressed interests. This relatively open structure has obviously been favourable to the involvement of women.

Table 1
Overall Participation of Females and Males in CSSA Sessions

Year	Number of Females	Number of Males	Number Sex Known	Number Sex Unknown	Percentage Females
1965	4	39	43	37	9.3
1966	2	9	11	1	18.2
1967	6	78	84	14	7.1
1968	8	51	59	6	13.6
1969	17	120	137	9	12.4
Subtotal	37	297	334	67	11.1
1970	23	175	198	18	11.6
1971	47	259	306	15	15.4
1972	75	267	342	24	21.9
1973	54	225	279	27	19.4
1974	71	303	374	29	19.0
Subtotal	270	1229	1499	113	22.0
1975	71	320	391	25	18.2
1976	71	264	335	33	21.2
1977	118	307	425	14	27.8
1978	122	304	426	18	28.6
1979	153	357	510	43	30.0
Subtotal	535	1552	2087	133	25.6
1980	108	259	367	20	29.4
1981	135	218	353	14	38.2
1982	101	199	300	15	33.7
1983	183	245	428	17	42.8
1984	147	217	364	24	40.4
Subtotal	674	1138	1812	90	37.2
1985	130	213	343	21	37.9
1986	185	227	412	11	44.9
1987	196	289	485	21	40.4
1988	174	231	405	13	43.0
1989	165	225	390	14	42.3
Subtotal	850	1185	2035	80	41.8

Such climate of relative openness did not simply happen by itself, but is due to the dedicated work of a relatively small group of women (Drakich and Maticka-Tyndale, in this volume). These women kept the issue of women and sex equality in the forefront of the collective mind of the Association, through a variety of means. Drakich and Maticka-Tyndale identify five phases of activism:

In the first phase, 1970-74, feminist activism utilized a primarily mainstream politic in both its locus and content. The second phase, 1974-77, saw the addition of the first clear steps toward disengaged activism. Spontaneous, grassroots organizations of women added a more far ranging feminist critique to the continued mainstream praxis within the Association. Eventually, in the third phase, 1977-79, many activist women disengaged from the Association itself. The disengagement was so complete, that some feared women's issues might disappear entirely from the agenda of the CSAA. During the fourth phase, 1979-85, activism within the Association was revived and the balance between mainstream and disengaged action was further developed. The fifth, and current, phase began with the institutionalization of a Committee on the Status of Women within the Executive structures of the Association in 1985 and the decision of the women of the Association to continue the grassroots, disengaged Women's Caucus.

Women's Executive Positions

The first female President, as Table 2 indicates, was in office during 1974 (Gillian Sankoff). Until 1979—for a fifteen-year period—she remained the sole female president. By contrast, between 1980 and 1991, there have been five more female presidents. Overall, this means that 23 per cent of all presidents have been female by 1991.[7]

By contrast, women's participation as conference organizers has been relatively low (see Table 3)—over the twenty-five year period it amounts to 12.5 per cent—while women have held 42.3 per cent of the positions of Secretary/Treasurer and 22.4 per cent of various editorial positions in the Canadian Review of Sociology and Anthropology (see Table 4) and Society/Société (see Table 5).

Comparing the CSAA to other learned social science societies in terms of their efforts to eliminate (or rather, reduce) sexism, the CSAA is clearly among the leaders in this area. In 1984, the Social Science Federation of Canada (SSFC) conducted a survey among its member associations on their awareness of a sexist bias in research. Only four of the 17 societies who were member associations of SSFC and who responded to the questionnaire displayed an awareness of this problem: the Canadian Association for Research in Home Economics (CARHE), the Canadian Psychological Association (CPA), the Canadian Sociology and Anthropology Association

Table 2
Association Officials by Sex, 1966-91: President and Secretary-Treasurer

Year	President Female	President Male	Secretary-Treasurer Female	Secretary-Treasurer Male
1966		Marc-Adélard Tremblay		Rex Lucas
1967		Marc-Adélard Tremblay	Céline Saint-Pierre	
1968		Reg Robson	Céline Saint-Pierre	
1969		Reg Robson	Colette Carisse	
1970		Richard Salisbury	Gillian Sankoff	
1971		Jan Loubser	Gillian Sankoff	
1972		Hubert Guindon		Kurt Jonassohn
1973		Pierre Maranda		Kurt Jonassohn
1974	Gillian Sankoff			Kurt Jonassohn
1975		Frederick Elkin		John Jackson
1976		Arthur K. Davis		John Jackson
1977		Peter Carsten		John Jackson
1978		Bernard Blishen		Dominique Legros
1979		Gordon Inglis		Dominique Legros
1980	Patricia Marchak		Patricia Fitzsimmons-LeCavalier	
1981		John Hofley	Patricia Fitzsimmons-LeCavalier	
1982	Brenda Beck		Patricia Fitzsimmons-LeCavalier	
1983		James Richardson		William Reimer
1984		Elliott Leyton		William Reimer
1985		Stewart Crysdale		William Reimer
1986	Thelma McCormack		Frances Shaver	
1987		John Jackson	Frances Shaver	
1988		G.N. Ramu	Frances Shaver	
1989		Robert Stebbins		Anthony Synnott
1990	Linda Christiansen-Ruffman			Anthony Synnott
1991	Margrit Eichler			Anthony Synnott

Table 3
Association Officials by Sex, 1966-91: Conference Co-ordinators
CSAA Meetings

Year	Anthropology		Sociology	
	Female	Male	Female	Male
1966		Lionel Vallee	Aileen Ross	
1967				M. Meissner & M.-A. Tremblay
1968				Ernest Landauer
1969				Richard Ossenberg
1970				Bernard Blishen
1971				James C. Hackler
1972		Richard Salisbury		John D. Jackson
1973		Jean Lapointe		John de Vries
1974		Tom McFeat		B.Y. Card
1975	C.J. Matthiasson			John Hofley
1976		Louis-Jacques Dorais		Michel de Seve
1977				James Richardson
1978		Mathias Guenther		Richard Henshel
1979		Doug Daniels		Alan Anderson
1980		Joseph Levy		Philip Ehrensaft
1981		Leonard Kasdan		Graham Morgan
1982		Jean Lapointe	Ann Denis	
1983		Michael Kew	Tissa Fernando	
1984		Frans Schryer		Sid Gilbert
1985			Frances M. Shaver	Marc Renaud
1986		John Matthiasson		Raymond F. Currie
1987		Richard Preston		Cyril Levitt
1988		Mahesh Pradhan	Mary Lou Dietz	Barry Adam
1989		Louis-Jacques Dorais		Daniel Gay & M. de Seve
1990		David Moyer		William K. Carroll
1991		Pieter de Vries		Robert M. Pike

(CSAA), and the Société québécoise de science politique (SQSP). The authors of the study conclude that such awareness is linked to the proportion of women in a discipline and/or the existence of a women's caucus or section (Christiansen-Ruffman et al., 1986).

Women's Publications in the Review

The *Canadian Review of Sociology and Anthropology* is the official refereed journal of the Association. By analyzing the sex of the authors or contributors

Table 4
Association Officials by Sex, 1964-91: CRSA Editors

Year	Editor-in-Chief Female	Editor-in-Chief Male	Acting Editor Female	Anthropology Editors Female	Anthropology Editors Male	Book Review Editors Female	Book Review Editors Male
1964	Jean Burnett						
1965	Jean Burnett						
1966	Jean Burnett						
1967	Jean Burnett						
1968	Jean Burnett						
1969		Frank Jones					
1970		Frank Jones					
1971		Frank Jones	Lynn McDonald				
1972		Frank Jones	Lynn McDonald				
1973		Frank Jones				Patricia Marchak	Yvan G. Simonis
1974		Raymond Breton				Marlene Mackie	Yvan G. Simonis
1975		Raymond Breton			Richard Frucht	Marlene Mackie	Pierre Dandurant
1976		James McCrorie			Richard Frucht	Rosalind Sydie	Pierre Dandurant
1977		James McCrorie			Richard Frucht	Rosalind Sydie	Pierre Dandurant
1978		James McCrorie			Richard Frucht	Rosalind Sydie	
1979		James McCrorie			Peter Carstens	Rosalind Sydie	
	Sociology Editors Female	Male					
1980		John Jackson			Peter Carstens		Gavin Smith, Lorne Tepperman
1981		John Jackson			Peter Carstens		Gavin Smith, Lorne Tepperman
1982		John Jackson			Louis-Jacques Dorais	Naciellen Davis, Emily M. Nett	
1983	Peta Tancred-Sheriff				Louis-Jacques Dorais	Naciellen Davis, Emily M. Nett	
1984	Peta Tancred-Sheriff				Louis-Jacques Dorais		Gail R. Pool, David A. Nock
1985	Peta Tancred-Sheriff				Pieter de Vries		Gail R. Pool, David A. Nock
1986		Robert Brym			Pieter de Vries	Constance de Roche	Don Clairmont
1987		Robert Brym			Pieter de Vries	Constance de Roche	Don Clairmont
1988		Robert Brym			Gail Pool	Constance de Roche	Don Clairmont
1989		James Curtis			Gail Pool	Paula Chegwidden	Tullio Caputo
1990		James Curtis			Gail Pool	Paula Chegwidden	Tullio Caputo
1991		James Curtis			Max J. Hedley	Paula Chegwidden	Tullio Caputo

Table 5

Association Officials by Sex, 1966-91: *Society/Société* **Editors**

Year	Female	Male
1975	Lorna Marsden	
1976	Lorna Marsden	
1977	Anne-Marie Ambert	
1978	Anne-Marie Ambert	
1979	Anne-Marie Ambert	
1980		Donald Willmott
1981		Donald Willmott
1982		John Goyder
1983		John Goyder
1984		John Goyder
1985		Neil Guppy
1986		Neil Guppy
1987		Neil Guppy
1988		Victor Ujimoto
1989		Victor Ujimoto
1990		Victor Ujimoto
1991	Arlene Tigar McLaren	

Note: Based on the editor for the last issue of each year.

to the journal, we obtain a different measure of the participation of women in one of the official Association activities (although publication is not restricted to Association members). The sex of authors was determined in a manner corresponding to that employed for the previous set of tables.[8]

Over the years the participation of female authors has increased, but there were, of course, yearly fluctuations. In order to provide a better overview of trends, I grouped the results in five-year periods, according to the nature of the publication. The difference between authorship in articles versus "other"—i.e., research notes, commentaries, etc.—is not substantial (21.1 per cent female authors for articles and 19.1 per cent for other publications). The results are contained in Table 6.

What is interesting here is the difference of female participation in the annual conferences as opposed to the female participation as authors in the *Review*. The differential female participation is graphically represented in Graph 1. Female participation in the meetings seems to be about ten years ahead of that in the *Review*. This may be due to a variety of factors, which will be examined below. First, it is interesting to compare the authorship in the *CRSA* with the authorship in the other major Canadian sociology journal,

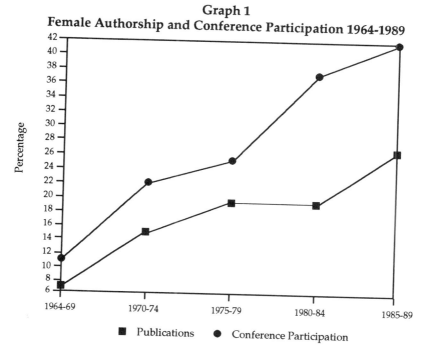

Graph 1
Female Authorship and Conference Participation 1964-1989

■ Publications ● Conference Participation

the *Canadian Journal of Sociology (CJS)*, and with the two leading American sociological journals, the *American Sociological Review (ASR)* and the *American Journal of Sociology (AJS)*.

In a comparison of the *CRSA* with the *Canadian Journal of Sociology*, women fare better as authors in the *CRSA* than in the *CJS*: the female authorship in the *CJS* between 1975 and 1980 was 13.0 per cent and between 1981 and 1985 it was 13.5 per cent (Mackie, 1986:Table 1). The comparable figures for the *CRSA* were 15.8 per cent and 20.8 per cent, respectively.[9]

Table 6

Authorship in CRSA by Sex and Type of Publication, 1964-89, in 5-Year Periods

Year	Vol.	Number of Articles	Female Authors	Male Authors	Unknown Authors	Number of Known Authors of Articles	Percentage Female Authors of Articles	Number of Other Published Items	Female Authors	Male Authors	Unknown Authors	Number of Known Authors All Published Items	Percentage Female Authors All Published Items
1964	1	16	2	14	0	16	12.5						12.5
1965	2	14	0	14	0	14	0.0						0.0
1966	3	14	1	15	0	16	6.3						6.3
1967	4	14	0	18	0	18	0.0						0.0
1968	5	16	0	16	2	16	0.0						0.0
1969	6	14	5	10	1	15	33.3	6	0	8	0	23	21.7
Subtotal		88	8	87	3	95	8.4	6	0	8	0	103	7.8
1970	7	15	0	17	0	17	0.0	7	2	5	1	24	8.3
1971	8	14	3	11	0	14	21.4	3	1	2	0	17	23.5
1972	9	14	3	11	1	14	21.4	7	3	4	0	21	28.6
1973	10	15	2	15	0	17	13.3	8	1	7	0	25	12.0
1974	11	16	2	19	3	21	9.5	4	0	5	0	26	7.7
Subtotal		74	10	73	4	83	12.0	29	7	23	1	113	15.0
1975	12	32	17	28	0	45	37.8	8	6	16	1	67	34.3
1976	13	30	6	28	2	34	17.6	6	2	8	0	44	18.2
1977	14	22	3	40	3	43	7.0	12	3	19	0	65	9.2
1978	15	20	7	16	3	23	30.4	18	1	23	0	47	17.0
1979	16	21	6	19	1	25	24.0	11	0	15	0	40	15.0
Subtotal		125	39	131	9	170	22.9	55	12	81	1	263	19.4
1980	17	20	5	20	1	25	20.0	7	1	6	0	32	18.8
1981	18	22	9	21	1	30	30.0	12	3	13	0	46	26.1
1982	19	17	5	16	1	21	23.8	13	2	15	0	38	21.1
1983	20	13	3	14	0	17	17.6	10	0	11	0	28	10.7
1984	21	14	4	13	0	17	23.5	9	2	9	0	28	21.4
Subtotal		86	26	84	3	110	23.7	51	8	54	0	172	19.8
1985	22	21	5	21	1	26	19.2	7	2	10	0	38	18.4
1986	23	21	7	21	0	28	25.0	5	1	5	0	34	23.5
1987	24	22	5	25	0	30	16.7	5	4	5	0	39	23.1
1988	25	21	12	14	0	26	46.2	6	1	8	0	35	37.1
1989	26	26	14	25	0	39	35.9	4	0	6	0	45	31.1
Subtotal		111	43	106	1	149	28.9	27	8	34	0	191	26.7
Total		484	126	481	20	597	21.1	168	35	200	2	832	19.1

If we compare the sex composition of authors in the *CRSA* with that of the *American Sociological Review (ASR)* and the *American Journal of Sociology (AJS)* we find that female authors in the *CRSA* are *very slightly* ahead of their U.S. counterparts (see Table 7).[10] The differences are, however, no more than

Table 7

Sex of Authors in *ASR*, *AJS* and *CRSA*, 1970-72 and 1985-87

	ASR 70-71 AJS 70-72		CRSA 70-72		ASR 85-86 AJS 85-87		CRSA 85-87	
	N	%	N	%	N	%	N	%
Male	247	87.9	43	86.0	242	80.4	67	78.8
Female	30	10.7	6	12.0	54	17.9	17	20.0
Sex Unknown	4	1.4	1	2.0	5	1.7	1	1.2
Total authors	281	100.0	50	100.0	301	100.0	85	100.0

Source of American data: Carden, 1990, p. 11, Table 1.

one to two percentage points. In both cases, the female authorship in the official journal of the respective national organization is significantly lower than the overall presence of sociologists (in the Canadian case, as expressed in the participation of women in Association meetings).

Carden suggests that there are three possible explanations for such discrepancy for the American case: what might be termed the *seniority hypothesis*[11] (women are on average less senior since newer to the field and therefore do not publish in similar proportions to the more established men in the two highest prestige journals), the *placement hypothesis* (women are less likely to teach in graduate departments where publishing is fostered more) and the *age hypothesis* (younger scholars, whether male or female, are less likely to find the type of article that is publishable in the *ASR* and *AJS* appealing and therefore prefer to publish elsewhere). A fourth hypothesis that could be added might be called the *discrimination hypothesis*: women's submissions are treated less positively and have therefore a lesser chance of being accepted for publications than men's. It seems interesting to examine these hypotheses for possible explanations of the differential found here in Canada.

With respect to the *seniority hypothesis*, it is still the case that women are, compared to their male counterparts, more clustered in the lower ranks than in the higher ranks: while 38.4 per cent of all male anthropologists and 31.1 per cent of all male sociologists were full professors in 1985-86, the same was true for only 23.1 per cent of the female anthropologists and 15.3 per cent of the female sociologists, as is shown in Table 8 (Guppy, 1989:15, Table 1). However, this hypothesis hinges on the correctness of the assumption that professors in senior ranks publish more than professors in junior ranks.

Table 8
Rank Distributions by Sex for Anthropologists and Sociologists 1985-87

Rank	Anthropology		Sociology	
	Female %	Male %	Female %	Male %
Full	23.1	38.4	15.3	31.3
Associate	42.3	47.4	41.2	48.7
Assistant	29.5	12.2	37.6	18.7
Lecturer	5.1	2.0	5.9	1.3
Total	100.0	100.0	100.0	100.0
N's	78	255	170	636

Source: Guppy, 1989, Table 1

Unfortunately, the CRSA does not publish the rank of its authors (as some journals do) and this analysis does not permit a direct test of whether higher rank is positively associated with proportionately more publications. This would require a separate study beyond the scope of this paper. It should be noted, however, that these days pressure to publish is pretty high on professors in junior ranks—and even on graduate students who are about to enter the job market. Until we have evidence that higher rank is associated with a higher rate of publication for both sexes for Canadian professors, we cannot consider this hypothesis as confirmed.

Table 9 presents information relevant to the *age hypothesis:* While, on average, female anthropologists and sociologists were four years younger than their male counterparts, (average age for women 42, for men 46, for anthropologists, and 41 and 45 years for sociologists), the differences do not

Table 9
Average Age by Rank, Sex, and Field, 1985-86 (in Years)

Rank	All Faculty		Anthropology		Sociology	
	Female	Male	Female	Male	Female	Male
Full	52	51	48	51	49	50
Associate	45	44	45	43	42	45
Assistant	38	36	40	38	38	39
Lecturer	36	34	35	42	33	38
Average	42	46	42	46	41	45

Source: Guppy, 1989, Table 2

seem significant enough to present a convincing explanation, especially when looked at by rank (see Guppy, 1989:15, Table 2).

With respect to the *placement hypothesis*, the stratification between Canadian universities is in no way comparable to that of American universities, and should therefore be a lesser factor than could be expected for the United States. If anything, the issue would be one of regional location. The annual reports of the sociology editor of the *CRSA* (Tancred-Sheriff, 1986, Brym 1887, 1988, and 1989) do not suggest a systematic discrimination against authors from the Atlantic regions, the Prairies, and B.C.[12] This hypothesis therefore does not seem applicable to the Canadian situation.

We then turn to the *discrimination hypothesis*. In Table 10, we do have data for the sex of submitters, reviewers, and authors of articles in the *CRSA* for 1985-88.[13] Four years (and not entirely complete data) do not constitute a sufficiently long period of time to make observations about trends, but it

Table 10

CSAA Membership and *CRSA* Reviewers, Submitters, and Authors by Sex

	Members		Reviewers		Submitters		Authors	
Year	Female %	Male %	Female %	Male %	Female %	Male %	Female %	Male %
1985			17.0	83.0		27.0	73.0	
1986			22.0	78.0	30.0	70.0	22.0	78.0
1987	42.6	57.4	46.9	53.1	45.8	54.2	43.8	56.3
1988	41.4	58.6	32.2	67.8	38.6	61.4	44.1	55.9

Sources: Annual reports of the editors of the *CRSA*
Note: Years may not correspond to calendar years, but indicate largest portion of an academic year

is interesting to note that there seems to be some correspondence between the proportion of female reviewers and authors. As the proportion of female reviewers increases, so does the proportion of female authors with the exception of 1988, where female authors exceed female reviewers. This period includes the review and acceptance of articles for a special issue on feminist scholarship, thus explaining the particularly high proportion of female authors.

These data suggest that discrimination does not explain the difference in female-male authorship. If discrimination were the explanation, the female rate of submissions would greatly outdistance the female authorship. While that is so for one year for which we have data (1986), it is not the case for the other two years (1987 and 1988). Indeed, in 1988 the reverse is the case: women have a better rate of acceptance of manuscripts than men in that year.

Another way of approaching this issue is to look at the role special issues play. In special issues typically some authors are invited to contribute, although articles are reviewed in the normal manner.[14] If women were systematically discriminated against, their authorship participation rate should be lower in special issues than in regular issues, since the special issue editors influence the selection of authors through their selective invitations.

If we divide the authorship in the CRSA by whether or not authors published in regular issues versus special issues, a surprising difference emerges. Over the twenty-five-year period we find that the overall female authorship drops to 16.7 per cent if we exclude special issues, whereas female authorship in all special issues is 35.2 per cent![15] The fourteen special issues include two special issues on women and feminist scholarship respectively, which boost female authorship, since they have a dispropor-tionately high number of female authors. In order to see whether the difference in authorship remains even when the special issues on women and feminist scholarship are excluded from consideration, I calculated the female authorship of special issues without the two female-oriented special issues. Female authorship drops considerably, but is still higher in special issues than in regular issues: 23.1 per cent of all authors are female in the remaining special issues. It seems that special issues of the CRSA are good for female authors.

Where, then, do we stand? We have four possible explanations for the lower participation of women as authors in the CRSA as compared to the annual meetings, but none of the four hypotheses explored—the seniority, placement, age, or discrimination hypothesis—presents a convincing ex-planation of this pattern. Let us, then, look at the issue from a different perspective.

So far, we have compared the participation rate of women within the annual meetings and as authors in the CRSA.[16] If, alternatively, we compare the overall representation of women in university faculties, in 1985-86, we find that 17 per cent of all university faculty were female, as compared to 24.1 per cent of all anthropologists and 21.7 per cent of all sociologists (Guppy, 1989:14). Taking the 22 per cent of female sociologists as a benchmark for measuring their authorship in the CRSA,[17] women authors are repre-sented proportionately to their overall representation in university facul-ties[18] (see Table 6). This is the same conclusion Mackie (1986) reached for an earlier period of time.

Given that this is so, a fifth explanation for the discrepancy between female participation in annual conferences and as authors seems reasonable. As was noted, female authorship seems to lag by about ten years behind conference participation. This may be a generational phenomenon (as distinct from an age phenomenon): more students are likely to be Association members and to participate actively in terms of presenting papers, and organizing and chairing sessions, than are likely to publish. Especially if they do so as M.A. students, it may well take them ten years to finish their M.A. as well as their Ph.D. and to start publishing in scholarly journals. Besides, not all of them will go on to become professors or end up in other jobs that reward publishing. This hypothesis remains, of course, to be tested.

Seen in this light, then, women authors are reasonably well represented in the official journal of the Association, in spite of the fact that their participation is significantly lower than in the annual conferences. It is generally easier to present a paper than to have a paper published in a scholarly journal (any scholarly journal). If this explanation is correct, we should see a continuing increase of female authors in the CRSA up to about 40 per cent by the end of the next decade.

So far, we have only looked at the question of female participation in the CSAA and of authorship in the CRSA. We have not looked at the issue of how sociology and anthropology as disciplines treat women in their content as well as in their organization.

The Role of Feminist Scholarship in Anthropology and Sociology

There is, unfortunately, ample documentation that sociology and anthropology have been every bit as sexist as the other disciplines. (See, for example, Annama, 1984, Dagenais, 1981, Daniels, 1975, Eichler, 1988, Gailey, 1987, Huber, 1976, Lorber, 1975, Mascia-Lees et al., 1989, Millman, 1975, O'Brien, 1983, Smith, 1979, Sydie, 1987, Yawney, 1982.) Sociology's founding fathers are "sexists to a man" (Schwendinger and Schwendinger, 1971). The challenge to this type of "malestream" thought has come from feminist scholarship. It is therefore useful to ask oneself how receptive sociology and anthropology as disciplines have been to feminist scholarship.

Fortunately, there is now a data source that allows us to shed some light on this issue. The Canadian Women's Studies Project has collected a large amount of information on women's/feminist studies professors in Canada, and in what follows I will draw on data from this project.

The project involved four phases of data collection: phase 1 consisted in collecting data through registrars' offices on women's/feminist studies offerings at all Canadian universities in 1987; phase 2 involved identifying and administering a questionnaire to all professors who had ever taught a credit course on women's/feminist studies at a Canadian university in 1988; phase 3 involved qualitative follow-up interviews with one hundred of the women randomly selected from our population and all of the men who could be reached (a total of 187 interviews) in 1989; and phase 4 involved in-depth telephone interviews with 30 thinkers across the world whose work had been identified as particularly useful by the total population (1989-91). I will here draw on information obtained in phases 2 and 3.[19]

Disciplinary Boundaries

The first thing one notices when trying to deal with disciplinary characteristics is that disciplines are messy. There seem to be no clear boundaries, no clear agreement whether something is a sub-field or a discipline: are media and communications studies, family studies, or criminology disciplines? sub-disciplines? if the latter, sub-disciplines of what? There also is no necessary correspondence between a person's discipline of work and the department in which she or he is working: a sociologist of medicine may work in a medical department, for instance, but that does not make her or him a medical doctor. In our survey, we asked people to identify their discipline themselves.[20] Under the circumstances, this seems the best way to classify professors in terms of their discipline, rather than, for instance, the discipline of their highest degree, the department in which they work, and so on.

In an earlier paper (Eichler with the assistance of Tite, 1990:Table 9) we found that if we look at the disciplines in which people take their master's degree, their doctoral degree, and in which they end up working, there are some significant shifts between disciplines. Judging from Table 11, sociology is the most receptive of all disciplines to feminist scholarship. This is based on two observations: in absolute terms, sociology has the single largest component of women's studies/feminist teachers of all the disciplines. Indeed, 20 per cent of all feminist/women's studies professors identify themselves as sociologists in terms of their first discipline of work.[21]

By contrast, anthropology is a relatively minor player among the eleven most important disciplines that supply feminist/women's studies professors—indeed, it ties with political science for the lowest place in the top group, with 3.3 per cent (n=27) of the total professors identifying themselves as working within anthropology as their first discipline of work.

Second, if we compare the number of people who have a Ph.D. in sociology with the number of people who work within sociology, we find that there are more people working within sociology than there are people who obtained their Ph.D. in sociology. The reverse is true for anthropology. This suggests that there is differential boundary permeability within the two disciplines.

Table 11 Disciplines of Master's and Doctoral Degrees and Work (a)						
Discipline	Master's		Doctorate		Work	
	n=793		n=623		n=809	
	N	%	N	%	N	%
Anthropology	34	4.2	31	4.9	27	3.3
Education	40	5.0	38	6.0	42	5.1
History	79	9.8	83	13.0	88	10.6
Modern & Mediaeval Languages	138	17.2	118	18.5	121	14.6
Philosophy	56	7.0	43	6.8	39	4.7
Political Science	39	4.9	36	5.7	28	3.4
Psychology	65	8.1	57	8.9	55	6.6
Religious Studies	42	5.2	33	5.2	50	6.0
Social Work	34	4.2	2	0.3	33	4.0
Sociology	136	16.9	127	19.9	162	19.5
Women's Studies	1	0.1	0	0.0	37	4.5
Other Humanities	36	4.5	24	3.8	45	5.4
Other Social Sciences	57	7.1	22	3.5	63	7.6
Other	47	5.8	23	3.6	39	4.7
Total	804	100	637	100	829	100
Missing Cases:	99		269		83	

a) Respondents who gave a double discipline were coded twice. The amounts by which the totals exceed the n's indicate the amount of double coding.
Numbers are based on total respondents.
Missing cases include those no longer at a university.

If we see the discipline of work as the end product, there are some net gainers and some net losers at the aggregate level. Anthropology ends up as a net loser (there are 31 professors who state that their Ph.D. was in anthropology, but only 27 declare it as their discipline of work) while sociology ends up as a net gainer (there are 127 who state that their Ph.D. is in sociology, but 162 state that their discipline of work is sociology).

Turning to shifts at the individual level, we can ask: for those people in anthropology and sociology whose highest degree was not in their discipline of work, which discipline was it in? And the reverse: if people with a highest degree in sociology or anthropology do not work in their own disciplines, which ones do they work in?

Sociology

Of the 158 respondents who state that their discipline of work is sociology,[22] 29 or 18.4 per cent have a highest degree in a discipline other than sociology. In order of frequency, the highest influx comes from education (5 people and 4 more who list sociology and education as their discipline),[23] anthropology (5 people), philosophy and political science (3 each), 2 from communication and media studies, 1 each from criminology, family studies, geography, social work, and social science, and 2 from some other combination.

Looking at matters the other way round, of the 121 people whose Ph.D. is in sociology, 16 people (or 13.2 per cent) work in a discipline other than sociology: 3 each in political science and social work, and 1 each in communication and media studies, criminology, family studies, management and business administration, medicine and health, religious studies, sports and leisure, urban and regional studies, and education/sociology.

Putting together the switchers both ways, then, for people in sociology: anthropology and education are the two most important feeder disciplines, with political science being next in importance both as feeder and recipient.[24]

Anthropology

The picture for anthropology is radically different and very simple. Of the 27 respondents who identify anthropology as their discipline of work, all but one (who has a Ph.D. in an unidentified double) have a Ph.D. in anthropology. Looking at the issue the other way round, of the 31 respondents who have a Ph.D. in anthropology, 4 are working in sociology, 1 in education, and 2 are not working in any discipline.[25]

Sociology and Anthropology Compared

It appears, then, that for women's/feminist scholars who work within the disciplines of sociology and anthropology, the permeability of their respective disciplines is very different. Whereas sociology has a high boundary permeability, allowing people to work within it who did not obtain their highest degree in sociology, as well as supplying professors who work in disciplines other than sociology, anthropology seems highly self-contained, that is, it has a low boundary permeability: while there is some switch from people who have studied anthropology to teach in sociology, otherwise chances are very good that a person with a Ph.D. in anthropology will also work in the field of anthropology, and, with the exception of sociology, anthropologists do not supply teachers for other disciplines. It must be remembered that none of this addresses the disciplines as a whole, but merely those professors within the disciplines who have taught women's/feminist studies courses.

Another relevant question is in what department the first women's/feminist studies courses were introduced: were anthropology and sociology early or late in the game? We have information in what year women's/feminist studies professors taught their first course in the area. Looking at this information in terms of their first discipline of work, we obtain a picture of the relative entry point of professors in different disciplines into teaching relevant courses.

Table 12 indicates that sociology was in an early lead. More important than looking at the cumulative percentages is to consider the absolute numbers. By 1975, there were already at least 38 sociologists who were teaching courses in the area. This compares to 5 anthropologists, 6 professors in education, 19 in history, 22 in modern and mediaeval languages and literature, 6 in philosophy, and so on. The critical mass of people is important when reflecting on what can be done within the confines of a discipline. Clearly, sociology was the one discipline most ahead of the others, and it has retained this relative advantage. Indeed, the number of sociologists teaching women's/feminist studies courses in 1975 was greater then than the number of anthropologists doing the same in 1988!

However, when we look at the problems encountered by sociologists when teaching their first course in women's/feminist studies and the effect of their involvement in women's/feminist studies on their careers (Tables 13-15), we find no advantage for female sociologists and only a very slight disadvantage of female anthropologists with respect to the frequency with which professors mention particular problems.[26]

One point is particularly noteworthy in Table 13. The single most frequently mentioned problem for all female professors still in the university system as well as for all female sociologists is lack of materials (43.1 per cent for all women and 44.6 per cent for all female sociologists). By contrast, only 16.7 per cent of the female anthropologists mention this as a problem—a rather unique and advantaged situation, and reflective of the fact that some of the early famous anthropologists were women.

By comparing problems encountered in teaching the first and the most recent course for anthropologists and sociologists (Table 14), we find rather minor changes for anthropologists and a greater improvement for sociologists.[27] However, this may be partly an artefact of the situation that more sociologists started teaching earlier, therefore had more difficulties than anthropologists who started teaching later (see Table 12), and therefore note a greater improvement over a greater span of time.

With respect to the effect of their involvement in women's/feminist studies on their career, as Table 15 points out, sociologist women are more likely to see their involvement as an advantage (26.3 per cent) than an-

Table 12

Year First Women's/Feminist Studies Course Taught by Discipline of Work (a)

Year	Anthropology		Education		History		Languages and Literature		Philosophy		Political Science		Psychology		Religious Studies		Social Work		Sociology		Women's Studies		Other Humanities		Other Social Sciences		Other	
	N	Cumulative %	N	Cumulative %	N	Cumulative %	N	Cumulative %	N	Cumulative %	N	Cumulative %	N	Cumulative %	N	Cumulative %	N	Cumulative %	N	Cumulative %	N	Cumulative %	N	Cumulative %	N	Cumulative %	N	Cumulative %
1967					1	1.4	1	0.9											1	0.7					1	1.7		
1968						1.4		0.9							1	2.3				0.7						1.7	1	1.3
1969					1	2.8		0.9	1	2.9						2.3			1	1.3						1.7		1.3
1970						2.8		0.9	1	5.9					1	4.7			1	2.0	2	8.3				1.7	1	2.7
1971					2	5.6	2	2.7		5.9			2	4.0		4.7			5	5.3		8.3			3	6.9	1	4.0
1972			2	6.3	1	7.0	3	5.3	1	8.8	1	4.2	6	16.0		4.7			8	10.5		8.3	1	2.3	1	8.6	2	6.7
1973	1	3.7	3	15.6	5	14.1	4	8.8		8.8	2	12.5	1	18.0		4.7	2	6.1	9	16.4	2	16.7		2.3	1	10.3	5	13.3
1974	1	7.4		15.6	4	19.7	4	12.4	1	11.8		12.5	4	26.0		4.7	2	12.1	7	21.1		16.7	2	6.8	2	13.8	2	16.0
1975	3	18.5	1	18.8	5	26.8	8	19.5	2	17.6		12.5		26.0	1	7.0		12.1	6	25.0		16.7		6.8	3	19.0	2	16.0
Sub-Total	5		6		19		22		6		3		13		3		4		38		4		3		11		12	
1976	2	25.9		18.8	12	43.7	7	25.7	2	23.5	1	16.7	1	28.0	2	11.6	1	15.2	6	28.9	2	25.0	1	9.1	1	20.7	2	18.7
1977	1	29.6	2	25.0		43.7	2	27.4	1	26.5	1	20.8	2	32.0	3	18.6		15.2	8	34.2	1	29.2	4	18.2	1	22.4		18.7
1978	2	37.0	1	28.1		43.7	8	34.5	2	32.4		20.8	1	34.0	1	20.9	3	24.2	6	38.2	2	37.5	4	27.3	2	25.9	4	24.0
1979	3	48.1	1	31.3	4	49.3	4	38.1		32.4	2	29.2	6	46.0	1	23.3	1	27.3	7	42.8	1	41.7	3	34.1	2	29.3	4	29.3
1980	2	55.6	2	37.5	5	56.3	5	42.5	5	47.1	2	37.5	7	60.0	6	37.2	3	36.4	10	49.3	5	62.5	5	45.5	5	37.9	5	36.0
Sub-Total	15		12		40		48		16		9		30		16		12		75		15		20		22		27	
1981	3	66.7	3	46.9	5	63.4	6	47.8	2	52.9	1	41.7	6	72.0	4	46.5	3	45.5	11	56.6	1	66.7	1	47.7	1	39.7	5	42.7
1982	2	74.1	3	56.3	3	67.6	5	52.2		52.9	2	50.0	5	82.0	2	51.2	4	57.6	11	63.8		66.7	3	54.5	4	46.6	9	54.7
1983	2	77.8	2	62.5	5	74.6	8	59.3		52.9	2	58.3	1	84.0	6	65.1	5	72.7	10	70.4		66.7	3	61.4	5	55.2	5	61.3
1984	2	85.2		62.5	4	80.3	16	73.5	4	64.7	4	75.0	2	88.0	3	72.1	1	75.8	7	75.0	3	79.2	6	75.0	9	70.7	8	72.0
1985	1	88.9	3	71.9	4	85.9		73.5	6	82.4	3	87.5	2	92.0	8	90.7	3	84.8	15	84.9	1	83.3	3	81.8	4	77.6	8	82.7
Sub-Total	24		23		61		83		28		21		46		39		28		129		20		36		45		62	
1986	3	100.0	6	90.6	4	91.5	15	86.7	3	91.2	2	95.8	2	96.0	2	95.3	1	87.9	10	91.4	2	91.7	5	93.2	6	87.9	7	92.0
1987			3	100.0	5	98.6	13	98.2	2	97.1	1	100.0	1	98.0	2	100.0	4	100.0	13	100.0	2	100.0	3	100.0	7	100.0	3	96.0
1988					1	100.0	2	100.0	1	100.0			1	100.0													3	100.0
Total	27		32		71		113		34		24		50		43		33		152		24		44		58		75	
Misc.					2		5		1		3		2						6		1		1		5		3	

(a) Based on full population, including those no longer at a university

Table 13

Problems Encountered in Teaching First Women's/Feminist Studies Course, by Sex and Discipline (a)

| | Anthropology | | Sociology | | | | All Respondents Still in University | | | |
| | Female n=24 | | Female n=134 | | Male n=23 | | Female n=711 | | Male n=108 | |
	N	%	N	%	N	%	N	%	N	%
1 Lack of Male Faculty Support	8	33.3	38	29.2	5	21.7	225	33.1	14	13.2
2 Lack of Female Faculty Support	5	20.8	18	13.8	3	13.0	124	18.2	9	8.5
3 Resistance from Male Faculty	5	20.8	26	20.0	4	17.4	159	23.4	12	11.3
4 Resistance from Female Faculty	2	8.3	12	9.2	2	8.7	58	8.5	5	4.7
5 Lack of Interest from Male Students	9	37.5	40	30.8	12	52.2	208	30.6	41	38.7
6 Lack of Interest from Female Students	5	20.8	15	11.5	4	17.4	93	13.7	12	11.3
7 Resistance from Male Students	5	28.8	41	31.5	6	26.1	174	25.6	17	16.0
8 Resistance from Female Students	4	16.7	16	12.3	5	21.7	96	14.1	13	12.3
9 Lack of Support from Administration	1	4.2	23	17.7	1	4.3	126	18.5	5	4.7
10 Resistance from Administration	2	8.3	12	9.2	1	4.3	52	7.6	2	1.9
11 Lack of Materials	4	16.7	58	44.6	6	26.1	293	43.1	25	23.6
12 Defined as Not a Serious Scholar	8	33.3	40	30.8	2	8.7	211	31.0	8	7.5
13 Nobody Cared	5	20.8	27	20.8	6	26.1	138	20.3	15	14.2
14 Other Problems	4	16.7	11	8.5	1	4.3	64	9.4	6	5.7
Missing Cases	4		4							

(a) Based on population of professors still at a university

Anthropology males (n=3) omitted, only 1 checked one problem (#11)

Table 14

Problems Encountered in Teaching First as Compared to Most Recent Women's Studies/Feminist Course by Sex and Discipline (a)

| | Anthropology Women | | | | Sociology Women | | | | Sociology Men | | | |
| | 1st Course n=24 | | Most Recent Course n=24 | | 1st Course n=134 | | Most Recent Course n=118 | | 1st Course n=23 | | Most Recent Course n=23 | |
	N	%	N	%	N	%	N	%	N	%	N	%
1 Lack of Male Faculty Support	8	33.3	9	37.5	38	29.2	28	23.7	5	21.7	2	11.8
2 Lack of Female Faculty Support	5	20.8	5	20.8	18	13.8	13	11.0	3	13.0	1	5.9
3 Resistance from Male Faculty	5	20.8	3	12.5	26	20.0	16	13.6	4	17.4	3	17.4
4 Resistance from Female Faculty	2	8.3	1	4.2	12	9.2	5	4.2	2	8.7	1	5.9
5 Lack of Interest from Male Students	9	37.5	9	37.5	40	30.8	32	27.1	12	52.2	7	41.2
6 Lack of Interest from Female Students	5	20.8	4	16.7	15	11.5	12	10.2	4	17.4	1	5.9
7 Resistance from Male Students	5	28.8	4	16.7	41	31.5	32	27.1	6	26.1	1	5.9
8 Resistance from Female Students	4	16.7	3	12.5	16	12.3	17	14.4	5	21.7	1	5.9
9 Lack of Support from Administration	1	4.2	3	12.5	23	17.7	12	10.2	1	4.3	2	11.8
10 Resistance from Administration	2	8.3	1	4.2	12	9.2	8	6.8	1	4.3	1	5.9
11 Lack of Materials	4	16.7	2	8.3	58	44.6	22	18.6	6	26.1	3	17.6
12 Defined as Not a Serious Scholar	8	33.3	2	8.3	40	30.8	28	23.7	2	8.7	2	11.8
13 Nobody Cared	5	20.8	5	20.8	27	20.8	23	19.5	6	26.1	3	17.6
14 Other Problems	4	16.8	3	12.5	11	8.5	10	8.5	1	4.3	1	5.9
Missing Cases					4		16		4		6	

(a) Based on population of professors still at a university
Anthropology males (n=3) omitted, only 1 checked one problem (#11)

Table 15

Career Effects of Teaching Women's Studies Courses, by Sex and Discipline (a)

| | Anthropology | | Sociology | | | | All Respondents Still in University | | | |
| | Female n=24 | | Female n=134 | | Male n=23 | | Female n=711 | | Male n=108 | |
	N	%	N	%	N	%	N	%	N	%
1 Helped Promote Career	5	20.8	35	26.3	4	17.4	193	28.3	21	19.6
2 Hindrance	2	8.3	6	4.5	1	4.3	29	4.2	1	0.9
3 Helped & Hindered	10	41.7	42	31.6	3	13.0	244	35.7	12	11.2
4 Not Relevant	2	8.3	23	17.3	8	34.8	108	15.8	49	45.8
5 Unsure	5	20.8	27	20.3	7	30.4	109	16.0	24	22.4
Total	24	99.9	133	100	23	99.9	683	100	107	99.9
Missing Cases	1		1				28		1	

a) Based on population of professors still at a university

Anthropology males (n=3) omitted

thropologist women (20.8 per cent) and a bit less likely to see it as a hindrance (4.5 per cent vs. 8.3 per cent) or as both a help and hindrance (31.6 per cent vs. 41.7 per cent). Overall, in terms of sheer quantity, feminist scholars seem to have a slightly harder time in anthropology than in sociology—although women in the two total fields are more likely to be full professors in anthropology than in sociology (see Table 8).

It remains to turn to the epistemological bases of the disciplines to explain the relative receptivity of sociology, and the lesser receptivity of anthropology. In our telephone follow-up interviews we asked respondents whether there was anything within their own discipline that makes it particularly easy or difficult to introduce a feminist perspective. To a person, both the anthropologists and sociologists reply that within their two disciplines it is comparatively easy—although difficulties are noted. One possible explanation of this finding is that everyone in every discipline who has, in fact, engaged in the process of trying to integrate women and/or a feminist perspective will say that it is particularly easy within their own discipline. Such is not the case. It is beyond the scope of this paper to attempt an analysis of the responses of all the people to this particular question, but a scan of all the answers makes it clear that the answers are differentiated by discipline and that members of some disciplines—e.g, political science— are more likely to claim special difficulties rather than special ease with which to introduce a feminist/women's perspective into their own discipline than are sociologists and anthropologists.

In general, the consensus is that the social sciences generally lend themselves particularly well to introducing a women's/feminist perspective, and that within these, anthropology and sociology lend themselves especially well to this. Beyond this general statement, there are some interesting differences. One concerns the intellectual origins of the two disciplines. An anthropologist notes that "a number of great early anthropologists were women." Another one mentions specifically Margaret Mead and Ruth Benedict in this same context. This is reminiscent of the fact that fewer anthropologists than sociologists and others mentioned "lack of materials" as a problem in either their first or most recent courses.

By contrast, every sociologist who touches on this issue agrees that "There's certainly nothing in classical sociology to facilitate women's or feminist studies.... Just like everything else, it's the old dads and the weight of many traditions that have absolutely discounted women."

One female sociology professor recounts how as a student

> I went through all of my undergraduate and most of my masters programme, not even knowing that...women [and]...gender existed as a category.... Nothing in sociological theory would ever allow you to assume that there would be such a thing.

Nevertheless, she, like the other sociologists in our sample, believes that it is fairly easy to introduce a feminist perspective into sociology, but adds that it is a lot harder to do so in sociological theory courses and methodology courses. The sentiments expressed by anglophones and francophones are similar on this count, in spite of the fact that there are two distinct sociological traditions to draw upon.

> ...il fallait remettre en question presque toute notre formation de sociologue pour poser des questions féministes. Il y avait un travail de déconstruction très long à faire...

Besides a sexist tradition in classical sociological thought, the second problem that is mentioned, by both female and male sociologists, are their male colleagues. No one mentions female colleagues as a problem![28] As one male sociologist who finds it quite easy to introduce a woman's perspective into his teaching states simply, "...the level of interest or commitment on the part of the overwhelming majority of the faculty is not there." Another man ties the two problems together:

> The department is still controlled by men and the perspectives are still fundamentally male, and the paradigms within our discipline from Weber to Marx are not informed by feminist understanding.

Yet another man states:

> The main problem I see is that a lot of my male colleagues,...despite sort of a superficial expression of interest and sympathy, don't really change their own conceptions in a noticeable kind of way. I think that really does constitute quite a serious barrier.

What then makes it easy, or qualifies sociology as "an ideal discipline in which to do it"? It is not the people—who are (if they are male) identified as the problem—but the characteristics of the discipline. As one of the female sociologists suggests:

> The topics that the men have chosen have been male-oriented and...women's experiences have been excluded, but I am not sure that it is the nature of the discipline that has done that, rather than the people who control the discipline.

There are three types of answers to this question. The first set centres on organizational principles. Several sociologists mention the flexibility that characterizes sociology departments. Professors typically design their own courses, choose their own readings, and "bring in pretty well what they want...to." This matches with the boundary permeability that we have observed previously.

Beyond organizational aspects that allow the individual professor to follow her or his own interests in pursuing research and teaching, the second set of responses make statements about the nature of sociology as well as of sociologists *per se*. Two aspects are particularly mentioned as making it relatively easy to introduce a feminist perspective in sociology: first, a "tradition of oppositional points of view" and a "long-standing interest in issues related to social inequality"; second, the fact that sociology is "sort of about life" and contemporary developments, such as "the flood of married women" into the paid labour force, make it relatively easy to introduce questions of systemic inequality between the sexes. Sociologists want to look pretty contemporary, according to our respondents, and so they are open to contemporary developments.

The third type of response is related to professional age and describes the momentum that can develop due to early efforts. Several of the women made the point that "the reason I went into sociology in the first place is...there's a lot of good feminists in sociology...." There is agreement that there is now a critical mass of materials available—which certainly was not the case when the early sociologists first started teaching their first courses twenty or more years ago.

Conclusion

When the organizers of this session invited us to prepare papers to critically assess the Association's activities over the past twenty years, the emphasis was on "critical." We were assured that there was no need to pretend that everything was well, that we could and should freely point out problems.

The image that has emerged from this *tour de force* through twenty-five years of Association activities and the extended work of feminist/women's studies professors shows the CSAA in an unusually rosy light: Comparatively speaking, the association has been relatively open to feminist demands, to integrating women in its various associational activities, and more is to be hoped for.

Looking at anthropology and sociology as two disciplines, some startling differences emerge: sociology seems to be a lot more receptive to feminist thought and action than anthropology. Why this should be so is a puzzle, since in many ways anthropology had a head start over sociology as well as other disciplines as far as integrating women into its theoretical underpinnings is concerned.

Carmen Lambert, in a critical reply to an earlier version of this paper, suggests that while sociology has a tradition of courses about social groups (women, ethnic groups, black studies, etc.), anthropology courses, by contrast, tend to be organized by cultural areas (Cultures of Latin America) or modes of production (Peasant Societies). This militates against introducing courses that are specifically about women. Anthropologists can and do, of course, teach their courses from a feminist perspective.[29] She further argues:

> Il faudrait aussi voir de près le développement historique des études sur les femmes (Women's Studies) et les orientations prises par ces programmes au niveau de l'enseignement comme de la recherche. Il y a dans le milieu une préférence, réelle quoique souvent inavouée, pour les sociologues et les historiennes. Les Women's/Feminist Studies sont devenue la marque de la sociologie. On est plus concerné par les questions considérées "contemporaines" qui nous touchent "nous" plus que les "autres," qui touchent "notre" culture et "notre" société plutot que les femmes dans d'autres cultures et d'autres sociétés. La sociologie comme discipline se voit ainsi favorisée et ensuite l'histoire qui apporte directement une réflexion sur notre propre société. La recherche en anthropologie est quelquefois loin de certaines préoccupations ponctuelles de notre propre milieu. Il est dommage que les apport de l'anthropologie féministe ne sont pas encore bien connus en dehors de la discipline. C'est un peu la faute des anthropologues elles-mêmes. Mais il leur est quelquefois difficile de briser cette barrière entre l'étude des "autres" et l'étude de "nous" alors que les préoccupations de très nombreuses féministes ne s'attachent qu'a ce "nous."

My hunch is that the current difference is primarily due to the concerted efforts of an early group of very active feminist women who happened to be sociologists, and who worked both within the association as well as in the total discipline towards improving the status of women in a large number of different ways. This does not contradict Lambert's comments. If true, further research should show that in other countries, in which a number of early feminist scholars happened to belong to a different discipline, the pattern is different rather than the same.

To put this relatively positive picture into its proper perspective, it is useful to turn the picture around: if sociology is the *easy* discipline within which to conduct women's/feminist studies—how much harder yet must it be for all our struggling colleagues in the other disciplines, including anthropology? For with all the talk about comparative ease, it must never be forgotten that the stress is on the word "comparative" rather than "ease." There are sufficiently heart-wrenching examples of problems encountered in our research to banish forever the thought that anything was given to anybody, rather than won through extraordinarily hard work and commitment.

Nor can we rest on our laurels. A lot of sociology is still very sexist, and although the position of women in Canada has improved in some ways (e.g., in the legal system), changed in an indeterminate direction in others (e.g., more women earn money, but the income differential remains very high while the work output for women has jumped enormously), and possibly become worse in others (there is some evidence that the problem of violence against women has increased rather than decreased, and the horrible shootings in Montreal in December 1989 are only one small example of this).

Nevertheless, it is appropriate to acknowledge the effect of the work of feminist sociologists and anthropologists, within the association and within their respective disciplines. All was not in vain.

NOTES

1   This is Report #8 of the Canadian Women's Studies project. Various aspects of the overall project have been financially supported by the following grants: SSHRC grants #482-86-0007 and #482-88-0016 (M. Eichler and R. Lenton), OISE SSHRC grant #0920 (M. Eichler), grant #234.02 of the Ontario Women's Directorate (M. Eichler), a McMaster Arts Research Board grant (R. Lenton), a grant from PAFACC UQAM (Louise Vandelac). In addition, special data were collected for this paper with the help of two small-scale grants from OISE, #3297 and #3321. I would like to thank Linda Christiansen-Ruffman and the other members of the editorial team for helpful editorial comments on this paper.

2   All of this work—a massive job—was performed by Barbara Center, over the period of October 1989 to March 1990.

3   It is possible that some errors of sex allocation occurred, since some names are ambiguous as to their sex (e.g. Gail, Marion, Robin, Keith, Pat, and names from cultures with which we were not conversant). Quite a number of people used initials only. We compiled a list of all those whose sex we could not identify, specified the participation date and their affiliation at the time, and circulated it. I would like to thank Linda Christiansen-Ruffman, Raymond Currie, James Frideres, Pierre S. Hamel, Roxana Ng, Robert Stebbins, Anthony Synnott, Peta Tancred, and K. Victor Ujimoto for identifying about half of our indeterminate list by sex, thus significantly reducing the factor of unknown. If the proportion of females to males among the unknown is similar to their proportion among the known, no distortion has occurred; if it is different, some distortion will have taken place. Possible distortion is particularly a problem for the very first meeting, because most participants were listed on the programme with their initials rather than first names and so the number of unknown is similar to that of the known. For the year 1965, then, the risk of distortion of the sex ratio is substantial. For that reason, this year should be ignored for most practical purposes in any analysis.

4   If a person appeared on the programme more than once, even within the same session (and this was quite frequently the case), the person got counted twice.

5   No distinctions were made between authors and co-authors, chairs and co-chairs, sole discussants and multiple discussants, and organizers and co-organizers. There seemed to be no consistent differences between the sexes to serve as sole author, co-author, etc.

6 Session organizers appear only in three years in substantial numbers, not sufficient to mention here.

7 My thanks to Gabrielle Chabot who collected the information on which Tables 2 and 3 are based.

8 All the work necessary to identify the authors by sex was done by Fiona Hart. The same caveats apply as in the case of the identification of the sex of conference participants, although only 1.5% of the authors are classified as "sex unknown" since they tend to be more easily identifiable than session participants.

9 These are Mackie's figures, not mine, to keep the internal consistency. The differences between her figures and mine can be explained by four factors: first, she included research notes in her article count, while I included it under "other." I can therefore either add up only articles (excluding research notes) or all publications, including commentaries (but excluding book reviews under all circumstances). While, overall, this makes little difference, in particular years it may have a substantial impact. Second, we may have a different number of "sex unknown authors," thus changing the percentages. Third, either one of us (or both) may have made errors in assigning sex and/or in counting and computation. Fourth, the percentages refer to slightly different groupings of years. In any case, even with differences in average percentages, we end up with the same overall picture and basically the same conclusions.

10 In order to make the Canadian data comparable to the U.S. data, which are adapted from Carden, 1990, p. 11, Table 1, I recalculated the Canadian data and counted only articles rather than all types of publications in the *CRSA*.

11 These labels are mine rather than Carden's, although derived from her work.

12 Quebec is omitted from consideration, since for obvious reasons—language and intellectual tradition—francophone Quebeckers stand in a different relation to the *CRSA* than do professors in anglophone regions. Indeed, Quebeckers publish mostly within Quebec, and when publishing outside Quebec, are more likely to publish in France and the United States than in any other Canadian media (see Juteau and Maheu, 1989:371).

13 Some information is missing, as seen in Table 10. I would like to thank Robert Brym for making me aware of the fact that this information existed, and James Curtis for searching through boxes of materials in order to find the relevant reports for me. I greatly appreciate the help. The data have been compiled from Tancred-Sheriff and de Vries, 1986, and Brym, 1987, 1988, and 1989. They do not correspond to the data contained in Table 6 because the years do not correspond exactly and the report data include accepted authors rather than only printed authors. They are therefore differently distributed through the various years. Table 10 is more interesting for its internal comparison between reviewers, submitters, and authors than as trend data for publication by sex.

14 It is beyond the scope of this paper to determine how many authors were actually invited to contribute and how many simply submitted a paper. We can, however, assume that this would vary from one special issue to the other, depending on the special editor, overall editorial policy at the time, and the subject matter.

15 The detailed breakdown of the authorship by issue on which this figure is based has not been included for reasons of space. It can be obtained from the author, by written request.

16   I have not compared authorship with membership in the CSAA since the Association has a number of members who are less likely to engage in publication: sociologists and anthropologists who are placed in institutions that neither place a premium on nor facilitate research and publication. In addition, the Association actively recruits students as members, who are also less likely to publish.

17   I am concentrating on sociologists because, first, sociologists outnumber anthropologists 2.5:1 (Guppy, 1989:14), and second, sociologists clearly dominate the authorship in the CRSA. They therefore have a disproportionate impact.

18   Of course, authorship in scientific journals is not restricted to university faculty, but they do constitute the overwhelming number of authors.

19   For more information on the project, see Eichler, 1990a and b, Eichler with the assistance of Tite, 1990, Eichler with the assistance of Vandelac, 1990, Eichler, forthcoming, Lenton, 1990a and b, Tite with the assistance of Malone, 1990, and Vandelac, 1990.

20   The exact wording of the question was: " In what discipline(s) do you work? (If more than one, list all in order of importance.)"

21   A reasonable hypothesis might be that sociologists are over-represented due to the fact that the research team was entirely composed of sociologists and therefore had better access to or more knowledge about sociology than all other disciplines. We do not believe such to be the case, first, because we guarded to the greatest degree possible against under-representing the other disciplines, second, the second largest category is modern and mediaeval languages, a cluster of disciplines with which none of the research team have any particular associations. If the representation of the sociologists was an artefact of personal links, one of the other social sciences, e.g., history or education or psychology, with whom the various team members have closer personal connections, should have been shown as more highly represented among the total population.

22   This analysis is conducted for the entire sociology population rather than by sex since there seem to be no systematic differences between the sexes in this instance.

23   This figure may be inflated due to the role of the Department of Sociology in Education at the Ontario Institute for Studies in Education. The department defines itself as feminist in orientation.

24   There are, of course, still other ways of looking at the boundary permeability between disciplines. One other way would be to look at second (and even third) disciplines of work identified by respondent. For sociologists, second disciplines are women's studies (6), history (5), political science, medicine and health (4 each), demography, law, family studies, psychology (3 each), education, communication and media studies, social work (2 each), education/sociology, anthropology, area studies, management and business administration, philosophy, women's studies/philosophy and one other double (1 each).

[25] Looking at their second discipline of work, one each defines archaeology, biological sciences, modern and mediaeval languages and literature, and women's studies as their second discipline of work. Looking at the issue the other way round, one of the people working in sociology and one working in education define anthropology as their second discipline.

[26] The patterns in terms of the nature of the involvement and its various effects is markedly different for women and men. This is being explored in a separate paper. For this reason, although I have supplied the figures for the men wherever it made sense, the discussion focuses on the women only.

[27] The absolute numbers for anthropologists are so small that not much can be made of the patterns found.

[28] Surprisingly, this is true for the men in the sample as well. See Eichler, 1990b on the issue of who creates problems for whom in women's studies.

[29] Carmen Lambert, personal letter, November 4, 1990.

CANADIANIZATION:
A JOURNEY COMPLETED?

John R. Hofley[1]

With apologies to Dickens, one could describe the state of sociology and anthropology in the late 1960s as "the best of times, and the worst of times." Best because the disciplines were growing and worst because we had few Canadians to fill the positions. What became known in 1972 as the Canadianization movement has been hailed and assailed; it has been the subject of a number of analyses. More recently, in a book by Robert Brym, it has been partially blamed for the state of the discipline in Canada or, as in the Marchak report on the future of the CSAA, it has been ignored.

Looking ahead is a very difficult task; looking back isn't easy either because our glasses become fogged with events, biases, and intermixtures of personal experiences and empirical observations. A twenty-fifth anniversary, whether of an Association such as the CSAA or of a marriage, is the time when we should not only look to the future but remember our past — more importantly, to remember to examine our past in an historical context. I'm reminded of Morag Gunn in Margaret Laurence's *The Diviners:*

> Morag walked out across the grass and looked at the river.... The waters flowed from north to south, and the current was visible, but now a south wind was blowing, ruffling the water in the opposite direction, so that the river, as so often here, seemed to be flowing both ways. Look ahead into the past, and back into the future, until the silence.

Laurence didn't stop *The Diviners* here but continued: "How far could anyone see into the river? Not far. Near shore, in the shallows, the water was clear.... Only slightly further out, the water deepened and kept its life from sight."

When I think about my own involvement with Canadianization, the water is clear. As I distance myself and try to comprehend it as a movement, the water darkens and I'm not sure if I can see its life. For me, the Canadianization movement was a search for an authentic voice—not someone else's, not borrowed, but one that emanates from deep within my own soul. I share Symons' remark in *To Know Ourselves:* "I would have thought it should be reasonably clear that a society, like an individual, needs to know itself and its place in the context of the world" (Symons, 1975:13).

I also believe that all societies, all cultures, are ethnocentric; they must be. The issue in Canadianization wasn't saying "No" to others such as Great Britain or the United States, but "Yes" to ourselves.

In this paper, I wish to do four things: (1) Locate myself within the Canadianization movement in order for you to understand the "voice" I am using; (2) Locate the origins of the movement within a very broad historical context; (3) Examine briefly and critically some analyses of the Canadianization movement and in so doing consider the involvement of the CSAA; (4) Suggest that the current constitutional crisis in our country is partly the result of the failure of Canadianization, viz., the absence of a curriculum and research agenda within sociology and anthropology whose central focus would be the analysis of the distinctive combination of economic, cultural, ecological, and demographic conditions that have formed Canada.

I went to undergraduate school at United College, University of Manitoba, and graduated in English and Philosophy in 1960. I attended graduate school at the University of North Carolina in Chapel Hill from 1962-1966 and did my work with Lenski and Blalock. I was hired in 1966 as an assistant professor at Carleton University. This was my good fortune, because the people there were all remarkable. In addition, the Department of Sociology at Carleton was unusual in that of the nine persons on staff, only one was an American. Three (Burshtyn, McFarlane, Vallee) graduated from McGill as undergraduates; two (Valentine and Frumhartz) from Toronto; one (Irving) from St. Pat's in Ottawa; one (Whyte) from Manitoba; and Porter had gone to London after the war. None of them received their Ph.D.s from a Canadian school. As I became acquainted with them, I heard about scholars such as Dawson, Gérin, and Hughes at McGill; Clark, Innis, Hall, and others at Toronto, as well as persons such as Laski and Titmuss at London, and about works done on Canada by people such as Hawthorne, Jenness, Ouelette and The Social Credit Series done between 1950-1959. I knew nothing about any of this, and I wanted to know why this was so new, and why I had not encountered these writers in my undergraduate education. Also, as I began my teaching career I wanted to tell my students about Canada and I found very little about Canada in the sociology texts that were available.

I left Carleton in 1970, spent a year in India as a Shastri Fellow, and returned home to the University of Winnipeg in 1971. In 1973, I became a Counsellor on the executive of the CSAA. I had participated in the debate at McGill in 1972 on Canadianization motions. I spent the years 1973-76 on the Executive. Here I was privileged also because Pierre Miranda, Gillian Sankoff, Sally Weaver, Gordon Inglis, Richard Ossenberg, Dorothy Smith, Bernard Arcand, Kay Herman, John Jackson, Fred Elkin, Kurt Jonassohn all served the CSAA during those years in which Canadianization issues dominated the Annual General Meetings. All were active scholars and committed to the issues underlying Canadianization.

This was also the time (August 1974) when the CSAA censured the University of Toronto for hiring seven Americans for eight new positions; this occurred after the Executive had discussed the issues with Professor Zeitlin, the Chairperson of the department at Toronto, a year earlier!

Between 1974 and 1981, I also pursued some activities that flowed from my involvement in Canadianization. I presented a brief to the Social Science Federation of Canada (SSFC) encouraging research support for smaller universities; this led to the SSHRC programme of Grants to Smaller Universities. I also lobbyed the federal government to tighten immigration laws regarding academic appointments; this resulted (effective May 1981) in the current law that gives priority to Canadian citizens and landed immigrants.

In 1980-81, as President of CSAA, I was asked to help David Mandel in his fight against McGill University. Mandel was a Canadian citizen, fully bilingual, with a Ph.D. in sociology and russian studies from Columbia. The McGill University search team twice recommended that he be hired and both times the political science department turned him down. An American was hired and Mandel let go.[2]

Finally, I, along with Wallace Clement and Dennis Forcese, persuaded the CSAA to establish the John Porter Award. I think it is clear that my "voice" in this issue of Canadianization was, in some small way, to bring Canadian cultures to self-consciousness (Rex, 1976:512).

What was the situation like in Canadian universities in the 1960s and early 1970s regarding sociology and anthropology? What was happening in our universities that eventually forced Canadian schools to hire so many non-Canadian scholars? There were three factors involved in this situation: (1) Enrolments at our universities increased dramatically during the 1960s. In 1960, there were 113,700 students enrolled full-time. By 1970 this figure increased to 309,500; there were also 156,600 part-time students in 1970 (Symons, 1984:26). Thus, more than three times as many students were attending post-secondary institutions in 1970 as in 1960. In addition, graduate enrolment increased six-fold during the same period. (2) The number of faculty members required to teach these students was enormous. The total number of full-time faculty in our universities went from 7,760 in 1960-61 to 24,612 in 1970-71. In sociology and anthropology, the increased demand for faculty was even more dramatic because disproportionate numbers of students flocked to courses in the social sciences, particularly sociology and psychology. Thus, in 1963 there were 106 sociologists and 30 anthropologists in Canadian universities. By 1969 we had 548 sociologists. By 1981 there were 1,427 persons teaching in these disciplines! (3) Where did all these new faculty members come from? Were we producing them in our own graduate programmes? In many disciplines we had an adequate supply, but not for sociology and anthropology. There were very few sociology and anthropology Ph.D. programmes in Canada in 1969. As Hiller (1979:129) notes: "...only 19 Ph.D.s in sociology were given in Canada in the 1960s whereas sociology needed 50-60 annually." We had to find faculty members quickly and we did so by looking mostly South. (Brym, Grayson, Hiller, Magill, Mathews, Millett, Steele, Symons, and Symons and Page all provide us with considerable data on these matters.)

The vast majority of persons hired were from outside Canada. In 1969, for example, Canadian universities hired 2,642 persons of whom 86 per cent were non-Canadian. (Given that non-Canadians did not have to pay taxes for two years, this is not surprising.) Between 1968-1971, more than 6,000 non-Canadian faculty members were hired. In 1973-74, 60 per cent of full-time faculty in anthropology and 45 per cent in sociology were non-Canadian (Symons, 1975:72). These figures were even higher in the Atlantic and Prairie provinces. Also, most Canadians hired were trained outside of Canada. Thus, in 1973, 77 per cent of all Ph.D.s in sociology were earned outside Canada.

In the late 1960s, then, our classes were full. We began looking for textbooks and journal articles on Canadian society. Those of us on the faculty who were Canadian also started looking at the courses being offered and what was taught in them. For example, courses on social inequality and/or ethnicity often used American books and talked about black/white relations in the United States. There were almost no courses on regions in Canada, on French Canada, on ethnic relationships in western Canada, or on de-industrialization in the Atlantic provinces. Consequently, Canadian students knew more about race relations in the United States than they did about French-English relations in Canada; they knew more about American and British literature than Canadian literature. Courses on Canada were in a minority in university social science curricula of the 1960s.

It was these yawning gaps in our curricula that in 1968-69 led two Carleton University professors of English, Robin Mathews and Jim Steele, to agitate for a stop in hiring non-Canadians. This debate at Carleton spilled over into the whole country, including the annual meetings of the CSAA at McGill University in 1972; the discussions were very intense and emotional. The Canadianization movement had begun.

While analytically the issues of Canadian content and Canadian citizenship can be separated, it is, de facto, difficult to do so. The two weave in and out of one another. This was why Steele and Mathews saw the issue of the absence of Canadian content empirically linked to the need for faculty members who were raised and/or trained in Canada. They, and others such as myself, argued that such persons were more likely to be committed to the establishment of a curriculum that would be Canadian-focused. (See Symons, 1975:11-20 for a further elaboration of this viewpoint.) The personnel issue was an outgrowth of the need to revise university curricula.

If I, as a person born and educated to the B.A. level in Canada, felt ignorant of Canadian history and society and ill-prepared for the task of illuminating that history, how could persons with no experience or knowledge of Canada solve the silences in our curricula? As these realities slowly sank in, many Canadian scholars became angry. As Harriet Lerner points out in her remarkable book *The Dance of Anger,* "Anger is a signal and one worth listening to" (1985:1). Sometimes we listened; often we did not.

While faculty and graduate students in other disciplines spoke out about the situation, sociologists, anthropologists, and their graduate students were the most outspoken. The CSAA was very active in addressing the dual issues of content and personnel. Yet, sociologists who have written about the Canadianization movement to date[3] have tended to stress that until 1975 the Canadianization issue was dominated by personnel issues. I suggest that this is only partially true as is indicated both by the Symons Report and by CSAA motions passed before 1975 (see Appendix to this paper).

The Symons Report was initiated in response to questions raised by Mathews and Steele about the lack of Canadian courses in the curricula, such as the low priority given to courses on Canadian literature and society. This lack of content in the curricula of Canadian universities continued with the result that, in 1972, the Association of Universities and Colleges in Canada (AUCC) commissioned the President of Trent University, Thomas Symons, an historian, "to study, report and make recommendations upon the state of teaching and research in various fields of study relating to Canada at Canadian universities" (Symons, 1975:1). The idea for such a commission came out of the AUCC's 1970 meeting in Winnipeg. The interest in this lack of research and Canadian content was very strong, as witnessed by the fact that during 1972 and 1973, the Commission received over 1,000 written briefs, heard from more than 1,200 persons in public meetings, and received more than 30,000 letters. All of this immense involvement in content issues occurred between 1970 and 1975.

Meanwhile, at the CSAA, from the late 1960s to 1981, considerable attention was being focused on the issue of Canadianization (see Appendix to this paper). The discussions and motions were not focused exclusively on personnel matters. In June 1969, the Executive established a "Future of the Disciplines" committee. Its task was to look at the strengths and weaknesses of each discipline as well as at the "needs of Canadian society." This committee was served by Jan Loubser, Frank Vallee, Rémi Savard, Guy Rocher, Ted Harvey, Claude Gousse, Jim Turk, and Tom McFeat.

In addition, when one examines the motions passed at the Annual General Meeting on May 31, 1972, one finds that their emphasis is clearly on research and teaching, not on personnel. They read as follows:

WHEREAS this Association expresses support for the encouragement and development of Canadian content in research and teaching in the social sciences and recognizes that there are grave problems of Canadianization that should be faced and worked on constructively in our two disciplines,

THIS ASSOCIATION APPROVES the establishment of two subcommittees: one on Canadianization and one on Canadian Studies as proposed in the "Postscript to the CSAA Brief on the Rationalization of Research Presented to the AUCC."

It is true that the motions passed in May 1973 at Queen's University focused on a hiring moratorium of non-Canadians. It was passed; it stated that if more than 50 per cent of persons in a department were non-Canadian, only Canadians were to be hired. At the 1974 Annual General Meeting, there was a motion to change the figure to 25 per cent. This was defeated.

In 1974, four Canadian Studies symposia were proposed by Dennis Magill. Each focused on content, not personnel matters. To my knowledge, two were completed, one on Development in the Atlantic Provinces and the other on Social Welfare Policy and the Marginal Work World. That much content work needed to be done in sociology and anthropology was reflected in the Symons Report released in 1975:

> Sociology and anthropology as taught at many of our universities are not sufficiently attuned to Canadian conditions and problems.... The charges are made...that scholarly writings in these fields at Canadian universities are uninspired by the major problems of our age, are not relevant to the social issues we face in our own society, do not contribute to an understanding of the dynamics of our institutions, ignore regional variations in the culture and social structure of this country and contribute little to the study of nation-building and of collective identity formation in Canada. The Commission's inquiries revealed that many of these criticisms are well-founded" (Symons, 1975:75).

Frank Jones reinforces the Commission's conclusions when he notes in his paper in this collection that when the *Canadian Review of Sociology and Anthropology* began in 1964, Jean Burnet, the editor, found there were so few acceptable manuscripts that the journal could not maintain a regular schedule of publication; this was not rectified until the early 1970s.

In addition, textbooks dealing with Canadian issues were almost non-existent in the late 1960s. For example, to my knowledge, the first introductory texts were published in 1968, viz., D.W. Rossides' *Society as a Functional Process: An Introduction to Sociology*, and Guy Rocher's *Introduction à la sociologie générale*. There were collections of articles published in 1961 (M. Oliver's *Social Purpose for Canada* and Bernard Blishen et al., *Canadian Society*), and W.E. Mann's *Canada: A Sociological Profile* (1968), as well as monographs such as John Porter's *The Vertical Mosaic* (1965), but they were scarce. Beginning around 1970, sociologists and anthropologists began publishing more and more monographs and texts on Canadian society. There is, thus, considerable evidence that the Canadianization movement was not dominated by personnel issues prior to 1975, either inside or outside the CSAA.

Brym, in addition to the argument that the Canadianization movement was dominated by personnel issues prior to 1975, makes a number of assertions about those of us who supported the movement that are, at best, partially true and, at worst, incorrect. Brym suggests that from 1975 on the

Canadianization debate focused more on "broad questions of method. Is it possible to produce a universally valid sociology? If not, exactly how should English Canadian sociology differ from the dominant American model of the discipline?" (Brym, 21-22)

He notes that many of the proponents of Canadianization took positions on the above questions that left them "open to the charge of parochialism" (23) and "minimizing the need for rigorously testing theories." (24) Unfortunately, he gives no specific citations as to who did these things. However, it is true that many in the Canadianization debate were being critical of abstract empiricism, were encouraging the study of history, and were attacking the ahistorical aspects of American structural-functionalism. This, however, was not confined to Canadianization types. French structuralists, British neo-Marxists, and many American sociologists were saying the same thing. For example, Nisbet (1976:17) wrote that "the great harm of the present consecration of method...is that it persuades students that a small idea abundantly verified is worth more than a large idea still insusceptible to textbook techniques of verification." A British writer, Raymond Williams, also noted that "persuasive empiricism [the search for facts] is founded...on the assumption that the facts can be made to stand still, and to be...disinterested" (1980:16).

Brym argues that as a consequence of these trends by some Canadian nationalists, sociology as a discipline suffered because it failed to incorporate the more useful elements in the American and international sociological traditions. However, once again, he does not tell us what these were other than a vague reference to the need for sociologists to do comparative analyses and to search for universal validity (for a fuller discussion of the issues of internationalism in the world of scholarship, particularly the American version, see Symons and Page, 1984: 48-50).

What many of us, including S.D. Clark, in the Canadianization movement said was that *before* we can do comparative studies of Canada and other societies, we must first have knowledge of ourselves (see Symons, 1975:13-18). If we had continued to adopt American sociology and hired American sociologists into the 1970s and 1980s our universities' curricula and research agendas would not have provided the impetus needed for self-knowledge. Ironically, in 1991, we are more ready to do what Brym urges, that is, more comparative, empirical studies, precisely because the Canadianization movement rejected the 1960s American model of doing sociology. Consequently, during the past fifteen years we have produced a considerable body of literature on Canada. This sociological literature, enriched by feminist and political economy perspectives, is not, as Brym says, "sullied by both parochialism and subjectivism" (172).

Hiller's comments on Canadianization deserve more attention than can be given in this paper. In his analysis of Canadianization, Hiller identifies a number of factors that might account for the rise of the Canadianization movement: increase in number of students, employment anxiety, some anti-American sentiment, consciousness raising, and most importantly a "new wave of national awareness and a nationalist consciousness" brought about by increasing industrialization, "the rapid expansion of the post-secondary educational system, and the growth of multi-national foreign corporations" (Hiller, 1979:126). These factors are important but I think they need to be expanded.

I hope that by briefly discussing some issues that have been ignored in the literature on Canadianization that others will take on the task of elaborating this important part of our history. Let me suggest four such issues.

The reasons for Canada having to import large numbers of foreign academics in the late 1960s and early 1970s

The increase in enrolments and the growth of post-secondary institutions that took place in Canada also occurred in the United States and in western Europe during the 1960s. However, other countries, unlike Canada, avoided having to hire many non-citizens. (One country that did follow the Canadian path was Australia.) For example, in 1976, the citizenship of the professoriate in Great Britain was 92 per cent British, in the United States, 98 per cent American, in France, virtually 100 per cent French. The comparable figure for Canada was 72 per cent. When undergraduate enrolment increased 500 per cent between 1955 and 1975 Canadian universities were not prepared for this expansion. Canadian graduate programs (their enrolment had increased 1200 per cent in the same time period) could not produce enough faculty to meet the demand. For example, between 1960 and 1970, there were 8,684 Ph.D.s awarded in Canada, of whom about 67 per cent (5600) were employed in our universities. We needed approximately 19,000! Thus, in three short years, 1968-71, over 6,000 non-Canadians were hired.

These demographic figures on enrolments and faculty size that Hiller and others provide do not answer the question, "Why did we have no qualified personnel in place?" These demographic patterns occurred in the United States and Western Europe; the hiring of many non-citizens did not occur. Two factors may account for the differences. The first is language. I recall that between 1973 and 1976 the francophone members of the CSAA Executive told me often that the requirement of French gave them an opportunity to "solve" their problem without having to hire too many non-citizens. They also told me, "You would have to find ways to solve *your* problem." (Of course, another advantage that Quebec French-speaking universities had was that the two graduate programs at Laval and Université de Montréal were well established.)

In Canada, the presence of non-Canadian faculty varied by region from a high in 1976 of 36 per cent in the western provinces to a low of 21 per cent in Quebec. Further underscoring the importance of language is the fact that between 1977 and 1981, at Quebec's anglophone universities, only 53 per cent of first appointments were Canadian; at francophone universities the figure was 88 per cent. Language is important but it does not explain all the variance; the percentage of non-Canadians hired during the same period in Ontario was just 5 per cent higher than for Quebec.

The second reason for Canada's lack of preparedness and its need to hire non-Canadians was its colonial history, a history that continued long after 1867 and was not confined to our economic structures. Prior to the late 1960s, bright Canadian students were encouraged by their professors to go to American or European schools. This was true for both English- and French-speaking universities. This meant that we did not feel we needed our own graduate programmes (Symons and Page, 1984: 34-35). We need to explore the implications of this colonial intellectual history more fully, particularly as it impacted upon the need for the Canadianization movement.

The extent to which the initial negative reaction by senior faculty and administrators was affected by their own experiences in World War II and the horrors of the holocaust.

A number of faculty, deans, and university presidents of the 1960s had fought in the Second World War or had families victimized by fascist forms of nationalism. For some, the Canadianization movement had an emotion that struck a chord deep in their own souls; this chord was very negative. All forms of nationalism were deeply suspect because they often ended up excusing totalitarian repression. I am convinced that one of the reasons for the emotional intensity of debates at Carleton University and at the Learned Societies stemmed from these sources. The initial cool response of university presidents to Canadianization and their perception that the movement was a threat to academic freedom and the free expression of ideas may well have come from their experience with, or knowledge of, fascism.

The impact of the Quiet Revolution, begun in Quebec in 1960, upon the attitudes of both francophone and anglophone sociologists

Hiller has mentioned this factor, and he noted that "some Anglophone sociologists have found an affinity with those Francophone sociologists who relate sociology to the quest for independence and national sovereignty" (134). While English Canada did not have a Quiet Revolution, it did experience some deep concerns about its own future. Three other developments were occurring during the late 1960s, one in the United States (Vietnam War) and two here (the Waffle Movement and the Student Movement). How these movements intersected with and influenced the Canadianization movement requires exploration and analysis. The Waffle and Student movements produced a critique of multinational corporations, a desire to learn more about Canada and less about the United States, and a fear that, just as many Quebecois felt that they had been colonized, so too were we in English Canada vulnerable to American colonization. What was worse was that this process was taking place right within our classrooms. Students not only flocked to universities, they overran the social science courses; they were looking for answers to their questions about Canadian history and yet, by and large, they were being given non-Canadian materials by non-Canadian faculty.

The extent to which the feminist movement and the resurgence of Marxism/political economy influenced the Canadianization movement

Very early, within the Executive of the CSAA, the issues of Canadian content and hiring became intertwined with the issues of feminism. The executive and the membership also felt that their energy should be more focused on developing social policies and a code of ethics. Discussions about hiring became focused increasingly on gender equity. The code of ethics tended to stress what behaviours were or were not appropriate in our relationships with colleagues and in our conduct of research. If we wish to know why the CSAA took such a strong stand on Canadianization and why it slowly died out around 1981, we need to interview the women and men who served on the Executive during the years 1970-81. I recall many a late-night discussion with colleagues on the Executive about the interrelationship between hiring, content, equity, and political goals. It is important to remember that we met over weekends in Montreal, and spent a lot of time in the wee hours of the morning discussing and arguing these issues. Much of the talk was about epistemological concerns, especially those raised by the emerging feminist and neo-Marxist/political economy movements.

I believe that as the perspectives of feminism and political economy gained prominence, the issues surrounding Canadian nationalism, Quebec, immigration, and bilingualism faded into the background. Feminism, of course, focused on issues of and for women. Political economy focused on class, capitalism, and inequality. Neither of these perspectives talked about bilingualism and little was said about ethnicity. Works done on regions tended to ignore language, charter groups, and so on.

A lot of us, including myself, thought that if class and gender issues were adequately addressed the need for the emotions/debates around nationalism (in Quebec or the rest of Canada) would evaporate. Even francophone sociologists were stressing the importance of class in the Quiet Revolution. The "No" vote in 1980 seemed to support these impressions. How wrong we were!

We began the Canadianization journey in the late 1960s, a journey that had two components: hiring Canadians and developing a knowledge base on Canada that would somehow forge a Canadian identity or a sense of nationhood. As I have argued, the movement lost its momentum around 1981-82. The hiring issue was dormant, partly because there were fewer jobs and partly due to the increasing number of Ph.D.s being produced. Regarding the second component, the judgement as to how well we did in terms of developing our knowledge of Canada and a strong sense of nationhood is more difficult to make.

The journey of Canadianization is not complete. The promise of a sociology that would examine closely the nature of Canada is unfulfilled. Some have argued that sociology during the 1970s made a significant contribution to our collective knowledge about Canada.[3] Others (Brym) acknowledge the immense growth in research on Canada, but think that "there has been an over-reaction in some circles to the valuable empirical and universalizing tendencies of American sociology" (1989: 172).

Yet, here in 1991, amidst the constitutional debate, the failure of Meech Lake, and the events of Oka in the summer of 1990, can sociologists point to a corpus of research that would enlighten these debates? Can we point to our curricula in both the undergraduate and graduate programs in sociology and anthropology and demonstrate that our disciplines have been in the forefront of understanding the complex dynamics of Canada? I think not.[4]

In order to evaluate the extent to which sociology and anthropology in Canada have fulfilled their mandate to analyze the distinctive combination of economic, cultural, ecological, and demographic conditions that have formed and continue to form Canada, we need to remind ourselves of the historical context in which the Canadianization movement started. A short list of some significant events between 1965 and 1971 should suffice:

1965 - John Porter's *The Vertical Mosaic* was published
1965 - George Grant's *Lament for a Nation* was released
1967 - Royal Commission on Bilingualism and Biculturalism
1969 - Mathews and Steele published *The Struggle for Canadian Universities*
1969 - White Paper: The Statement of the Government of Canada on Indian Policy
1969 - Harold Cardinal published *The Unjust Society*
1969 - Official Languages Act
1970 - Royal Commission on the Status of Women
1970 - October Crisis
1971 - Senate Report on Poverty in Canada

Implicit in this list was the opportunity to do two things: (1) give our graduate students the necessary skills to understand and explore the issues raised in these books and reports; (2) develop a research agenda whose core would be the study of "nation-building" (Symons, 1975). We lost this opportunity. As Guy Rocher remarked in "Les Deux Solitudes":

> Le Canada offre aux sociologues un riche laboratoire de cohabitation à la fois de deux grands groupes culturels et linguistiques, et aussi d'Amérindiens et d'Inuits, les premiers occupants du territoire, et de toutes les autres communautés ethniques, linguistiques et culturelles qui se sont ajoutées et multipliées, particulièrement depuis la 2e guerre mondiale. Nous avons négligé une occasion extraordinaire d'approfondir et d'étendre la connaissance de la société canadienne, et aussi d'apporter une contribution tout à fait unique au progrès des connaissances dans notre discipline. Partout dans le monde, la sociologie contemporaine souffre terriblement de la pénurie de recherches comparatives; celles-ci auraient pu être la marque par laquelle la soiologie canadienne se serait distinguée et aurait ainsi gagné une identité exceptionnelle.

One of the skills we could have given our graduate students was knowledge of both official languages. Surely such knowledge is as important to sociology in Canada as theory and methods? We did not; the solitudes continue.

Our graduate programmes burst onto the scene in the early 1970s and, unfortunately, adopted mostly the American model of graduate training— courses and individualized committees. Students could do a Ph.D. in the same department and after four years of graduate work have almost no common ground on which to hold a discourse. Perhaps one commonality should have been a seminar on the works listed above? The same process of individualization and privatization that characterized graduate training became dominant among faculty members during the 1970s. These processes meant that concepts such as language, culture, charter groups, class, region, and gender that are so integral to an understanding of Canada were left to the whims of individual choice. Some were elaborated quite extensively (class, for example), and others largely ignored. For example, we know what Porter meant when he talked about charter groups, but do we know how people in different regions, in their everyday lives, understand this concept?

Or, to take another example, what is meant by the term "Québécois culture"? How does it manifest itself? How has it been changed by the Quiet Revolution in Quebec? To what extent do upper-middle-class persons in different regions of Canada live different lives, possess different or similar values et cetera? Brym rightly points out the need for more comparative work between Canada and other countries, but what we need also is more comparative work *within* Canada. Regional studies, for example, have focused on economic variables or on questions of dependency; they are seldom ethnographic. Thus, other than language, we need to ask whether rural persons in the Maritimes, Quebec, and the Prairie provinces practise different cultures. Does the speaking of another language automatically mean that one is a member of a different culture?

These are just a few of the questions that could have formed the core of major innovations in research and curricula emanating from the Canadianization movement. However, when we look at our universities and departments, the curriculum is a pot-pourri of courses. For most courses, we have little idea as to what is really being taught. Do we really know what our colleagues in sociology are teaching? Are there mechanisms within departments and universities to find out? Do we wish to? Is it an infringement on academic freedom to ask?

What priority has Canadian literature in English departments? How much do our students know about our writers and poets? How much Canadian history, economics, political science, geography, and anthropology do we know? What about our knowledge of French and English? We need to recover Canadian content, but it will not come about without collective efforts.

In the fight for Canadianization, we spent too little time talking about and doing research on the type of society we think we can become, and how to get there. As Rex noted in his 1976 article on nationalism in the *Canadian Journal of Sociology:*

In [their] choice of problems for investigation, [social scientists] highlight features of [their] own national culture and help to bring that culture to self-consciousness. It would seem to me that in this area there is undoubtedly a role for nationalists' concerns in social science. (512)

Anyone familiar with Canadian history and Canadian literature knows that one of the dominant themes in Canada has been survival, the importance of place in our lives. Atwood says that the crucial question is not "Who are we?" but "Where is here?" or as Raymond Williams has put it: "Out of the ways in which we have interacted with the physical world we have made not only human nature and an altered natural order; we have also made societies." (1980:84) It is our task, in our research and teaching, and in the design of our curricula, to search out the nature of the societies we have produced and are producing right now. This journey was not taken.

Conclusion

Although I am a westerner, I am very much taken by the approach to understanding developments in Canadian sociology put forth by Quebec sociologists such as Guy Rocher and Fernand Dumont. Rocher argued in 1974 that anglophone sociology in Canada basically followed American sociology because they both shared the same premise: that the continuing existence of their society was not problematic. Francophone sociology could not accept this premise, and thus developed a more collective and critical independent stance. Until the rise of a more critical sociology in English Canada in the mid-1970s, I think Rocher was correct. Rocher wrote: "Le mur des silences qui sépare les communautés anglophone et francophone canadiennes se retrouve à l'intérieur de la sociologie." (1974:3)

However, by the 1970s we had lost our naiveté. We began to see two things: (1) our, that is, English Canada's, continuing existence might be problematic, and (2) just as Third World scholars and activists began to explore the extent to which their thinking was dominated by colonial and imperial powers, Canadian scholars began to see parallels for Canada. We began to think out loud and collectively about American hegemony, including that found in our universities and social sciences. The interior of English-speaking sociology began to change, but it didn't last. Other forces such as the development of political economy, and the struggle of women for equality inside and outside academia, affected the journey. Most of us thought the journey had been completed. In terms of hiring it probably was; in terms of content, we had hardly dipped our toes in the water.

If we are to renew the journey, to move away from the shallow waters, sociologists and anthropologists must take seriously the challenge of developing research and curricular innovations that are more focused on issues that bear directly on the future of our country. This is not an easy task. Canada is made up of memory and distance, of time, space, being, and of many cultures. Dumont in his *The Vigil of Quebec* captures this powerfully (Weinstein, 1985: 116): "To discover and confer *sens;* that is the promise. To acknowledge and suffer *absence* with `terrible patience'; that is the present demand."

How can we say the journey is completed when all around us there is no life in the deep water, only darkness sown by people and politicians who do not know our histories, our lands, our many nations. I weep for the promise unfulfilled by the Canadianization movement. Has the river stopped or is it just momentarily dammed?

APPENDIX
KEY MOTIONS ON CANADIANIZATION APPROVED BY ANNUAL GENERAL MEETINGS

I. MAY 31, 1972, MCGILL UNIVERSITY

Whereas this Association expresses support for the encouragement and development of Canadian content in research and teaching in the social sciences and recognizes that there are grave problems of Canadianization that should be faced and worked on constructively in our two disciplines,

This Association approves the establishment of two subcommittees: one on Canadianization and one on Canadian Studies as proposed in the "Postscript to the CSAA Brief on the Rationalization of Research Presented to the AUCC."

Terms of reference of the above two committees:

CANADIANIZATION SUBCOMMITTEE

A. 1) To raise the level of discussion of the issue within the profession;

2) To ask the Ethics, Social Policy, Future of Sociology, and Future of Anthropology subcommittees of the CSAA to investigate and analyze the problems of Canadianization within their own terms of reference and to recommend courses of action to the executive;

3) To define the components of, and gather data on, the problems of Canadianization in our universities, museums, government agencies, community colleges, and high schools from coast to coast, in terms of

a) hiring practices,

b) graduate student admission policies,

c) course content,

d) research needs and support, and

e) other aspects deemed relevant by the subcommittee members by others that may bring matters to its attention;

4) To receive comments and be available for consultation when called on by individuals;

5) To give careful consideration to issues raised in the CSAA Brief to the AUCC, including its recommendations, plus any other relevant submissions;

6) To generate guidelines and draft solutions to be proposed to the CSAA executive for presentation to the 1973 Annual General Meeting;

a) That the CSAA Canadianization and Canadian Studies Subcommittees recommend a set of temporary measures for approval at the December 1972 CSAA Executive meeting. The purpose of these temporary measures is to help ameliorate some of the more critical problems (as to be defined by the two subcommittees) concerning the Canadianization of our professions. These measures are to be applied until such time as the Canadianization and the Canadian Studies Subcommittees can present a more complete set of recommendations;

b)   That these temporary measures be published in the January issues of the CSAA Bulletin;

7)   To prepare materials for a Guide to Canadian Departments of Anthropology and Sociology in our Universities, museums and government agencies, Community colleges, and high schools (see Recommendation 2); and

8)   To receive an initial budget of $500 for the year beginning June 1, 1972 and to prepare a research proposal to be submitted by the Administrative Subcommittee of the Executive to Canada Council and to the Secretary of State.

B.   That the CSAA instruct the secretariat, in cooperation with the Canadian Studies Subcommittee, to prepare for publication and sale as soon as possible a comprehensive guide to Canadian departments of anthropology and sociology, in our Universities, museums, government agencies as applicable and in Community Colleges and High Schools where Sociology and/or Anthropology is taught.

1)   The guide should include for each department information on faculty, specializations offered, degrees offered, the number of registered students per degree, the approximate number of new faculty expected to be hired, the level of appointment, the area of specialization, and new candidates expected to be admitted for the next academic year, etc..

2)   Each department that is listed should be charged a fee to cover costs.

CANADIAN STUDIES SUBCOMMITTEE

1)   To encourage and help organize a series of symposia for anthropologists and sociologists which are designed to define and explore Canadian social issues;

2)   That symposia be designed to provide basic background knowledge of Canadian society in the form of ethnographic and historical information, thereby requiring assistance from members of other fields such as history and related social sciences;

3)   That the three broad areas within which specific topics should be organized are: national, regional, and ethnic issues;

4)   That whenever suitable, symposia include resource personnel from the community as active members;

5) That edited transcripts of the symposia be printed and distributed at cost to libraries, students, faculty, and other members of the Association, when feasible;

6) That the Subcommittee prepare proposals for the Executive to submit to funding agencies to support these activities;

7) That there be several symposia each year in different parts of the country and that the pilot period of this recommendation be three years.

II. MAY 30, 1973, QUEEN'S UNIVERSITY

Recognizing the importance and point of the studies of the problems of Canadianizing the practice of sociology and anthropology already undertaken by the CSAA committee on Canadianization,

Recognizing as well the fact that unless prompt remedial action is undertaken by the profession, the delay in enacting policy will render future solutions irrelevant,

Be it resolved that this Association recommend to those Canadian sociology and anthropology departments with more than 50 per cent non-Canadian faculty a moratorium on the hiring of non-Canadians for any regular academic appointment at or above the rank of Assistant Professor.

The above policy recommendation is to be viewed as an interim, emergency measure to operate until the results of the projects initiated by the Canadianization Committee have been reported to the Association and acted upon.

III. AUGUST 1974, UNIVERSITY OF TORONTO

Recognizing the failure of Canadian Departments of Sociology and Anthropology to hire both Canadian citizens and graduates of Canadian Departments,

Further, recognizing the failure of the 1973 CSAA "Canadianization Motion" to effect the desired changes in both hiring practices and the granting of tenure,

Moved that

a) a full list of the names and research interests of graduate students in Canadian Departments, Canadian graduate students at foreign universities be compiled by the CSAA;

b) this list be circulated with all possible speed and updated yearly in time for the meetings of the CSAA;

c) the persons on this list be contacted concerning job opportunities before alternate sources of recruitment are tapped;

d) a full report on hiring policy and hiring practice at each department be circulated and read at a special session at each forthcoming CSAA annual meeting;

e)   certain hiring criteria—specifically that of having completed a Ph.D. dissertation—be relaxed if necessary for people falling into the categories specified in clause (a). Persons who have not finished their Ph.D. dissertations should be hired at a reduced salary and given a reduced teaching load, thus permitting them to complete their degrees while teaching;

f)   that this resolution and the 1973 "Canadianization Motion" be adopted by all Departments as policy.

Recognizing the difficulties experienced in implementing the 1973 Resolution of the General Meeting which called for a moratorium in the hiring of non-Canadian staff, and

Reiterating the urgent need for effective, affirmative action in ensuring reliable growth in the Canadianization of our disciplines,

Resolved that the General Meeting endorses a policy on recruitment during 1974-75 which:

1)   establishes that at a minimum 75 per cent of all departmental hiring in Sociology and Anthropology during the year be committed to candidates who are Canadian nationals, and/or are engaged in fulfilling advanced degree requirements at a Canadian university; and

2)   urgently requests all Departments of Sociology and Anthropology to endorse and implement this policy; and

3)   charges the Executive of this Association to support the work of an *ad hoc* committee with responsibility to review the principles and practices of hiring, and to develop national programmatic initiatives in this area.

IV. MAY, 1981, DALHOUSIE UNIVERSITY

Moved that

A.   In view of the large numbers of Canadian graduate students in Canadian departments of sociology and anthropology; in view of the decreasing number of tenure stream positions available in Canadian universities and colleges; and in view of the under representation of women in departments of sociology and anthropology, it is recommended:

1.   That for a five-year period there be an absolute moratorium on the hiring of other than Canadian citizens for any positions available to sociologists or anthropologists in universities, colleges, museums, and other organizations that employ sociologists and anthropologists.

2.   That first priority in hiring be given to competent Canadian women; that second priority be given to competent Canadian men.

3.   That when competent Canadian citizens are unavailable, hiring decisions be deferred pending the availability of suitable Canadian citizens.

B.   That the CSAA urge the federal Minister of Employment and Immigration to ensure that, for the next five years, no foreign academics be allowed entry into Canada to assume positions in sociology and anthropology except for limited term visiting appointments of not more than one year, but the latter must not be renewed or translated into regular appointments.

C. That the CSAA take appropriate steps to ensure that Statistics Canada collect information on citizenship, country of final degree and discipline for persons at non-university institutions of post-secondary education.

D. That while there has been improvement in Canadian content in many programmes of sociology and anthropology, the CSAA encourage governments, funding agencies, universities and colleges to further the development of Canadian oriented courses of study.

E. In view of the expressed need for Canadian textbooks and Canadian materials in general, it is recommended that the CSAA State of the Art Committee examine the necessary steps to:
  1. Encourage the publication of integrated textbooks with a Canadian focus.
  2. Solicit editors in sociology and anthropology to co-ordinate publications synthesizing existing knowledge in various substantive areas as it pertains to Canada and obtain appropriate project funding to ensure publication within two years.

F. That the CSAA take whatever steps are necessary to obtain increased funding for the research and publication of sociological and anthropological materials.

G. In view of the crisis in commercial scholarly publishing, that increased funds be obtained for the *Review* to expand the number of pages.

H. That the CSAA urge that in matters of tenure and promotion, research and publication in Canada be considered the equal of all other research and publication and that a strong national reputation be accepted as evidence of scholarly excellence in the field of Canadian studies or in such sub-fields of sociology and anthropology where the primary scholarly community resides in Canada.

I. That the CSAA Canadianization Committee monitor the implementation of "A" through "H" and that such individuals report to the Executive on a regular basis.

NOTES

1   I would like to thank the editors of this volume for their critical comments and helpful suggestions.

2   The CAUT did not take a hard stand in this case because it dealt with hiring, and, by definition, all persons about to be hired are not members of faculty associations or unions and therefore not covered by collective agreements. This meant that departments and universities could hire non-Canadians with little fear of being asked to justify their decisions. This situation led many of us to ask the federal government to tighten the immigration laws. Thus, since 1981, universities that wish to hire a person who is not a Canadian citizen or landed immigrant must provide a written justification and show they have looked for a qualified Canadian.

3   Of all the pieces devoted to analyzing the Canadianization movement and the CSAA's involvement, there are two that deserve careful attention, viz., Harry Hiller's *The Canadian Sociology Movement: Analysis and Assessment* (1979) and Robert Brym's recent book (with Bonnie Fox) *From Culture to Power: The Sociology of English Canada* (1989). They deserve attention because they are studies that attempt to grasp the complexities of the Canadianization movement as a whole. I think the best is Hiller's; the most misleading is Brym's.

4   A political scientist, Stephen Bornstein, remarked in the Fall 1991 issue of *McGill News* that "When I first arrived (1979) at McGill, I was astonished at how little teaching and research was done on Canada/Quebec issues."

Part Two
The Constitution of Knowledge

REMAKING A LIFE, REMAKING SOCIOLOGY
REFLECTIONS OF A FEMINIST

Dorothy E. Smith

In 1988 I drove with a friend from Toronto to Atlanta, Georgia, to go to the meetings of the American Sociological Association. The meetings were held in a hotel that is part of a major complex of post-modern malls and hotels built in the shambles of a declining inner-city. I stayed in one incredible, amazing, delightful post-modern hotel—a circular tower with fairy-tale structures within a structure that at night-time was eerily enclosed in a cover of low cloud. The meetings were held in another post-modern hotel, wholly different in style, with swooping balconies, tier on tier to the distant roof, surrounding a vast central lobby (with the standard hotel coffee shop selling the standard indifferent coffee and the standard mundane salads). The meetings were held in the basement and there, in a standard conference meeting room rather like a plum wall-papered and carpeted interior of a large safety deposit box, we discussed sociological theory.

In that peculiar space, we were divorced from the life of the streets; we moved from architectural fantasy to architectural fantasy by underground malls and overhead walkways. The whole complex was an immense turning-away of consciousness from the world of poverty outside on the streets. Discussing sociological theory entombed in the basement of this complex, I found analogies. I listened to papers reflecting on theory, theories of theories, seeking some ground of unity, a way of reconstructing the multiplicities of sociologies endemic to American sociology, building theoretical walkways, underground malls, sky-displacing interiors, suturing the raw edges, to create a wholly enclosed and enclosing intellectual structure.

There we were inside a theoretical box within a box, within a box, within a box. The world outside was closed off to us, not only in the everyday/ everynight of the week we lived in those hotels and malls, but also in the ways in which we were addressing the world conceptually and in the substance of theoretical discussion.

I was returned there to the sociology that I was educated in at the University of California at Berkeley as a graduate student, a highly professionalized sociology that I learnt very well, I think. I had forgotten what it was like to be immersed in it as fully as I had been (though it had always made me uneasy). For later in Canada, during a period of nine years when I taught at the University of British Columbia, I had undergone a major personal and intellectual transformation, in which those intellectual practices were displaced and replaced.

In Canada at the University of British Columbia I discovered that I was teaching in what I came to think of as a colonized institution. So far as sociology was concerned, the University of British Columbia was a colony of the American sociological establishment. No doubt this applied in other fields. I did what I had been trained to do with considerable thoroughness, namely to reproduce the discipline of sociology as I had learned it at one of the major American centres. I reproduced it regularly, faithfully, and thoughtfully, with due care for the students who at second-hand were getting the message from the centre. I remember teaching a six-month course on deviance—it was a little trying teaching deviance for six months, but one manages. Fortunately, sociology in that field was far from uniform. There were a number of contending theories of deviance that could be presented, critiqued, explored empirically, and so on. I taught what I was taught. We kept busy. Within two or three years of my being there, the influences of Canadianization began to be felt in the Canadian academy. These have been very important to the sociology we have in Canada today. Our sociology, however much it shares methods and theoretical practices, differs in important ways with the sociology prevailing in the United States.

The Canadian critique contributed to my discovery of the colonial character of the world that I was putting forward to my students. I discovered the very distinctive role for which I had been trained. It is rather like that of the docent in museum or art gallery. She (it is usually she) has learnt her piece and faithfully repeats it to the crowd who follow her round the gallery. It is not up to her to have independent opinions about the materials displayed. As docent she has no mind of her own, cannot innovate, has no opinions other than those that have been scripted for her. She may share them, but it is not her place or role to dispute them if she does not. She speaks what she has been taught to speak. I spoke what I had been taught to speak.

The Canadianization critique of the social sciences and the humanities in Canada showed us the colonial character of the intellectual regime we practised. For me, this was important as precursor to the further intellectual, personal, and political moves that became the radical divorce I experienced in Atlanta, between where I'm coming from and the theoretical sociology of the basement of the Marriott Hotel. Canadianization began to free me for the possibilities of thinking from a different space in the society than I had been trained for.

I had been trained in my own work to reproduce sociology as I had learned it and also to get my students to reproduce the sociology that I reproduced. You get these characteristic essays (we're all familiar with them, but they're always irksome) in which a student reproduces the theories that s/he has been taught but does not know how to think them or does not have any conceivable use for them as a means to think with. It is a pathology of the social organization of a colonized and colonizing sociology. For sociological theory as I had learnt it has its uses for sociology but, as Canadianization taught us, it may effectively insulate us from knowing the world we live.

These became problems for me in the context of the Canadianization critique. They were also problems raised directly for me by students. Students, I found, wanted to understand what was going on around them, and it seemed to me that sociology only had the kinds of answers that weren't answers. It didn't offer much as a means to know and think about the world. But these issues became acutely problematic for me in a different way with my involvement in the women's movement.

The women's movement begins and belongs outside the academy. We started somewhere outside the academy with our own lives, our own experiences—as wives, as mothers, as women employed outside the home, as young women growing up into a society that was, and in many ways still is, a very sexist society. Our first major discovery was that we had no language. This was not an abstract matter. It was very concrete, very practically immediate to the possibility of organization.

We needed a way to talk, as women among women. What we knew was the masculine colonizing discourse that displaced, subdued, and marginalized our consciousness as women. To speak it was to be subdued and marginalized again. We needed a way to talk and to imagine. We needed language and images. Women's studies entered the University of British Columbia through the back door out of this need. It wasn't invented by academics. A group of women students started a course in the student union for women in general, students, women from the community, academics. They gave the impetus to women academics' initiative for a women's studies course as a regular part of the curriculum in the Faculty of Arts.

The women academics who were active in this believed—certainly I did—in the university as a place of rational discourse. We believed that its processes were governed by canons of logic, evidence, cogency, objectivity. We encountered a strangeness. We were deeply disillusioned by our experience of attempting to get a women's studies course in place. We did succeed, but in the process we encountered prejudice, questioning of our professional competence, insults and threats variously veiled and unveiled. We went through thirteen committees when the normal process was two or at most three. We began to get an idea of what we were up against. Call it patriarchy.

That women's studies course was a profoundly transforming experience. It was entirely different as an experience of teaching than any other I had had. Even to describe it as teaching is not quite apt. There was at that time nothing to teach in the ordinary academic sense because there was no literature (this was one of the more rational objections to our course proposal.) We had an intensifying sense of how deeply the intellectual practices of our disciplines (they were indeed our own intellectual practices) were contaminated by exclusions and subordinations of women. Yet there wasn't anything to teach from as an alternative. I think when we started I had about three books on my shelf (including Jessie Bernard and Mirra Komarovsky). We used whatever we could find. So we used our experiences as women, whether student or faculty, to challenge our disciplines, to challenge ourselves, to explore, contend, expand, discover. All of us.

We taught an interdisciplinary course in which we made a critique of our disciplines on the basis of experiences as women that we discovered together with students in the classroom. It was an amazing experience. The critique from women's experience was powerful. We could begin to see gaps, absences, distortions, alienations. But perhaps most extraordinary was the three-times-weekly experience of entering a totally different discursive world than the one we normally inhabited. We thought of that class as the "real university," the place of intellectual challenge, of intense argument, of a class in which everyone participated in discovery, debate, questioning. We were doing a hard thinking and a hard inquiry together. I have this image of the Pied Piper of Hamelin playing his pipe through the city, gathering up the children, and leading them through a hole that opens up in the mountain to the golden country beyond. Three times a week, collectively rather than conducted, we went through a hole in the mountain into the other world of the real university of women.

This was a very major experience in my life. It was a transforming experience. It challenged me to think very differently about my sociology. I came more and more to see the male biases built into standard sociologies. I also saw in sociology a more fundamental problem, namely its inability to explicate for women, indeed for anyone, the ways in which our lives are embedded and structured by complexes of powers and relations beyond the scope of our experience. I wanted a different sociology, one that would live up to the potentiality that my commitment to it had seen. I also felt, in my teaching and my other scholarly work, a quite different responsibility. Previously my responsibility had been professional. I had undertaken responsibility to serve up to my students a sociology that could name but could not explicate the social relations and organization of their lives, that could not tell them how to know and explore the world for themselves. To be responsible was to deliver that profoundly male-biased sociology impersonally and competently. I had been brought up to be responsible. I had been a good girl for a long time. I had taught sociology responsibly. And now I could not do it any more.

In this women's studies course I learnt a new responsibility. It was in direct contradiction with the responsibility I had undertaken before. Getting rid of the old responsibility was also discovering an entirely different responsibility to the students in the class and not just to the students, but to women in and beyond the classroom. Rather than teaching sociology, I was now committed to telling the truth, to being able to say "this is how the society works," "this is what's happening to us." I found that the sociology I had been trained in didn't lend itself to that. It did not provide a way of speaking to women about the society. It did not provide a way of understanding the society from the point of view of women's actual experience. Here was a powerful impetus to remake sociology so that it would in fact do what we were called upon in that setting to do.

Sociology, as I had learned it, bound us to its texts. What we could talk of in the classroom as part of its business circulated through the textbooks and other readings. This early women's studies course worked entirely differently. We began with what we knew in ordinary and experiential ways. In building the intellectual life of the classroom, we were never bound by the texts. The classroom was never insulated from the society in which it existed. Women pulled into it from their lives beyond topics, knowledge, concerns, questions, angers, desperations, and humour. The political fortifications that have been built in this century to insulate the university from the local society it is set down in were breached. The university's political isolations, built in small increments over fifty years, has cut it off from its potential relationships with working class, with women, with non-white peoples in the community. We sought to break out of this isolation. We made connections beyond the classroom because the classroom was part of the women's movement and the connections were already there. And though in the classroom we did not organize action beyond the classroom, women went from the classroom into action.

Now in women's studies we face the severing of those relations beyond the classroom that were in the early stages such powerful presences *in* the classroom. At that early period those relations were integral to what we did. There was no separation. We did not talk, as now my students do, of the conflict between doing scholarly work and activism, because that contradiction had not emerged. The classroom of women was in the women's movement. As you went from one site of work in the women's movement to another, you found an open interchange between practical issues of organization and the disciplinary and theoretical issues of the classroom. The debates that were central in the formation of the political directions (and they were always multiple) of the women's movement were the debates of the classroom, and what we could do in the classroom illumined those debates. In academic contexts we learned skills that had their uses elsewhere. We set up an organization called the Women's Research Centre, designed not to study women, but to do research for women. It was designed to do research responding to the situations women were encountering in the community and involving them in the research process. It was directed towards what they needed to know in order to be able to act; it was not directed by the characteristic social scientific stance of what we needed to know about them.

We deliberately set this up outside the university because we could not see otherwise how to escape the characteristic way of relating built into the university. Universities suck knowledge out of people outside the university, put it through a filtering procedure provided by social science, and confine it to specialists. Knowledge produced by universities is not designed by the people in whose lives it originated. It is not spread about for them. It travels rather in the discursive relations of disciplines and the media of the intelligentsia. It serves the organization of ruling people, rather than serving people. The rejection of a mode of relating to people and of relating knowledge to people became an essential part of how I began to work, both within and outside the university. It became essential to how I began to reconstruct my thinking as a sociologist. It did not seem sufficient just to work outside the university. So long as we operated with standard social scientific procedures we found that our work converted the women we wanted to work with and for into the objects of ruling. Therefore, it seemed to me, a different way of thinking was needed, a thinking that would begin with women as subjects, rather than converting them into objects. I was not rejecting what the academy could do. Rather my notion was to create a conceptual transformation reconstructing social scientific knowledge to enable a leakage from the academy to the sites where people really need to know. At the outset, the women's movement in the academy was deeply subversive because it insisted on this dual relation between within the academy and beyond: on the one hand drawing women's experience in the world into the academy if only as a critique of established disciplines; on the other, expanding a knowledge that could be brought into women's lives to use, to think with, to know the world. In important ways we can transform, and to a considerable extent have transformed, the knowledge that is available to women in the society. If sociology has seen the world from a particular viewpoint, namely men's, we can envisage its expansion to other bases of consciousness—women's, working class, native peoples, black people. Much more than an expansion of subject-matter is entailed. Also at issue is the method of looking at the world that is built into the established sociological method of thinking and enables the particular perspectives and interests of male participants in ruling to be reproduced as objective.

I do not claim that my own work was exceptional. All of us involved at that period took these issues up, each in her own way, for there were no standards, no precedents, no guidelines, no canon. If anything is distinctive in what I've done, it is perhaps to have been more grandiose, to have wanted to claim for women not just a sociology for women in the sense of specializing in women's concerns, but the equivalent for women of the sociology for men that has been the established sociology—that is, a sociology knowing the world from the standpoint of women.

Canadianization showed me a colonized sociology; it showed me a sociology written from a centre located in the United States; the standpoint of women, which we practised in this early women's studies course, showed me a sociology written from the position of men; the intersection of the two pointed to structures of power built into sociological theories and methods. The standpoint of women was not at that time the abstract coinage of feminist debate. It was a classroom practice, a way of working, a critical strategy. It transformed relations in the classroom. I thought it could provide a method of remaking sociology. We could have, I thought, a way of knowing society from a standpoint that was outside the abstract and abstracting organization of ruling in which established sociology participates. I thought we could explore society from the places that people actually lived and from a ground in their actual experience of living. We could have a sociology beginning from where women were situated in their everyday/everynight lives. We could have a sociology responding to people's lack of knowledge of how their everyday worlds are hooked into and shaped by social relations, organization, and powers beyond the scope of direct experience. Repression operates in part through the management of ignorance.

Located in the actualities of our everyday lives, we cannot grasp how it is put together. The objectified knowledge of social science does not connect up with our immediate realities. An intelligentsia that works within the objectified forms of knowledge of the relations of ruling does nothing to change that problem, no matter what its politics. A position in the relations of ruling is built into standard conceptual practices and methods of research. Established sociological theories and methods produce knowledge about people for the institutions of ruling—the sociology that we inherited from the American establishment does just that. A sociology for women, indeed a sociology for people, would work in the opposite direction, developing strategies for knowing that could disclose to people how things happen to them as they do.

The subversive practice essential to women's studies at that time was important to me personally in many ways. I discovered, among other things, the possibility of quite different kinds of relationships than those normal to the academy and profession. Relying on the collocation of many women's experience to critique and question made the classroom an open place. No one woman's experience could be privileged over another. Standard top-down pedagogic practices were called into question. We're talking about a society we're all part of, that we all know in different ways and from different angles. The work of the instructor was in part the co-ordination of difference within the developing matrix of the discipline in which she worked.

The pedagogic practices of the sociological docent described above was exactly opposite. If the sociology I had learned in graduate school was to be transmitted to students unsullied and more or less exactly replicated, the instructor needed to act as authority. She needed to be able to impose the version of society built into her discipline. She needed to drive out others. She needed to pre-empt the "naive" understandings of the world that students learned in their everyday/everynight living. She needed to replace them with the disciplinary understandings. In the classroom, therefore, however genially mediated, she exercised authority and required conformity.

The early days of women's studies challenged these assumptions about what it is to have a knowledge of society. We began with a tacit understanding that the classroom speaking of society and the social is part of what it speaks of, and that those who are present have all kinds of knowledge of the social that they bring with them. Usually it is unspoken. In the early women's studies classroom, it was not only permitted, it was essential, it was relied on. I do not, of course, imagine a sociology that always remains at this point. A body of knowledge, structured otherwise, does develop. Women want to learn, to go beyond their experiential knowledge. The point of developing a sociology of knowledge is that there would be a knowledge capable of expanding experience into zones it does not reach. At the same time, what people bring to the classroom as an everyday/everynight knowledge of the world is never excluded. Rather, it is encouraged and invited. There is always more to be known. There are critiques to be made. There should be a dialogue between a developing knowledge in the academy and the actualities of women's/people's lives. Knowledge of the society doesn't begin and end with the teacher's knowledge. It incorporates the knowledge of those who are, for this time and this place, the students of that teacher. Their experience, their knowledge of the society, is part of what can come into the classroom and be given an active presence as part of a process of discovering the society we live.

As they must be, such changes in my thinking and practices were also personal transformations. For I discovered that the relations of power built into my profession were not altogether outside me. They were an integral part of who I was. Including the masculine positioning that I took on in thinking sociology as I had been taught to think it. I had to go through a long and sometimes painful process of divestment. Learning to work as a feminist in sociology has not been a purely intellectual work. It has also been a transformation of a way of being as a woman in society, my transformation of my way of being as a woman. In this to understand differently was to be different, to be a different woman, a woman who related to society in very different ways. I was also becoming a woman who wanted to discover how to move directly from the everyday/everynight world of experience into the intellectual constructions of society created by sociology. Both had to change.

Before the beginnings of this change, I had a hard time writing papers. I had a particularly hard time if I thought that I was going to say anything that was significantly innovative. It caused me acute anxiety. I used to drink a glass or so of brandy to get going. Looking back, I see that as the mark of the profound alienation of my located subjectivity and the mode in which I had to write. I had no ground from which to write into the objectified male-grounded textual ordering of sociology. It was a difference between myself and male colleagues. Garfinkel has written of how the formal theoretical terminology of sociology always depends for its sense on the background knowledge of society that the reader (or writer) brings. Lacking that background knowledge, that participation as a member in the male-order of ruling, it was not easy to write in that mode purely as an abstraction. Every paper was a performance before an alien other, a judge, who shared an intimacy of understandings with male sociologists that was never mine. Among other matters, it took for granted my absence *as a woman* from sociological discourse, most obviously as object, but also as subject.

I discovered as a feminist a very different way of writing. Somewhere around 1972 I drove south from Vancouver with a group of other feminists to attend a meeting of the American Academy for Political Science at the University of Oregon in Eugene. I had written a little paper out of my experience of the critique of sociology that emerged from women's experience. It was called "Women's Perspective as a Radical Critique of Sociology." I made mimeocopies of it myself and took a bunch of them with me. So we drove south on Interstate 5, crammed in a car and feeling bold. In those times passing through the border had elements of risk. We did not, of course, say where we were going or for what.

Giving this paper had an extraordinary outcome for me. Because it travelled. Tattered, and increasingly indistinct through many copyings, it went all over. I got letters from many places in the United States, and beyond, and one even from Hungary. I saw then that the professional academic media of sociology could be used in a totally different way than I had conceived them. They could be used as a medium through which feminists could exchange messages. You could write to be read by people who wanted to read your work. You could write differently (I modified the structuring of my papers to conform sequencing more closely to how I wanted/needed to put things together). Your work, rather than claiming finality as a status, could be opened-ended, opening up dialogue, written at the point at which your work had arrived, at which you needed to hear from others. The ways in which I could work and write within established sociology were transformed. I did not have to perform for the American sociological establishment or its Canadian outpost. The media of professional discourse could be used by women to reach women.

The Canadianization of sociology has also transformed Canadian sociology, perhaps not quite so profoundly as a feminist sociology, but in the same direction. Whereas American sociology strove for supra-national generalization, and/or for universal scientific theories, Canadian sociology took as its foundation a commitment to speak of the society it was and is part of. That we are speaking about Canadian society is always somewhere present in Canadian sociological writing. In the multiplicity of issues and questions raised at the annual sociological meetings in Canada, we can see Canadian sociology's ongoing connectedness with the society. It is continually responding to and incorporating problems and questions that come from what is happening in Canadian society. They are not derived from the internal logic of the sociological discourse. This means, of course, that we carry back from Canadian sociological meetings news about our own society to enter it into our research and teaching.

I believe this to be a powerful and vital aspect of Canadian sociology. I long for us to hold on to it. Sometimes I fear it may be in jeopardy. I long for us to hold on to this because in our reported research, our debates and disagreements, we are learning as sociologists to know better the society we live in. Through these means our sociologies maintain contact with the actualities of peoples' lives. Sociologists come more and more from different places in the society and speak for people situated elsewhere than in a white male establishment. Canadian sociology is challenged and renewed in this process and its capacity to address the realities of this society are enhanced. The women's movement has played a leading part in insisting on a different basis in experience of the society as a different basis for speaking of it, and in anchoring Canadian sociology in the same world it is part of.

FACTICITY AND DOGMA IN INTRODUCTORY SOCIOLOGY TEXTS: THE NEED FOR ALTERNATIVE METHODS

Sylvia Hale

There are times in life when the question of knowing if one can think differently than one thinks, and perceive differently than one sees, is absolutely necessary if one is to go on looking and reflecting at all.

In what does [philosophy] consist, if not in the endeavor to know how and to what extent it might be possible to think differently, instead of legitimating what is already known?

–Foucault, 1985:8-9

Introduction

This paper explores issues in the philosophy of science as they apply to sociology, with specific attention to the role of textbooks in initiating students into the discipline, the influence such texts may have, and the possibility that they promote theoretical closure and dogmatism rather than openness and debate.

The ideas of Kuhn and Feyerabend represent opposite poles in the debate on the nature of scientific knowledge and progress. Kuhn maintains that knowledge develops most when a community of scientists share a common paradigm and work collectively to test elements of that paradigm against an ever-broadening body of factual evidence. Textbooks epitomize mature science in initiating students into the concrete problem-solutions acceptable within the discipline. Feyerabend's counter-argument is that any unifying paradigm threatens to lock science into the intellectual straightjacket of well-confirmed theories. He enjoins scientists to work with a plurality of theories, and preferably to seek theories that contradict the factual character of whatever is considered already known. His critics respond that if his arguments are correct, then science disintegrates into solipsism, implying the impossibility of making any factual claims.

This paper explores the utility of social constructionism as an alternative approach to knowledge that takes into account its context-dependent character and the essential interpenetration of theory and evidence. The factual character of knowledge is sought in what people do to produce the appearance of factual evidence rather than in the conceptual conclusions that they draw from it. Dorothy Smith's extensive research on accounting practices in sociology is used to guide analysis of knowledge claims in a standard introductory textbook. This analysis suggests that much of what is regarded as the body of factual knowledge in sociology needs to be re-evaluated as theoretical conjecture. It further suggests the need for radical change in the format of introductory textbooks to present sociology as a body of theories that are used to conceptualize, or to factualize, evidence, rather than a body of facts about which we theorize.

Thomas Kuhn: The Functions of Dogma in Science

Thomas Kuhn's analysis of the structure of scientific revolutions (1962) challenged the conventional view of science as the objective, open-minded search for truth, with scientists as uncommitted researchers, owing allegiance only to bare and objective facts. In practice, Kuhn argues, the scientific enterprise is essentially closed. Regardless of whether their work is pre-dominantly theoretical or experimental, researchers generally know before they begin their work all but the most intimate details of the results that the projects will achieve (1970:357). Far from seeking novelty, scientists are predisposed to reject it as an error in conceptualization or methodology that can be corrected by more careful research. New scientific truths, Kuhn suggests, rarely appear sufficiently convincing to persuade practising scientists to abandon established theoretical paradigms. More commonly, opponents of the new truths gradually die off, while the younger generation becomes committed to them from the start.

Kuhn's central thesis is that such intellectual closure is not anathema to the scientific enterprise, but rather an essential component of normal science. To be fully productive, scientists must be committed to a shared world-view that tells them what is worth researching, what are acceptable solutions, and where the important trouble spots are. Such commitment ensures the concentration of collective efforts to pursue knowledge at the boundaries of the discipline. Without it, efforts tend to be dissipated in floundering between competing theories. Individual scientists feel they need to start back from the beginning with a research problem. Experiments are constantly repeated, discoveries made but promptly lost, because scientists lack sufficient clarity in their predictions to distinguish real findings from accidental effects. With the clear foundation of an established paradigm in place, scientists can push ahead, using all their skills to articulate it, to apply it to new areas, and to develop the highly specialized research techniques needed to penetrate and resolve anomalies.

Kuhn thus acknowledges that "scientific education remains a relatively dogmatic initiation into a pre-established problem-solving tradition that the student is neither invited nor equipped to evaluate" (1970:359). Textbooks are designed to train students to become competent practitioners of their disciplines, not to be independent critical analysts. At the same time, however, Kuhn is emphatic in rejecting the notion that the practical outcome of such scientific education is dogmatism. Empiricism, the relentless testing of theory against empirical evidence in experimental research, provides a defence against dogma. He argues that a well-developed paradigm allows scientists to predict with great precision the expected outcome of research, provided the guiding paradigm is correct. This very precision means that any error should become glaringly obvious, especially when a community of scientists is collectively struggling to solve the puzzles and make the paradigm fit. These are the times of crisis that portend paradigm change or scientific revolutions. Kuhn asserts, in effect, that dogma performs a critically important function in science education. Textbooks train students to operate as competent puzzle-solvers from established rules. But, at the same time, scientific education instills allegiance to objective, factual evidence as the basis for evaluating theories and revising paradigms. Kuhn acknowledges that this process of revision is far from straightforward, since older scientists tend to cling doggedly to their favoured paradigm until the end of their careers, but their work is destined eventually to be overthrown by the "young Turks" and the weight of contradictory evidence. In principle, the tension between professional skills on the one hand, and the professional ideology of empiricism on the other, should combine to ensure the success of the scientific enterprise.

Empiricism as Dogmatic Metaphysics

The success of Kuhn's defence of theoretical closure in science rests on the power of empiricism—the systematic evaluation of theory against objective, factual evidence—to expose flawed paradigms and so to prevent dogmatism. This defence rests on the critical assumption that facts are available independently of theory. Hence, theories can be tested against known facts and their credibility or confirmation can be further advanced by experimental research that generates additional facts.

It is this faith in the independent facticity of evidence over against theories that is challenged by Feyerabend's critique of empiricism (1970, 1975). The core of Feyerabend's argument is that no factual data can be independent of the theoretical assumptions that guide the process of defining and searching for them. Any description of evidence necessarily presupposes a theoretical perspective and hence cannot at the same time stand as a test of that perspective.

This does not mean that experiments are useless. They play a decisive role in deciding between alternative theories in that they test the compatibility of generated data with theoretical predictions. Theories are shown to be flawed when experimental data are not in accord with predictions. Such tests, however, work only at a low level of generality where the nature of what constitutes factual evidence itself is taken as given. The possibility of any crucial experiment to decide among competing theories depends on prior agreement concerning what will be accepted as constituting objective, factual evidence, as against conjecture, opinion, interpretation, fantasy, illusion, or deception.

It is at this fundamental level that Feyerabend launches his critique against contemporary empiricism as leading to dogmatic metaphysics. Feyerabend insists that the background interpretive theory or ontological assumptions that define how evidence becomes recognizable as factual must itself be subject to test (1970:321). Crucial experiments, he argues, cannot test such background theory because they necessarily presuppose it. When scientists in the puzzle-solving tradition insist on consistency and meaning invariance as basic rules in developing and testing any new theory, they preclude the possibility of generating alternative conceptualizations of observation sentences such that their status as objective factual statements could be questioned. They never test the background theory that determines what they conceptualize as factual evidence. Their conjectures become "facts." Those secondary theoretical explanations that are consistent with the facts as given appear as more and more highly confirmed. The unquestioned and untested background assumptions produce their own confirmation. The possibility that scientists will challenge such facticity becomes more and more remote as the body of evidence expands. For Feyerabend, the problem of scientific dogmatism goes far deeper than the rigidity of aging scientists who resent having their life's work challenged by their juniors. The nature of experimental research itself and the interdependence of theory and evidence leads to "establishment of a dogmatic metaphysics and the construction of defense mechanisms which make this metaphysics safe from refutation by experimental inquiry" (1970:320). The uniformity of theory and empirical evidence that Kuhn praises as the sign of mature science appears to Feyerabend as self-deception.

The alternative approach to empirical sciences that Feyerabend advocates is diametrically opposed to Kuhn's ideal of puzzle-solving within the dominant paradigm. Feyerabend advocates developing a plurality of theories, and the more radically they differ in basic assumptions from the dominant paradigm, the better. Feyerabend's central argument is that there exist facts that cannot be unearthed except with the help of alternative theories. The ideal is to strive for theories that are so totally different from the prevailing theory that the background conceptualization of what constitutes factual knowledge itself comes into question. Such theories are "incommensurable" in that the nature of what would constitute evidence is so different that no single test can decide between them. Feyerabend argues further that the meaning of concepts and their operational referents is determined by the theories in which they are embedded. Hence, such meanings cannot remain invariant as theories change. He gives the example of the concept of mass, not as a property of objects in classical physics, but as a relationship, involving relative velocities, between an object and a co-ordinate system of other objects in relativity theory (1970:326). The ultimate goal in developing alternative theories is to make possible radically different visions of the nature of the factual world that will free ideas from the closed box of immutable facts and well-confirmed theories: for Feyerabend, then, the problem of dogmatic metaphysics in science is rooted in the very reliance on factual evidence that Kuhn sees as shielding science from dogma. Textbooks, in so far as they present a body of factual knowledge, cement that theoretical dogma in place prior even to students knowing what the implicit theory framework is. Only that theory in terms of which the facts were constructed will become visible. Alternative theories are not available to be thought because the facts preclude them.

Feyerabend's critique of contemporary empiricism has been widely rejected by traditional scientists as leading to anarchy. They argue that, at best, the plea for a multiplication of theories seems destined to lead backwards to the state of premature sciences described by Kuhn, where researchers continually circle around without ever making progress. And at worst, Feyerabend's assault on the facticity of evidence seems to make it impossible to assert anything (Hattiangadi, 1977; Tibbetts, 1977). The fundamental issue raised by such criticism is whether it is possible to challenge respect for facts and still have science. If Feyerabend is taken seriously then what can be said? How can empirical research proceed? How might it be possible to have a non-dogmatic approach to science education that would still recognizably be science? Is it possible to produce textbooks that will "train practitioners" in the Kuhnian sense, and at the same time promote openness in critical theoretical questioning as envisioned by Feyerabend?

Social Construction: A Re-vision of Empiricism

Once the facticity of evidence is acknowledged as compromised, then a retreat into a reliance on that evidence as a defence from dogma in science is no longer possible. It forces a search for an alternate approach to empiricism that can take into account the essential interpenetration of theory and evidence and the context-dependent character of knowledge. One important form that this re-vision has taken in the social sciences, as in other disciplines, may be loosely referred to as social constructionism. Dorothy Smith's work explores the implications of this approach in sociology.

Smith first addresses the question of how we can distinguish science from ideology (1974a:39-40). Specifically, she identifies ideology as "the interested procedures which people use as a means not to know" what people are actually doing in the processes of producing what we come to see as factual knowledge (ibid.:40). The ideological practice of sociology is a critical procedure that separates a corpus of statements about the world from the subjectivities of those who have made them. In any science, the research practices structure accounts in definite ways (1974b:262). The problem of ideology arises when the outcome of such structuring and interpretive practices is presented as facts that were discovered, as if they were there prior to and independently of the scientist's inquiry.

An ethno-methodological study of astronomers engaged in the process of "discovering" an optical pulsar, shows how this ideological practice works (Garfinkel, Lynch, and Livingstone, 1981). In the conventional scientific account of the research, the pulsar is depicted as the cause of everything seen and said about it. It is described as existing prior to and independently of any specific method of discovering it. The scientists through proper, lucid methods, come upon the pulsar that was otherwise hidden due to ignorance, sloppy work, and so on. The account is in the third person, as if the personal presence of the scientists were irrelevant. The factual discovery of pulsars is objectively and neutrally there. The ethno-methodological study writes the process in reverse. The authors explore the tape recordings and notebooks kept by the scientists to show how they collectively talked themselves into believing that the ambiguous readings they were getting in their research equipment constituted a finding. Before the "discovery" was made it was by no means obvious how to interpret these surface appearances. Many different underlying patterns could be and were proposed to account for the details, with the option of optical pulsars only one among several. Perhaps if the shop-talk between the scientists had gone differently, the conclusions drawn about what they were looking at would have been different, and pulsars would not have been discovered at all. In other words, it is not the factual existence of pulsars that produces the account, but the accounting process that produces the pulsars.

From the perspective of social constructionism, the bedrock facts consist of what the people were doing—how they set up their research equipment, and the haggling and arguing that produced the conclusion that a concept like "pulsar" could be used to make sense of the blips that appeared in their data. These humanly scientific practices become ideological when these accounting processes are omitted from the final report, so that the concept "pulsar" becomes the cause of the results.

Smith argues that this practice of converting concepts into "facts," while obscuring the true factual evidence of what people do to produce them, is pervasive in contemporary society. Most of what we know comes to us second-hand in the form of documents produced by others. The main features of our society, such as illness rates, crime rates, class structures, occupations, job satisfaction, and the like, are the products of the reporting and documenting procedures of earlier researchers. Most of our knowledge is thus already "worked up" or socially constructed before we acquire it. The factual character of statements that we find in such documents is not intrinsic to the statements themselves, but imposed on them by the way in which the statements are structured or presented (Smith, 1974b:258). Some statements insist on a factual usage by being presented in the form of an announcement—Pulsars are a kind of star—or they are introduced by such words as "in fact." This is typically the form in which scientific statements are presented. Such statements convey the impression that their content is an external, fixed entity, objectively the same for everyone, and independent of the subjectivity of the teller. Institutional credentials, and publication in scientific journals and textbooks, add to their aura of facticity. Other ways of writing statements preclude a factual interpretation by their being introduced in the form of "I think," "I believe," or "the argument we find plausible here is...."

Smith draws particular attention to the very different social relations between the teller and the receiver of information generated by the two kinds of statement. The factual form brooks no argument. The statement appears as objectively neutral revealed truth, the state of affairs. The opinion form, in contrast, includes both teller and receiver as participants in the definition of what happened and how it might be interpreted. It invites further questioning from the receiver.

Smith's central argument is that the subjective interpretation of the person presenting any statement is necessarily involved in the accomplishment of facts. The teller must impose some conceptual and temporal organization onto the raw experience of "what happened" in the process of communicating the account. Any account necessarily intends its own interpretation in the sense that the teller formulates the telling in a manner that makes the raw experience make sense, or seem "accountable" as some event. The problem is that this structuring appears to the recipient of the communication as intrinsic to the event being described. The sense imposed by the teller becomes part of the structure of "what happened" as known to the recipient. This is especially so when statements are constructed in factual form, the form typical of scientific reports. The challenge for social science is to make visible these structuring processes.

Relations of power and control, or what Smith refers to as the apparatus of ruling, are embedded in the production of knowledge that appears to define the major features of our society (Smith, 1974b:259). Much of the work of producing documents occurs as part of routine work activities in organizations. What happens as spontaneous events in peoples' lives becomes structured as factual knowledge in documentary form through the routine record-keeping activities of bureaucracies. The sense that such a document makes is determined by the relevancies of the organization producing it. At the point when evidence enters this "document time" all the subjective selection processes and interpretations that are intrinsic to the categorization of data into statistics disappear. Data are summarized in documents as objective statements of fact. Researchers who begin with these documents as evidence remain bound by these hidden construction processes.

The implications of Smith's analysis for textbooks in sociology parallel those of Feyerabend's work, while also pressing beyond them. The requirements of traditional empiricism, that theories account for the facts as known and that concepts be invariant with respect to such facts, mean that science remains locked into the formal organization or apparatus of ruling that generates the documents providing factual information. Sociologists who begin with documentary evidence and seek to account for it in theoretical terms become part of the apparatus of ruling itself. Even supposedly radical critiques remain locked into this ruling framework so long as the facticity of the documentary evidence itself remains unquestioned as the starting point for theoretical explanation.

Smith's special contribution is that she proposes certain methodological procedures for resolving the impasse noted by critics of Feyerabend's work—the seeming impossibility of making any warranted scientific assertions once the facticity of evidence is placed in doubt. Smith argues that to break free from the constraints of documentary reality researchers must focus directly upon the social processes through which documents are constructed. In the social sciences this necessarily includes analysis of the practices of routine, everyday work in organizations that produce the documents, including social science textbooks, that constitute knowledge about society.

Fact and Theory in an Introductory Sociology Text

The remainder of this paper examines a standard introductory sociology text to uncover how the relationship between fact and theory is treated, and its implications for theoretical pluralism or closure. It also addresses the question of how a science of sociology is possible, and how it might be introduced in textbooks, when the facticity of evidence is constantly in doubt.

The text edited by Robert Hagedorn, *Sociology* (second edition) 1983, was chosen principally because of the editor's explicit commitment to incorporate three major theoretical perspectives in each of the seventeen chapters devoted to specialized sub-fields of sociology. The nineteen contributors were asked to utilize conflict theory, structural functionalism, and symbolic interactionism as an integrating theme for the chapters (Hagedorn, 1983:1 and Preface).

In principle this approach promised to be compatible with Feyerabend's appeal for non-dogmatic, theoretical pluralism in science. In practice, however, this goal seems elusive. For the most part, debates between theories throughout the text tend to be resolved into differences in emphasis within a generalized consensus. The central message is one of unity with variations, with few contributors straying far from the dominant functionalist paradigm. This homogenization of theory became more pronounced as the text evolved from the first edition in 1979. A few of the early contributions adopted a more exclusively Marxist orientation, such as those by Cuneo, Kopinak, and Grayson, in their treatment of class and stratification, the polity, and social movements. But these were replaced by contributions that fitted more closely into the model of consensus around three perspectives.

This pattern is by no means unique to the Hagedorn text. Ben Agger, in his review of American sociology textbooks, refers to "the illusion of sociological heterogeneity" (1989:365). American texts, he suggests, "canonize three (and only three) theories: functionalism, symbolic interactionism, and conflict theory" (ibid:367). An important problem that he identifies with this approach is that the supposedly diverse theories are quickly collapsed into each other in an effort to maintain synthesis. Symbolic interactionism is not a theory at all, he suggests, but a research strategy in microsociology. Textbook Marxism loses all its critical political edge to become a safe, respectable variant of functionalist conflict theory. In this "Boy Scout Marxism" conflict is an unavoidable fact of social and economic life that must be dealt with piecemeal by the capitalist welfare state. Girl Scout feminism, on the other hand, is domesticated in the gender, family, and sex role chapter(s). It too becomes another variant of mainstream conflict theory, with women urged to work "with men" to sort out their mutual problems. The potential for Marxism or feminism as radical critiques of conventional theoretical wisdom is lost.

The central question addressed here is how and why this theoretical closure occurs, using the introductory chapter from the Hagedorn text as a test case. The argument explored below is that pressure towards consistency and meaning invariance in comparing alternative theories with what are taken to be established facts leads inexorably to the closure of debate. To break this closure I will develop the implications of the alternative theory of ethnomethodology and its macrosociological equivalent of social constructionism, to challenge the facticity of the evidence to which the three mainstream theories are constrained to conform. My point is not to demolish all evidence, but rather to illustrate that all evidence is necessarily structured by theoretical assumptions.

It is not my intention in the following analysis to privilege ethnomethodology or social constructionism as necessarily superior to all other sociological perspectives. They are used here because they are useful for reconceptualizing old "facts." Similar challenges to the factual character of certain evidence might be mounted by Marxist and feminist theories— although not of the Boy-Scout, Girl-Scout varieties. But they would run a greater risk of sidetracking the debate on epistemology into an argument about politics or value bias, which is not central to the present analysis.

Sociology—The Study of Facts and Constraints

Important clues to how the closure of debate comes about are contained in Chapter One of the Hagedorn text, entitled "What is Sociology," written by Hagedorn himself. Hagedorn outlines what he sees as the major theories in sociology, grounding them in work of the classical theorists Durkheim, Weber, and Marx. He begins with a discussion of Durkheim's emphasis on sociology as the study of social facts, facts that are external and coercive with respect to individuals. Durkheim's study of suicide rates provides a classic example of social facts. Certain suicide rates appear stable across different countries and time periods. Married people, for example, commit suicide less frequently than divorced or single people, and Catholics less than Protestants. The explanation for these data is the social fact of level of social integration. People who are members of families, or of the Catholic church, are part of more integrated social groups than single people or non-Catholics. For further information on methods of measurement Hagedorn directs readers to Chapter 17 on research methods, written by himself and Alan Hedley, which presents detailed practical information on how sociologists gather objective, factual data. Other examples of social facts include a discussion of political institutions in which the position of Prime Minister of Canada "exists independently of a specific individual. In a real sense, it is out there external to any individual. Further, it is coercive or constraining upon any individual elected to the position" (1983:6).

Hagedorn's subsequent presentation of the ideas of Weber and Marx shows them to be fully compatible with this view of external and coercive social facts, notwithstanding important differences in approach and emphasis. Hagedorn cites Weber's definition of sociology as "a science which attempts the interpretive understanding of social action in order thereby to arrive at a causal explanation of its course and effects. 'Action' refers to all human behavior to which an actor attaches subjective meaning" (1983:7). Hence, sociology should proceed by imputing motives and meanings to actions. Weber's view of sociology has the potential to provide a radically different and subjective interpretation of social reality. However, his ideas are introduced here in a way that retains the view of social facts as external and coercive. The example given of subjective meaning is that of a foreign traveller in Spain who must know the typical, culturally defined meaning of hand movements in order to correctly understand directions (ibid:7). The third classical theorist, Karl Marx, is noted for his central concern with establishing a science of society with the ultimate objective of changing it. The primary social fact for Marx is the division of society into two basic and antagonistic social classes, and the historical struggle between the "haves" and the "have nots" to change this structure.

In the next section of the chapter, the work of these three classical theorists is systematically linked to current perspectives in sociology. Hagedorn begins with macrosociology, which he defines as referring "to a set of factors, characteristics, dimensions, or variables that exist in society independently of individuals" (ibid:12). Structural functionalism, associated with Durkheim, focuses upon the social system in dynamic equilibrium, while the conflict perspective, associated with Marx, focuses upon conflict and struggle around these structures. Weber's interpretive perspective is associated with microsociology, concerned with the meaning and significance that people attach to social facts.

In the final section of the chapter, concerned with sociology and science, these three perspectives are shown as compatible with the application of natural science methods to the study of behaviour. Science seeks to explain patterns or relations between variables by reference to objective scientific laws. Objectivity is based on the three critical attributes of (a) verifiability of evidence, (b) unbiased observation, and (c) unbiased interpretations.

In summary, the paramount message in this introductory chapter is that sociology consists of the study of social facts that are external to individuals and that exert coercive causal force on behaviour. Statistics constitute one form of social fact, as do indices of group integration, formal organizations, and prestige rankings. They are all amenable to objective and verifiable scientific measurement. Macrosocial institutions and organizations such as political structures exist independently of individuals and function as principal determinants of behaviour. Individuals function as role incumbents within them. Interpretive sociology, concerned with subjective meanings, applies primarily, if not solely, at the level of microrelations, operating within the constraints of macrostructures. Culture, as subjective meaning, constitutes a set of typical, external facts that have to be learned and correctly interpreted by individuals. Scientific method generates verifiable evidence and unbiased observations and interpretations, marred only by distortion introduced by biased researchers. Explanations take the form of law-like relations between variables.

This overview of sociology is very much within the mainstream tradition in textbooks. Teevan and Blute, in the Teevan text (1989, Chap. 1) provide a closely comparable discussion of the origins of sociology as the scientific study of social facts, and a description of the three theoretical perspectives. Allahar, in the Tepperman and Richardson text (1986, Chap. 1) repeats similar themes. Hagedorn's introductory chapter is appealing as a coherent and readable account that provides clear illustrations of ideas and makes reference to a variety of approaches. It cannot be faulted for inaccuracies in presentation of the three perspectives. They are described very much as they are used in the mainstream tradition.

So what is the problem? The issue raised here is not with quality but with form. We are reminded of Ben Agger's awkward question: "Do books write authors?" Agger warns that college textbooks exert a major influence on present and future sociologists. They do much to structure the general discourse of the discipline, and this discourse tends towards theoretical closure. There is heavy pressure, especially within introductory textbooks, to present sociology as a mature science in Kuhn's terms, a science that has a unified body of knowledge and theory endorsed by the community of scholars. Diversity within the discipline is characterized as a form of dynamic equilibrium in which Marxism and symbolic interactionism give the illusion of theoretical openness but with the end product of mature consensus largely attained. The critical questions that we raise below are: Does sociology appear in dogmatic form as a body of facts about which we theorize or as a body of theories through which we conceptualize, or factualize, evidence? Can we see the theoretical assumptions, the haggling and the arguments, through which the blips in the sociological research technology become worked up into "facts"?

Facts as Problematic

The argument explored below is that the body of social facts and constraints noted in Hagedorn's introductory chapter are derived from an underlying epistemology that privileges structural analysis. Other theoretical perspectives such as conflict theory and symbolic interaction are forced to conform to this mould or to appear to be contradicted by the facts and therefore false. Alternative visions of social reality find no grounds for expression. Of particular importance is the unquestioned assertion that macrosocial institutions exist as factual structures that function as causal determinants of social behaviour. Theoretical debate seems confined to arguing over the extent to which such structures determine or shape or influence behaviour, depending on one's preference for more deterministic conflict theory or more flexible interactionism. But any argument that implies that such structures do not exist at all seems doomed. Similarly with respect to culture, we seem able to debate the degree to which culture determines, structures, or merely frames choices, but any argument that implies the non-existence of culture seems ludicrous. The challenge, therefore, is to elevate the ludicrous to the status of an equally plausible theoretical perspective in terms of which social structures and institutions are not entities but concepts, ideas that sociologists and other people have found useful in accounting for certain experiences, but not facts.

Suicide Rates

Durkheim's classical study of suicide rates provides an ideal example for such reconceptualization because it has been the focus of extensive criticism from the standpoint of ethnomethodology theory. Douglas (1967) argues persuasively that suicide statistics do not provide objective, factual measures of the incidence of intentional self-death. Rather, they are the outcome of complex decision-making processes by coroners or other official record-keepers trying to classify probable causes of death. The patterns that Durkheim found within the resulting statistical data reflect the theoretical assumptions and interpretations that coroners and their informants used to make their decisions. A common theory, for example, is that "happily" married people with children are less prone to suicide than "lonely" divorced or single people. This leads to a strong predisposition to conclude that ambiguous deaths by people in the former context were probably accidental, but were probably suicide for those in the latter context. The lower suicide rates among Catholics can readily be accounted for by the Catholic proscription against suicide as mortal sin. Such beliefs form a powerful incentive for relatives and local priests to give a dead Catholic the benefit of any possible doubt and to label ambiguous deaths as accidental rather than suicide. Douglas points out that the suicide rate jumped by as much as fifty per cent in one year in one region when the persons responsible for classifying deaths changed from local priests to government bureaucrats. Such a change due to methods of counting exceeds the differences in rates upon which Durkheim relied for testing the theoretical link between suicide proneness and social cohesion. The taken-for-granted assertion that married people or Catholics generally enjoy higher social integration than unmarried people or Protestants is also challenged by Durkheim's own evidence of higher suicide rates among married women, and Douglas's observation that while Catholics had lower recorded suicide rates than Protestants they made up for it in higher accident rates.

Douglas's critique of Durkheim's study has far-reaching implications for traditional sociology. The interpretation of statistical rates as the outcome of subjective decision-making processes by people who compile them is incommensurate with the interpretation of the same rates as an objective count of numbers of instances. No simple experiment will decide between these theories because they do not agree at the basic level of what would constitute evidence. Durkheim's functionalist argument about the relationship between social cohesion and propensity for unhappiness or suicide relies on finding correlations between measures of cohesion and measures of suicide. Douglas's ethno-methodological argument reconceptualizes all such evidence as indications of the accounting processes used in categorizing deaths. The apparently factual character of the statistics is revealed as theoretically constructed rather than as given in advance of theory.

This begs the question raised by critics of Feyerabend: what is it possible for sociology as a science to say about suicide once the factual character of suicide rates is called into question? From the standpoint of ethnomethodology and social constructionism as theoretical perspectives, the answer is that we need a very different kind of evidence. In order to understand what suicide rates mean we need to study the routine everyday practices of coroners as they do their work of investigating and categorizing deaths.

Smith (1983) goes further than Douglas in demonstrating the essential circularity of theory and data in studies of suicide. She cites work to show how not only coroners but witnesses and family members themselves rely upon theories about motives for committing suicide when they produce accounts of what happened. She emphasises that accounts always and inevitably *intend* their own conclusions. The intentions of the teller structure how the details of each account are presented so that the listener/reader is likely to come to the same conclusions as the author. Smith gives the example of two different accounts of the suicide of Virginia Woolf, one written by her nephew, Quentin Bell, the other by her husband, Leonard Woolf. Bell's account leads readers to see Virginia's suicide as a rational and fully reasonable act of a sane woman trapped in an unbearable situation. She had coped with the outbreak of the Second World War, the bombing of her London home, a serious quarrel with her sister, the threat of a Nazi invasion of Britain, and the probability that she and her Jewish socialist husband would be tortured if the Nazis ever caught them, and hence the suicide pact to which they both agreed, should their capture seem imminent. She appears to have coped with circumstances that would have defeated many of us. The last straw, suggests Bell, was the evidence that her husband and her friend thought she was sinking into psychotic depression and should be hospitalized.

The alternative account, given by Leonard Woolf, reads more like a psychiatrist's clinical report. Virginia's earlier psychotic illness is given prominence rather than the external conditions in wartime England. We learn that she is depressed, openly talking of suicide, and manifesting cyclical mood swings. We are drawn into seeing Virginia as a psychotic, and her suicide as the foreseeable and probably unavoidable act of a mentally ill person.

The issue here is not which account is correct, but how the author's interpretive scheme or theory directs how each account is put together. We have no possibility of knowing "the facts of the matter" listed in some uninterpreted form. All that we have are the patterns that the tellers unavoidably impose in their efforts to make the vague flux of experience accountable, to themselves and to others, as "what happened." As with the earlier discussion of the discovery of the concept of pulsars, the bedrock facts are the accounting practices, or what people do in the process of coming up with conclusions, not the conceptual conclusions that find their way into statistics.

Organizations as Fact or Conjecture?

Belief in the factual existence and constraining character of complex organizations is much more deeply entrenched in sociological claims to knowledge than are statistical rates. In traditional textbook accounts, such as that provided by Hagedorn, it is taken as fact that bureaucracies exist, comprising more or less rigidly defined systems of roles or jobs, arranged in a hierarchy, and with each role having a reasonably well-defined set of duties. That a position such as Prime Minister of Canada exists independently of a specific individual and exerts a coercive and constraining influence upon any elected incumbent seems self-evident. The only room for theoretical debate seems to be how well people's informal behaviours fit with their formal duties (symbolic interaction) or how oppressive or miserable some jobs are relative to others (conflict theory). From the perspective of social constructionism, however, everything is turned around. Notions or concepts like "bureaucracy," "hierarchy," "job descriptions," "duties," and the like appear as just that—concepts. They are the outcome of people's accounting practices, ideas that sociologists and others use to make sense to themselves and to others of what is going on. They are not factual entities or external constraints that cause, determine, limit, or influence what people do.

The belief in the factual existence of bureaucracies is so pervasive that constructing and communicating an alternative theoretical perspective in terms of which such entities do not exist is a Herculean task. We will tackle only a tiny bit of it here, exploring the social construction of what comes to be seen as the hierarchy of roles and duties in a formal organization. A study by Reimer (1987) suggests that there is commonly a wide gap between what clerical workers are supposedly doing, according to their formal job description, and what they are doing according to their own practical accounts. The job description for clerical workers in the government bureaucracy defines their work as "routine delegated duties" requiring limited educational skills or responsibilities. The practical accounts by clerical workers, however, reveal that much of their work requires independent thought, initiative, considerable skills, and comprehensive knowledge of the operations of the organization in which they work. Clerical workers frequently carry out important managerial functions, including, in one case, actually preparing her department's annual budget.

A study by Cassin (1980) suggests similarly that the work of clerical staff in the British Columbia civil service can be usefully conceptualized as managerial work. When we attend to what these workers actually do in the ostensibly routine work of opening and sorting mail, for example, we see that they are actively structuring their bosses' jobs, making key prioritizing decisions before the boss even gets involved. If they make mistakes, like putting on the back burner what should have received prompt attention, the ramifications could be serious.

What we begin to see from the perspective of social constructionism is that the notion of bureaucracies as a structured hierarchy of roles with defined skills and responsibilities is a fiction. It functions as ideology, an interested procedure that people use as a means not to know what people are actually doing. This function cannot be resolved into the familiar distinction in functionalist theory between formal and informal behaviour, because this reduces to a tautology. Bittner (1965) raises the critical question, What is the difference between formal and informal organization? The answer is circular. Any behaviour that fits the model or the organizational chart is formal, and all the rest is informal. The meaning of the concept of "formal organization" is contained in how it functions as part of the accounting practices of the people involved, and the reports of sociologists that piggy-back on such accounts. Reimer's study illustrates some of these accounting practices by showing how terminology borrowed from job descriptions serves to obscure the skills of clerical workers. The same task that is termed "research" when done by managers or professionals is termed "routine getting of files" when done by clerical staff. The questions used in job interviews, again structured by the job descriptions, typically leave no scope for clerical workers to display their knowledge outside the routines listed as their duties. The end products of their work are attributed to those defined as responsible for such work, so that any contribution by clerical workers becomes invisible. Any behaviour that does not fit the rational, bureaucratic model will not appear anywhere in any formal organizational records or minutes of meetings, because it is defined as only informal behaviour and therefore irrelevant. Job classification workers evaluate the organization chart itself, labelling and classifying what role incumbents are supposedly doing, according to the relevant job descriptions, while the reality of what people are actually doing does not enter the picture.

These multiple ways in which people actively use job descriptions in their accounting practices together constitute the social processes through which the concepts of formal organization and bureaucratic hierarchy gain their appearance as facts. These classification schemes are in turn used by other workers to produce the labour-force statistics on the percentage of professional, managerial, para-professional, clerical and semi- or unskilled workers. Statistics Canada records these convenient fictions in neat tables. Sociologists then use these tables to produce their accounts of the occupational class structure of Canadian society, and such secondary statistics as the proportion of females doing managerial work. The gender-class structure of Canadian society might look very different if the managerial work of people in non-managerial job categories actually gained recognition, along with the non-managerial work that some people in managerial job categories do. How different we do not know. Our knowledge of what people do comes to us so totally worked up by bureaucratic accounting procedures, guided by the fiction of organization charts, that what is actually going on is almost impossible to know. We might have to start from scratch.

In summary, the structural functionalist definition of organizations as presented in Hagedorn's introductory chapter identifies bureaucratic roles and positions as external structures or social facts that determine the behaviour of role incumbents. Such a view is incommensurate with the social constructionist reconceptualization of bureaucratic structures as the outcome of accounting practices. From this perspective the very factual descriptions upon which functionalism relies constitute fiction that reinforce the dominant ideology that legitimizes the apparatus of ruling.

The apparent integration and consistency of the dominant theoretical paradigm in sociology begin to crumble as soon as we begin the exercise of reconceptualizing apparent social facts as interpretations in the light of structuralist theory. The paradigm loses its aura of well-confirmed concreteness and we are forced to confront both theoretical pluralism and incommensurability of basic assumptions regarding what constitutes relevant evidence for theoretical tests.

Subsequent chapters in the Hagedorn text closely replicate the approach adopted by Hagedorn in his introduction to sociology. All the contributors share a commitment to presenting large bodies of evidence within their distinct sub-fields of sociology. Such evidence is treated as objective, factual information that is known independently of theory. The three theoretical perspectives of structural functionalism, conflict, and symbolic interactionism are introduced after the description of facts, and with the same commitment to consistency and meaning invariance with respect to the facts as given. The insight of ethnomethodology—that the factual character of evidence is dependent upon the theoretical perspective through which it is viewed—is not developed.

Conclusion

The central aim of this analysis has been to accomplish the transformation of familiar statements about social facts into theoretical conjectures, thereby freeing up intellectual space for different kinds of questioning than is possible when factual statements prevail. The critical difference between statements of fact and statements of theory is in the kind of response that they promote. Facts appear as neutral, objective, and independent of the subjective interpretations of speaker and listener, writer and reader. Theories are constrained to be consistent with them or to appear to be false. Conversely, statements of theory or conjecture expose the subjectivity of the thinker and invite the listener to share in the questioning process.

Critical relations of power, or what Smith terms "relations of ruling," are embedded in the transposition of conceptual statements into statements of fact, organized around theoretical consensus. Dis-sensus is silenced or made to seem ludicrous because it appears to fly in the face of demonstrable empirical knowledge. Tight brackets are set around what can be reasonably thought. In Feyerabend's view, our main defence against such closure is to work with a plurality of theories, and to actively search for those that challenge the factual character of what is currently known. But this process is extremely difficult. In Hagedorn's text the authors actively struggled to incorporate three theoretical perspectives into their analyses, but for the most part the factual statements held firm and the theories bent around them into a muddled but recognizable consensus.

The goal of social constructionism is to make visible the accounting practices of social scientists and others that produce the appearance of the factual character of evidence, thereby changing statements of fact into concepts. This does not mean that concepts such as bureaucracy, hierarchy, culture, or socialization are no longer useful. But their meaning emerges through how they are used in the accounting practices of the people involved. Nor does this mean that sociology slips into solipsism, where nothing can be said beyond one's own opinions. Social constructionism draws on a different kind of empirical evidence in which the meaning of knowledge statements rests in the practical activities of those who produce them. When we can see the interpretive processes that go into the construction of evidence, then we know in a different kind of way the meaning that evidence entails.

Smith's central argument is that this is what knowledge means. Knowledge is always human knowledge, and hence always actively put together from an interested standpoint: "There is no theory, no method, and no knowledge as a product of these which is not made by men and women and made in the interests of those who make it" (Smith, 1974a:40). There can be no such thing as disembodied facts separate from the interpretive processes that give them meaning. Consequently, there can be no sociology textbooks that provide factual knowledge of society without theoretical perspectives, implicitly or explicitly, pervading all aspects of the account. We therefore need to explore what it is that people do in their everyday lives to produce the patterns and the classifications that sociologists and others subsequently identify as culture, norms, statistical rates, and the like.

These observations together suggest the need for far-reaching changes in the character of introductory textbooks in sociology. We need to shift the focus away from sociology as the study of social facts and constraints that are somehow known independently of theories, and to focus instead on sociology as a body of theories that uncover and structure evidence in particular ways. This approach entails fundamental change in the relationship between students and texts. The goal is to encourage students to challenge and debate competing theories, to explore evidence critically, to see how it is put together, and to search for alternative interpretations and new questions. It is upon such critical skills that the advancement of science depends.

In closing, I would like to reply to Ben Agger's question, "Do books write authors?" with a resounding "yes!". The discourses of the discipline seem so firmly embedded in the introduction to sociology as the study of social facts and constraints defined in advance that any dis-sensus is kept on a tight rein. The effort of trying to hold up other interpretations against the weight of this material has felt like trying to stand firm in the path of an avalanche. Think about how it must feel for students!

WHAT IS GOOD FOR ANTHROPOLOGY IN CANADA?

David Howes

"Canada has always been a cool climate for heroes."
— Northrop Frye, *Divisions on a Ground*

To speak of "British Anthropology" as opposed to "French Anthropology" or "American Anthropology" makes immediate sense. Each of these designations refers to a recognizable tradition of inquiry with its own litany of great names: Malinowski/Radcliffe-Brown/Evans-Pritchard, Mauss/Lévi-Strauss/Godelier, Boas/Mead/Geertz. But "Canadian anthropology"— what is that? It is only very recently that we have begun to discover its history (McFeat, 1976; McKillop, 1987; Barker, 1987), or taken a serious look at its social organization (Preston, 1983). And the conclusion that results from these studies is that as far as a tradition is concerned, there isn't one, or not very much of one anyway.

Who would a roll-call of Canadian anthropologists begin with? Suppose one wished to construct a canon, what texts would it include? Bailey's *The Conflict of European and Eastern Algonquin Cultures 1504-1770* (1937)? Dunning's *Social and Economic Change among the Northern Ojibway* (1959)? Dewdney's *The Planiverse: Computer Contact with a Two-Dimensional World* (1984)? Trigger's *Natives and Newcomers* (1985)? Boddy's *Wombs and Alien Spirits* (1989)?

The task of constructing a canon is perhaps as difficult as determining the answer to the question "As Canadian as _?" Every Canadian knows the answer to "As American as ___." But "As Canadian as _?" The reason no immediate answer comes to mind is simple. The answer would depend on whether one were English-Canadian or French-Canadian, and the matter is further complicated by the fact that one could well be neither. It seems the best answer to date remains the one given in response to a *Morningside* survey: "As Canadian as possible under the circumstances."

This response is exemplary of the contingent character of the Canadian identity (Howes, 1988). It also goes a considerable way towards explaining why there can be no such thing as *a* Canadian anthropology. To speak in such a singular way would be to exclude everything that has been accomplished in Quebec (Gold and Tremblay, 1983). To put this another way, the expression "100 per cent American" is familiar enough, but there is no such thing as "100 per cent Canadian," except perhaps for the new airline (formerly Canadian Pacific), which substituted a ">" sign for the "a/e" in Canadi>n. When I use the term Canadi>n in what follows, I mean to underline the contingent character of the tradition I am evoking, Canadi>n anthropology being "a tradition that is not one," like the identity of which it is, in part, an expression.

To pursue this idea of a canon of Canadi>n anthropological literature further, it is surely the case, as the reader will have remarked, that some titles belong there and that others—in particular, *The Planiverse*—do not. There is nothing anthropological about a work of "science fantasy," which is how *The Planiverse* is described. However, its form *is* that of an ethnography—an ethnography of the nature of social life in a two-dimensional universe—and there are other reasons for seeing it as a classic of Canadi>n anthropology, as will be shown in the next section. Besides, we are said to live in an era of "blurred genres" (Geertz, 1983). Witness the extent to which a distinctly literary sensibility has invaded anthropology through the works of Marcus and Cushman (1982), Clifford and Marcus (1986), and Geertz (1988), usurping the place of the older paradigm of structural linguistics (as in Lévi-Strauss, 1963). So why insist on a strict separation between anthropology and science fantasy?

Frankly, I think it is important to keep literature and anthropology separate, and that we can and should be using anthropological techniques to analyze literature, but not (as is more and more the case) the other way round (Howes, 1990a). My more immediate point, however, is that it should not be by reference to content that we decide whether a book belongs to the canon. What we need, in order to make such judgements, is a set of *formal* criteria. Otherwise, we would be forced to exclude not only *The Planiverse* but also Boddy's *Wombs and Alien Spirits* because, being about a community in northern Sudan, the latter work has no "Canadian content." There is no more preposterous notion than that of "Canadian content," though I think it is possible to speak about a Canadi>n structure, and it was, I suggest, in recognition of the profoundly Canadi>n structure of the ideas expressed in Boddy's book that it was nominated for the Governor General's Award.

The aim of this essay, then, is to identify a set of criteria that could be used to decide whether a given work belongs to the canon. The criteria I propose are by no means the only ones, but I would emphasize that they do have the advantage of being general (as we shall see, they permit us to tell what is good in other fields of endeavour besides anthropology, such as the visual arts), and they also have the merit of being constitutional (that is, they are legal and cannot therefore be dismissed as "purely political").

A Classic Canadi>n Ethnography

The Planiverse was written by Alexander Keewatin Dewdney, a professor of computer science at the University of Western Ontario. Its plot is summarized (on the back cover) as follows:

> Dr. Dewdney created a hypothetical two-dimensional universe as an exercise for his computer science students. They developed a program

called 2DWORLD to model a detailed, though somewhat primitive, planet. Then one day in May 1980, something extraordinary happened.

The "something extraordinary" was that the 2DWORLD program some-how connected with a real two-dimensional world, Arde. The rest of the book is taken up with describing Dewdney and his students' odyssey across the face of Arde in the company of a creature by the name of Yendred.

Given that the idea behind *The Planiverse* is so obviously borrowed from the English writer Edwin Abbott's 1884 classic *Flatland*, while the drawings of Yendred of Arde are so obviously modelled after the American film director Stephen Spielberg's "E.T.," hence the "Canadian content" of Dewdney's fantasy is not very apparent; and given that *The Planiverse* is a work of science fantasy, not anthropology, the reader may well wonder how the present writer could possibly see it as "a classic of Canadi>n anthropology." But this difference of opinion is easily resolved. The reader has only to stop thinking "literarily" —that is, in terms of genres (fantasy/realist, history/ethnography, etc.) and in terms of "influences" (or as some contemporary theorists prefer to say, "relations of inter-textuality") —and *start thinking anthropologically*. A properly anthropological, as opposed to literary, analysis of how *The Planiverse* came to be written would delve *behind* these other texts and attempt to specify what was unique about Dewdney's life experience such that the ideas of *Flatland*, and transforming E.T. into a two-dimensional being, appealed to him.

Significantly, *The Planiverse* is dedicated to "my father Selwyn Hanington Dewdney, artist, writer, scholar" (Dewdney, 1984:5). In real life, Selwyn Dewdney was even more complex than this glowing dedication would imply. As Christopher Dewdney (Alexander Keewatin's brother) recalls:

> when I was six or seven or eight years old, [father] dragged me [and A.K.] around every summer on...canoe expeditions [in the Keewatin District of Ontario] and he'd introduce me to shamans and we'd be documenting Indian rock paintings. So I was steeped in Amerindian lore. My father, I realize now, had actually converted from Anglicanism to Amerindianism. I think he believed something intrinsic about the Amerindian identity was one with his own set of beliefs.... And this became my matrix (quoted in O'Brien, 1985:91).

It has been suggested that the highly unique style of Christopher Dewdney's poetry may be attributable to his early exposure to the mysteries of the rock art of the Canadian Shield (O'Brien, 1985:90). A similar argument could be made regarding the sources of A.K.'s inspiration—that is, that he became obsessed with the idea of documenting life in a two-dimensional universe as a result of all those summer-long canoe-trips with his amateur archae-ologist father.[1] In point of fact, the drawings of Yendred and the other creatures of Arde are closer stylistically to the X-ray style pictographs one encounters on the rock faces of the Canadian Shield than they are to Spielberg's E.T. The problematic of the book, 2-D existence, is also directly related to Shield rock art, since the original producers of that art restricted themselves to thinking and drawing in two dimensions as well, and not a single pictograph shows any interest in, or knowledge of, how to represent things or people three-dimensionally.

There is a further sense in which *The Planiverse* may be regarded as a quintessentially Canadi>n ethnography, though I am rather uncomfortable with the essentialism of the Jungian-type analysis we are about to embark on. Essentially speaking, Dewdney's narrative conforms to the archetypal pattern laid down by Margaret Atwood in *Surfacing*, perhaps the most formulaic Canadian novel there is. That pattern may be described as follows: child follows in footsteps of father to discover meaning and salvation inherent in an alien universe.

Surfacing is a novel about a woman who returns to her childhood home—a cabin on an island in northeastern Quebec—in order to solve the mystery of her father's disappearance. In the cabin, she discovers a map with crosses on it, and a stack of papers with numbers scrawled alongside drawings of, among other things, "hands and antlered figures, a half-man with four sticks coming out of it" (Atwood, 1973:101). At first, the narrator interprets these drawings as signs that her father had gone insane. Later, she comes across a few pages from a book entitled *Rock Paintings of the Central Shield*, by a certain Dr. Robin M. Grove, and she realizes that her father was, in fact, engaged in charting and recording the "signs" left by "the original ones," the Indians. "The Indians did not own salvation but they had once known where it lived and their signs marked the sacred places, the places where you could learn the truth" (Atwood, 1973:145).

The narrator goes to one of the places marked on the map, but cannot find any evidence of rock painting. Suspecting that this might be because of a change in the level of the lake, she dives underwater and there experiences a vision of "a dark oval trailing limbs" (Atwood, 1973:142). Such a motif is typical of the pictographs of the Shield (see Dewdney and Kidd, 1967), but it also has a personal significance for the narrator: it is the soul of the foetus she had been compelled to abort by her ex-husband. This vision leads her to confront her own and her civilization's "capacity for death," which is seen as resulting from that civilization's drive for technological mastery over nature (Atwood, 1973:147). The vision also awakens in her a longing "to be whole" (Atwood, 1973:146). The narrator finally achieves this "wholeness" or "salvation" by rejecting everything that "divides us into fragments"—language, society, technology—and becoming one with nature.

Surfacing may be said to revolve around the theme of having to erase what George Grant has called "the mark within us" left by our "conquering relation to place." As he observes:

> When we go into the Rockies [or the recesses of the Shield] we may have the sense that gods are there. But if so, they cannot manifest themselves to us as ours. They are the gods of another race, and we cannot know them because of what we are and what we did. There can be nothing immemorial for us except the environment as object (Grant, 1969:17).

Selwyn Dewdney expressed similar sentiments in his "Ecological notes on the Ojibway Shaman-artist" (1970), even though as we learned earlier from his son Christopher's testimony, he came closer than most any other Canadian to overcoming the "conquering relation to place" and communing with these "gods of another race."

To make a long analysis short, Selwyn Dewdney was the real-life exemplar of Atwood's father-figure. This should be understood not in the sense that Dewdney was the model for Atwood's character, for she knew nothing of him, but that his life was *as prototypical* as that of the character she constructed. Selwyn Dewdney does not appear in the pages of *The Planiverse* any more than Atwood's father-figure appears in *Surfacing*, but in both cases the absent father guides his progeny to a point where contact can be made with an alien universe. Beyond this, however, the archetypal pattern we have been tracing breaks down, since Atwood's female narrator achieves grace, or illumination, by abandoning technology, whereas A.K. attains wisdom by experimenting with technology.

Is it not "more than just coincidental," as a Jungian would say, that there is such a strong resemblance between the two father-figures? Was Selwyn Dewdney the archetypal Canadian father? Frankly, I think that to pursue this psychologistic line of reasoning any further would be pointless because, as Lévi-Strauss (1963:208-9) would say, it is "pre-scientific." According to Lévi-Strauss, it is the relations *between* images or ideas, not the relation of an image to a putative archetype, that we should be studying. Meaning emerges out of difference.[2] A Jungian analyst would be powerless to explain why the fates of the two narrators diverge (one embracing, the other rejecting technology), because Jungian analysis has no space for difference. By contrast, the proportional analogy that emerges from a structural analysis of the two works—namely, *woman is to nature as man is to technology*— does tell us something about the Canadian imaginary.

We shall be developing this structural analysis of the Canadi>n imaginary further in the next section, where the scope of our inquiry will be widened to include the American imaginary, so as to permit what is distinctive about the *kinds of relations* that inform the life of the mind in Canada (as distinct from the U.S.) to emerge more clearly. Our analysis will depart from Lévi-Strauss's, however, for whereas the latter sees all minds as being wired the same way, and conceives of the laws of logic as universal, the method advocated below, which derives more from the work of Durkheim and Mauss (1970), views operations of mind (including logical relations between ideas) as grounded in the social relations between persons, as determined by a given constitution. Thus, minds can be configured differently, depending on the society in which they mature.

But before proceeding, let me sum up what I think we have learned from studying Dewdney's *The Planiverse* as if it were typical of a certain national genre of anthropological writing. What we have learned is that irrespective of the *de facto* otherness of the Ardreans, what inspired and enabled A.K. to construct them as he did, was his experience as a youth. A certain distinctly Canadi>n structure for the acquisition and articulation of experience was instilled in A.K. by his father, and *The Planiverse* was a projection, or better, the *realization*, of that structure.[3] What Ardreans are like in and of themselves is, obviously, not something we are ever going to know.

The Constitution of Mind and Society

In recent years, anthropologists have become increasingly conscious of how their position in their own society may influence what they come to know and write about other societies. While few have gone so far as to explore how their childhood experiences may have influenced the selection of the issues that engage their interest as adults (as we have just done for A.K. Dewdney), many now feel it necessary to identify their sex, ethnic background and social class. The implication is that each of these factors somehow mediates their experience of the Other.

In what follows, I would like to explore the significance of another factor that is of relevance to the formation of the anthropological imagination—namely, the constitution of the anthropologist's society of origin. The word "constitution" has a variety of senses. It can refer both to the "mental character" of an individual and to the "mode in which the State is organized." The double meaning of the word "constitution" would have appealed to Durkheim and Mauss, for as they argued in *Primitive Classification* (1970), the life of the mind is always structured after the life of individuals in society. According to Durkheim and Mauss,

> The first logical categories were social categories,...the first classes of things were classes of men; not only the external form of classes, but also the relations uniting them to each other, are of social origin; and if the totality of things is conceived of as a single system, this is because society itself is seen in the same way...the unity of knowledge is nothing else than the very unity of the social collectivity extended to the universe (Needham, 1970:xi-xii).

In illustration of this thesis, Durkheim and Mauss give the example of the seven-fold classification of space, and the association of certain species of totemic animals with each of the seven regions so discriminated, among the Zuni Indians of the south-western United States. This arrangement can be seen as modelled after the division of the tribe into seven clans. Thus, among the Zuni, there is a "classification of things by clans" (Durkheim and Mauss, 1970:55). It is the space occupied by the divisions of the tribe in the camp—the form of society—that provides the model for the Zuni representation of the cosmos.

Following Durkheim and Mauss, I take it as given that the form in which one thinks is mediated by the form of one's society. I would further argue that the excellence of any given representation (be it a painting, a poem, or a monograph) consists in the degree to which the representation gives expression to the *archai*, or first conceptions and principles, of its producer's constitution—in both the mental and the legal senses of that term. The last point is inspired by Alasdair MacIntyre's (1988) trenchant critique of the Enlightenment ideal of a tradition-independent rationality. No such rationality exists, as MacIntyre very convincingly demonstrates. MacIntyre goes on to develop the thesis that every tradition is predicated upon some conception of "the good" for human beings, even those traditions that do not recognize themselves as such (e.g., liberalism, or Canadi>n anthropology). It is the articulation of that good that constitutes the *telos* of intellectual inquiry within the tradition or community in question.

If MacIntyre is correct, it follows that *what* is structural is good. What I meant by "structural" is "tending to conform to the constitution." Thus, a given work may be judged good if the relations between the ideas expressed in it can be seen to agree with the relations between persons and between groups established by the constitution. As should be apparent, I am treating the constitution as both necessary to the production of knowledge (i.e., as providing a form for thought) and as the standard against which such productions may be judged (i.e., as providing a measure of the good). As should also be apparent, "the good" is not something that exists or can be appreciated in the abstract, but only in relation to a particular constitution.

Let me illustrate this theory by taking the Canadian and American constitutions, comparing them, and proceeding on the basis of this comparison to determine what is good for intellectual inquiry in the two societies. Basically, whereas the "ultimate end" *(ultimus finis)* of human life under the U.S. Constitution is to be free from government interference, to enjoy the equal protection of the laws, and to participate in a "unity of we," under the Canadian Constitution it is good to subject oneself to a regime of "peace, order and good government," to enjoy the proportional protection of the laws, and to participate in a "unity of you and I."[4]

The first two contrasts between the two constitutions (pursuit of liberty as opposed to order, and equality as opposed to distinction or deference) have been remarked upon by numerous scholars, and are not controversial. The third contrast, however, "unity of we" versus "unity of you and I," is somewhat mysterious, and requires further clarification. Where does the U.S. ideal of joining in a "unity of we" come from, and what does it mean? It comes from the Preamble to the U.S. Constitution: "*We* the People of the United States, in Order to form a more *perfect* Union, establish Justice,...and secure the Blessings of Liberty to ourselves and our Posterity," etc. But the idea is actually older than that. It was already present in the Declaration of Independence (1776). As James White (1984:238-39) explains:

> The "one people" the Declaration seeks to create is not a diverse people, different in talents and interests, in mode of life, in character and manners— not a nation as [Edmund] Burke has taught us to conceive it. It is a single whole, a single person, as it were, with a single set of sentiments and determinations... "We" are blended into a single "one," the stated ideal of equality among people becomes an ideal of a very different sort, of merger into a common identity.

I would underline what White says about the ideal of equality as providing the ground for the emergence of a singular identity, because of the way it abolishes distinctions.

What is the origin of the Canadian ideal of participating in a "unity of you and I," and what does it imply? As Edwin Black (1975:173) observes:

> the Canadian federation was inspired by a purpose altogether different from that which animated the American union. This purpose...was to safeguard the permanence and to promote the expansion of two national cultures. It is here, in the essential partnership of two linguistic and cultural groups that one finds the dominant fact of Canadian nationhood. Here too, says the historian Arthur Lower, "is the most resounding note in our history, the juxtaposition of two civilizations, two philosophies, two contradictory views of the fundamental nature of man." To Malcolm Ross, "we are inescapably, and almost from the first, the bifocal people." The characteristic prudence of the Canadian [according to Ross] "derives from the necessity for taking second thought, for having one foot on each bank of the Ottawa."

The bifocality, or better *bicentricity*, of the Canadian Constitution explains why there is no Canadian equivalent to either "American individualism" or "American nationalism." "Canadian individualism" simply makes no sense. There is occasional talk of something called "Canadian nationalism," but it has never succeeded in overcoming either "Québécois nationalism" or the various regionalisms (western, Maritime, and so on). One would need a civil war, as in the United States, for these divisive tendencies to be negated.

A Bicentric Imagination

Having determined certain key respects in which the unity of the American collectivity differs from that of the Canadian collectivity, can we detect any similar differences in the way the Canadian and American imaginaries operate? A good place to start is with the following quotation from a *Time* article commemorating the 200th anniversary of the U.S. Constitution: "Walt Whitman wrote, `I contain multitudes.' That is what the Constitution does, an astonishing feat considering the variety of multitudes that have landed on American shores, and continue to land" (Morrow, 1987:21). What is remarkable about this quotation is the way in which "the variety of multitudes" is reduced to, or engulfed by, a single person, an "I." A related example would be the American song in aid of famine relief for Ethiopia, *We Are the World*. The title speaks volumes. What both of these examples evidence is a mind that tends to operate synthetically (or better, *concentrically*): an "I" or "we" that expands to encompass the whole world. As will also be apparent, what is missing from the constitution of the American imaginary is any sense of proportion, of limit.

The Canadian consciousness, by contrast, is hamstrung by its sense of proportion. It has difficulty arriving at the notion of a whole that is not divided internally. This is apparent from a consideration of the lyrics of *Tears Are Not Enough*, the Canadian song in aid of famine relief for Ethiopia. One of its couplets goes: "And if we should try, together you and I, Maybe we could understand the reasons why." This invites comparison with the line from *We Are the World* that reads: "Let's realize that a change can only come when we stand together as one." The American song declares and enacts a realization concerning which there can be no doubt, while the Canadian song is pervaded by doubts and "maybes". The "we" of the American song also differs from the "we" of the Canadian song: in the latter case, it must be specified that "we" means "you and I." The bicentric or "diathetic," as opposed to synthetic, character of the Canadian song is also reflected in the fact that *Tears* contains two lines in French. The American song, by contrast, is monolingual, as if English were *the* universal language (see further Howes, 1990b).

The difficulty the Canadian mind has in arriving at the idea of a whole that is not divided internally could be regarded as a sign of weakness, a "failure of the imagination." But this is only from an American perspective for, as will be recalled, the Canadian constitution prescribes that the "two civilizations" *not* merge—that is, that they remain juxtaposed. Far from signalling a weakness, then, this bicentric propensity, this refusal to synthesize, is a manifestation of the strength of the Canadian Constitution, and, to pick up MacIntyre's point again, it follows that the more bicentric a work is, the better it must be, by Canadi>n standards.

The Best We (You and I) Can Do

The preceding discussion enables us to formulate a "local" theory of the good and the best, which is also a theory of representation. That theory may be put as follows: the best that any Canadian can do is to represent things *bicentrically*, while the best that an American can do is to portray things *concentrically*. These, then, are the biases, but also the conditions for the achievement of excellence in the production of any given representation, in the two settings.

We can test this theory by considering the work of the most prominent or well-known Canadians in a series of different fields of endeavour, such as the visual and recording arts, political theory, and theory (or "thought") in general, and seeing how their work fits our description. In each case, we shall ask: Who is the most prominent Canadian in the field of? (assuming that well-known-ness provides some index of greatness, however rough).

The visual arts? Alex Colville has been described as "our painter laureate." What most stands out about his paintings is their measured quality, and the uncanny juxtaposition of opposites. Think of *Horse and Train*. Colville's paintings of couples, such as *June Noon, January*, and *Couple on Beach*, are also interesting in this connection: in each case, the attentions of the man and woman are turned in different directions.[5] Thus, one cannot think a Colville as a "unity of we" or a "single whole," only a "unity of you and I." His paintings are eminently bicentric.

The recording arts? Glenn Gould, perhaps, and what he is best known for is his recording of Bach's *Goldberg Variations*. This makes sense, for Bach was a master of counterpoint. The essence of counterpoint is simultaneity of voices: "a melody is always in the process of being repeated by one or another voice...the voices always continuing to sound against, as well as with, all the others" (Said, 1983:45). Gould's renown as a recording artist also makes sense in terms of the pattern, discussed earlier, of Canadian men tending to reject the "oneness" of nature and immersing themselves in technology. Significantly, as Said (1983:52) notes, in 1964 Gould left the concert world and was "reborn as a creature of the technology he exploited to permit more or less infinite reproduction, infinite repetition ('take-twoness' he called it)."[6] To interpret: the oneness of the concert world did not appeal to Gould: he excelled at doing "what came constitutionally."

Political theory? C.B. Macpherson, perhaps. A constant theme in Macpherson's work is the idea that there are two competing models of the human essence. The first model is based on the assumption that human beings are above all consumers; the second, that human beings have a desire to better themselves intellectually as well as the ability to transcend materialism. It is in terms of these two models that Macpherson (1973) describes the different historical/philosophical periods of liberalism, and also challenges contemporary liberal democratic society to strike a more adequate balance between the two. The fact that Macpherson wrote *the* critique of individualism makes sense in terms of the bicentrism (hence "dividualism") that would have informed his thought as a Canadian.

Finally, who is the greatest Canadian thinker? Would this not be Marshall McLuhan, the "most important thinker since Newton, Darwin, Freud, Einstein, and Pavlov," as they say on the back cover of *Understanding Media*? McLuhan is remembered more for his eccentricity than his bicentricity, but that there was a strong streak of bicentrism to his thought is undeniable. Marchand (1989:245-48) has called it "dichotomania," a good example being McLuhan's use of the figure/ground analogy. McLuhan often illustrated the point of a lecture by referring to those sketches that look either like a lamp or two profiles, depending on the part of the sketch one focuses on. The part one sees would be the figure, the part one does not see the ground:

> McLuhan's point was that most people are trained not to look for the ground in any situation. They focus on one part and ignore the rest. If people consider the motorcar, for example, they focus on the car itself, rarely perceiving the network of gas stations, highways, neon signs, parking lots and all the altered habits and perceptions that arise out of the existence of the car—the ground, in other words, of the automobile. True perception, according to McLuhan, is the ability to hold both figure and ground in one's attention, in a dynamic and resonating relationship, to perceive the total situation, background vibrating against and subtly changing the image one happens to focus on (Marchand, 1989:248).

Interestingly, it is not normally considered possible to perceive both figure and ground at once (see further Howes, 1991b).

Having acquired some appreciation for what is good across a broad spectrum of intellectual and artistic fields of endeavour, let us now use this knowledge in an attempt to answer the question with which we began. What is good for anthropology in Canada? Four authors' works will be presented and commented upon in terms of the ways in which they exemplify the features we have come to recognize as distinctive of the national genre.

David Turner's *Life Before Genesis* (1985) represents the culmination of many years of research into the social organization of hunter-gatherer band societies. He contrasts the "movement towards two" type of social organization of the Australian Aborigines of North Queensland with the "movement towards one" type characteristic of the Cree of Northern Manitoba, and suggests that these two "primals" can be discerned behind the whole subsequent course of human history. This is bicentrism at its purest.

Michael Lambek's *Human Spirits* (1981) offers a cultural account of the practice of spirit possession on the isle of Mayotte, Madagascar. This work is noteworthy for its insistence upon the idea that: "Spirit and host are two entirely different persons.... This opposition between two discrete identities, host and spirit, is the single most crucial element, the axiom, upon which the entire system of possession rests" (Lambek, 1981:40-41). Lambek's views on spirit possession stand opposed to the dominant, instrumental view. According to the latter, the host pursues his or her own personal ends by adopting the identity of a spirit (this second identity is simply a cover). Thus, Lambek sees double where others see one.

Janice Boddy's *Wombs and Alien Spirits* (1989) is partly about spirit possession and partly about the construction of gender in a northern Sudan community. She describes how women and men, like humans and spirits, "occupy a single physical plane but separate though contiguous realities" (Boddy, 1989:6)—shades of *The Planiverse*. Of particular relevance is her discussion of the meaning of female circumcision for the women of Hofriyat:

> By removing their external genitalia, female Hofriyati seek not to diminish their own sexual pleasure—though this is an obvious effect—so much as to enhance their own femininity. Pharaonic circumcision is a symbolic act which brings sharply into focus the fertility potential of women by drastically de-emphasizing their sexuality.... Village women do not achieve social recognition by behaving or becoming like men, but by becoming less like men, physically, sexually, and socially (Boddy, 1989: 55-56).

Other analysts see the practice of genital mutilation not as the expression of a cultural logic of gender complementarity, but rather as a blatant expression of patriarchy, and are, of course, quick to denounce it.

Finally, there is Bruce Trigger's *Natives and Newcomers* (1985), a work of immense scholarship, which takes a cool look at Canada's "Heroic Age" (the period from Discovery to 1663). Rather than provide us with yet another chronicle of the pursuits of a chosen few (such as Cartier, Champlain, Brébeuf), Trigger seeks to show how it was the Indians who set the stage for this period, and how it was they who (in considerable measure) directed the actions of the other characters. *Natives and Newcomers* thus presents a two-sided view of the history of the "Heroic Age," in contrast to the lop-sided view that has traditionally prevailed. This balancing of views represents a significant historio-graphical breakthrough, but it also conceals a flaw: there is no attempt, for example, to delve into how the Indians themselves conceived of "history."

Other titles could be added to this list, but it is perhaps more pressing to explore how the Canadi>n modes of representing the Other already considered contrast with the ways in which the Other is constructed in American anthropology. In place of a tendency towards bicentricity, we would expect to find evidence of a tendency towards concentricity. One of the most striking examples of concentrism in American anthropology is Lee Drummond's (1986) treatment of James Bond as an *American* culture hero. Another fine example of concentrism is the explanation given for the focus on the American scene in Marcus and Fischer's *Anthropology as Cultural Critique* (1986). The authors assert that their focus "reflects a historical development in which anthropology in the United States seems to be synthesizing the three national traditions"—i.e., British, American, and French (Marcus and Fischer, 1986: viii). A Canadian, who would "naturally" (read: constitutionally) regard the idea of synthesis with some suspicion, might not agree.

Casting our glance back, we can also find evidence of this tendency to represent things concentrically, or what is to say the same thing "individually," in the work of the Culture and Personality School (see Bock, 1980 for an overview). It was one of the central tenets of that School's work that cultures can be seen as (individual) personalities writ large.[7] Of course, in recent years, this conception of cultures as bounded individuals has come undone. But only to be replaced by a totalizing conception of a higher order—Wallerstein's "world-system theory" (see Marcus and Fischer, 1986:80-81). According to Marcus and Fischer's treatise on the state-of-the-(American)-art of ethnography, it is now essential that a monograph

> register the constitutive workings of impersonal international political and economic systems on the local level where fieldwork usually takes place. These workings can no longer be accounted for as merely external impacts upon local, self-contained cultures. Rather, external systems have their thoroughly local definition and penetration, and are formative of the symbols and shared meanings within the most intimate life-worlds of ethnographic subjects (Marcus and Fischer, 1986:38).[8]

Curiously, at the same time American ethnographers have grown less inclined to recognize any distinction between "We the people" and "the World" (given the assumption that a single "world-system" embraces us all), they have also grown more inclined to focus on individual lives. This is manifest in the numerous "life histories" (the biographies as opposed to ethnographies) that have been appearing recently, as well as the emphasis on treating the individual as an actor rather than a robot in a structure. This individualistic thrust, which may seem to run counter to the holistic thrust of world-system theory, is in fact nothing more than the other face of the American commitment to individualism, or the "single whole," as discussed previously.

A few die-hard structuralists in America, such as Emiko Ohnuki-Tierney (1981), have criticized the burgeoning notion of the "individual as an actor." But her critique is scarcely heeded because of the obligatory contemporary "incredulity towards metanarratives"—particularly, structuralism (Marcus and Fischer, 1986:8). Indeed, American ethnography is said to have entered

> a period of experimentation...characterized by eclecticism, the play of ideas free of authoritative paradigms, critical and reflexive views of subject matter, openness to diverse influences embracing whatever seems to work in practice, and tolerance of uncertainty about a field's direction and of incompleteness in some of its projects (Marcus and Fischer, 1986:x).

In point of fact, there is a paradigm that undergirds this "experimental moment"—namely, American Pragmatism, with its doctrines of "eclecticism," "transience," "meliorism," and "the truth is what works" (McDermott, 1986). Were the proponents of experimentalism a bit more reflexive about their approach, they would recognize that their abandonment of theory (read: metanarratives) has had the effect of foregrounding the unexamined premises of a distinctly homespun philosophy. Surely, there is no intrinsic reason why American pragmatism should replace British empiricism and/ or French rationalism (not to mention Canadi>n bicentrism) as a global research methodology and strategy.

Conclusion

The preceding analysis of the constitution of knowledge in the United States and Canada, and of how the single standard of American scholarship contrasts with the double standard of Canadi>n scholarship, admittedly suffers from a certain "legal formalism," and needs to be completed by a more contextual approach.[9] For all its weaknesses though, I think it does illustrate Kenelm Burridge's (1983:318) remark to the effect that "the ways in which Americans live and organize themselves and their intellectual endeavours," and the ways in which Canadians do likewise, have "played their parts" in lending a distinctive bias to the two traditions of anthropological inquiry. Both traditions could profit greatly from reflecting further on how they each in their own way "constitute the Other."

Another thing I would emphasize in closing is how different the constitutional approach to the analysis of ethnographic texts put forward here is from the increasingly literary approaches to ethnographic writing which have emerged within anthropology itself (e.g., Clifford and Marcus 1986; Geertz 1988). I think the "flight from theory to style" (Howes 1990a), which is manifest in the greater attention now paid to alternative "styles of text construction" as opposed to the study of other forms of social organization, is regrettable. As the present essay has shown, there may be a very intimate link between discursive style and social structure, but only a *social* analysis can bring that out.

NOTES

1 Though he was not a professional, it must be said that Selwyn Dewdney's *Sacred Scrolls of the Southern Ojibway* is first-rate ethnology, and *Indian Rock Paintings of the Great Lakes* (Dewdney and Kidd, 1967) an important contribution to Shield archaeology.

2 Jungian analysis, like linguistics before de Saussure, assumes that there is an intrinsic relationship between a symbol and its referent (i.e., some archetype), or the signifier and the signified, but this is quite wrong. The relation is arbitrary. See Macklem (1991:125-32) for a fine discussion on this point, as well as an attempt to do for law what the present essay seeks to do for anthropology.

3 It would be interesting to compare Dewdney's *Planiverse* with Urszula K. Le Guin's science fiction (LeGuin being the daughter of the great American anthropologist, A.L. Kroeber), but space does not permit.

4 For a fuller discussion of these contrasting features, and of how the structure of Canadian federalism differs from that of American federalism, see Howes (1990b and 1991a).

5 This arrangement reflects Colville's personal philosophy of relationships: "I am inclined to think that people can only be close when there is some kind of separateness," he says. This is also the philosophy behind the Canadian Constitution.

6 While Gould might sound "post-modern" on this account, what he was doing, in fact, was simply fulfilling the purpose or *telos* of the Canadian confederation.

7 For a more recent example of this sort of reasoning, see Richard Handler's (1988) analysis of Quebec nationalism.

8 For a penetrating critique of this view, see Solway and Lee (1990) and Coombe (1991).

9 As Gilles Bibeau observes, "En se limitant à la constitution on se risque de s'emprisonner dans l'univers des lois et d'ignorer des lieux de constitution des lois et ce que les gens font avec la loi" (personal communication). Bibeau also notes that the increasing presence of representatives of ethnic groups not comprehended by the constitution has precipitated a "débalancement des rapports fragiles qui s'étaient historiquement institues entre les francophones et les anglophones (ou mieux entre les français et les anglais)." Pursuant to this, it will be interesting to follow how the "indigenous ethno-graphers" who come to take up positions in Canada as opposed to the United States inflect their discourse differently in response to the dominant (disappearing) paradigm.

CAUGHT IN THE RIPTIDE:
FEMALE RESEARCHER IN A PATRICENTRIC SETTING

Janet M.C. Burns

Dissertations are collective efforts: products of long and sometimes painful negotiations between student and supervisory committee. Questions asked, ways of searching, and answers obtained are true only under existing or specified conditions. Completion breeds ambivalence. The problem I posed, the method I chose, and the solutions I found left me troubled (Burns, 1990). One thesis was defended. Another lay hidden in the richness of field work experience. This account is aimed at recovering that knowledge.

Research interests drive graduate programmes. Student choice of programme is guided by the availability of faculty advisors and funding. That summer, I was preoccupied with choosing among a number of universities. One morning the mail brought good news. It was a letter that offered, in addition to the regular student stipends, one year of research funding. An interview was requested. The writer proposed that we meet to discuss my interest in researching the Pacific coast commercial fisheries. Here was a potential dissertation topic and supervisor. Getting to that appointment involved about five hours' travel to the top of a mountain. Ultimately, that destination would take me many more miles from home.

I was spurred on by thoughts of doing research among a community of persons who live on the margins of urban industrial society. I saw the fishery as a last frontier of individualism, untouched by the apathy and boredom typical of most wage labour jobs. As independent commodity producers, fisher(men)s[1] were imagined to be autonomous, self-motivated and fulfilled workers, still free from the degrading impact of the capitalist mode of production. I thought that they worked hard in a demanding physical environment, but that this kind of productive labour was the essence of the good life. Fishing in the morning would bring philosophy after dinner. Fisher(men)s exemplified the declining class of petite bourgeoisie. The fisher(man) embodied the ideal of the craftsman and was a type of labour destined to wither away. The idea of sitting on the dock of the bay to document and help preserve the way of life of this endangered species was my inspiration.

I was also critical of the economic determinist argument that workers were virtually helpless in protecting themselves from the onslaught of capital. Determinism seemed irreconcilable with emancipation. I hoped that culture was the vehicle through which workers were able to resist economic exploitation and pursue their own interests. I expected that fisher(men)s, because of peculiar working conditions, participated in an occupational culture that could form the basis of class consciousness.

The tenacious unmasking of one falsehood entailed the shrouding of another. From inception through to final conclusion, I studied men as fishers. I didn't recognize there were potentially two important sociological categories: fishers as workers and fishers as men. I even failed to seriously consider that my entrance into that context added two more variables: myself as woman and woman as researcher. Unawares, I had adopted a patricentric standpoint. I reproduced the "scholarly and institutional practices that reproduce sexism and androcentricism in scholarship and in our daily lives—practices that underlie the invisibility and undervaluing of women and women's lives" (Christiansen-Ruffman, 1989:128). I overlooked the argument that women were the dupes of patriarchy, ignored the issue that gender may create some insurmountable problems for women field researchers,[2] and failed to situate myself in the context of my research. This is an account of that deception.

I entered a doctoral programme and began researching the fishery. My academic concerns were neatly bounded by seminars, the library, and a few lingering questions from a masters' thesis. I completed the required courses and established a supervisory committee. All three women on faculty were indifferent to my project; my teachers and advisors were and continued to be men. I busied myself trying to learn the ways of two alien milieus: the university and the fishery. In both contexts I was an outsider and neophyte struggling to achieve acceptance and mastery.

Research begins with asking questions. I narrowed my focus with time, persistence, and coaxing from advisors. My question emerged. What is the relationship between technology, social organization, and work culture in the harvesting sector of the fishing industry? This was relatively straightforward. It conformed to the thesis format and would contribute to a broader theoretical debate. I recognized the necessity of doing some field work.

Field work can be a most rewarding and frustrating research activity. The recording of everyday life brings the researcher/researched into intimate contact. Genuine and gratifying friendships may evolve on the basis of shared knowledge and experience. While field researchers presume and often have a superior formal education, the researched have greater experience in the research setting. The participants exchange information from different but equal social positions.

Gender-neutral contexts facilitate mutual accommodation because social distance is minimized. Indeed, Oakley (1981) points out that women interviewing women is a contradiction in terms. When the researcher is a woman in a woman's world, she is simultaneously an insider and outsider. Hierarchical relations become indefensible. The result is a deepening of mutual understanding. When the researcher is a woman in a man's world these dynamics are confounded.

Cross-gender contexts encourage social distance because traditional, asymmetrical gender roles intervene. It may be that women interviewing men is also a contradiction in terms. When the researcher is a woman in a man's world, she is an outsider on two counts. Egalitarian relations become quixotic. The masculinity of the researched may assume dominance and jeopardize researcher privilege. Participants exchange information from different and unequal social positions.

I assumed researcher privileges and hoped for the type of relations that Oakley envisions. Confronted by masculine prerogative I was denied such a privilege. Normal power relations between the researcher and the researched were reversed. The researched contested my identity as researcher and imposed my identity as woman. There were few guarantees of reciprocity, let alone egalitarian relations. At the time, I did not recognize the possibility of my subordination.

The question of the impact of my gender on the field work was raised during a graduate seminar. A male faculty member disputed that I could undertake participant observation among fisher(men)s. He argued that my femininity would create reactivity and alter the presumed naturalness of the research setting. He suggested that I abandon the project and leave it to a male to complete. Femininity made me incompetent. Only men could study men. Women must therefore study women. I replied that if sex is an ultimate barrier to human understanding, then there is a real problem with the social science presumption of "objectivity." This firmed my resolve to tackle this project.

"Objectivity" in field work is maintained by avoiding the pitfall of over-rapport. This is accomplished by forcing a distinction between the researcher and the researched. Social distance is encouraged. The subjectivities (i.e., emotions, beliefs, and values) of the researched are observed and collected as datums for logical examination. Observers assume a rationally privileged standpoint. This is also a surreptitious means of establishing research and researcher credibility. In adopting the stance of "objective" researcher, I suppressed my individual subjectivities and hoped to establish some academic and personal legitimacy.

Participant observation also requires that the investigator establish empathy and rapport with the research subject. My aim was to participate in the fishery to understand the beliefs and values of fisher(men)s. I intended to submerge myself into a foreign life-world, uncover its inner meaning and logic and then reconstitute it in an academic text. The only way for women to accomplish this is to adopt a patricentric standpoint. I hoped to camouflage my feminine self and become one with the masculine social surrounding. This tactic was not unfamiliar. I was accustomed to negotiating my femininity in many social situations.

Once the original research question and approach was formulated, the second step was to establish contact. The Department of Fisheries and Oceans mailed a letter introducing the study, and requesting the participation of all licensed commercial fisher(men)s residing in the Greater Vancouver area. Roughly 200 indicated a willingness to participate in the study. A total of 80 interviews were completed. The mass of accumulating data was bewildering.

In the months preceding the interviews my imagination kindled many colourful images of fisher(men)s. I was seduced by dreams of adventure. I anticipated real-life enactments of the John Wayne masculine stereotype: handsome, hard working, and hard playing. They might have a tough exterior and probably be poorly educated but they would also be astute and, in the last analysis, honourable. I suspected there would be a commitment to fishing forged by a long family tradition in the industry. I thought fishing crews would have camaraderie. I anticipated stories telling of bravery in the face of natural catastrophe. I also foresaw a Captain Ahab: angry, driven, nasty, and cruel. As I crisscrossed the lower mainland of British Columbia, from elite districts to East Hastings Street tenements, and anchored alongside wharfs I had these images. What I found proved to be an entirely different matter.

Work history was the main-line of my enquiry. Often I was sidetracked to discuss family matters and personal lives. Fisher(men)s complained of problems synchronizing home and work concerns during the fishing season. They reported relying on their wives at home to attend to business and household finances while they were away at sea. Some were distressed by their wives' access to social activities and by their own social and sexual isolation. While at the time I didn't recognize the sexist and racist allusion, one fisher(man) graphically depicted his burden this way: "You don't get a lot of mermaids out here. If you're lucky you might get the odd blueberry blond."[3]

I let his comments go unnoticed and asked questions on length of fishing time away from home. I considered my knowledge of racism and sexual frustrations among fisher(men)s as irrelevant. Nor did I deem relevant that the fishery was buoyed up by the "domestic labour" of women. These were minor deviations. I continued my quest.

I was sensitive to informants scolding my lack of fishing experience. Many stated that to truly understand fisher(men)s, one had to go fishing. One fisher(man) ending the interview remarked: "all this is lies you know...just telling lies...only my opinion. To really know you have to go out there." Others informed me that females were considered good deckhands. One remarked that "girl deckhands are ten times better than guys." Someone else mentioned that "...most boats now have state rooms, two crew sleep in one state room and they have showers...my crew sleep with their clothes on, so I imagine that's what a woman would do." Field work became imperative.

My entrance into the field setting was provided one afternoon during a lengthy home interview with a married couple. We talked comfortably over coffee while sitting at the kitchen table. Their stories of the fishery were enchanting. His grandfather had been a fisher(man) and she went fishing with her husband. They told me of the early days, fishing in row boats on the Fraser River. How going fishing every year was a dream come true. As the conversation progressed, the wife made some chilling comments. She remarked:

> ...single young men up on the trolling fields always get a deckhand. Well, of course, the ideal person to have for a deckhand among young, healthy males is a young healthy female... But the minute that a woman walks on a guy's boat, it's, it's immediately presumed by the old gossip types that this is a sexual arrangement... There was a girl come up the coast last year and ah, they no sooner got the groceries put away, and took off from land and one thing and another, and over into and anchored into a little bay. Then this, this repulsive old man, came down, took his clothes off, and expected that this was going to be the arrangement.

Her comments momentarily invoked a sense of disgust. We proceeded to discuss other topics. They encouraged me go fishing and recommended their nephew. He hired female deckhands and he could be trusted. We were quickly introduced. He too declared that first-hand experience was essential for the kind of knowledge I sought. He offered to take me on the herring fishery and proposed that I help with the cooking and cleaning. I liked and trusted these people. My assigned role seemed "natural" and would provide some form of reciprocity. I readily accepted the offer.

The offer came from someone with a long family history in the fishery. He was well connected and recommended. He was also charming and a good conversationalist. I surmised that we were close in age and probably shared some common life experiences. He evinced an interest in my research project. I was convinced that my willingness to help with the work, even if it was in the galley, would legitimate my presence. Being from a middle-class family, having no brothers, a father with post-secondary education and an office job, I expected relatively egalitarian relationships between men and women. I also expected some respect for higher education and the goals of social science.

The interview took place in January. The field trip was set for February. The setting would be the roe herring fishery on the west coast of Vancouver Island. Further arrangements would be discussed about two weeks before departure.

As time drew nearer, I wondered what problems might be encountered and there was some self-doubt. I dismissed these misgivings as stage fright. Fears were minor irritants to my curiosity. My knowledge of the industry was extensive. I trusted my informants. I was invigorated. Here was my long-awaited opportunity to learn the reality of commercial fishing. Time to put away the books and take up experience. Enough of theory, it was time for praxis.

Field work began. Knapsack in hand and long underwear prickling, I arrived at the dock at 2:00 p.m. I expected to be assigned any of a number of limitless identities: goffer, mascot, acceptable incompetent, honorary male. Much to my chagrin, my gender would become the defining factor. The traditional female domestic role was immediately assigned and "naturally" assumed. As I arrived at the wharf, I was confronted by two fisher(men)s. Both were in their mid-thirties and dressed in old clothes. Their greeting was: "You got here just in time to stow the gear and clean the galley while we go to the bank!" I familiarized myself with the boat and put supplies away. It was a dirty mess. They returned and began working on the fishing gear. I began cleaning the galley. That evening was spent at the skipper's house. His wife cooked dinner. He told fishing stories. After dinner they went out and left me alone to my field notes. The next morning we left the wharf at 7 o'clock. It was ominously grey, cold and windy.

Spirits were high as we entered the Gulf of Georgia. Environment Canada issued a "Small Craft Warning." Little talk was heard over the din of engine and the VHF radio. The sky darkened. We feared "hitting the rocks" and fought the urge of "puking one's guts out." Eight hours brought an end to the day's journey. We berthed at the government wharf in Victoria. Once the boat was tied up, while unpacking the skipper quipped: "So did you bring your black lace negligee?"

The thought was incongruous, given the context, and resulted in general laughter. Although possibly indicative of the "joking relationship,"[4] aimed at establishing rapport and intimacy, it was not a comment a male deckhand would have received.

One further incident on the first evening set the tone for future interactions. Expecting to leave port early the next morning, I went to visit friends and returned early to sleep. The fisher(men)s set off for the bar, returning inebriated at about two in the morning. Coming on board they called to me and proceeded to recount the exploits of their evening. The next day we stayed in port. I began to notice jokes about my research. Note writing was a cause for humour. A nickname was assigned; I became "girl." My feelings of discomfort intensified.

The next night they also went to the bar. They returned in a torrent of obscenities, sexual jokes, and innuendos. I seriously considered abandoning ship. They left to visit another fish boat and I sighed with relief. The skipper returned at about 5:30 a.m. and woke me. He began explaining how partying was a tradition on the first night in port and then shifted to talking about sex. I fancied he intended to provide some much-needed consolation but the booze was clouding his thought. Negative reaction is considered improper field work strategy. I wanted to study the fishery and would have to grow accustomed to such talk. A male researcher might also find this behaviour offensive. He would also be less inclined to terminate the research. The other fisher(man) returned about 10:30 a.m. We left port a half-hour later.

The next stop was a desolate bay about six hours' travel up the coast. That evening passed uneventfully. The next day another eight hours' travel to a small fishing community. That night again they went to the bar. They returned early and sober. The morning brought news of a possible strike, and talk turned to criticizing the union. More fishing boats arrived. We waited, listened to radio news and dockside gossip. We kept busy: they fixed the boat, I cleaned the galley. Tensions and frustrations started to mount. No one knew if, when, or where the fishery would open. After a few days we left on a two-day journey to the proposed fishing grounds. By now I was firmly ensconced in my role as galley slave: "three squares a day, a bunk, wash the dishes, do some cooking and keep the cabin and galley clean."

On the fishing grounds, we endured what seemed to be an endless wait for the fishery to be declared open. For almost two weeks we, and the other members of the fleet, waited at anchor in an isolated bay.

I struggled to maintain the identity of researcher but it was largely unrecognized or ignored. My identity as a young single woman predominated. I had difficulty maintaining an identity of "self" as researcher. I asked appropriate questions and listened intently. The undercurrent of gender always surfaced. One fisher(man) from another crew took it upon himself to tell me a story about a skipper who always hired female deckhands—promised them $100 a day for working but expected to have sex with them. I began to wonder if that was my presumed role. I started to feel like a fool. Later that day I asked the skipper's partner if he found my presence disturbing. He said no, that anything was a relief that kept the skipper preoccupied.

Some believed that I was looking for a husband or boyfriend. One fisher(man) suggested that I "should chase after...or.... They've got money. You gotta be here looking for a husband." Another asked if I was an undercover fishery officer. It seemed that previously a young woman nicknamed Sockeye-Sue had used feminine wiles to enter the ranks of the fisher(men)s, only to report violations of fishery regulations. Being a woman I was an anomaly and my motives were suspect. My status as researcher was of dubious merit.

A fishing boat is a jail. There's no escape. The inmates are given subsistence and a few places to exercise. The worst part of it is coping with the other inhabitants. No one believes you're innocent. Telling tall tales is a good way to pass the time. As we waited for the fishery to open, other fisher(men)s would often come to our boat to retell fishing stories in superb acts of what Spradley and Mann (1975) have termed "masculine display." They came to tell stories of sexual exploits or other fishing seasons, and gossip about each other. Time wore on and frustrations mounted.

On our boat, one of the fisher(men)'s responses to the building tensions was to initiate a game of strip-poker. I agreed to play to a certain limit, my long underwear. Here again, I doubt that such a game would have occurred without my presence. Men do not play strip-poker among themselves. Predictably, given my limited knowledge of poker playing, I lost and the game ended. The skipper got in the dinghy and departed. The remaining fisher(man) and I discussed the situation—the stupid things people do, the problem of the government mismanagement of the industry, and the wives back home.

I asked the skipper what he thought about women deckhands and how this might affect his relations at home. He remarked:

No double standards! I'm not a jealous man. Another woman cheated on me once. All I care about is that I have a room when I get home. All that would bother me is if there were three men in the kitchen drinking beer, one in the spare bedroom and one my bed. All with numbered cards!

What was interesting in his remark is that he viewed the sexuality of his mate in his own terms. He imputed his values to her and thereby justified his own sexual orientation. Having met his wife, I had no sense that there was any possibility of the scenario he described ever occurring. It fuelled his fantasies.

The above was typical of many remarks. Much talk on our boat was what some would consider obscene. My field notes record references by the fisher(men)s of their being sexually frustrated and the desire for "skin magazines." Indicative of my naiveté, this was the first time I perceived the connection between sexuality and pornographic magazines. Like a prosti- tute or "erotic" dancer who provide turn-ons for money, I started to feel expected to provide turn-ons for information.

One evening after dinner and over drinks, the skipper made overt sexual advances. He claimed that because of my presence he was sexually aroused, frustrated and feeling impotent.[5] I was being hustled. I interpreted all of this to be unavoidable. Some men typically felt it necessary to make sexual advances towards women. In confinement the persistent hustler is difficult to avoid.

A lone female in a patricentric setting, I was impelled to negotiate the sexualization of the setting. One means of avoiding personal involvement is to shift the focus of interaction. The previously mentioned game of poker fulfilled this outlet. The skipper of the boat became angry with the end of the game. The other fisher(man) and I flirted. The skipper's anger intensified. Our merriment escalated. The skipper left in a huff. Manipulating femininity to my advantage, I drove a wedge between the two fisher(men)s, diverted the skipper's attention, and enjoyed a short reprieve from his overt sexual advances. I relied on the complicity of the other fisher(man) in this manoeuvre. He also benefited in diffusing the skipper.

After an endless wait, the fishing season opened and "work" began. During this time of four days of sleeplessness, I watched and listened to the radios and the fisher(men)s' stories between "sets." I was not allowed to participate in the hauling of nets and was confined to the boat. Being excluded provided some advantages to the research. As the fishing activity was in close proximity to the boat I could observe the actual process. Given that government announcements were always over the CB or VHF radios, I was assigned the task of listening for important information on future openings and closings. Between "sets," other fisher(men)s came to tell more stories. They appeared at all hours; sometimes with bottles of rye. The talk was fishing, fishers, past glories, money, and sex. I participated, listened, taped conversations, asked questions, and between visits made notes.

In the end, our boat had sold approximately $6,000 worth of fish and we began our three-day return trip to Vancouver. Now that I was leaving the field, I could begin the process of interpreting my experiences. Coming back was as much disengagement and re-entry for the fisher(men)s as it was for me. Longing for home, we motored into the mouth of the Fraser River, and Canadian urban society opened up to us.

The fishing season and field work terminated simultaneously. All participants had embarked and terminated the same journey with different thoughts and experiences. On our departure, there was the excitement of an adventure: the possibility of the fisher(men)s making lots of money, and my anticipation of collecting good field notes. On the grounds, there were the never-ending fishing schemes and fish stories, chasing fish and evading the fisheries officers. On arriving ashore, there were bills to pay, rest to catch up on, and for me tapes to transcribe and field notes to interpret. All three participants began the process of disengagement from the field setting. On the horizon, Vancouver was cloaked in smog.

We returned to the local wharf and went our separate ways. There was a farewell drink at the nearby fishermen's bar. I was offered a job as a deckhand for the upcoming salmon season. I maintained personal contacts in the fishery for two years after this initial field trip. Returning home, I showered, changed, and with my female roommate shared dinner and a therapeutic bottle of wine. It was great to be on familiar, and stable, ground. Unwinding, I recounted to her the events of the recent past.

In the few weeks after returning from the field, I happened to meet two women students who had just returned from field work in developing countries. We all reported encountering sexual dilemmas in the field. One woman was raped. The other, frightened for her life, found refuge in an intimate liaison with a male informant. We came to collectively define our experiences as one of the many pitfalls that women encounter in daily life both in and out of the field. Nothing extraordinary.

Field notes and interviews take an eternity to transcribe. Coding can become sheer tedium. Analysis can seem hopeless. Peers and mentors are solicited to read countless drafts and endure endless talk about the research. This accounting and recounting generates reams of written text. Stubborn persistence brings final results. The research is judged acceptable by the examining committee. Finally, the dissertation takes a place on the bookshelf, testimony to a series of scholarly and institutional practices made in the pursuit of particular knowledge claims. What in the end becomes defined as a significant contribution to our knowledge of society is an inscription of particular social constraints located in time and place.

Patricentricism is an invidious problem. It permeated my practices from the beginning until long after the conclusion of the field work. Alone in a patricentric setting, I was made to feel uncomfortable. While I attempted to deny my femininity and assert a researcher identity, the fisher(men)s laughed at such presumptions and imposed my "natural" role as woman, domestic labourer, and sexualized object. In a graduate seminar a male faculty member had instructed me to abandon the project because femininity would cause reactivity in the presumed naturalness of the research setting. In conducting interviews I ignored the absence of women in the harvesting sector of the fishery and left unquestioned the fact that the industry is buoyed up by the domestic labour of women. In formulating my research question I neglected to consider the gender dimensions underpinning class society. In sum, I reproduced the institutional and scholarly practices that underlie the invisibility and undervaluing of women and women's lives.

Looking back on our mistakes, we can usually see how it could have or should have been different. The point of this essay is not this kind of second-guessing. Rather, it is a re-visioning of a field work experience from a different perspective. In conducting the original research, I adopted a male-centred and "objective" viewpoint. The project contributed to furthering that kind of knowledge. As my awareness of gender and the research process developed, I became increasingly critical of the patricentricism of my viewpoint and context as well as the presumption of objectivity.

I am less inclined today to formulate, conduct, and report research findings in the same way. Instead, I recognize that as a woman in a man's world, both in and out of the field, I am a special kind of outsider. This status is not merely an annoying source of bias, it is at the very heart of the experience of being a woman. It is also an extremely valuable and insightful point of view. As a field researcher, I am obliged to locate myself in the research context, participate, observe, record, and retell. Part of the story is about the relations of power and gender.

NOTES

[1] Throughout this discussion I have adopted the convention of referring to fishers as fisher(men)s to indicate that although the generic term fishermen is rejected as sexist and one that renders invisible the participation of some women in the industry, the predominant persons in the harvesting sector are men and it is this phenomenon that is relevant in this study. Despite the growing gender egalitarianism in many occupations, this is not the case for owner-operators of commercial fishing vessels on the Canadian Pacific coast. In the Greater Vancouver area during the 1980s approximately 2 per cent of these fishers were females. However, female deckhands across the entire fleet were more common. It is possible to estimate their proportion around 25-30 per cent. It must be kept in mind, however, that the majority of these women were either wives, or long-term companions of the fisher(men). In this regard, I strongly disagree with Kaplan's (1988) argument that women in the harvesting sector of the fishery do not come from a fishing background, or have anticipatory socialization for the fishery. The data she provides indicate that of the ten current fisher(women)s in her study, 4 were married and 2 were cohabiting with fishers and one other came from a fishing family. The status of the remaining 3 can be surmised from her statement that "the majority became interested in fishing through casual friends or...if they knew the captain or a member of the crew." These connections are indicative of at least some anticipatory socialization, as well as predisposing personal background.

[2] When this field research was initiated the first edition of Peggy Golde's (1970 and 1986) *Women in the Field* was the source for discussions on the problems female researchers might encounter in the field. Unfortunately, the main concern of the text was exotic cultures; there was no direct advice for women in patriarchal white North America. Golde's objective was to depict the personal side of field work for neophyte researchers. The first edition reads much like a book of etiquette and is not informed by feminism (an acknowledgement Golde makes in the 1986 edition). Unfortunately, with only two new chapters, there is little progress in the second edition. There are two new journal articles by women doing field work in male-dominated settings (Gurney, 1985; Hunt, 1984). Again, the primary concern is with survival

strategies and not contextual analysis. Finally, the contemporary neophyte also has two additional texts (Warren, 1988; Whitehead and Conaway, 1986). All told, the cross-cultural bias and the emphasis on survival strategies remain the dominant concerns. Warren (1988:65) attempts more than a book of manners but ends with the warning and advice reminiscent of well-intentioned mothers to daughters: "Go into the field, and live, and think, and write. Listen to what we others have said, but do not let our voices become too much the shaper of yours."

3   For others who are unfamiliar with this argot, "blueberry blondes" is a derogatory term for native women.

4   Radcliffe-Brown (1952) developed the concept of the joking relationship to identify the process by which social actors sanction group deviants, whether they be insiders or as in this case outsiders, and socially construct and thereby impose normative definitions. In the functionalist terms characteristic of his approach the joking relationship is seen to *function* to reduce and prevent social structural tensions and conflicts. He also observed that these relationships may be either symmetrical or asymmetrical. In the asymmetrical case, one member may initiate and maintain the relation without the consent or participation of the other. This latter form occurs between persons of unequal status. One example would be a joking relation between family members from different generations as between grandparents and grandchildren.

5   One of the impacts of feminism has been to change sexual expectations in male-female gender roles. One criticism of feminism has been that men are unfairly threatened by the new woman. Perhaps a more accurate interpretation is that provided by Haas & Haas (1990:486),

"(a) generation ago, the double standard dictated that women were expected to be sexually attractive but passive. Men were expected to be the aggressors. Single women and men followed a fairly precise dating ritual.... The women's movement in the last two decades has meant both greater equality for the two sexes and recognition of female sexuality. Women no longer necessarily confine themselves to traditional gender roles, and they may want more in their sexual lives. These new developments can threaten both sexes. Some men see their masculinity challenged. Others perceive the new woman as less sexually available but more demanding of satisfaction. Women may believe that they are expected to be more know-ledgeable and also more readily orgasmic."

Hite (1975) suggest that these perceptions and attitudes often lead to distrust and self-doubt.

STAR WARS: THE SOCIAL CONSTRUCTION OF REPUTATION IN ANGLO-CANADIAN SOCIOLOGY

David A. Nock

The Social versus the Contemplative Account of Knowledge

One traditional representation of scientific work is the image of the researcher with flashlight in hand (i.e., ever more sophisticated research methods), uncovering the new facts of nature which sit passively on the shore awaiting discovery. Barry Barnes refers to this as "the contemplative account" of knowledge accumulation in which it is supposed that knowledge is accumulated by "disinterested individuals, passively perceiving some aspect of reality, and generating verbal descriptions to correspond to it..." (Barnes, 1977:1-2).

A key assumption is that individuals "intrude minimally between reality and its representation," and this is encouraged by the fostering of detachment and value neutrality in the scientist. The development of scientific knowledge is seen to be cumulative, with researchers each contributing to the completion of a giant jigsaw puzzle. The development of scientific knowledge is seen as directed by the nature of nature. As Barnes puts it, this account puts a stress "on the objects of knowledge almost to the extent of excluding the role of the knowing subject" (Barnes, 1977:10). In this traditional account, it is held to be possible for the scientist to approach the object of knowledge without preconception or prejudgement, without prior values, and without consideration of the standpoint of the researcher. A strong emphasis on method and methodology is considered to be a check on the biases of the investigator. In this traditional account, the subject (i.e., the researcher) is seen as "an isolated contemplative individual without social dimensions or historical situation..." (Barnes, 1977:10). Barnes calls for this traditional account to be replaced "by a more down-to-earth account which treats knowledge as the actual product of people as they live and work in society" (1977:10).

One of the earlier authors to emphasize the social versus the contemplative accounts of knowledge was the doctor-scientist Ludwik Fleck in his *Genesis and Development of a Scientific Fact* (1935; 1979). The substantive topic in this work was the analysis and treatment of syphilis. More important in the long run was its presentation of a theory of knowledge that emphasized the communal nature of knowledge. Ignored at the time of publication, this work was a major influence on Thomas Kuhn's *The Structure of Scientific Revolutions* (1962). The modern edition was edited by Robert Merton and contained an acknowledgement by Kuhn himself. However, whereas Kuhn has pondered publicly the extent to which his ideas fit with the social sciences, Fleck had no such doubts. He explicitly discussed his theory of knowledge in relation to both the social *and* natural sciences and he chastised sociologists and proto-sociologists for committing "a characteristic error. They exhibit an excessive respect, bordering on pious reverence, for scientific facts" (Fleck, 1979:47). He objects to the "special position of current scientific statements" which suggests that natural science is "in complete contrast with all other ways of thinking" (Fleck, 1979:50).

Fleck attacks the positivistic conception of "fact," that it is something immutable and external to the observer. A fact, he says is not something "fixed and absolute," it "is relative" (ibid.). A change in styles of thought creates new facts and renders others of little importance.

Knowledge for Fleck is "the most socially-conditioned activity of man [*sic*], and knowledge is the paramount social creation" (Fleck, 1979:42). Personal interests invariably play a role in the creation of knowledge and factors such as "propaganda, imitation, authority, rivalry, solidarity, enmity, friendship begin to appear..." (Fleck, 1979:43).

Fleck emphasizes that ideas create polarization and identity among actual social groups. "Words which formerly were simple terms become slogans; sentences which once were simple statements become calls to battle" (Fleck, 1979:43). Nor can the social factors that go to make up knowledge or its interpretation be easily overcome as he suggests that "those who consider social dependence a necessary evil and an unfortunate human inadequacy which ought to be overcome fail to realize that without social conditioning no cognition is even possible" (Fleck, 1979:43).

In this paper it is my aim to analyze the structure of citations in Robert J. Brym's (with Bonnie J. Fox) volume *From Culture to Power: The Sociology of English Canada*. The choice of this particular book is due to the fact that it represents one of the few treatments of Canadian sociology over the past fifty years. In its first years of mature expansion in the 1970s and 1980s, Canadian sociology was more interested in developing particular sub-fields and tended to be non-reflective, compared to Québécois sociology. Brym's portion of the book was originally written for an international audience as a representation of Anglo-Canadian sociology (Brym, 1986)[1] and its impact in both its monographic and book form is likely to be great. Brym himself underscores the ambition behind the book as he claims that it describes "the main controversies that have animated sociology in English Canada since the 1960s" (Brym, 1989:1). He also suggests that he is being governed by an objective response to "the results of several reports that show where English-Canadian sociologists concentrate their research and teaching efforts" (Brym, 1989:2).

My operating hypothesis is that the choice of citations is related to more than just a reflex reaction to the accumulated literature, and will reflect deep-seated social influences on the production of knowledge. I particularly wish to emphasize the issues of regionalism, personal network, and graduate school. In order to ensure that these relationships are more than accidental, I have extended the analysis to Robert Stebbins' *Sociology* (1990).

The choice of regionalism for analysis would seem obvious in Canada, where it is a deep-seated part of Canadian identity. Regionalism, however, is discussed as an important factor in sociological production by Straus and Radel (1969). Crane (1967) has discussed the importance of doctoral training and graduate school in advancing personal networks. Nicholas Mullins (1973) discusses more comprehensively the influence of networks in the construction of sociological paradigms. Berkowitz suggests that there is "strong theoretical and empirical cause to believe that there is real interaction between the structure of these theory groups and the kind of work they produce" (Berkowitz, 1984:11).

I believe it is important to analyze this text for several reasons. English Canadian sociology has not been overly reflexive in the past, in part because of the inductionist and positivistic biases of key practitioners. John Porter, perhaps English Canada's single most widely known and read sociologist, expressed a viewpoint that seems widespread. He writes, "the facts often speak for themselves, regardless of the framework within which they are presented" (Porter, 1975:x).[2]

The explanation that the fields chosen by Brym for consideration are just "mirror" representation of objective reports seems unlikely in that the fields chosen for discussion seem related to Brym's own areas of publication. A glance at his own listings in the references (pp. 184-85) reveal his own publication in each of these fields except feminist sociology. Moreover, many sociologists in Canada will wonder if other fields were of any less interest. The emergence of a radical-critical criminology will amaze anyone who remembers the empiricist-functionalist bias of the sub-discipline even into the 1970s. The emergence of a solid core of critical Canadian criminologists who have established a strong tradition of their own (signalled by the call at the 1989 Ontario Association of Sociology and Anthropology meetings by Carleton's Tullio Caputo to undertake a redefinition of themselves as no longer a beleaguered minority but as a new mainstream) seems as important as anything Brym chooses to discuss. Let me hasten to add that I find the Brym-Fox book excellent: it reads very lucidly; it comments intelligently on a veritable mass of material relating to recent Canadian sociology (it cites no fewer than 148 journal articles by currently practising Canadian sociologists, not to mention books or research reports) and it does so in a volume that is a handy, easily usable size. It is sure to become, and deserves to be, a classic of its type.

However, it is my contention, one taken from the sociology of knowledge and post-modernist debates, that there is no final "positivistic" presentation of reality, and that, in some way or another, all social science is about "representation" as it is constructed in the mind of the scientist-sociologist (as much as it is in terms of pre-existing "fact"; see Hayden White, 1973; Aronowitz, 1988; Murphy, 1988).

Regionalism and the Production of Canadian Sociology

One enduring factor of polarization in Canada is regionalism. In Canada it seems true that differences in population, language and ethnic origin, climate, size, political traditions, and type of economic base are such as to contribute a major impact to Canadian identity. It seems no accident that one complete chapter in Harry Hiller's *Canadian Society: A Macroanalysis* (1986) is devoted to regionalism and that after the normal introductory chapter it is preceded only by the issues of national dependency and inequality. Hiller makes the point that regionalism is "also a consequence of a *comparative relationship* among regions...[and that] *power relationships* become obvious" (1986:107).

Although Canadian sociologists have paid a great deal of attention to the issue of regionalism in the larger Canadian society, it is less than obvious that this issue has been noticed in relation to sociological production itself in Canada. In part this has to do with the underdeveloped state of the sociology of sociology in Canada. In part it may be due to an empiricist notion that publication decisions are simply reflex responses to the quality and quantity of what is submitted. Also the fact that the majority of sociologists are not indigenous to their region of employment must play a role.

In the United States this issue of regionalism, unequal power, and publication rates was discussed by Straus and Radel (1969). Their interest in the topic was roused by a revision to the constitution of the American Sociological Association that had been stimulated in part "by the objection of sociologists in certain regions to what was believed to be a regional bias in the control of the association" (Straus and Radel, 1969:1). They commented with surprise that the controversy had been undertaken "without benefit of empirical data" and this they wished to provide. They did find that there was some deviation from a mirror reflection of ASA officeholders, with such leaders coming disproportionately from the Pacific and Mountain and Northeast regions, with the Midwest and the South under-represented (Straus and Radel, 1969:2). The authors went beyond this finding into the issue of publication by region as they assumed that "officeholding...is not expected to be strictly representative" and that "professional eminence" plays a role and "it is quite clear that centers of professional excellence are not equally distributed by region" (Straus and Radel, 1969:2). They found that the Northeast was most productive, followed "fairly closely" by the Pacific and Mountain region and the Midwest, followed rather distantly by the South. On the basis of a citation count, the pattern was the same, with the Northeast and the Pacific-Mountain states at the top, the Midwest a *close* third, and the South far behind. The conclusions from this study were that although election to higher ASA office is related to productivity somewhat (especially in regard to the South), the Midwest had been overlooked, "severely under-represented" as the authors put it (Straus and Radel, 1969:4), in relation to the more important ASA offices.

Ironically, this overlooking of the Midwest was to allow for some representation of Southerners at the highest levels (despite the average lower production of the latter region). The article concludes by raising the question of why an equity principle of representation should have been achieved "at the expense of the Midwest rather than the other regions" but stated that the answer was "unclear" (Straus and Radel, 1969:4). It seems important to note that the Midwest was a close third in terms of publication rates and citations as opposed to the more distant South.

In the current study of citations in Brym with Fox, it was decided to break the data down into the following regions: the Atlantic provinces, Anglophone Quebec, Ontario, the Core Five Universities (Toronto, York, OISE's Department of Sociology in Education, McMaster, Carleton), the Rest of Ontario, the Prairies, and British Columbia. In distinguishing the Core Five universities in Ontario from the rest of Ontario, I am influenced by Arthur K. Davis's article on hinterland-metropolis. He defines metropolis as "the centres of economic and political control located in the larger cities" and hinterlands as "relatively underdeveloped colonial areas which export for the most part semi-processed extractive materials" (Davis, 1971:12). Davis is careful to identify "hierarchies of metropolis-hinterland relationships" and to view the metropolis-hinterland distinction "as a *series* of oppositions" (Davis, 1971:12).

Seen from this perspective, it makes sense to define Toronto and Ottawa as the core of economic and political power. From a professional point of view, these cities and Hamilton are all in urban populations of over half a million, each of the departments has a doctoral programme with many graduate students, and each has or is very close to major libraries. The University of Ottawa has not been counted with the Core Five as its department is heavily francophone and, more importantly, it does not have a doctoral programme.

There is some argument to include Waterloo and Western Ontario as core universities as they both maintain doctoral programmes and are in relative proximity to the core. However, I have chosen to include them in the rest of Ontario since they both are some distance from the political-economic cores and, in fact, are situated in southwestern Ontario, a region historically with its own sense of identity distinct from the core. This is confirmed by the Province of Ontario, which maintains separate administrative districts for Southwestern Ontario, Eastern Ontario, and Northern Ontario apart from the "Central Region" (i.e., Toronto). As noted above by Davis, metropolis-hinterland relationships are categorized on a continuum and London and Waterloo can be categorized as closer to the centres of economic and political power than, say, Sudbury or Thunder Bay. Nevertheless, London and Waterloo are still not quite the core. McMaster's location as a core university is justified by its Ph.D. programme, by its location in a belt of continuous population adjoining Toronto, and by its own census metropolitan area population of over 550,000. Despite its location, the University of Ottawa is not included as a core university because of its lack of a Ph.D. programme.

Divided up in the fashion, we find that the Core Five amount to 25 per cent of English Canada's sociologists, the rest of Ontario accounts for about the same, the Prairies for a little less at 24.2 per cent, the Atlantic region at 14.6 per cent, and B.C. and Anglophone Quebec at 5.8 and 5.1 per cent respectively. The total number of sociologists in English Canada at universities seems to have remained constant at just a bit more than 700. I depended in this analysis on the 1986 National Museum's Guide to Sociologists and Anthropologists in Canada (see Herman and Carstens, 1986). This I think is justified on the grounds that the kernel of the Brym with Fox book originated in a 1986 monograph published by Brym alone in *Current Sociology*. Brym has updated and extended his text somewhat since then and Fox's contribution was written after 1986 by invitation of Brym. Where the National Museum overlooked a number of English Canadian sociologists and departments at university level, I have added them to the analysis (e.g., Athabaska University, Algoma and Nipissing University Colleges, University College of Cape Breton). Although I am aware that a number of sociologists have found employment at community colleges, it has not been necessary to consider them as Brym and Fox have been rather traditional in citing university-based sociologists operating in sociology departments.

Table 1

Number of Pages Mentioned in *From Culture to Power*, by Sociologist

No. of Pages	Sociologist
37	John Porter
21	Michael Ornstein
18	S.D. Clark, B.J. Fox, W. Clement
17	R.J. Brym
12	W.K. Carroll
11	J. Fox, M. Boyd, J. Curtis
08	M. Cohen, C. Cuneo
07	P. Pineo, P. Connelly, R. Breton, J. Goyder
06	W. Kalbach, D. Magill, (including Wilcox-Magill), M. Luxton, R. Ogmundson, P. Ghorayshi, G. Laxer, G. Darroch, J. Reitz, M. Porter
05	M. Pinard, H. Hiller, J. Myles, A. Richmond, [J. Niosi]
04	H. Friedmann, A.A. Hunter, W. McVey, D. Olsen, H. Rich
03	K. Anderson, P. Armstrong, H. Armstrong, V. Burstyn, D. Dasko, M. Eichler, M. Gillespie, J.P. Grayson, Roberta Hamilton, B. Neis
02	R. Apostle, D. Clairmount, C.A. Dawson, C. Gannage, J. Gaskell, N. Guppy, Richard Hamilton, J. Harp, I.C. Jarvie, Wm. Johnston, R. Lambert, C.M. Lanphier, R. Lenton, P. Li, T. Makabe, J.G. Morgan, M. O'Brien, J. Sacouman, D. Smith, D. Stasiulis, P. Stevenson, K.W. Taylor, L. Tepperman, F.G. Vallee, B. Wellman, D.R. Whyte, S.D. Berkowitz, R. Morris

Source: Brym with Fox, 1989

I would like to begin with Tables 1 and 2 which show the pattern of citation in Brym and Fox by individually named sociologist. Table 1 shows by sociologist the number of pages on which the sociologist is named; Table 2 shows the number of studies (individual articles, books, research reports, chapters) cited by each sociologist. The second table is somewhat complicated by the pattern of co- or multiple-authored studies. I have counted all studies in which an individual is named, not just studies where the sociologist is first named.

Table 2

Number of Studies Authored or Co-authored as listed in the references
of *From Culture to Power*, by Sociologist

No. of Pages	Sociologist
16	M. Ornstein
15	R.J. Brym
09	R. Breton, J. Curtis
08	B.J. Fox, W.K. Carroll
07	R. Ogmundson, S.D. Clark
06	M. Boyd, G. Darroch, A. Richmond
05	P. Pineo, M. Pinard, J. Fox
04	W. Clement, C. Cuneo, J. Goyder, Marilyn Porter, J. Reitz, H. Hiller, J. Myles, B. Blishen, Dorothy Smith
03	J. Porter, P. Connelly, G. Laxer, T. Makabe, Roberta Hamilton, Richard Hamilton, P. Armstrong, C.A. Dawson, P. Stevenson, D. Magill

Source: Brym with Fox, 1989

Just over 100 sociologists are cited for at least one research report. The number of studies cited per person ranges from 1 to a high of 16, and the number of pages a person is cited on ranges from 1 to 37 (Table 1). It may come as no surprise that from Table 1 we see that the Canadian sociologist cited on the most number of pages was John Porter, with S.D. Clark and Wallace Clement in the top group. However, the high rankings of some other individuals may be more controversial (such as the authors themselves), especially if one maintains an empiricist argument that such patterns of citation are a mirror of the pattern of production. In all about 14-15 per cent of English Canadian sociologists are cited at least once. Of course, many English Canadian sociologists publish nothing that is directly relevant to the study of Canada, or publish nothing at all, so that the total number of persons cited in relation to the actual pool of English Canadian sociologists who have published items relevant to the study of Canadian society would be much higher. At any rate, one cannot fault the authors for lack of industry, as in a relatively short work, 148 journal articles and scores of books and other sources are cited.

Table 3

The Top 10 and the Top 29 Most Cited English Canadian Sociologists in *From Culture to Power*, by Region (based on page citations, Table 1)

Region	General Distribution	Top 10	Top 29
Core Five	25.0%	80%	65.5%
Prairies	24.2	0	10.3
Rest of Ontario	25.4	10	6.9
Atlantic	14.6	0	6.9
British Columbia	5.8	10	6.9
Anglophone Quebec	5.1	0	3.4
	100.1% (rounding procedure)	100%	99.9% (rounding procedure)

Source: Brym with Fox, 1989; Herman and Carstens, 1986-87

In Table 3, we look at the top 10 and the top 29 most cited sociologists in Brym and Fox as measured by the number of pages an author is cited on. Of the top ten most cited sociologists, 80 per cent come from the Core Five universities, and of the top 29 most cited sociologists, almost two-thirds (65.5 per cent) come from the Core Five. This compares to their actual share of all sociologists in English Canada, 25 per cent. By this measure, the Prairies, the rest of Ontario, and the Atlantic provinces are all considerably undercited compared to their general distribution. The top 10 most cited sociologists are cited on at least ten pages of text, the top 29 on at least five pages of text.

Table 4

Percentage of Sociologists by Region Cited in *From Culture to Power* (cited at least once)

Region	% Cited in Brym with Fox
Core Five	.27
Atlantic	.18
Anglophone Quebec	.17
British Columbia	.10
Rest of Ontario	.08
Prairies	.06
Canada	.15

Source: Brym with Fox, 1989; Herman and Carstens, 1986-87

In Table 4, we see the nature of regional citation in Brym and Fox in terms of the rate of faculty in each region who are cited at all (i.e., on at least one page) in *From Culture to Power*. Thus 27 per cent of the Core Five faculty are cited, 18 per cent of the Atlantic sociologists, 17 per cent of those from Anglophone Quebec, 10 per cent of those from British Columbia, 8 per cent for the rest of Ontario, and only 6 per cent for sociologists from the Prairie provinces are cited on at least one page or more. The average for all sociologists in English Canada is 15 per cent. Thus the Core Five sociologists are more than 400 per cent more likely to be cited at least once than Prairie sociologists, and about 300 per cent more than their colleagues in the rest of Ontario. What is valid is to compare each regional percentage with the Canadian average of 15. Basically all Ontario sociologists outside the metropolitan core of Ontario are under-cited, as are sociologists in British Columbia and the Prairies. On the other hand, Anglophone Quebec and the Atlantic provinces are slightly "over-cited" in terms of their general distribution.

Empiricists may retort that such a pattern of citation is simply a mirror reflection of relevant publication. One way to estimate this is by looking at regional rates of publication in the *Canadian Review of Sociology and Anthropology* and *The Canadian Journal of Sociology* (referred to as the *CRSA* and the *CJS* henceforth).

Table 5

Journals Cited in *From Culture to Power* by Number of Articles and by Geographical Location

Canada	Number of Articles Cited
Canadian Review of Sociology and Anthropology	65
Canadian Journal of Sociology	26
Studies in Political Economy	09
Canadian Ethnic Studies	03
Journal of Canadian Studies	02
Atlantis	02
Society/Société	02
CHA Historical Papers	02
Canadian Historical Review	01
Labour	01
Queen's Quarterly	01
Sociologie et sociétés	01
Newfoundland Studies	01
Alternate Routes	01
Canada	**117**

Foreign	
American Journal of Sociology	04
Social Forces	03
American Sociological Review	02
Sociological Focus	02
The American Sociologist	02
Sociology Inquiry	02
Comparative Social Research	02
British Journal of Sociology	01
Signs	01
Administrative Sciences Quarterly	01
Sociological Analysis	01
Ethnicity	01
Current Sociology	01
The Insurgent Sociologist	01
Comparative Studies in Society and History	01
International Migration Review	01
Journal for the History of the Behavioral Sciences	01
Social Science Information	01
Studies in Comparative International Development	01
Research in Social Structure and Mobility	01
Population Studies	<u>01</u>
Foreign	**31**

Source: Brym with Fox, 1989

In Table 5 is given the total number of articles cited from each journal in Brym and Fox. Thus, 65 articles from the CRSA, 26 from the CJS, and 9 from Studies in Political Economy (SPE) were cited in From Culture to Power. The greatest number of articles cited in Brym and Fox authored by Canadian sociologists had been published in these Canadian journals. It might be argued that Canadian sociologists were publishing more prestigiously elsewhere but as the table shows, only relatively few articles cited by Brym and Fox appeared in the American Journal of Sociology or the American Sociological Review. As Table 5 demonstrates, whereas 100 articles cited in Brym and Fox came from the top three most cited Canadian journals, only 9 were cited from the American trio of ASR, AJS, and Social Forces.

Table 6

Canadian Journal of Sociology 1975-88 and *Canadian Review of Sociology and Anthropology* 1975-84 by Region of Authors

Region	General Distribution	CJS	CRSA
Core Five	25.0%	31.8%	35.9%
Prairies	24.2	28.0	22.7
Rest of Ontario	25.4	18.4	20.5
Atlantic	14.6	10.7	10.0
British Columbia	5.8	8.0	7.3
Anglo Quebec	5.1	3.3	3.6
Total	100.1% (rounding procedure)	100.2% (rounding procedure)	100.0%

Source: Herman and Carstens, 1986-87; Indexes, 1986 and 1989 (Anon.), for *The Canadian Review of Sociology and Anthropology* and *The Canadian Journal of Sociology*.

In Table 6 we see the publication of article by region of author for the two core Canadian journals concerned from 1975 through 1984 or 1988. In this table it is valid to compare the General Distribution column with the *CJS* and *CRSA* columns. It might be argued that Core Five publication rates are three to four hundred per cent higher in the two major English Canadian journals. Table 6 shows that this is not the case, although it is true that there is some over-representation of Core Five authors. This is most marked for the *CRSA*. However, it is clear from these data that although Prairie and rest of Ontario authors are *somewhat* under-represented in the *CRSA*, this scarcely amounts to three or four hundred per cent. In the case of the *CJS*, both the Core and Prairie authors are somewhat over-represented. The drastic under-representation of Prairie authors noted in Brym and Fox may in part be due to their relative neglect of the *CJS* compared to the *CRSA*. Brym alone authored or co-authored three papers in the *CJS* and if these are excluded from consideration, only 21 *CJS* papers were cited. However to get back to the main point, the Prairies and the rest of Ontario were only slightly below the general distribution but were drastically under-cited in Brym and Fox. On the other hand, Atlantic sociologists were somewhat under-represented in both the *CRSA* and the *CJS* but were slightly over-cited in Brym and Fox.

Personal Networks and Theory Groups

Turning aside from regional considerations, we now turn to a consideration of personal networks and theory groups. Let us review one article by Diana Crane that goes beyond empiricist-positivistic assumptions about the construction of knowledge: "The Gatekeepers of Science: Some Factors Affecting the Selection of Articles for Scientific Journals" (1967:194-201). This article looked at the practices of journal editors in the social sciences (sociology, economics) and in the case of the *American Sociological Review* did so before and after anonymous refereeing was introduced in 1955. She found that: "It appears that the evaluation of scientific articles is affected to some degree by non-scientific factors" (Crane, 1967:200).

She suggested two factors that might apply, that "editorial readers respond to certain aspects of methodology, theoretical expression and mode of expression in the writings of those who have received similar training" and that "doctoral training and academic affiliations influence personal ties between scientists which in turn influence their evaluation of scientific work..." (Crane, 1967:200).

Another extra-scientific factor that Crane investigated was the "unearned increment" that is accorded to highly productive colleagues at major universities. She points out that "Evidently, productivity did not make the scientist as visible to...colleagues...as did a position at a major university" (Crane, 1965:710). Her study revealed that high producers at minor universities received only slightly more recognition than low producers at major universities and far less than high producers at major universities (see Crane, 1965: Table 10). Crane herself talked about a possible "halo" effect (1965:713; 1967:195) that a major university confers on the receptivity of work even if it may be undeserved.[3] Thus to use her term, "non-scientific factors" do come into play in the construction of what is accepted as legitimate knowledge and in the construction of scientific reputations.

The citation pattern of Brym and Fox, then, is revealed in a context that is consistent with the sociology of science and knowledge literature. The Core Five universities are located in the major metropolitan centres of economic and political power, all have complete graduate programmemes up to the doctoral level, and all are in urban centres of high population in a favoured region. The two authors themselves are from the Core Five universities and we see by turning back to Table 1 that the two authors and the husband of one (John Fox) are represented among the top ten most cited authors by number of pages. Michael Ornstein, who emerges as one of the top two most cited sociologists from Tables 1 and 2, was a supervisor of the seventh most cited William Carroll's Ph.D. dissertation and a former collaborator of John Fox, and Robert Brym acted as an examiner of Gordon Laxer's dissertation.

Rather than referring to personal networks influenced by friendship and kinship, let us look at the pattern of citation as evinced among University of Toronto and University of Alberta doctoral graduates. Both of these universities have had large doctoral programmemes since the mid-1960s. Robert Brym received his own doctoral degree from the University of Toronto in 1976, spent two years at Memorial University of Newfoundland, and then commenced as a faculty member at Toronto in 1978. Fox received her Ph.D. from Alberta in 1980 but spent a minimal amount of time there and had taught at several universities in several regions until her appointment with the University of Toronto in 1985. Where Brym is clearly tied to the Toronto connection, this is less clear with Fox.

In the period from 1967 to 1984, Alberta graduated 81 Ph.D.s compared to 130 for Toronto. From 1973 to 1984, the numbers were 69 and 112 respectively. Since Brym entered the Toronto doctoral programmeme himself in 1973, and since the only break he has had with Toronto was a two-year stint at Memorial, he has demonstrably close ties to Toronto. Table 7 shows that Brym with Fox were twice as likely to cite Ph.D. graduates from Toronto as from Alberta, thus 10 per cent of Toronto doctoral graduates in the entire period from 1967 to 1984 were cited at least once in Brym and Fox as opposed to just about 5 per cent of Alberta graduates. In the period from 1973 to 1984, when Brym at least would have known personally many of the Toronto graduate students, the percentage goes up to almost 12 per cent compared to just under 6 per cent for those with Alberta Ph.D.s.

Even when Alberta doctoral graduates wrote on topics very relevant to *From Culture to Power*, such as Heather-Jo Hammer's dissertation "Mature Dependency: The Effects of American Direct Investment on Canadian Economic Growth" (1983-84), they were likely to be ignored by Brym and Fox, even though Hammer, for example, has published in high-prestige journals (Hammer and Gartrell:1986). One of the four Alberta graduates cited in Brym and Fox (not counting Fox) was A.R. Gillis, a colleague of the authors at the University of Toronto and thus within their orbit of proximity and connections.

Table 7

Pattern of Citation in *From Culture to Power* by Location of Doctoral Degree, Universities of Alberta and Toronto

University	Dates	Ph.D. Graduates	Number Cited	As a %
Alberta	1973-84	69	4	.057
Toronto		112	13	.116
Alberta	1967-84	81	4	.049
Toronto		130	13	.10

Source: Helmes-Hayes, 1988; Department of Sociology, University of Alberta, 1984.

Once more the empiricist may suggest that the pattern of citations is simply a mirror reflection of the "state of the art." Apart from considering publication in the two major English Canadian sociology journals, one way to investigate this issue would be to look at citations. The best available measure is the *Social Science Citation Index (SSCI)*. There are some criticisms of this tool in the literature, especially as it may be partially unsatisfactory for Canadian scholarship (Assheton-Smith, 1979:52). On the other hand, its use as an indicator of esteem, prestige, and even of that elusive concept in the social sciences, quality, is well known.

Jonathan and Stephen Cole, two well-known contributors to the sociology of science and knowledge, write: "The data available indicate that straight citation counts are highly correlated with virtually every refined measure of quality...the value of using them as rough indicators of the quality of a scientist's work should not be overlooked" (Cole and Cole, 1971:28).

Using *SSCI* cites is, for the Coles, a means to measure quality that relies on Kuhn's recognition that science is a social construction. In other words, they proceed from the view that it is impossible to ascertain "absolute truth" but instead truth in scientific work is that which is considered useful by scientific colleagues (Cole and Cole, 1973:24).

They also go on to argue against the view that critical citations indicate a lack of quality in authors so criticized; rather, for the Coles, "all publicity is good publicity" in the sense that criticized work is work that has still been found useful in the advancement of science (Cole and Cole, 1973:25). They suggest that it is "unlikely...that work which is valueless will be deemed significant enough to merit extensive criticism. If a paper presents an error which is important enough to elicit frequent criticism, the paper, though erroneous, is probably a significant contribution. The significance of a paper is not necessarily determined by its correctness" (Cole and Cole, 1973:25). This is a rather important point to consider given the fact that most of the citations by Brym with Fox to Porter, Clement, and the Carleton School are critical in nature despite their high placing in Tables 1 and 2. It is perhaps difficult to agree with the Coles that the number of citations is itself a sufficient indicator of objective quality, since it seems clear that the number of citations in any field depends partly on the number of researchers in the field and partly on whether a particular text partakes in the popular assumptions of any given age. Thus, other things being equal, articles dealing with American and British studies will draw more citations than Danish or Costa Rican studies. However, measures of citations do indicate the extent to which a person's work is known and found useful in a particular scholarly community.

The Coles themselves present some evidence to counter such criticisms of citation measures. They found that "at least in physics" there was "no relationship between the size of a specialty and the number of citations to the work of men [sic] in that specialty" (Cole and Cole, 1973:29). They found that in 1966 there were 4,593 solid-state physicists and only 1,833 elementary particle physicists. Yet the latter group actually had a few more citations, on the average, than the larger group. However, the Coles did recognize the issue as possibly relevant (1973:28). It may be that research in the humanities and social sciences differ, since they do *not necessarily* use the building block method of natural science.

There are a number of strange anomalies. Perhaps the strangest is the complete failure to cite the work of Patricia Marchak, a former president of the CSAA. From 1981 through to September 1989, she garnered 88 citations in the literature, which puts her in a high category with more than Brym himself (especially when it is remembered that about half of Brym's 71 *SSCI* citations are to topics *not* relevant to Canadian macrosociology). It is also surprising since Marchak has published on most of the topics relevant to *From Culture to Power*. Furthermore, it should be pointed out that Marchak was a presenter at the conference on "The Structure of the Canadian Capitalist Class," held at the University of Toronto, November 1983. Brym was one of the organizing group behind this conference, and was editor of the two volumes that came from it. Marchak's article from the conference was published in the second of the two volumes to come from it (see Marchak, 1986).

The omission of certain authors by Brym with Fox despite prominence in the *SSCI* at times is due to the selectivity of topics discussed earlier. Thus Reginald Bibby, Canada's most cited sociologist of religion with 70 *SSCI* cites, and Kenneth Westhues with 43, remained uncited although both authors have published material relevant to Canadian macrosociology.

Other western authors not cited in Brym and Fox despite many *SSCI* citations or important publications include Alan B. Anderson (40), John Conway (17), Arthur K. Davis (27), James Frideres (55), Marlene M. Mackie (61), and Emily Nett (16). In another case, a distinguished author on ethnic studies, Leo Driedger with 74 *SSCI* citations, is quoted on one page only of Brym and Fox. On the other hand, an author such as J. Reitz, a Toronto colleague of Brym's interested in ethnic studies with 48 *SSCI* cites, is mentioned on six pages.

Another point worth mentioning is the overlooking of Prairie authors even when they publish articles relevant to the topics chosen by Brym with Fox and even when such articles were in sources close to hand. Thus Harry H. Hiller's "Internal Party Resolution and Third Party Emergence" from the *Canadian Journal of Sociology*, 1977, was not cited, nor were James McCrorie's article "Change and Paradox in Agrarian Social Movements" and Arthur K. Davis's chapter "Canadian Society and History as Hinterland Versus Metropolis," both published in Richard Ossenberg's book *Canadian Society* (1971). The article by Davis has been reprinted several times, even recently in one reader (Curtis and Tepperman, 1990), and between 1976 and 1985 was cited 24 times in the *SSCI*. Nor were John Conway's articles on populism, published in the *Journal of Canadian Studies* (1979) and the *Canadian Journal of Political Science* (1978), cited; neither was his book *The West* (1983).

It is not the case that Brym is ignorant of these articles, as most of them are cited, but not quoted, in his article on "Social Movements and Third Parties" in *Models and Myths in Canadian Society* (1984). Conway's *The West* is placed in an annotated bibliography by Brym (1986:208). In some cases, the failure to cite in *From Culture to Power* may be due to theoretical or methodological considerations. Thus a paragraph from page 23 could well be said to summarize A.K. Davis's views without mentioning his name.

The method followed in this paper may be applied generally to other works in sociology. If the assumptions of the sociology of knowledge are correct, that knowledge is a social enterprise in which social factors play a role in determining what constitutes knowledge, then similar findings should be discovered for works other than *From Culture to Power*.

Let us take a look at the second edition of Robert Stebbins' volume on *Sociology: The Study of Society*. Stebbins teaches at the University of Calgary and is a former president of the Canadian Sociology and Anthropology Association. He is in origin an American with a Ph.D. from Minnesota but has spent his career since 1965 in Canada, except for three years in Texas. He spent 1965-1973 at Memorial University of Newfoundland before moving to his current location in 1976 (Jaques Cattell Press, 1978:1144).

Table 8 and 9 show respectively the pattern of citation for eight English Canadian sociologists who were cited on three or more pages and the pattern of regional breakdown for those cited on five pages or more and for the fuller list of twenty-five cited on these pages or more. The lists of Canadian sociologists were taken from the *ASA 1989 Guide to Graduate Departments* supplemented by the *Commonwealth Universities Yearbook 1988* and by a few individual university calendars when necessary.

Table 8

Number of Pages Mentioned in R. Stebbins' *Sociology* (2nd ed., 1990)

20	R. Stebbins
9	J. Porter
6	E. Lupri, J. Frideres, A. Hunter, W.B.W. Martin
5	R. Bibby, M. Mackie, R. Prus
4	P. Pineo, H. Hiller, W. Clement, R.J. Brym
3	J. Hagan, J.D. House, M. Boyd, M. Eichler, J.P. Grayson, N. Guppy, H. McRoberts, P. Marchak, A.B. Anderson, G.S. Lowe, F. Elkin, A.J. Macdonell

Source: Stebbins, 1990.

Table 9

The Top 9 and Top 25 Most Cited English Canadian Sociologists in R. Stebbins' *Sociology* (2nd edition, 1990) by Region

Region	General Distribution	Top 9	Top 25
Core Five	24.8	22.2	44.
Prairies	23.3	55.6	32.
Rest of Ontario	25.5	11.1	04.
Atlantic	14.6	11.1	12.
British Columbia	6.0	0.0	8.
Anglophone Quebec	5.8	0.0	0.
Total	100.0	100.0	100.

Source: Stebbins, 1990; *ASA Guide to Graduate Departments 1989*; *Commonwealth Universities Yearbook 1988*.

From looking at Table 9 we see that the Prairies, far from being grossly under-cited, are considerably over-cited compared to the general distribution in Canada. The Core is actually a little under-cited, or at least at the expected statistical figure for the top 9. They again are over-cited for the top 25; the rest of Ontario, the Atlantic region, B.C., and Anglophone Quebec are all under-cited to varying degrees. However, it should be noted that the

Atlantic region is only marginally under-cited and it will be remembered
that Stebbins spent a number of years there in the early 1970s. The three
Atlantic sociologists cited in the top 25 are all veterans in the area. A.J.
Macdonell was listed at New Brunswick as of 1971, and House and Martin
were both listed in the 1978 edition of the *National Museum's Guide to Departments of Sociology* (see Herman and Carstens, 1978-79). (It should be
noted for the benefit of those who wish to replicate these tables that S.D.
Clark is listed in the index as cited on three pages, but this is incorrect as one
of the citations is a work by his son, Samuel D. Clark, a member of the
Department of Sociology at Western). The point of the above analysis is to
show that the effects of region and personal network are not unusual, but
frequent and common.

Table 10

Percentage of Sociologists by Region Cited in Brym with Fox and
Stebbins (cited at least once)

Region	Brym and Fox	Stebbins
Core Five	.27	.22
Atlantic	.18	.09
Anglophone Quebec	.17	.05
British Columbia	.10	.15
Rest of Ontario	.08	.12
Prairies	.06	.18
Canada	.15	.15

Source: Stebbins, 1990; Herman and Carstens, 1986-87.

In Table 10, we look at the percentage of sociologists cited at least once
by region in Brym with Fox as compared to Stebbins. This analysis reveals
that the Prairie-based author Stebbins cited Prairie sociologists three times
as often as Core authors. The Core authors were most likely to cite themselves at least once, with eastern Canadian authors next most favoured. The
Prairies stood at the foot of the citation nexus. In Stebbins' case, Western
authors (including B.C.) were cited at or above the Canadian average. The
Prairies were actually the second most cited regional group, with the Core
most cited. Certainly the Prairies were not significantly ignored, as in the
case of authors Brym and Fox. Aside from the obvious regional effect, the
tendency of a none-Core sociologist to cite Core authors heavily is noted.
The CSAA discussant of this paper, Claude Denis (1990), mentioned to me
the possibility that non-Core authors feel a need, even if unconscious, to
recognize Core authors even if the reverse is not the case. No matter how

regionalist we may be, keeping up with the sociological Joneses is better expressed by citing Core authors than by citing those in Moose Jaw or Chebucto.

Returning to our original aims, I have shown in this analysis that social factors in citation do play a role. This has now been shown in two books by different authors in different parts of the country. In addition, these two books are somewhat different in their respective aims. One (Stebbins) is an introductory textbook, the other a more specialized survey that endeavours to be an analytical summary of Canadian sociological history over the last forty years. The fact that the two books, despite their different aims and origins, show the influence of their social construction (since according to the strict positivist or "contemplative" accounts, such factors should not be present, most especially in textbooks that purport to be simply a summary of research facts) presents itself strikingly. I now leave it as a challenge for further research to replicate such an approach to other works by Canadian sociologists.

Conclusion

In examining these examples of sociological writing, it is clear that geographical location, personal networks including graduate school, methodological and theoretical biases, and reputation of authors all intersect in dictating which authors are cited and which are not. Sociologists who are physically close to the authors, who are at departments distinguished by relative largeness and by advanced graduate programmes, who write on topics of interest to Brym with Fox in approved styles, are likely to be cited. Yet we notice that Atlantic authors are cited somewhat above what their number (Table 4) would warrant and three hundred per cent as much as Prairie authors.

It is my contention that this hardly represents a mirror image of sociological production given the emphasis on research at several large Prairie universities such as Calgary, Alberta, Manitoba, and, increasingly, Saskatchewan. Rather, it has a lot to do with Brym's own background: brought up in New Brunswick, B.A. and M.A. from Dalhousie, two years as a faculty member at Memorial, and a prominent role in giving rise to a political economy orientation in Atlantic research (Brym and Sacouman, 1979).

In the introductory pages, I stressed that the sociology of knowledge acknowledges the social nature of the production of knowledge and rejects extreme empiricist and positivist views. It is likely that much, if not all, of the empirics of this paper will be a surprise to authors who may suppose that factors of objective merit or intrinsic interest alone influence their citation decisions. There is no reason to suppose that sociological authors themselves are clear in their own minds about the rationale of citation choices. But if the sociology of knowledge has validity in analyzing sociology itself (as it claims it does), we should be wary of accepting any sociological interpretation as the final word in representing our social world. All writing is hermeneutic, all writing is selective, all writing proceeds through conceptual filters of one sort or another. One hardly expects citation patterns or interpretation or cognitive evaluations of a Dorothy E. Smith to be that of a Talcott Parsons, but perhaps it will still surprise us that an account produced by two centrally located Core sociologists with extensive Atlantic experience will differ from the more western orientation of a Harry Hiller, a John Conway, a Patricia Marchak, or a James McCrorie.

As far as specific implications for readers of the Brym and Fox text is concerned, my conclusion is not to suggest that the book should be avoided (as all books are written from specific social locations); rather, the regional, personal, and professional choices of the authors should be kept clearly in mind when assessing and evaluating this particular rendering of Canadian sociology. In addition, I believe that I have shown the relevance of the sociology of knowledge to understanding sociology itself, and this hypothesis regarding the social construction of knowledge has been extended by our consideration of Stebbins' book. The fact that none of the authors concerned was born in their area of current employment just heightens the importance of the phenomenon—it occurs even without the roots of birth and upbringing.[4]

NOTES

[1]   It should be noted that this earlier monograph and the Brym and Fox book (1989) differ in several aspects. Most importantly, there was little or no mention of women sociologists or feminine sociology in the Brym monograph. This adds an ironic note to Fox's critique of the "adding on" process (1989:123).

[2]   For a more explicit and philosophical treatment of the nature of science from an empiricist-positivistic standpoint, see Nettler (1970), especially on *Scientific Explanation*, 85-111.

[3]   Some readers may feel that "the American model of hierarchy between universities" is inapplicable in Canada where there is not so blatant a distinction between "major" and "minor" schools. In the sense that Canadian universities are more dependent on the State, there may be an important comparison to the U.S.A., where many important universities are privately funded. Yet my own experience in Canada suggests the major-minor distinction is still valid. A number of universities in Ontario with a "major" reputation have been calling for a different funding formula than the rest; in teaching sociology of education last year my own students showed themselves quite knowledgeable about minor-major university reputations in Ontario; on another subjective

level, professors from so-called "minor" universities sometimes find that colleagues from better-known universities are confused about the identity or location of the lesser-known university. See Lynne Ainsworth, "'Favoritism' Urged in Funding of Universities," in which a Queen's University official calls for a two-tiered university system based on the number of "Ontario scholars," the number of first-class graduate programmes, and solid reputations in research (31 January 1990). In an article of April 13, 1990, President George Pedersen stated that

> "he doesn't care if Western appears elitist—smaller universities like Lakehead and Brock can meet the province's accessibility demands if they want, but established universities like Western and Queen's should emphasize academic excellence" (Bass, 1990).

4 This paper was read at the CSAA meetings held at Victoria, B.C. in 1990. It was read by a number of people not mentioned in the paper including Richard Helmes-Hayes and Tom Palantzas. I would also like to thank the anonymous referees, Deborah Harrison and Bill Carroll.

Part Three
The Academic Milieu

WHISTLING WOMEN:
REFLECTIONS ON RAGE AND RATIONALITY[1]
Dorothy E. Smith

When a dreadful event erupts into the life of a society, a great deal of work is done to bring it interpretively into the zones of what already makes sense. People seek to restore the everyday order that has been breached. Some events resist. We use notions of madness to incorporate them. We make sense of them by insisting that they don't make sense.

After the massacre at the École Polytechnique in Montreal in December 1989, official and unofficial sources defined Marc Lépine as mad and the massacre as an act of madness. Such an interpretation refuses to allow the act of killing young women engineering students to reflect on the established order and powers of the society. It isolates Marc Lépine: his act is all his own; it has nothing to tell us about other men, about men's violence to women, about the contemporary forms and relations of patriarchy. Coherence within established order is restored by representing his act as outside our methods of making sense.

The representation of Marc Lépine as insane has been disputed by the women's movement. We have claimed precisely that his act is not his alone, that it has much to tell us and society about other men and men's violence to women, about the forms and relations of patriarchy, and specifically about the rage that follows women's move into a sphere of power/knowledge traditionally the monopoly of men. My own reflections here pursue the latter theme. I remember not only that fourteen young women were killed but that they were engineering students, that this was a institution of post-secondary learning, that Marc Lépine had also been a student there. I ask: "How could such rage arise in the context of the learning of a rational knowledge? How could gender be found to ground the order of reason at so fundamental a level that a man would massacre fourteen women who had elected to become members? What does this frightful murder have to tell us of the social organization and relations of science, the life of mind, and the university?"

Rage, Regimes, and Anomalies

A saying from my youth in northern England goes like this: "A whistling woman and a crowing hen, lets the devil out of his pen." The saying equates the order of nature (cocks and hens) with the gender regime (men and women). Anomalies are created when hens act as cocks and women as men. Gender reversals disrupt a natural (social) order. The penned-up devil of disorder is unloosed. I use this saying as a clue to introduce an analysis of what I call here the "regime of rationality."

The notion of a "regime" is that of an order imposed and regulated. Using the notion of a "regime of rationality" takes us beyond rationality as a mode of thinking and discourse, or as a paradigm for ordering the relation between thought and action. The "regime of rationality" shifts attention from rationality as ideas, concepts, methods, in general as a matter of mind, to rationality as a social order, as social organization concerting the activities of actual individuals. And hence as ordering, among other matters, relations among women and men.

I had at one time the illusion, shared no doubt with many, that the university was a place where rational order prevailed. I learned that this was an illusion when we women sought to redress inequities in it. We had thought of the university as a place where reason prevailed and injustices could be addressed.[2] We discovered that rational processes of argument, evidence, and reasoned persuasion disintegrated when issues of women were raised. Those of us who embarked on women's action in university settings rapidly learned that the rules that we had believed to govern institutional discourse did not operate once issues of women's place were broached. At the University of British Columbia, where I was working in the 1970s, we found that even such an apparently straightforward matter as trying to get a women's studies course in place plunged into astonishing irrationalities. Objections were raised that were never otherwise raised; rather than a routine passage through two or three committees, we were bogged down in thirteen. In forming a women's action committee and beginning to raise issues of women's inequality, some of us were subjected to extraordinary personal attacks, let alone the barbs and sometimes outright hostility of colleagues whom we'd thought of as allies. Nor was this hostility restricted to colleagues and administrators; male students also could on occasion assume the male privilege of policing the boundaries securing male privilege—I remember a male student who attended a women's studies course to ensure that what we (the four women instructors) taught was "on the rails" and another who pinned me down in my office for two hours to rant about the inequities of what he believed was being put forward in women's studies. I have heard much more frightening accounts of intimidation and even violence from other universities.

The movement of women to displace the consolidated male consciousness that was, and still too much remains, the substance of university teaching and research was a deeper challenge than we knew. We discovered that the supposedly rational order was grounded in an order of another kind altogether. We had unknowingly attacked the obscured but vital levels of a regime articulating gender and sexuality with intellectual and personal dominance—a regime assuming men's right to dominate sexually and to command the discounted and devalued services of women as colleagues, secretaries, and wives. We discovered a gender irrationality foundational to the regime of rationality.

Sheila McIntyre's experience at the law school at Queen's University teaches us this lesson again and more acutely, partly because the attacks on her were exceptionally savage and partly also because they took place in the context of a discipline and discourse explicitly committed to rational argument and to principles of justice. She too had believed that in such a context her work as a feminist would be supported.

> I thought that what I consider the male "tilt" of law was largely unreflective and was rarely grounded in intentional bias or overt anti-feminism (McIntyre, 1987:7).

When she suggested in one of her courses that students address a particular case including a woman as the legal subject as well as men, male students undertook a campaign of harassment policing the masculinist foundations of law. McIntyre writes:

> The details of what happened in class are difficult to describe. About six men were deliberately disruptive, uncooperative, interruptive and angry...they...belligerently tried to prevent students who disagreed with their position from speaking by a combination of insult, interruption, hostile gestures and increasingly voluble but untenable argument. When I tried to legitimize the contributions of other students, they were equally abusive to me. Their bottom line, albeit only indirectly conveyed, was: we don't want to talk about gender; and we won't; and we won't let anyone else either (ibid:7).

This incident was only one event in a campaign to undermine McIntyre's position in the law school and to intimidate women students who had aligned or might align themselves with her position—they "no longer felt it safe to speak." These responses were not confined to students. Shortly after McIntyre had circulated a memo in which she discussed issues of gender bias in recruitment:

> I was publicly and privately attacked by a male colleague. He sneered at me in a faculty-wide memo, dressed me down publicly in the halls and then rebuked, insulted and threatened me in my office for about 45 minutes (ibid:9).

Such incidents tell us that active repression is not strange. They are not unusual. It would be easy to add to the list. It is, in fact, in writing this, hard to decide which incidents to omit and which to include. I think, for example, of the President of the University of Western Ontario's public rage in response to a critique of sexism in the university. The list could be very long. Men's rage is not an unusual experience for women who have been activists in the university context—as elsewhere. Masculinist culture is repressive. Jean Gordon and Helen Breslauer describe some recent incidents as follows:

> Recent well-publicized incidents on university campuses across the country have illustrated that life on our campuses is far from non-violent. These incidents have taken a variety of forms: violent reactions to an anti-rape campaign; vilification of a female engineering student who had dared complain about the treatment of women in her faculty; vilification of female faculty who had dared to ask questions about their female colleagues' experiences and publish their answers. What these and similar incidents had in common was a male response of outrage over female challenges to their authority. Women are first victimized and then blamed as the creators of their own problems (Gordon and Breslauer, 1990:6).

I take this rage as a clue to the social organization and relations of a regime of rationality. I take this rage as arising in an irruption of the unfamiliar into the familiar practices of the regime, the disruption of a taken-for-granted ordering of power.

As Mary Douglas has shown us, any social regime embeds anomalies and contradictions in its order (Douglas, 1966). In creating its coherence, every regime contains and represses the restless entopic possibilities of the actual. The very coherence of a social order generates anomalies, sites of contradiction, and its distinctive sources of danger and disorder. Anomalies endanger the coherence of a regime and are experienced as a threat, and hence it must exclude, repress, avoid, prevent. Its methods and practices of exclusion, repression, avoidance, and prevention sustain the moral valence of the regime[3] and the moral commitment of its members.

People come to count on such order as the everyday ordinariness of their lives. This is the order they take for granted; in which they know themselves and others; in which they find their privileges and deprivations. Anomalies are threats to who and how they are. More than mere deviations, they attack the very character of the order itself, the presuppositions on which it is based, its internal coherence. Crowing hens and whistling women let loose disorder on the world. Women who act in ways identified with men are anomalies, are dangerous, must be repressed for the sake for the regime. Anne Hutcheson was exiled from the Massachusetts Bay Colony as she who had "stepped out of [her] place" and had "rather been a husband than a wife." Women leaders of women's organization in the French Revolution were guillotined for engaging in cross-sex behaviour—she, for example, "who wished to be a statesman," or she whose "desire to be a savant" led her to "forget her sex." Their behaviour was dangerous; it was their dangerous behaviour, not the men, that led the law to punish them and the guillotine to execute them. Their actions caused their punishment, we are told. It is the crowing hens and the whistling women who let the devil loose.

Ascribing characteristic types of behaviour to one sex or the other is the effect of a regime and not of nature. If gender differences in behaviour aren't a matter of nature, potential anomalies are always present, always a potential threat to the regime that depends on such differences, particularly, of course, to its ordering of privilege and prerogative. Anomalies are an ontological threat to those identities constituted by the regime. Hence the rage of those identified with power and privilege. The rage is not experienced as individual but on behalf of the regime. Characteristically the rage is only expressed by a few individuals; it is, however, permitted, even tacitly supported, and sometimes explicitly justified, by other men. McIntyre's colleagues depreciated the significance of their colleague's attack on her. In general they ignored, side-stepped, and discounted issues of gender bias, repression, and harassment from students and others. Men's rage is sometimes treated as elicited by women's breach of patriarchal order (Gordon and Breslauer, 1990). This is the message of the north English saying of my youth: The whistling women, the women appropriating for themselves the privileged activities of men, endanger the regime. Pain and punishment exacted by men in its support flow from women's own actions.

The Gender Foundations of the Regime of Rationality

The notion of a "regime of rationality" formulates an organization of actual practices among actual people. Rationality and objectivity are understood here as ongoing aspects of an organization of relations among members of a discourse or discourses, that is, extended conversations mediated by texts. Actual people are at work, are active, orienting their daily/nightly practices to the specific forms of argumentation, evidence, reasoning, that others know how to interpret in the same modes.

Emphasis upon actual people at work shifts attention from abstract principles or concepts or procedures to rationality and objectivity as modes of organizing relations among people. We are talking then about actual practices of thinking and communicating, including the theories and methods through which participants constitute what they recognize as rational behaviour, rational discourse, objective accounts, and so forth. People are at work in actual settings and under definite material conditions and a regime of rationality is no exception. It must embed a gender order of some kind and in some way (not necessarily dichotomous, of course). The institutions of objective knowledge and rationality have built distinctive relations between men and men and between women and men, and also, as Mary Wollstonecraft insisted, among women; those relations have become, and still to a large extent remain, foundational.

An existing institutional form is taken for granted as it is; it seems merely to "be there." But its being given to us just as it is, its ordinary presence, is the outcome of complex historical processes. Tracing the history of the regime of rationality enables us to locate elements of explicit design in the establishing of its gender order. Men, many of them philosophers, wrote gendered constitutions for the regime of rationality. There was no conspiracy, but over a couple of centuries or so, constitutional conventions were established bonding together men within the collegial relations of rationality to the exclusion of women. Indeed, the bonds among men came to be defined by women's exclusion.

The Enlightenment constructed a male community of science and intellect whose internal relations (among men) were governed by reason, not by passion, myth, or prejudice, and were directed to producing an objective knowledge, a knowledge constituted as the same for all participating subjects. I emphasize its social relations and organization, not just its ideas, and I suggest we can explore how the philosophers of and after the Enlightenment wrote the gender constitution of that community. Philosophers have set the terms of rational discourse; they have been its architects and regulators. But the standpoint of women does not confine us to the boundaries they have written. The regulators of discourse are also the regulators of its gender order. Their work can also be read for its constitutional force in organizing and regulating the relations among women and men in the regime of rationality. We will look at instances from the work of those who wrote the constitution of the regime of rationality in the sixteenth, seventeenth, and eighteenth centuries in Europe and Britain.[4]

Caroline Merchant describes Bacon's sexual imagery. Nature is female. Domination of nature is the scientist's objective. She is to be "hounded" remorselessly so that she can be led or driven to the desired place. Some of his imagery is strikingly sexual. He tells us, for example, "Neither ought a man to make scruple of entering and penetrating into these holes and corners, when the inquisition of truth is his whole object...." (from De Dignitate et Augmentis Scientiarum, quoted in Merchant, 1980:168).[5] The classic Aristotelian opposition between men as active and women as passive is deployed to define the relation between scientist and nature. The male thing is to bend the woman to his desire; she is elusive and mysterious; chase and capture, entering and penetration, flow from his desire exclusively—she is always and only an object, never a subject.

Such images of gender are more than a gendering of men's relation to their scientific object. They are constitutive of the subject of scientific discourse. By this I mean that they write a design for the motivational, moral, and jural status of the subjects (speakers/writers/ agents) of scientific discourse. Bacon wrote prescriptively; he was the architect of scientific discourse. His images tell men of science how to be as such. His masculinization of the scientific subject prescribes for science a remorseless insistence on penetrating and dominating his object, indifferent to any consideration other than pursuit and conquest, concerned exclusively with screwing the truth out of nature (Merchant, 1980).

Another component of the gendered architecture of science was contributed by Descartes, who designed rationality's transcendent subject, the proper speaker/writer of the abstracted forms and relations increasingly vested in textually mediated discourse. Descartes's design for the discursive subject separates him from the particular local sites and experiences of his bodily existence. His transcendent subject is divorced from, and yet secretly dependent on, the world of women's work oriented to the particularities of people's existence, towards their bodies' subsistence and care.[6] This new design introduces a new and distinctive effect, namely the formal substitutability of one subject for any other. For the transcendent subject is detached from the particularities of his history, the settings of his work, his actual relations, the conditions and forms of co-operation that produce his work, and so on. Descartes saw reason as the universal instrument of humanity and designed a universalized subject corresponding to (and necessary to) it. Understand this not merely as prescribing a practice, a method, for individuals to pursue, but as constituting a mode of relating among subjects (readers/writers) who are co-participants in a discourse.[7] The subject-site thus constructed was and is indifferent to time, place, and the particularities of biography; anyone could enter who could enter; the discursive relations flowing from this were indifferent to differences of rank and person; internal to the discourse, they were relations of equality. It is indeed a striking moment in the organization of the regime of rationality, establishing that equality among members of the scientific discourse that is constitutively foundational of the objectivity of knowledge. Correlatively, that objectivity is reflexively constitutive of the equality of subjects who know how to participate in it. Thus a community among rational subjects is designed.

In this period of emerging scientific discourse, the principles and practices of rational discourse were also being applied to the organization of civil society (Schiebinger, 1989). The regime of rationality extended into the ruling of society, into military practice and organization as well as its technology, into the design of and organization of government, into the strategies of princes, into the principles and practice of impartiality in law, into the conduct of commerce. Formerly pragmatically rational ways of getting things done are systematized in discourse, designed rationally on the page, debated, expanded logistically, supplemented with tables, measurements, and statistics, and in general subject to systematic and discursively situated design and evaluation. Weber viewed rationality as a powerful principle at work in history, but examined from the standpoint of women it appears not as a principle but as a specialized organization of actual practices of ruling among men and by men and excluding, though depending on, women. The regime of rationality is a distinctive organization of patriarchal power.

The Gender Designs of the Enlightenment Philosophers

In the earlier years of the Enlightenment, and despite Bacon's decisively masculinist construction of the scientific subject, scientific discourse, so Londa Schiebinger argues, was not yet monopolized by men (Schiebinger, 1989). Though Descartes set up a "vertical" division, constituting the specialization of mind by calling into question the very existence of the particularized, localized, embodied sphere of traditional women's work, his discursive subject is gender-neutral.[8] He represented reason as the "universal instrument of mankind" (Schiebinger, 1989:171). During the Enlightenment in France, women intellectuals were active and influential. The salons of aristocratic ladies were settings for gentlemanly dispute regulated by the leading women intellectuals of the period. Schiebinger describes a major transition in women's relation to science and rationality in which Rousseau played a significant part, seeking to redesign the relations of rational discourse as an exclusively male preserve.

Though Enlightenment philosophers were not, of course, the sole source of the changes in women's roles in the eighteenth and nineteenth centuries, they wrote blueprints prescribing women's relation to the regime of rationality and ascribing to women a mode of being antithetical (yet complementary) to it. Rousseau attacked the gentlemanly character of the scholarly discourse of his period and was profoundly opposed to the styles of discourse prevailing in salons. In his view, scholarship should be vigorous and strong and could only be so in the context of conflict. Truth could only arise out of conflict and debate. Therefore combat was essential to relations among scholars, for it was thus that "the mind gains passion and vigor" (Schiebinger, 1989:157). The theme of truth arising out of conflict recurs in Hegel. Whereas Descartes had relied on a divine guarantor of the self-certainty of the transcendent subject, for Hegel self-certainty emerged out of a life-and-death struggle of opposing consciousness. It is a struggle among men—a kind of duelling relationship in which life is at risk. Self-certainty arises at that moment when one of the two caves in and becomes "other" to the successful and now paramount subject; the other becomes abject, the other's consciousness is denied, subordinated, suppressed, and disappears. For Hegel, the moment of self-certainty arrives in the overcoming of the other and opposing consciousness through conflict in which men hazard their lives. For Hegel, as for Rousseau, certainty is determined by conquest and truth is a matter between men.

The philosophers of the Enlightenment take for granted the masculinity of the relations of rationality. They prescribe complementary roles for women subordinate to and excluded from the male bonded circuits of contest and community. Susan Okin suggests that the seventeenth and eighteenth centuries see the emergence of what she calls "the sentimental family" (Okin, 1981). The sentimental family constitutes the gender supplement to a regime of rationality extending into the political sphere. Rousseau designed an education to produce the fully autonomous individual capable of independent judgement and reason. The individual is male. Rousseau's Émile depends upon a Sophie whose complementary educational discipline shapes her "nature" to subordinate her to Émile's needs, to function as his support, and to bear and rear his child. The proper rearing of Sophie must ensure her exclusion from the community of reason, hence she is to be denied participation in rational discourse (Rousseau, 1979; Martin, 1985). When Kant takes up his pen to prescribe for women, the gender order of the regime of rationality is already in place, and it remains for him to explicate and expand on the distinctive qualities of women in contrast to those of men. He too writes prescriptively: Women should not venture on to the terrain of reason. "Deep meditation and a long-sustained reflection," "laborious learning or painful pondering....destroy the merits proper to her sex" (Kant in Agonito, 1977:131). "Her philosophy is not to reason, but to sense" (ibid:132.).

The eighteenth century, Okin suggests, celebrates families as private sanctuaries of sentiment, inserting a sharper division than had before existed between the domestic sphere, in which women preserve the values of love and sentiment, and the public and political sphere of rational male action as citizens, and "women increasingly come to be characterized as creatures of sentiment and love rather than of the rationality that was perceived as necessary for citizenship" (Okin, 1981:74). Women, according to Hegel, could not have direct access to transcendence through reason. Occupying the private sphere of family, their access to the public sphere, to the sphere of transcendence, is always mediated by men.

Of course the power of the philosopher to redesign the role of women must not be exaggerated. No doubt they refined and elaborated new forms of social relations already emerging. But philosophers spoke of and on behalf of the regime of rationality; they wrote its constitution and its constitution included conventions governing membership as well the conduct of relations among members. The "sentimental family" was designed in a sense that no familial order had been designed before. The emergence of a print culture in Western society brings a wholly new order of relations into being (Smith, 1990b). Kathryn Shevelow has explored the significance of print culture for the construction of femininity during the eighteenth century in Britain (Shevelow, 1989). Of course there was no simple and direct transfer from design to actual practice, but print culture established common and universalized ideals, standards, and norms. Print is indifferent to circumstance and situation. Given the ability to read, any reader could take herself to be addressed and herself, her friends, her neighbours to be equally subordinate to standards, prescriptions, and ideals, given textual presence in print. Topics, criteria, and references are thereby generalized across local sites and particular cases.

Like Rousseau, Kant did not view the qualities natural to women and men as spontaneous developments. They had to be nurtured and cultivated through education and instruction.

> ...one expects that....all the other merits of a woman should unite solely to enhance the character of the beautiful, which is the proper reference point; and on the other hand, among the masculine qualities the sublime clearly stands out as the criterion of his kind. All judgments of the two sexes must refer to these criteria, those that praise as well as those that blame; all education and instruction must have these before its eyes, and all efforts to advance the moral perfection of the one or the other.... (Kant in Agonito, 1977:130).

But as Mary Douglas stresses (Douglas, 1966), the very constitution of order creates anomalies, contradictions, potentials for disorder. The gender order foundational to the regime of rationality established by the Enlightenment created a deep contradiction between its gender exclusiveness and its claim to universality and the equality of reasoning subjects. The generalization of text-based discourse through print meant that anyone who read could have access to it, as readers and potentially as writers. Descartes's design of the discursive subject was non-exclusive. Women could and did imagine a discourse open to anyone, to us as well as them. The exclusionary practices of the regime did not appear at the surface of the text. The regime of rationality itself installed the convention of reading the masculine subject as the impersonal. In the absence of women as contending subjects, the pretence of universality was not contested. But women readers too could avail themselves of the openness of the text to its readers. Participation in the regime of rationality as it became accessible in print was available to just anyone who had the necessary skills.

If the text itself had no barriers, barriers had to be inserted at the juncture between discourse and the social relations in which it was embedded. Women who were enchanted with the freedom of the text and delighted in the exercise of reason were actively repressed. Schiebinger describes an astronomer of the eighteenth century who was deprived of access to the tools of her trade (Schiebinger, 1989). The education of women became an issue and site of struggle in denying women's access to the life of mind and enforcing their commitment to domesticity. Also from the eighteenth-century period comes Ellen Weeton's account of her mother's disciplining of her mathematical and creative inclinations.

> ...my mother continually checked any propensity I showed to writing or composing; representing to me what a useless being I should prove if I were allowed to give up my time to writing and reading, when domestic duties were likely to have so frequent a call upon me. (Weeton in Murray, 1982:204-5)

Mary Somerville (from whom Somerville College at Oxford, England, was named) describes how she pieced together a scientific and mathematical education, combing bookshelves at home for anything that would instruct her. Her family and the servants of the household combined to obstruct her; there were fears that she would go mad if she continued her mathematical studies; she was deprived of books and candles to read by (Somerville in Murray, 1982:207-10). Though we may ridicule the threat to sanity Somerville's parents saw in her studious proclivities, there may be a reality here. Certainly Virginia Woolf saw and felt a profound conflict between a woman's genius and the practical, moral, and social constraints on her freedom to exercise it (Woolf, 1929). Elizabeth of Bohemia, a correspondent of Descartes, wrote to him

>...that the life I am constrained to lead does not allow me enough free time to acquire a habit of meditation in accordance with your rules. Sometimes the interests of my household, which I must not neglect, sometimes conversations and civilities I cannot eschew, so thoroughly deject this weak mind with annoyances or boredom that I remain for a long time afterwards, useless for anything else.

Kant's dictum, quoted above, insisting that meditation, reflection, learning, and pondering "destroy the merits proper to her sex" regulates specifically this contradiction. His legislative stance eliminates the other term of the contradiction and is wholly external, displaying a total absence of appreciation of how such a denial might be experienced or what the cost of it might be to its practitioner. Connecting his dictum with Elizabeth of Bohemia's experience of the incompatibility of modes of consciousness required by household and social duties and those of rational meditation brings the masculine interest in denying women's participation in the regime of rationality into view. Men were the regulators; their interest was in a female sex competent to produce the well-ordered household and the civilities of social life on which ultimately the conduct of rational discourse must depend. It is not hard to imagine that the costs of this deprivation for some women were too great or that the enforcement of modes of consciousness wholly at odds with a powerful creative intellect might drive her mad.

Nineteenth-century struggles for women's education arose in the matrix of the contradictory claims of the universality of the rational subject and the masculine monopoly of subject positions sustained by the regime of rationality. They were largely resolved in major compromises institutionalizing the striking limits on women's access to science and mathematics[9] that our contemporary universities inherit.

The Regime of Rationality in the Contemporary University

Jessie Bernard in her early and path-breaking work on *Academic Women* (Bernard, 1964) described what she called the "stag" effect, men's orientation as scholars exclusively to other men. Though women scholars might be known and recognized, they were not identified as members of the discourse to whom scholars were oriented in their work and debates. Women's exclusion may be experienced, as some women have reported, as a "chill" factor in universities; they have found "their male colleagues condescending, insensitive, hostile" (Gordon and Breslauer, 1990:7).

The "stag" effect as an ordering of academic discourse defines relations among teachers and students as well as among university faculty. In universities in North America, practices restricting women's participation in the classroom have been widely observed and reported. Women in the classroom are less likely to be addressed, less likely to have an opportunity to speak, more likely to have what they say discounted and dismissed, and more likely to have instructors whose attention is primarily directed towards men students. Men students take for granted that the public space of the classroom is their domain, and exchanges between male instructors and male students is the norm, while women's interventions may be ignored or treated as frivolous or irrelevant (Sandler, 1988). At York University a study done by Linda Briskin during the 1989-90 academic year describes a growing concern among students and faculty about the increasingly difficult climate between male and female students, which effectively silences women (Briskin, 1989). As women we have not been members of the circle of scholarly speakers; our voices have had no authority; the camaraderie, factions, enmities, and competitiveness of science and scholarship have not included us. As we resist the old ways, we are resisted.

At the university, masculine defence of the established gender order of the regime of rationality works at multiple levels. Part of this defence involves a recognition of women's sexuality which defines them as objects of male desire and denies them equal presence as co-participants in learning and discovery. The fear and sometimes anger that has greeted the raising of sexual harassment as an issue attest to the normal pervasiveness of the masculinist regime.[10] The boundaries, I argue, of the "stag" effect were, and to a significant extent remain, boundaries marked by the sexual objectification of women. Young women were viewed by men (and probably by many young women too) as normally available to the male faculty member. Relations among men were affirmed and defined on the terrain of university and rational discourse by reducing women to their sexual value. Women whose age or stylistic refuges repudiated their status as sexual objects might find that they had indeed no place, that they were not fully subjects, not fully present. They were "battle-axes," "old witches," "neurotic spinsters," in need of a "good fuck." Sally Hacker's study of the culture of engineering at MIT found that of jokes told in classrooms at MIT, those ridiculing women were second in frequency only to those ridiculing technical incompetence (Hacker, 1990: 118). Schools of engineering have ritualized the sexual demeaning of women: the parading of Lady Godiva naked on a horse through campus; an orientation event at which engineering students "passed a life-sized inflated female doll from hand to hand, shoved a beer bottle in and out between its legs, then threw it to the ground where several men jumped on it in simulated rape" (Dagg and Thompson, 1988).

Such practices must be seen, as much as establishing relations of gender-based camaraderie among men, as defining women. Defining women exclusively in degraded sexual terms determines the significance of what women could mean among men and hence what men can mean to one another. Hacker links the decisively masculinist character of engineering culture to the part engineers play in the impersonalized and bureaucratized modes of domination of large-scale business organization. She relates this masculinized culture to a practice of engineering that "is essential to leadership in bureaucratic organization—[requiring] control of sensuality, emotions, passion, one's very physical rhythms. Dominance in such rationally ordered institutions is indeed inscribed on the body" (ibid., 1990:209).[11] The organization of a regime of rationality excluded women as *significant* sexual objects (Hacker tells of engineers recommending immersion in technical processes as a remedy for love—[ibid., 1990:207]) and excluded the dimensions of human existence—sensuality, emotions, passion—with which women became peculiarly identified during the seventeenth and eighteenth centuries.

The contest relations prescribed by Rousseau call for a male cast. At least one contemporary writer on science, describing relations of conflict, contest and competition among scientists, shares Rousseau's view that such relations are essential to science. David Hull believes that "the altercations that arise in science from its competitive aspects are as intrinsic to it as is the camaraderie that result from its more cooperative side" (Hull, 1988: 163).

> Scientists acknowledge that among their motivations are natural curiosity, the love of truth, and the desire to help humanity, but other inducements exist as well, and one of them is to "get that son of a bitch." Time and again, the scientists whom I have been studying have told stories of confrontations with other scientists that roused them from routine work to massive effort. No matter what the cost, they were going to get even (Hull, 1988: 180).

Hull's cast of characters is almost exclusively male. He describes "periodic warfare" among bands of bioscientists and remarks that though rarely degenerating to physical violence, contests among scientists can involve "vicious" verbal exchanges (Hull, 1988:180). Susan Sherwin suggests that conflict has become foundational to philosophical method.

The logic of the argument is the most important feature of a philosophical position, far more important than the plausibility of the claims or the usefulness of the insight to other questions. In commenting on a philosophical thesis, one may identify a logical flaw in it, challenge its underlying assumptions, or note the inadequacy of its explanatory power. It is taken for granted that the task of colleagues discussing this work is to test the thesis along these logical dimensions, seeking to demolish it to make room for their own clever innovations (Sherwin, 1988).[12] By Rousseau's and Hegel's rules, truth is a product of conquest and the "stag" effect circumscribes those eligible to compete and hence those whose defeat counts as the winner's success.

Such an organization of the subject is deeply implicated with the social organization of the stag circuit as the gender underpinnings of rational discourse. What can be thought, what participants can recognize within the conventions of discourse as thought, observation, inquiry, sense, significance, reason, is bounded by the shared severance of modes of consciousness from being "in" nature. Being excluded from the stag circle of competing egos can create a special freedom, for the stag circle is structured by hierarchies and standards enforcing normative and paradigmatic conformity.[13] Thus Evelyn Fox Keller did not argue, as she has often been held to have, that Barbara McClintock's style of inquiry, relying on "intuition, feeling, a sense of connectedness and relatedness" was characteristically female; many male scientists also work with such methods (Keller, 1989:38). Rather Fox Keller suggests that McClintock was free, as men scientists are not, to occupy "a place" where "the matter of gender drops away" (ibid:38).

> However atypical she is as a woman, what she is not is a man—and hence is under no obligation to prove her "masculinity" (Keller, 1985:174).

McClintock was not hampered in deploying her style of inquiry by conformity to the norms of objectivity determining what counts as masculine among male scientists. The proof of masculinity in science is in the pudding of conflict among men for the winning discovery. What could be a discovery is already set by the paradigm in terms of which contest is conducted. The conformism of the stag effect limits as well as drives scientific practice.[14] Luce Irigaray writes of a "'subjective' revolution that has not [yet] taken place."

> The epistemological subject has undergone but not yet acted upon nor gone beyond the Copernican revolution?.... The scientist now wants to be *in front of* the world, naming, legislating, axiomatizing it. He manipulates nature, utilizes it, exploits it, but forgets that he is also in nature, that he is still physical and not only in front of the phenomena whose physical nature he fails to recognize. Advancing according to an objective method that would shelter him from all instability, from all moods, from all emotions and affective fluctuations, from all intuitions that are not

programed in science's name, from all interference by his desires, especially those that are sexed, he settles himself down, in his discoveries, in the systematic, in what can be assimilated to the already dead? Fearing, sterilizing the imbalances that are in fact needed to arrive at a new frontier. (Irigaray, 1989: 64)

Freud's *Civilization and its Discontents* charts the psychic costs in anxiety and in the potentiality for loving relationship of such an economy of consciousness. The pornographic rituals practised by student engineering societies produce, as social organization, the reduction of men's and women's sexual relations to those of pure appetite without feeling, tenderness, or commitment. Such rituals of degradation practised by young engineers enforce modes of subjectivity (as the currency of professional discourse) that forget that the scientist "is also in nature." They institutionalize a consciousness that denies the "imbalances" that make it possible to "go beyond the Copernican revolution" (ibid.) while also denying the human implications of rational forms of organized domination (Hacker, 1990).

Other denials are created. The constitution of objectivity as a feature of the regime depends on them. Practices severing body, sex, and feeling from the subject constituted within the regime of rationality deny women presence as subjects. The gender order established in the seventeenth and eighteenth centuries in Europe assigned to women the zones of subjective being cut out from the regime of rationality. But the rational, objectifying subject does not lose its gender grounding. Rather the centrality of masculine consciousness in the scholarly world is assured, permitting the transposition of masculine sub-texts to the status of the objective—for example, the insistent interest of male scientists in supposed sex differences in cognitive function.[15]

This boundary becomes visible as such as women challenge it. Women's studies may be acceptable when it is parked at a distance from the "real" intellectual world, but when it intrudes, as in Sheila McIntyre's case, the response is anger. For example, reports from a sociology course in which students who incorporated feminist interpretations into assignments got back comments saying, "I want standard sociological interpretations. None of this feminist nonsense." Or, from another university, a faculty member tells a student, "If you put any of that feminist rhetoric in your paper, I shall not mark it." From yet another university a student reported that when she asked questions challenging traditional views in other courses, her professor walked out of class.[16] Only by organizing gender exclusiveness could the illusion of a fully objective world of knowledge be sustained; only by denial and repression could a single socially constructed order of consciousness be read as truth.[17]

Rage and the Regime of Rationality

Thus rationality has been much more than an intellectual practice, it has been a highly masculinized organization of social relations on many dimensions. It has been for its practitioners in universities a social world excluding and demeaning the "trivial" world of women's existences. "Despite reason's articulated stance of separation from emotion and imagination, it has embedded itself in an emotional and imaginative substructure characterized largely by fear of, or aversion to, the 'feminine'" (Rooney, 1991:98). Its ongoing being as a social reality has aligned itself on a gender boundary; gender has been integral to its reality for participants and the gender boundary has been policed and defended in defence of rationality itself, for rationality has been well understood, though not theorized, by its practitioners as gendered regime. The rational subject has been constituted and sustained in gendered circuits dividing the scientific mind from experiencing being "in," rather than external to and dominating, nature. How men have known and know, have valued and value themselves and each other—who they have been and are—has relied and relies on, and is not separable from, the ongoing practical realization of the regime of rationality in their and other's lives. Men have come to count on the regime of rationality as the everyday settings and relations in which they exist as scientists, philosophers, public servants, and other participants. Its gendered organization has been taken for granted; it is the way the world is. A woman who claims, as a woman, to be a full participant in the regime of rationality has been and is a threat, an anomaly. She is more than deviant, she puts in question the very character of the order itself, the presuppositions on which it is based, its internal coherence. Crowing hens and whistling women let loose disorder on the world.

Rage is there as a response not from the outside but from within the university. Returning to Mary Douglas, we can begin to see what is at stake in what seems sometimes an extraordinary resistance in universities to full and equal intellectual participation of women. True, only the few express the rage, but tacitly they act representatively, they act for those whose silence is a tacit acceptance or whose attribution of responsibility to women supports them.

Feminist activists within the university have encountered the rage that arises from a threat to an order in which people's deep beings as subjects are implanted. Sheila McIntyre encountered that rage where principles of reasoned disputation are held most to apply. She is not alone. Rationality as a practice invites women to believe that it means what it says, but rationality as a gendered regime has defended itself savagely and irrationally against them.

Marc Lépine's rage was unleashed on women who had so far "forgotten" their sex as to be present and participating in the rational discipline of engineering. It surfaces for us a rage that is an endemic potential of the regime of rationality, a rage that responds to a threat to the modes of being men have taken for granted. Though official responses to the Montreal massacre have been of horror, grief, and dismay, elsewhere the massacre has added horrific force to expressions of repressive masculinity in university settings. In one such incident, among many, Celeste Brousseau, an engineering student at the University of Alberta, appeared shortly after the massacre on stage in an engineering school skit. She had been a public critic of sexism in the Faculty of Engineering. She was received by engineering students with chants of "shoot the bitch! Get her off stage!" (French, 1990). "Shoot the bitch" has a resonance post-massacre that it did not have before. It has been echoed on other university campuses in Canada. And though defining Lépine's act as the act of a madman is more decorous, such an interpretation carefully observes and reconstitutes the moral boundaries of an established order in which the gender-exclusive foundations of the regime of rationality survive. Other men are absolved and nothing changes.

But this has not been the only response. There is a contradiction between the principles of rational discourse and the gendered organization of the regime of rationality. As we've seen, it is this contradiction that has both given hope and in the past misled women into believing not just in reason but in the rationality of the regime in which rational discourse has been embedded. We believed that because the doors were open, we had only to step forward and through them. It has, of course, been this marvellous illusion that has led us women into this battle; it is a illusion that offered the promise of a truth it could not yet deliver.

The contradiction within the regime of rationality is real; if it is there for women, it is also there for men, and more and more men are aware of it. It is a contradiction that is experienced, though in different ways, by those excluded by their non-European origin. I am among those who believe that the universality of principles of rationality entail just those struggles that are currently sometimes conducted under the banner of post-modernity. I believe that rationality bears with it an implicit but necessary challenge to the irrationality of the gendered and Euro-centric regime that has been institutionalized in our universities and other sites of cultural and intellectual creation and reproduction. This isn't a battle to be fought only by women or members of non-European ethnic origins. We all have something at stake here; we all have something to win—the final opening up of the potential of what was, after all, in its time, an Enlightenment only for the few.

It is vital that men too become active in unpicking the gendered regime of rationality institutionalized in universities and colleges—the irrationality at the foundations of rationality: the masculinist privilege of treating young women as sexual objects rather than as colleagues or future professionals; the established conventions of classroom discrimination; the so-called "academic freedom" to speak sexism or racism in the classroom; the ordinary institutions of exclusion practices through hiring and promotion; the stag effect. The fabric is densely knitted[18] and will take some work to unpick. Women take and have taken risks with their careers and many have lost out because they have fought such battles from vulnerable positions. Yet the gains we have made, though slow and difficult, have been real.

We can work together, women and men, to remake these institutions. To men, I have this to say: This struggle is for the reality of what men in the past have denied themselves; it is a struggle to realize what the Enlightenment promised from the beginning—the rule of reason, not authority, the equality of reasoning subjects. To women, I have this to say: Do not be afraid. The saying I quoted at the beginning is a threat; it is telling women, if you act against patriarchal order, you will unleash an impersonal patriarchal rage. But the devil, the rage, the Marc Lépines succeed only if we are terrorized into silence and inaction. After all, we want a new kind of order in which hens may crow if they will and women can surely whistle. If the massacre in Montreal tells us what we are up against, it also tells us how effective we have been and how far we have come, we whistling women.

NOTES

1　This paper was originally presented as the "Hawthorne Lecture for 1990" at the annual meetings of the Canadian Sociology and Anthropology Association (CSAA), University of Victoria.

2　At this point as I spoke, I could see some in the audience laughing. They were asking, I suppose, "How could we have been so naive?" Ah well, we were. Perhaps it's just as well. We might never have got going if we had known just how tough it was going to be and what we were up against. But at that time we thought all we had to do was to explain the position clearly and to demonstrate the existence of injustices. I should have learned better from my experience at the University of California at Berkeley in the 1960s. The beginnings of the Free Speech Movement at Berkeley were entirely framed by the same belief. A leading figure, Mario Savio, a graduate student in physics, believed that the university authorities only needed to be convinced of the rationality and justice of the arguments for free speech on the university campus. The demonstrations were intended to appeal beyond the immediate obstructionism of the university authorities to a broader public commitment to these same principles. Progressive disillusion in the moral and political virtue and wisdom of established authorities was a profoundly significant component of the political transformations that followed.

3　See Émile Durkheim's discussion of reactions of deviating behaviour as constitutive of the moral order and as mobilizing the collective sentiments to sustain it.

4　I have depended quite heavily in this section on two books: one is an historical study by Londa Schiebinger called *The Mind Has No Sex? Women in the Origins of Modern Science* (Schiebinger, 1989) and the other is a book by Genevieve Lloyd called *The Man of Reason: Male and Female in Western Philosophy* (Lloyd, 1984).

[5] Thanks to Cathy Boyd-Withers for calling my attention to these passages quoted by Caroline Merchant.

[6] In Newton's life women appear twice, once as mother, and once as elderly women who cleaned his rooms at then celibate Oxford.

[7] Thus "mind" is constituted as a specialized mode of the activity of subjects embedded in discursive relationships that provide the social and material substructure of rationality.

[8] Descartes himself corresponded actively and without condescension with women who wanted to learn from him.

[9] A recent study of the teaching of mathematics and science to girls in British secondary schools describes forceful means adopted by boys to assert their monopoly of the science classroom:

> Our more qualitative observations showed that there were marked differences in the way girls and boys behaved in class. Where resources such as apparatus were limited, boys seemed to assume that they had automatic priority. They would exercise this priority by grabbing the equipment or, if a girl got there first, by breathing down her neck until she relinquished the desired object. Boys were reluctant to wait for the teacher's attention and frequently pushed the queues or called out answers before their turn (Kelly et al., 1984:33).

Such behaviour was apparently unrestrained and uncorrected by the teachers.

[10] See Claire Robertson, Constance Dyer and D'Ann Campbell's study of sexual harassment policies and procedures at "institutions of higher learning" in the United States. They write that "[t]here is a great deal of nervousness, bafflement, tension, fear, and sometimes outright hostility involved when the subject of sexual harassment is raised among university personnel" (Robertson, Dyer and Campbell, 1988:799).

[11] See also my discussion of masculinism as an ideology of domination in "Gender, power and peace" (Smith, 1989).

[12] See also an earlier paper on the same topic by Janice Moulton (Moulton, 1983).

[13] The gender sub-texts of Kuhn's theory of paradigms in science remain to be explored. O'Rand's exploration of the "thought styles" in the scientific construction of gender inequality is suggestive in this respect (O'Rand, 1989).

[14] The irony has been that what women on the margins may have done with their freedom has in the past been depreciated and appropriated, as Caroline Herschel's discoveries were appropriated by her brother.

[15] There are many feminist critiques. A recent critique of particular interest shifts from issues of reasoning and fact to problems of the "thought styles" involved (O'Rand, 1989).

[16] Constance Backhouse and her co-authors report a similar experience. A respondent who had extensive publications in the area of feminism and had received prestigious academic awards reported that graduate students were actively discouraged from working with her. One senior male faculty member told his class that she was "incompetent" and another cast aspersions on her

"academic integrity." Further, her department Chair had denied her the academic freedom to identify her area of research in the departmental graduate brochure, and she was refused permission to teach graduate courses (Backhouse et al., 1989:20). This situation was finally disallowed by the university.

[17]   The same reasoning applies, of course, to issues of race and class. They are, however, institutionalized quite differently.

[18]   Even felted.

THE DECLINE OF FACULTY INFLUENCE: CONFRONTING THE EFFECTS OF THE CORPORATE AGENDA

Janice Newson

Over the past year or so, some members of the academic community have expressed alarm about the corporate/business oriented direction being pursued by Canadian university administrations and encouraged by government policy. Although the trend in this direction has been underway for some time, it is only very recently that the effects of the trend appear to have created sufficient impact and visibility to draw the attention of these concerned academics.

For example, in his regular column in the OCUFA Forum, Professor Bill Graham of the University of Toronto and President of the Ontario Confederation of University Faculty Associations, has been arguing that the university needs to assume a more active and presumably independent role "in shaping public policy and culture," because "business, industry and government...are becoming more successful in defining the role of universities and the purposes of post-secondary education to suit their own interests" (1989:2). Graham argues that, as a consequence, intellectuals in society are not as effective sources of public information as they should be. He refers to Russell Jacoby's book, *The Last Intellectuals*, to support his argument. Jacoby believes that public intellectuals are a "dying breed," having been replaced by "high tech intellectuals, consultants and professors who may be 'more than competent' but who do not enrich public life."

Although Jacoby's book is about the state of intellectual life in the United States, Graham says the same danger exists today in Canada. He particularly cites as an example an Ontario report published by the Premier's Council, *Competing in the New Global Economy*. Among other things, the report argues that public culture needs to become an "entrepreneurial culture" and "while education and training are often seen as social programs, they are really investments in our economic future." Graham points out that the report says nothing about personal development, creativity, cultural enrichment, or fundamentally changing social relationships so as to ensure freedom and equality for all. Graham calls upon his colleagues—"the voices of university professors"—to become more involved in "forming and informing" public policy and thereby challenging the "narrow instrumental determinism of the predatory economic vision of the future."

In a similar vein, Professor John McMurtry, a philosopher at the University of Guelph, claims that the language and the methods of the corporate market have infested academe and transformed once ivory-towered academics into "players for sale." His argument for eschewing this trend is that the logic of the market and the logic of education don't mix, that in fact, they are contradictory. The principles that benefit markets undermine the objectives of education and, conversely, education that achieves its intended purposes cannot serve well as a marketable commodity.

Professor Michael Locke of the University of Western Ontario has also added his voice to the small but growing chorus of academics who are concerned about a corporate takeover of the university (1990:8-16). Locke's viewpoint is especially interesting since, as a zoologist involved in cell science, he is reacting from the perspective of a natural scientist who has carried out research that is instrumental in the creation of marketable products and who therefore might be more favourable than academics who work in the social sciences and humanities to links between the university and private sector corporations.

Locke refers to the present trend in universities as signifying "the rise of edubis." He defines "edubis" essentially as an approach to managing the university, one which "assesses the value of a university to society in figures on its balance sheet with the short term objective of feeding its graduates into the job market." He outlines the indications of this trend which have recently emerged at his own university but which members of many other Canadian university communities will easily recognize. For example, managerial expansion which, he argues, is advancing at a much faster rate than the increase in faculty members or students; a managerial campaign to get faculty member subscriptions to American Express cards; the installation of an expensive campus telephone system without consulting the faculty; the increase of in-house university publications devoted to "management empire building"; contracting business professionals to give seminars to faculty members on how to use their time more efficiently and productively; the increase in large, well-furnished, and well-serviced managerial office space in contrast to the small spaces allocated to faculty offices and the crowded and deteriorating classrooms. Locke views these developments as illustrating the degree to which the voice of the university no longer reflects the values of academe. Instead, the importation of business values by the excessive influence of business people is leading to a decline of academic influence and a decline in ethical standards.

It is indeed a relief to witness members of the academic community finally beginning to react to the impact of the advancement of "the corporate agenda"[1] for universities. When Howard Buchbinder and I first began to write in the early 1980s about a shift in higher education policy and the vulnerability of the academy to being carried along by it, we were often accused of overstating the potential effects of a relatively minor or marginal development and of speaking from an "anti-business" or, even worse, "turgid Marxist" position. Some of our colleagues argued that the university has always, or at least for a long time, served an economic/technological development purpose. Furthermore, they insisted that nothing is particularly different nor harmful about the renewal of a "societal" interest in ensuring that universities pay their way by contributing to economic growth and technological progress. Most important, the renewed attempt to forge new links between universities and the corporate sector will not prevent the university from continuing to serve its more traditional purposes as well, they argued. As to the changes in the organization of academic work that Buchbinder and I associated with the renewed emphasis on serving the needs of the corporate sector, some of our critics argued that these changes were perhaps more characteristic of our own university, rather than representing a pattern of changes that are affecting universities on a broad scale.

With regard to the latter point, Graham, McMurtry, and Locke's recent contributions to the debate suggest otherwise. Graham and Locke speak from the experience of two of the older, more established universities in the province of Ontario. As well, we have heard descriptions similar to Michael Locke's portrayal of edubis from colleagues at other universities across the country—some large and some small, some considered to be more prestigious and others less so. All of them support a major conclusion about the effect of changes in the organization of academic work that Buchbinder and I drew in *The University Means Business*. That is, that the viewpoint and collective interests of academic workers in universities are being increasingly marginalized in the emerging decision-making processes.

But what precisely does this process of "marginalization" mean or add up to, and how does the understanding of the political position of faculty members in the universities of the 1990s help us to formulate a political strategy in response to "the corporate takeover"? Is it the case that a more influential and centrally involved faculty would have responded differently to the pressures that led the university into the current situation as described by Graham, McMurtry, and Locke and, if that situation were rectified, would lead us in a different direction now, with those same pressures in place? Those who experience the loss of influence and who believe that the increasing attendance to corporate needs and business methods are leading the university in a wrong or too narrow direction will be tempted to respond in the affirmative. But such a conclusion can only be drawn if we ignore many of the underlying complexities. My purpose in this paper is to expose some of these complexities and thereby to show that simply enjoining faculty members to reassert their claims to professional or collegial dominance in the university is an insufficient strategy for reversing the process that is now underway.

The Roots of Marginalization

The process whereby academic interests have been increasingly marginalized in university affairs is not, as Graham and Locke imply, a recent result of "the corporate takeover" as much as it is a pre-condition of it. In fact, the decline in collective faculty influence[2] can be located, in the first instance, in the institutional changes that accompanied the financial turnaround of the 1970s. Two of these changes are of special importance: the expansion and differentiation of university administrations, and the development of collective bargaining within the university. Whereas the offices of presidents and deans have long existed as features of the administrative structure of universities, in the 1970s we find increasing numbers of vice-presidents, associate deans, and professional-managerial staff (a kind of university "civil service") supporting the activity of these major administrative offices. By the 1980s, whole departments in charge of such areas as Human Resources, External Relations, Research, Development—often under the direction of their own vice-president—became commonplace on most campuses. In the context of budgetary shortfall, administrative expansion might seem to have been an illogical or contradictory response. However, it was precisely the budgetary situation that provided the justification for the expansion. "Tough decisions" had to be made and those who held administrative posts, such as deans and presidents, often argued that "the collegium" had too much vested interest to be able to take these decisions. In order to survive the financial crisis, it was argued, administrative leadership was needed that transcended the particular interests of departments, programmes, divisions, and even faculties. As well as growing in size and in scope of decision-making, "the administration" began to establish an agenda that was distinct from the agenda of "the collegium"[3] and increasingly turned its face outward, to constituencies external to the university itself, in developing its managerial approaches and priorities.

Ironically, the creation of differentiated administrative agendas and activities was facilitated by the second major institutional change of this period, the introduction of collective bargaining into the university. On the one hand, the faculty and other university employees undertook collective bargaining as a means of protecting themselves from the dangers of budgetary cutbacks and of preserving their roles in the decision-making process in the face of increasingly interventionist and expansionist administrations. But, on the other hand, collective agreements also legitimated the existence of the administration as a separate entity and provided the vehicle for operationalizing its agenda, as one of the two contractual partners. The division of the academic work force into separate bargaining units or sections of bargaining units depending on part-time versus full-time status; the various methods of distinguishing the research, service, and teaching functions of academic work so that ultimately each could serve as the basis for different job categories with different pay scales, perquisites, and protections—all contributed to the fragmentation of the academic work force and the marginalization of academic workers.[4]

Buchbinder and I have argued that these institutional changes created a condition of political vulnerability for the university, in which the seeds of the "corporate agenda" could germinate and take root.[5] This political vulnerability is more complex than simply the result of overbearing administrators with wrong values who are able through increased numbers to outvote the faculty on various decision-making bodies. Such a narrow understanding of political vulnerability frequently underlies the diagnosis offered by faculty members who decry the current state of affairs in universities. They point to the expanding numbers of administrators and their increasing control over resources. They argue that these administrators not only have values and orientations towards the university that are significantly different from members of the academy, but also, do not consult sufficiently with the faculty in making their decisions. The proposed cure for the problem stated in this way is to re-establish the basis of faculty influence and to urge faculty members to renew their participation in various bodies and positions so that a uniquely "academic" perspective on decisions will be restored.

Locke's account of the rise of edubis is a good example of this kind of reasoning. For example, Locke argues that "a university inevitably comes to reflect the values of its administration" (1990:8). In other words, the administrators are "the key players" in shaping the ethos of the university and, hence, many of its activities. He says that in the past, university administrations were peopled by, often distinguished, academics "who understood history and the role of the university." Edubis has arisen because administrations are now comprised of professional managers who, even if they have academic credentials and experience, are "would be business executives." As well, with the expansion of the administrative structure, "minor managers" often speak on behalf of the university and are not censured from doing so by presidents even though their statements are often ill-informed and do not reflect an understanding of the historic role of the university. Locke also argues that the prevailing administrative approach in universities is not even good business. He characterizes the centralized decision-making that has been implemented by many self-interested university administrations as out of step with the more up-to-date decentralizing approaches advocated in the modern corporate world.

Locke's frustration with a style of management that reduces decisions about class sizes, faculty workloads, testing students' knowledge, and how to register students for courses to issues of technical efficiency undoubtedly speaks to the concerns of many faculty members. I agree with many of his observations about the current situation that support the view that administrators have increased their political influence within the university and are undermining the influence of the faculty.[6] However, I will outline several important reasons why the current emphasis of many Canadian universities on meeting corporate needs and mirroring corporate procedures cannot be simply reduced to the whims and values of a new breed of administrator-manager, and why the replacement of these managers with "more enlightened" academic leaders is not a sufficient strategy for counteracting what Locke and others see as the undermining of the real purposes of the university.

1. Why a New Managerial Style?

First of all, the changes in university administration cannot be explained in terms of a *coup d'etat* through which a new kind of administrator simply appeared magically or spontaneously on the scene. More important, what Locke and others tend to represent as a change of "style" needs to be understood more fundamentally as a new approach to, and purpose of, administration in the university. Specific social, economic, and political pressures underlie the emergence of this new system of managing universities. These pressures include the political priority that is being given to increasing Canada's economic competitiveness in the world market—a process often summarized in the term "globalization." Replacing university administrators with more enlightened people who understand the role and history of the university does not address these pressures, particularly insofar as they project a somewhat different role for the university in the twenty-first century, one which narrowly concentrates on developing co-operative links with the private sector in order to enhance worker productivity and technological innovation. These pressures will remain even for the more enlightened academic leaders that Locke envisages.[7]

The fact that even the most enlightened and academically dedicated administrator could not, in the face of these pressures, practise administration in a way that is organically connected to her or his local university community[8] was graphically brought home to Buchbinder and me when we visited British universities in 1985, following the budgetary cutbacks that seriously affected almost all universities in Britain. We interviewed twenty-five to thirty high-ranking university administrators at a variety of British universities. In almost every interview, we were told of the pressures on administrators to change their approach to administration from "serving the collegium" to being pro-active formulators of university policy directions. They repeatedly referred to the change from "administration" to "management," the former designating a more passive approach to implementing policy that is set by the British equivalents of academic councils and senates, and the latter designating an active role in formulating policies and objectives. And although some of these managers greeted this pressure to change with trepidation and concern while others greeted it with a sense of excitement and approval, all of them affirmed that the change in approach could not be resisted.

2. More than a Change of Style

Second, while certain aspects of the change in university administrations that have taken place over the past decade or so are easily recognized, some of the more important features are not. For example, the articles by Locke, Graham, and McMurtry identify a change in style and size. Locke points out that administrative offices have sprung up seemingly overnight. Many of these offices have been created to co-ordinate and control specialized services, some of which were once embodied in the work carried out by faculty members (e.g., student advising, co-ordinating research projects) and some of which are new creations of a more corporate-looking and outwardly directed administrative apparatus (e.g., public relations offices, technology transfer centres). But most academics have not recognized these changes as representing a whole new "system" of managing universities.[9] Marguerite Cassin and Graham Morgan's discussion later in this section focuses specifically on this system of management. It involves a significant transformation in the actual processes of making decisions in universities. I do not claim to be able at present to fully explicate this transformation but I will outline one of its most significant features.

Put simply, this transformation has consisted in a shift from oral contestation to textual manipulation and interpretation as a central tool for accomplishing the task of management in the universities of the 1990s.[10] Discussion and debates over objectives, priorities, and policies in the various fora of the university, such as departmental meetings, faculty councils and senates have been replaced by a complicated process of constructing documents such as five-year plans, mission statements, and collective agreements. Constructing and applying the texts of these documents are the means by which a wide array of actions are brought within the control of centrally guided policies. These documents do not only define, but they actually constitute, the relationships that exist among the various units of the university.

For example, the process by which a five-year plan is created defines and constitutes the relationship of academic departments to the higher level planning committees which are directed, if not chaired by, senior members of the administration. Whereas academic departments create versions of the five-year plan in which they make recommendations about curricula and staffing based on their own assessments of academic and pedagogic needs, the higher level planning committees construct the operative five-year plan, that is, the plan according to which resources are allocated.

Academics in most Canadian universities are by now familiar with these documentary forms of decision-making. But familiarity doesn't mean that the decisions which result make sense to them. On the contrary, many academics are mystified by the results of five-year planning processes. For example, they see little or no correspondence between the five-year plan they participated in creating and the five-year plan that actually controls the allocation of resources. Nevertheless, the process appears as one in that academics participate, as members of departments, faculty councils, senates, and various associated committees.

The political strategies previously adopted by academics to influence decision-making are not effective in relation to this kind of decision-making via documents. For example, ensuring that the representation of faculty members is not outweighed by administrators on bodies like faculty councils and senates assumes that the critical decisions are made in these bodies. Although these bodies continue to be assigned a final approval role in the "decision-making by documents" process, this approval is relatively inconsequential in the actual shaping of the text of the documents. For one thing, the fact that "decision-making" is taking place at all is obscured in a process that appears to be operating on its own.[11] Documents are shuffled from committee to committee according to each committee's prescribed terms of reference, and the contribution that a committee or body can make is restricted ahead of time by its specific mandate or function in the process. Faculty councils, senates, planning committees, and so forth are nodes in the process that is designed for transforming the document, rather than being institutional fora for debating matters of principle and policy.

Obscuring the decision-making process also makes it difficult to know where or how to apply political pressure. For example, the changes that take place in five-year plans between the time they leave academic departments until the time that the "operative" five-year plan is adopted cannot be explained simply in terms of how representatives voted in the bodies that approve the plan at various stages. These bodies usually do not have access to the original submissions on which the final plan is based and, if they do, they do not have access to the process by which the original documents were transformed into the document they are asked to approve.

3. Undermining Collegial Structures

A third reason that the current "business oriented" trend will not be counteracted simply by replacing managers with enlightened academic leaders or even by reasserting faculty influence is that significant changes are taking place in the internal political structures through which the faculty have exerted their influence in the past.[12] These changes are taking place privately, without fanfare or open debate. They are driven by the very instruments that are being used to forge new links between the university and the corporate sector.

For example, let us consider the effects of the participation of individual faculty members in specific partnerships with corporate clients. On the surface, these partnerships appear to be nothing more than a straightforward exchange of one kind of resource for another; namely, funding from the corporate client in exchange for the expert focus of a faculty member on a particular scientific innovation or application. The idea and the reality of such partnerships is not entirely new to the university. Contract research and consulting has been a source of additional income to faculty members for some time, especially those appointed to science faculties and professional schools. However, these partnerships are taking on new forms that have significant implications for the organization of academic work itself. I won't try to outline all of these new forms or all of their implications.[13] I will discuss only two examples here to make the point.

Faculty members become owners or part owners of private research companies that may be based in their own campus offices or labs. Graduate students who are taken on as their research assistants, at the same time are involved in an academic apprenticeship relationship as part of their educational programme, and in an employer-employee relationship as a research worker in a private company. As employees, the work they are required to do is aimed towards the creation of a product for sale, even though it may have little value as an aid to their education. As well, because the company is engaged in marketing its products in competition with other companies, the graduate students are sometimes asked, sometimes required, to maintain secrecy about their research in the lab/company, and even to delay publication of their theses until the patents can be obtained on discoveries that have a marketable application. The intellectual character of graduate education is compromised thereby, and academic policies and guidelines about the open publication of findings and free access to intellectual ideas are bypassed in the interest of enhancing the business potential of these hybrid research "companies."

Moreover, the host university may also own shares in these companies.[14] In such cases, serious conflicts of interest can arise—for example, in allocating resources within the university. Those who control the university's resources will be tempted to ensure the viability of companies in which they hold a financial interest as against other research programmes that show no financial profit. Even more threatening to the preservation of free inquiry is the possibility that other faculty members might be prevented from pursuing investigations that challenge or criticize the research being undertaken by the profit-making company.

Whether on campus or in nearby research parks, these private companies are staffed by faculty members and other university-appointed researchers such as doctoral or post-doctoral students, and by research scientists who are hired, or contributed to the company, by corporate partners. The non-university scientists, in turn, are often appointed as "adjunct" members of the university collegium, even though they have not been hired through an academic appointments process. They may even become voting members of the departments and faculties in which they hold adjunct status. However, as employees of a private company rather than the university, their political weight is most likely to be used to support the interests of their company. Their voting presence within departments and faculties can significantly affect the political balance within the collegium.

One specific case will illustrate how this shift of balance takes place and how established academic procedures can be undermined in order to accommodate the interests of these private companies. A professor who owns a private in-house research company wanted one of the industrial researchers involved in his company to be given adjunct status in his department and faculty. The advantage of having such status is that an adjunct can apply for research funds and thereby enhance the financial support available to the research of the private company. His department members refused to grant the status because they felt that the industrial researcher was not sufficiently qualified. The professor then sought the support of the administration who, over the head of the department, granted adjunct status to the industrial researcher. The administration then sent research applications submitted by the new adjunct to the departmental Chair to be signed. On the advice of his Executive Committee, the Chair refused to sign. Shortly thereafter, the central administration proceeded to create two new contractually limited positions in the department, specifying that the industrial researchers employed in the private company must be considered eligible for these positions because the positions were going to be funded by monies made available through the professor's private company. One condition attached to the creation of these two positions was that the professor who owns the private company must be a member of the department's hiring committee, thereby undermining the department's normal procedure of naming its own hiring committee.[15] Because the department was desperately in need of additional staff, the opportunity of having two new positions, even on a contractual basis, drew support from some. Others were opposed because they were concerned that the professor's area of research, which represented only one of a number of facets of their discipline, would acquire more political influence than it should have. As well, they were concerned that, if the employees of the professor were hired, they would always vote to support his views and would not be politically independent of him. Ultimately, in a close vote of a minority of department members, the department agreed to accept the contractually limited positions and the hiring conditions.

This case illustrates how these links between the university and the corporate sector introduce and support relationships between individual academics and corporate clients that supersede relationships among academic colleagues as members together of a collegial structure. These relationships are aided and supported in turn by that branch of the central administration that is mandated to encourage and develop collaborations with the corporate sector. The normal relations between the administration and lower level decision-making units are bypassed in these arrangements.[16] The central administration acts on behalf of those who participate in them, if and when their collegial units attempt to assert their interests in, and concerns about, the effects of such arrangements.

The undermining of normal collegial structures is further extended by the Centres of Excellence programmes developed by governments as means both of influencing, if not controlling, the research agendas of universities and of securing the financial and institutional involvement of private corporations. The distinguished Canadian metallurgist and spokesperson on science policy, Ursula Franklin, is especially concerned with the way that Centres of Excellence remove the accountability of academic scientists to their peers and to the public at large. Academic researchers are seconded to these centres, not as members of the collegium but as highly skilled experts in a field. The priorities of the Centre's research programme are established within the Centre itself in interaction between the academic researchers and the industrial scientists. Although the Centre is based in the university, it has no links to the academic policy-making structures. It is not accountable to these structures and it is not subject to the policies that normally guide research and scholarly work within the university.[17]

4. Shifting the Scholarly Agenda

Perhaps the most critical reason that the "business-oriented" trend will not be counteracted simply by changing the composition of university management is that the priorities and criteria of the corporate agenda are being embedded in the very judgements that are made about which research projects and intellectual quests will be taken up by academics; in other words, about the content of social knowledge itself. How intellectual questions are identified and selected is a very complex process, involving individual faculty members as well as their colleagues in peer reviews, administrations, members of granting councils, and others. I will not attempt to fully explore this issue here, but rather will especially focus on the implications of this "skewing" effect on the social sciences and more particularly sociology.

Many academics have not questioned how their own intellectual pursuits are deeply affected by the corporate direction in higher education policy. Social scientists, for example, may not see themselves on the frontline of scientific breakthroughs that will attract financial backing from corporate sponsors who foresee the possibility of a "marketable product" arising from specific scientific applications, and therefore, they may believe that they are insulated from these effects. Nevertheless, the language of "corporate relevance" and the emphasis on measurable "productivity" and "efficiency" have entered the domain of social science departments and research agencies.[18] For example, the "Centres of Excellence" concept has been incorporated into the social sciences and humanities community with the same rationale as is used in natural sciences, even though the justification for such centres[19] may not apply to, and may even undermine, the research processes of the social sciences and humanities. SSHRCC's recent adoption of "track record" as the means of determining which research applicants have the greatest chance of being "productive" flies in the face of what is known about scholarly work in the social sciences; namely, that many superior contributions have been made at advanced stages of career, when a scholar is able to synthesize and draw together the insights of years of study, reflection, and reading.[20]

Perhaps the most disturbing example of how the social sciences are being absorbed into the market-driven university model is in the transformed meaning of the word "relevance" as it is applied to the research interests of both faculty members and students in universities. In the 1960s, the term "relevance" became a watchword of the student movement in asserting that the university is only of value to society to the extent that it is able to shed light on the key issues of the time, including issues of social justice, militarism, economic inequality, and so on. However, in the age of the corporate agenda for universities, "relevance" has increasingly become a pseudonym for developing knowledge that will have a practical application in the service of economic growth and technological innovation. Claire Polster's paper in this section tracks these changes in the language, priorities, and rationales of higher education policy statements over the past two decades. The danger for sociology as for many other disciplines resides not so much in the way economic and technological priorities may come to define what research does get done, but also what does not get done. In the situation of resource scarcity that currently exists, the pluralist solution no longer holds sway: resources are not sufficient to support a variety of priorities. More importantly, resource scarcity provides a useful justification for rejecting research applications, graduate student admission files, and job applicants whose interests don't conform to the new orthodoxy of relevance, efficiency, and productivity.

I recently organized a workshop for graduate students on applying sociological insight to practical and political concerns. The approximately thirty Ph.D. and M.A. students were asked to state their current research interests and to indicate whether and how their interests related to practical or political concerns. Almost all of them indicated that their interests arose out of a practical or political concern, even though many of their projects also took up important, even abstract, theoretical issues within the discipline. Even more interesting, most students stated that they were involved with a community, social service, or political organization that was actively addressing these concerns. Yet, in spite of the fact that these students are already engaged in highly "relevant" investigations, some faculty members have begun to argue for the necessity of directing students towards more "practical" research interests through seeking out corporate clients who will be willing to fund their research. Clearly, the issue here is not "relevance" but who can pay! Most if not all of the groups that the graduate students are presently "servicing" are not able to financially support their research contribution. They are fledgling organizations struggling with volunteer labour and shrinking grants to pay for office space and equipment.[21] Certainly a student might take a research interest in a project of concern to a corporation, but why should the corporation have privileged access to research assistance from a publicly funded institution simply because it is able to pay for it? Moreover, it is extremely rare to find a corporate donor who wants to participate in these kinds of arrangements and who will not want to have considerable influence in the parameters of the research project and its objectives.[22]

Turning towards private paying clients as a way of solving the university's funding problems could seriously undermine the kind of "free" and free-wheeling research that has enabled sociologists for generations to develop an analysis of society that gives space to the "underlife," to the perspectives of the poor, of deviant populations, of the politically disenfranchised, of marginal communities, and of "the unofficial." This threat to sociology's critical edge is not only posed by the research priorities embedded in specific academic–corporate client partnerships. More pertinent, it is also posed by the emphasis on "efficiency," "productivity," "more bang for buck," and narrowly defined "relevance" which has entered into the distribution of public research monies.[23]

Conclusion

My main objectives in this paper have been to show, first, how the "marginalization of the faculty" in the decision-making processes of the university is rooted in complex changes that must be understood as more than simply the adoption by university administrators of a corporate style of management. Second, I have argued that these changes are closely interwoven with efforts to forge new links between universities and the corporate sector. Third, I have suggested that these changes are having a significant effect on the organization of academic work, its content, and the political ability of university-based intellectuals to maintain a critical perspective in the practice of their disciplines. I have also tried to show why the call to academics to renew their influence in formulating the policy directions of the university, although praiseworthy in some respects, is not a sufficient response to these changes.

That call is insufficient for a reason that is even more problematic than those I have already outlined, namely, that these changes have proceeded with the support and participation of academics themselves. Bill Graham's urging that academics become more involved in shaping public policy assumes that academics will oppose the present trend in higher education policy that he describes as being pursued by "business, industry and government." Yet many academics have been highly influential in arguing for the implementation of the "corporate agenda" and in policy directions that are closely linked to it. It is not new for academics to be the agents and even initiators of trends that appear to be located in political, economic, and social forces external to the academy. Dorothy Smith's analysis of the "regime of rationality" illustrates how the academic establishment has been implicated for several centuries in what she terms "the relations of ruling."

In the present context, for example, academics have all too quickly accepted the political and financial trade-off that was originally proposed by Judith Maxwell and Stephanie Currie in *Partnership for Growth*, namely, that government underfunding requires universities to be more willing to accommodate to corporate sector needs and to market-oriented pressures in exchange for corporate sector funding. They have actively helped to provide justifications for this new arrangement and to calm or dismiss fears that others may have about any potential negative consequences.[24] The participation of academics is also central to implementing the "corporate agenda": in forming corporate-university partnerships of various kinds, in developing the proposals for setting up Centres of Excellence, in participating in decisions about which research or teaching priorities ought to be pursued, and in establishing the rationales, if not the procedures, for the various documentary processes of decision-making that limit collective academic influence.

Most importantly, forging ties between universities and private corporations is part of a broader political-economic agenda in which the state has performed a critical role.[25] Academics have lent their expertise and scientific authority to justifying changes in government policies that go along with re-shaping the university to serve the interests of economic growth and technological innovation. For example, very recently in higher education circles in Canada, public policy in regard to tuition fees and the extent to which students and their families should be asked to bear the financial cost of university education has been a focus of renewed discussion. Leonard Minsky and David Noble, in discussing recent developments in universities in the United States,[26] argue that there is a direct link between the proliferation of university-industry research ties and increases in tuition fees charged to students. They say that the increased emphasis on commercializing academic research has required a reallocation of university funds to support increasingly expensive research personnel and equipment. At the same time, tuition fees have been increased to cover the higher costs of maintaining institutions of higher education even though cutbacks have taken place in the services available to students. Students are being asked to pay more for a lower quality education and, according to Noble and Minsky, members of racial and ethnic minorities have been experiencing reduced access to a university education.

This link between the proliferation of university-industry research ties and the broader social policy issue of access to higher education can be uncovered in recent discussions of tuition fees in Canada. Although I cannot pursue a detailed analysis of this link here, suffice it to say that academics on the whole have neither been outspoken in voicing their opposition to proposals for increasing tuition fees, nor have they been as quick as they might be about defending the broader and underlying issue of accessibility.[27] In fact, some academics have helped to provide a "scientific" basis for, in the first instance, de-coupling the consideration of tuition fee increases from their effects on accessibility and, in the second instance, replacing the priority once assigned to accessibility with a priority on "quality."[28]

For those who believe that academics need to reassert their voices in the formation of important public policies, the perplexing question is how we can be sure that the greater influence of academics will produce different, presumably "better" and "more enlightened," policy than that which is presently guiding the development of higher education in Canada? Those of us who share concerns about the potential and actual effects of current policy directions on the university must begin to confront the fact that the influence of academics as professionals is significantly different from their collective influence as academic workers within the institutional decision-making processes of universities.[29] And some, perhaps many, academics like it that way. Others, without really reflecting on it, have retreated from the more contentious and often discouraging institutional arena into the quieter, if not more rewarding, sphere of their own professional development. In the meantime, decisions about university objectives, programme priorities, and institutional connections continue to carry us more and more towards the market-oriented university that, only a few years ago, appeared to many as a "marginal" development—one that would have little if any impact on the nature of the university as an institution devoted to free inquiry and critical reflection.

NOTES

---

[1]   A description of this agenda is found in *The University Means Business: Universities, Corporations and Academic Work* (Toronto: Garamond, 1988). The use of the term "agenda" does not imply a consciously orchestrated conspiracy. Rather, it refers to a view of the role and functions of the university that gives priority and emphasis to meeting needs that will promote private sector economic development and technological innovation. This view is shared and actively promoted by a diverse collection of interest groups including members of the corporate community, policy makers, politicians, university officials, and academics.

[2]   This comment implies that a greater degree of faculty influence previously existed. Buchbinder and I have argued that the comparative affluence and expansion of the university system during the 1950s and 1960s created opportunities for the faculty collectively to formally extend their influence in university decision-making. This extended formal influence does not necessarily mean that the influence of power of individual faculty members was greater than in earlier historical periods.

[3]   Buchbinder and I have used the term "differentiated" to refer to this aspect of the change in administration. In previous periods, although presidents and deans wielded considerable power and influence in university decision-making, this power and influence usually claimed legitimacy in terms of the dean's or president's leadership *within* the relationship *to* the collegium; not, as has now become commonly accepted, as the "chief executive officer" or as holding the senior position in an administrative apparatus that often looks outside the university for direction.

[4]   This is not an argument against the unionization of the faculty. In the face of budgetary retrenchment and what at the time was perceived as only the threat of administrative expansion and encroachment, unionization was a necessary defensive manoeuvre. However, as I and Buchbinder have argued elsewhere, unionization also provided a means for dividing the academic work force and for legitimating the administration's claims to a separate role in decision-making. Moreover, it provided the means for articulating distinctively administrative criteria and interests in various decision-making processes.

[5]   This is not to deny the fact that the advance of the corporate agenda accentuates and extends further the marginalization process.

[6]   Locke's implicit model of how universities function is very similar to analyses contained in an extensive literature on the university as an organization that was produced in the 1960s and 1970s, largely based on the American experience. A major objective of these studies was to provide a rational account of the functioning of universities for policy makers and other interested outside observers who often perceived them as anarchic, irrational, and unmanaged

institutions. They tended to focus on describing the various "structures of decision-making" such as the collegial structure consisting of senates, faculty councils, and departments, and the "administrative structure" consisting of boards of governors, presidents, deans, and their staffs. As a whole this literature shared the view that universities are, or appear to be, inefficient and irrational because they embody different and inherently contradictory models of organization. Some authors defended this multi-structured form of organization even while conceding its inefficiency while others argued that change is needed. Not surprisingly, these investigations often provided policy makers with a scientific basis for viewing the crisis of the university as a result of the inefficient and irrational use of resources. The frequent conclusion drawn and acted on was that universities need to be organizationally streamlined and the administration needs to assert more effective leadership. George Keller's book *Academic Strategy* is a good example.

In spite of the fact that these studies purported to be about the way universities function, they did not explain the decision-making process itself; that is, they didn't explain how, and on what basis, decision-making and therefore management is accomplished, given the complex organizational features of universities.

[7]   Although I would agree with Locke that the relationship between presidents and deans and the academic collegium as reflected in departments, faculty councils, senates, and even individual academics that characterized pre-1970 universities is preferable in specific ways to the present situation, I don't want to join in romanticizing the associated style of academic administrative leadership. It was often patronizing, arbitrary, and reflected a hierarchical rather than a communal exercise of authority that favoured particular factions and cliques.

Nevertheless, another obvious observation, which is compatible with Locke's complaints about present-day university managers, is that it is not likely anyway that individuals who correspond to Locke's view of enlightened academic leaders will be successful in competing for senior administrative positions in the university. "Knowledge of the history and role of the university" are no longer high in the priorities of presidential or even decanal search committees, except perhaps in a highly technical sense. In fact, ads for university presidents are more and more explicit in describing the position in the language of business corporations as "chief executive officer."

[8]   I am grateful to Marguerite Cassin for sensitizing me to the importance of local versus translocal administrative practices.

[9]   Marguerite Cassin's work on personnel management develops the basis for distinguishing a "system of management" from the localized practices and activities of individual managers.

[10]   The work of Dorothy Smith has been seminal in pointing to the increasing centrality of a documentary-based ruling apparatus. Also, Marie Campbell's study of nursing work and Marguerite Cassin's study of personnel administrators have been especially helpful in directing me to the significance of new forms of documentary-based decision-making in universities.

[11]   I think it is interesting that, at the same time that decisions appear to be "made on their own," and that the process as well as results of decision-making are

increasingly mystified, faculty members also seem to attribute greater and greater powers to the administration, either with awe and admiration, or with a sense of resignation.

[12]   It is tempting to accuse the faculty of political apathy or of narrow self-interest in relation to their professional responsibilities. In some cases, these accusations may be justified. However, it is also true that what appears to be a "retreat" from service responsibilities in the university is actually the result of no longer knowing how to influence decisions and of dissipating the energy devoted to trying.

[13]   A more comprehensive listing of the forms of partnership and their general implications can be found in Buchbinder and Newson, 1990:355-79.

[14]   In exchange for the use of university resources such as the original research time of the faculty member or for special equipment that is needed. In some cases, university administrations also view such companies as good investments for some of their available cash.

[15]   In crude terms it can be said that, in view of the fact that the professor who owned the company could influence the supply of research monies to the university from his clients, he bought his place on the departmental hiring committee.

[16]   This especially makes it difficult to challenge these procedural alterations through the grievance mechanism of faculty unions and faculty associations. Collective agreements have been based on a structure of decision-making in which certain assumptions can be made about how key members of the administration relate to collegial units like academic departments, faculty councils, senates, etc. Links to corporate clients largely fall outside these relationships. New paths of communication and approval have been invented that connect individual academics directly with the central administration. When other academics insist that appropriate procedures ought to be followed, they are accused by their colleagues as well as senior administrators of being obstructive. Even more so, when faculty unions and faculty associations move in to protect the terms agreed to in collective agreements, they are accused of standing in the way of progress.

[17]   It is not surprising that Franklin and others would have identified the "slippage" of collective academic control which is embedded in the Centres of Excellence idea. After all, this is precisely the "advantage" that proponents of the Centres of Excellence had in mind. They argued that, in order to harness the expertise available in universities for the purpose of meeting the needs of private sector corporate development, the principles that guide research within the academy need to be overridden. They proposed the Centres of Excellence as a means of bypassing the normal relationship of academic researchers to the university. (See Panabaker, 1987:73-74.)

[18]   It is important to remember that the "corporate agenda" is not only being implemented through direct links between academic researchers and corporate clients who sponsor their research, but also through the funding policies of both levels of government and particularly through the funding policies of the major granting bodies in Canada, NSERC, SSHRC, and MRC.

[19]   For example, the "Centres of Excellence" concept is partly based on the presumed benefits of gathering together experts in a particular area in sufficient numbers (i.e., critical mass) with the ability to share the use of very

expensive lab equipment. Social sciences and humanities research rarely requires this kind of cost-intensive equipment.

[20] Even within the natural sciences, the "track record" approach to research granting is suspect. For example, concern in the United States about scientific fraud has raised questions about the pressures placed on scientists to show results in limited time frames in order to retain their "track record" position for obtaining further grants.

[21] In fact, this form of exchange of expertise is one way that a publicly funded institution can be seen as returning benefit to those who fund it, without at the same time encumbering the research process and limiting the free inquiry of the researcher. The corporate agenda prescribes a very different kind of relationship between the university and its funding public; in fact, the funding public subsidize research that increasingly benefits the corporate sector and related interests, while the corporate sector itself contributes only a very small portion of the budget of an extensive research development enterprise, the university system.

[22] In a recent study of corporate-university collaborations carried out in the United States by Yonkevich et al. at Cornell University, corporate executives said that their most important reason for participating in them is the ability they acquire to shape the research objectives. This study is reported in *The Scientist*, March 21, 1988:3.

[23] I am mainly referring here to the federal granting bodies and provincially funded research and development programmes, but I also want to include the many smaller competitions for release-time research fellowships which are carried out within universities. In the present funding climate, it would make some sense for these local campus competitions to compensate for the corporate biases of the federal and provincial policies, but my experience has been that they tend to mirror the same biases.

[24] It has been my experience on several occasions that academic colleagues have been the most adamant about defending the new emphasis on co-operating more with the corporate sector. These colleagues have accused others like myself, who have been concerned about the effects of such co-operation on the university, of being too politically biased against business, or of being "scaremongers" and nay-sayers. In fact, I have often found non-academic acquaintances–neighbours, people who walk their dogs in the same park as I walk mine, massage therapists, clerks and secretaries–to be more concerned about the implications of the changes I have described in this paper than I have found many of my academic acquaintances to be.

In some ways, this situation suggests that a remarkable shift of perspective has occurred in a relatively short period. The same generation of academics who adamantly defended university autonomy and the need to maintain arm's-length relationships with the "corporate-industrial-military complex" in the 1960s is now a largely passive witness to university-corporate "marriages" that are publicly celebrated from week to week in the in-house publications of many universities in Canada.

[25] I have not discussed in this paper the role of the state in developing social policies that encourage, indeed coerce universities and academic researchers to build links with the corporate sector. Buchbinder and I have emphasized

this aspect in our other work, notably, in chapter six of *The University Means Business.*

26   Leonard Minsky and David Noble, "Corporate Takeover on Campus," in *The Nation*, October 30, 1989:1.

27   Provincial student associations and the Canadian Federation of Students have been the major sources of opposition to tuition fee increases. They have faced a very hard struggle in maintaining their long-standing position on this issue because a number of campus-based student organizations have been won over to the "necessity" for increasing tuition fees. At the same time, many faculty members have also been persuaded that tuition fee increases is the only means for preserving the quality of education. At least, this is the rationale they publicly offer. A more cynical view is that tuition fee increases provide the means for maintaining the real value of their salaries.

28   A good example is the recent study published by the Council of Ontario Universities called *Focus on Fees*, written by David Stager, an economist at the University of Toronto. In a later paper, I will provide a more detailed analysis of the arguments that have been constructed by David Stager and others about the link between tuition fee increases and accessibility, and how these contribute towards a redefinition of the role of the university as a public institution in Canada.

29   I am suggesting here that at least two basis of occupational identity exist for academics: one is based in workerism and the other in professionalism. I am also suggesting that a tension exists between them. Although this tension is not new, the "corporate agenda" tends to accentuate it. For example, the idea of partnering academics with corporate clients creates a kind of entrepreneurial professionalism in which the university often intervenes as a bureaucratic inconvenience to those who want to advantage the partnership. At the same time, academics exist in a worker relationship to the administration and, in order to protect their collective interests as workers, participate in and become committed to the many practices which are otherwise viewed as "bureaucratic inconveniences." Much more needs to be said than is possible within the scope of this paper about this tension and its implications for the political practices of members of university faculty in relation to the changes in the university that have been outlined.

THE PROFESSORIATE AND THE MARKET-DRIVEN UNIVERSITY: TRANSFORMING THE CONTROL OF WORK IN THE ACADEMY[1]

A. Marguerite Cassin and J. Graham Morgan

"There is set up within the university an 'administration' to which I am held closely accountable. They steer the vessel, and I am one of the crew. I am not allowed on the bridge except when summoned: and the councils in which I participate uniformly begin at the point at which policy is already determined. I am not part of the 'administration,' but I am used by the 'administration,' in virtue of qualities that I may possess apart from my academic proficiencies. In authority, in dignity, in salary, the 'administration' are over me, and I am under them."

Anonymous Contributor, *Scribner's Magazine*, 1907[2]

Introduction

This paper provides a preliminary sketch of an issue awaiting investigation. Our purpose at this stage is to define the nature of the issue, to set it in a context, and to indicate certain directions in which we intend to move in order to understand it. The issue is control of the work of the professoriate in the university setting. We are interested in how such control is changing, the directions that such changes are taking, the assumptions that are undergirding the changes, and some of the ways in which the changes are being implemented.

In recent years there has been developing a whole field of discourse concerning the administration and management of organizations that heretofore were largely immune from corporate managerialism. The discourse derives largely from the latter sphere and has now become clearly evident, for example, in the fields of health care and higher education.[3] The extent to which this development has affected Canadian higher education has not been systematically studied.[4] At this stage, therefore, it can only be a matter of conjecture and of raising questions relevant to such an investigation.[5] We do this in reference to our own institution, Dalhousie University. This is a "full-service" university of about 10,000 students, with a wide range of graduate programmes and professional schools and a correspondingly diverse complement of faculty members. The examples and documents to which we refer are drawn from this milieu. At present it is impossible to say whether the Dalhousie case could be seen as "typical" in any sense, whether its march down the road to full-fledged managerialism is any further advanced than other places. Thus we do not attempt here to make comparisons in this regard. On the other hand it is clear enough that Dalhousie is in no way unique. Our description of the manner in which it is evolving presents an instance of a general trend of higher education in the direction of managerial control.

Support for this contention is to be found in the recent work by Janice Newson and Howard Buchbinder on the state of the universities in Canada. (Newson and Buchbinder, 1988; see also Newson's chapter in this volume). They have provided a cogent analysis and critique of the present state of universities in Canada by concentrating on the ever closer relationship between the corporate sector and the universities, and have shown some of the ways in which this relationship is consequential for the operation of the universities. We intend to focus on one facet of such consequences, namely those for the professoriate. We approach this by concentrating on the manner in which the assumptions and methods current in the corporate world have come to be adopted in the world of the academy.

Our interest in these matters is also, of course, experiential. What are the forces and expectations affecting our own occupational "life-worlds"? How do we make sense of them? How do we deal with them?

Transformation in University Governance and Orientations

Consonant with Newson and Buchbinder's characterization of the university as increasingly a business-oriented enterprise, we situate our issue in the changes taking place in how universities are organized and administered. The context of work for the professoriate is the university. The conception of the university that is traditionally dominant for the professoriate involves *collegiality*, the idea of a group of colleagues independently organizing and administering their affairs in the interests of scholarly pursuits. Such collegiality in practice has been subject to a changing milieu: it is not that in some respects it does not still exist but rather that its centrality has been eclipsed in important ways by different conceptions of organization and administration. How these affect the occupational role of the professoriate and its conception is the subject of this paper.

The modern university is not dissimilar from its predecessors in being embedded in a particular economic and political setting to which it is related culturally and ideologically. The particular embeddedness of the modern university, however, has come to entail some specific features whose rise to dominance requires a re-orientation of collegiality. This is a complex matter and only some of its characteristics can be touched upon here. Its main component, however, is the idea of *accountability*. Universities have come to be overwhelmingly dependent upon governments for the majority of their funding; governments have become more concerned to demonstrate that they are interested in getting "value for money" in what they fund. The result has been, on government's part, a more insistent call for universities to be "effective" in their use of funds, to exercise fiscal responsibility, and to be financially accountable. This governmental quest for demonstrated cost-effectiveness in higher education was explicit in the Nova Scotia case in 1988 when amendments to the laws concerning the Auditor General were formulated. The amendments involved the extension of "value for money" accounting to all recipients of government funding (that is, including universities). Similarly, in setting up the Nova Scotia Council on Higher Education the government described its functions as follows: to "...inquire into and review the delivery of all university programmes to determine whether they are being delivered in a cost effective manner."[6] Criteria such as value for money and cost effectiveness are redolent of the marketplace in making judgements about actions, decisions, programmes, and products, not of the academy. More specifically, they are terms appropriate to the objectives of certain players in the marketplace: entrepreneurs and managers. Thus an important part of our argument is that in so far as the external demand for accountability has taken hold in the academy and been responded to, universities have begun to transform their organization and administration into managerial, not collegial, functions.

What we have just alluded to is the appearance in the universities of a certain kind of thinking, a particular kind of language beginning to be applied. Its content naturally implies judgement and evaluation—to this we will return. At present, let us describe some relevant aspects of the university milieu that this thinking and language has affected.

First of all, we can note that the implementation of a managerial model is to some extent rendered possible by the professoriate's admission, not always tacit, that it is not interested in the details of administration—it should be "left alone" to get on with its real work of teaching and research. It has adopted the attitude that the administrator's job is to provide the professoriate facilities and resources for the effective carrying out of its dual mandate. The attitude is certainly understandable, but it is one that clearly facilitates the carving out of a distinct administrative role in the academy. The character of this role has been in process of definition in the last fifteen years or so, a period that has been marked by an increasing market orientation on the part of the major fund supplier (the government) which in turn is heeding the calls for greater fiscal responsibility and restraint from the business and financial community. Thus, the academy has begun to transform its administrative features to conform with various expectations and methods that are generated primarily external to itself in the worlds of business and of government: worlds where priority is ostensibly given to cost effectiveness, organizational efficiency, value for money, and so on.

Some manifestations of this transformation include:

- the employment of persons whose functions are exclusively administrative and managerial, creating within the academy a cadre of persons whose career path is divergent from the professoriate
- a consequent disjunction between the administrative cadre and the professoriate
- an increasing professionalization and hierarchization of the administrative cadre
- an increasing proportion of the academy's employees in managerial roles in relation to the proportion in the professoriate
- the increasingly important role that the non-academic administration plays in academic decision-making bodies such as the senate—the attendance at which by the professoriate, although it is their most important official arena for influence, is often minimal
- the tendency for the managerial cadre to see themselves as a distinct determinative body.[7]

The "infiltration" of the managers is not a superficial grafting on of a few ideas from different life spheres; it is the incorporation into the academy of specific assumptions about what is to be valued and devalued, what is to be promoted or let go. The assumptions are those of managerial control, the practical priorities of which have not been constructed in the academy (although of course discussed and formulated there in fields such as business adminstration and management studies). But it is these priorities that have come to be applied to the adminstration and organization of the academy, not least in respect of teaching programmes, research emphasis, and the conceptualization of the role of the professoriate in the whole enterprise.

Thus, we find the managerial cadre assuming a role of increased importance, a presence of greater prominence in shaping the direction and character of all aspects of the academy. In this respect it is interesting to note the changing manner in which the presidents of universities conduct themselves and the way they are valued inside and outside. Many of them are coming to see themselves as Chief Executive Officers rather than Vice-Chancellors; as people whose main concern, although often expressed in suitably academic terms, is with the established managerial priorities of efficiency, cost effectiveness, and the need for "flexibility" in the conditions under which they can get on with the business of running a tight ship.[8] This conception of the role of the university president has led, certainly in the Dalhousie case, to a wholly new bureaucratic phenomenon: The "President's Office." The latter used to be little more than a geographical designation; now it is a concept of organization that embraces a large complement of functionaries, a bee-hive of activities, a complex of interconnecting offices.[9]

One last thing to observe in connection with the transformation of university governance under the present political and economic conditions: a more "intrusive" approach to the construction of the character and operation of the university on the part of the board of governors. One example will suffice for the present purposes. The Dalhousie Board of Governors has established for itself a Financial Strategy Committee. The mandate of the Committee is very broad indeed, involving study of how the university can generate more income and how it can best spend the income it obtains. It has become an engine of studies and planning documents. Given its deliberately broad mandate it has become directly involved in the discussion of the university's priorities of an academic nature. It is chaired by a prominent, but young and vigorous, member of the local business community. Such involvement directly by the Board would have been all but unthinkable a few years ago.

In the foregoing section we have attempted to sketch some of the elements of the direction that university governance is currently taking. We have focused on the increasing prominence of managerial style and assumption in the academy, and have indicated that the development of such an orientation is filtering into the world of the professoriate. Before we examine this latter point more directly, let us first outline briefly some consequences of the orientation.[10]

Consequence of the Managerial Orientation: New Priorities

Implementation of a managerial organization requires that personnel and resources be deployed for purposes related to such organization. As this component of the university has grown it has absorbed a greater and greater proportion of the available funds: paid out in salaries, capital expenditures, operational expenses, and so on. The extent to which this proportional growth in personnel and fund allocation has occurred is a question that bears careful investigation. In our experience, the information that one would need in order to trace this growth is hard to come by: the ups and downs of the professoriate complement have been quite closely tracked by faculty associations for obvious reasons, but disclosures by administrations of their own growth is avoided. In any case, what has occurred has been the creation of a bureaucratic arm whose growth we strongly suspect outstrips that of the university in terms of student enrolments and in terms of full-time faculty complement.

The bureaucratic character of the university's managerial organization has involved, amongst many other things, the emplacement in the university of a concept of university administration involving careers and hierarchical responsibilities. This aspect of the university milieu is not at all well known to the professoriate and, again, the precise character of its development and present state is in need of detailed investigation. It is sufficient at the moment to observe that this bureaucratization has resulted in the emergence of a distinct occupational cadre whose style and expectations are distinctly different from, and not necessarily compatible with, those of much of the professoriate.

This newly important managerial presence in the university is profoundly affecting the way the university conducts its affairs. We have referred already to the great opportunities for control that have become available to the managerial administration. It remains at this stage to point out some salient characteristics of this control.

(1) It is predicated on the assumption that the methods and values associated with the world views of business and finance are appropriate and necessary in the world of the academy. In some respects this is saying that the important reference groups for the managers lie outside of the academy in these other worlds. Universities have, of course, always had connections to these other worlds through their senior administrators. The current relationship, however, is one that has come to involve the incorporation of the methods and values of these worlds directly into the orientations of the university administrators. This has resulted in the blooming of business and financially oriented talk (designating all areas of the university including libraries and academic departments as "cost centres," for example, the recipients of "budget envelopes") and, more importantly, an increasing generation of ways in which "effectiveness" can be objectified, reported upon, measured, evaluated, and rewarded. Such overriding concerns with "effectiveness" are managerial priorities; they are becoming suffused through *all* components of the academy.

(2) It is giving prominence to a view of the academy as a knowledge resource to be exploited in contrast, for example, to the more traditional view of the academy as a place for the diffusion and growth of knowledge for the public good. The conception of the university's utility, which has been so prominent in the orientation of governments of late, is one that the managerial orientation finds congenial indeed. It has led to a promotion of certain kinds of activities in the university over others; it gives a particular prominence to research activities that have a potential for market exploitation and hence entails the willingness of the managerially oriented administrators to encourage fields and abilities where market "value" is a possibility. There are many dimensions to this tendency. Here we will illustrate it by referring to one such encouragement: recent interest by universities in setting up offices of technology transfer. These offices are designed to increase the extent to which universities are able to "interface" with the market, to the mutual advantage of each. Dalhousie established one of these offices recently and stated in the appointment announcement of its "officer" that he [sic] would be facilitating the "commercialization of intellectual

property." This was not a Marxist hoax. Not incidentally, this announcement appeared in the *business section* of the local daily paper.[11]

(3) It is resulting in a comparative devaluation of the teaching function while at the same time encouraging technologically based teaching methods. The concern is with cost effectiveness and efficiency as operational criteria in the sphere of teaching. This has the tendency to devalue teaching, since resources have to be diverted away from this function in order to subsidize the more "marketable" aspects of the university's activities. From the managerial point of view teaching can be relegated to effective criteria of audit such as teacher/student ratios, or demands of the market for particular fields and classes. Decisions on curriculum and programmes that are based primarily on such criteria are to be seen as essentially managerial, not academic, ones. In the light of the increasing importance of such managerial criteria, it is understandable that the managers/administrators have shown a tendency to profess an interest in the "quality of teaching" and a "concern for students" in this respect. The most common remedy to the problems associated with larger classes and diminishing programmes is the managerial encouragement of more "cost effective" forms of educational "delivery," that is, greater use of teaching technology, audio-visual aids, and less expensive teachers (part-timers, graduate students, teaching assistants).

The Transformation of the Work Environment of the Professoriate

The consequences of the trends that we have outlined are not uniformly felt by all segments of the professoriate; many are poorly understood, and the directions of many are still only obscure. At this point, therefore, we want only to make some general observations about how the conditions of work are changing in the academy as control is becoming managerial-oriented control.

The overriding managerial consideration is for "effectiveness." This concern is applied increasingly to the various aspects of the work of the professoriate, requiring that the products of work and the extent of work be described in standardized ways using standardized criteria. "Effectiveness," therefore, depends upon methods of describing and quantifying those aspects of the professoriate's work that are deemed capable of accountability, and deemed "relevant" to the mission of the university. In addition, as we have indicated above, the managerial predilection is to encourage and support those activities in the university that can most readily result in reducing costs and/or in increasing revenues.

These components of the managerial orientation when put into practice inevitably affect the work environment of the professoriate. Some examples

include:
- encouragement of research activities that increase the revenue of the university; the larger the grants received the greater the academic rewards
- expectation that research work will result in quantifiable output, as in the form of published papers or reports, books, book chapters, and so on
- escalating demands for higher outputs in respect of research and publication
- escalating demands for increased teaching loads, especially on the basis of quantified comparisons between departments and other institutions, including increased class sizes and more classes taught per faculty member, greater contact hours
- encouragement for members of the professoriate to engage in entrepreneurial activity
- expectation that the professoriate will "make do" with decreased secretarial and administrative assistance.

For many in the professoriate the experience of this changing environment is one of increasing workloads: more teaching and more administrative work. The increase in these spheres has the effect of diminishing the efforts that can be put into research and other scholarly endeavours, the very components of academic work that form the basis for greatest rewards. The real problem tends to be that the demands on the individual academic are all increasing simultaneously: teaching has become more demanding and time-consuming as classes have increased, contact hours have increased, professorial replacements have not been made; service and administrative functions have increased as the university has become more bureaucraticized and as the professoriate has struggled to maintain collegiality; research and writing have become difficult to combine with the other aspects of the professoriate's work and thus for many have to be confined to the months of summer only.

Thus, the professoriate appears to be entangled in a series of ever-escalating expectations where work becomes constantly subject to scrutiny and evaluation.[12] This is occurring in a context where there is a strong managerial tendency to favour some kinds of "products" and activities rather than others—those that are most marketable, most "transferable," attract the most students, are most "cost effective," and so on. This is tending to create and sometimes encourage divisions in the professoriate, to put a premium on the most productive work (in managerial terms), to lead to a sense that certain work is not valued vis-à-vis other work.[13] It is also leading to efforts by members of the professoriate to reduce their teaching commitment (e.g., by "buy-outs" and research leaves) so that they can concentrate on the more immediately rewardable research activities. The reduction of teaching by some usually has the effect of increasing the teaching of those who remain to teach, thus further exacerbating work-load increases.

The Objectification of Work

The quest for accountability through the introduction of managerial organization into the university creates administrative centralization. Centralization depends upon and is enhanced by the production of accounts of the work organization. These accounts provide the basis to structure decisions about programme, work priorities, and allocation outside the settings in which work is actually conducted. The foundation for these accounts is the creation of reporting practices that objectify the work organization in terms that are compatible with financial management. We are seeing the creation of just such objectified reporting practices at our university. Increasingly the work of professors is being formulated through criteria that make it comparable and relevant to new financial initiatives. Two initiatives at Dalhousie illustrate the process of the creation of objectified reporting practices: the "comparative opportunities study on mixes: ideas and constraints" (COSMIC) and the annual reports of faculty. Both point in the direction of work-load management systems and cost accounting measures as methods of determining, controlling, and supervising the work of the professoriate.

COSMIC was initiated through the Financial Strategies Committee of the Board of Governors of the University. Rather than focusing upon financial matters directly, however, it focuses upon creating an inventory for the work of the professoriate and then studying universities of comparable size that are more advanced in professorial management. COSMIC begins with an apparently innocuous observation that "alternative academic mixes" have been used successfully at other universities without damaging reputation or programme quality. In the study design it becomes clear that "alternative academic mixes" means introducing and institutionalizing a division of labour into existing professorial work. The creation of an inventory of existing professorial work is a prerequisite for such institutionalization.

COSMIC does a "ground clearing operation." It uses applied social science techniques to create reporting categories for professorial work at the programme level. Professorial work is reported as research, service, and teaching. However, it is structured in terms of managerial/institutional criteria, which are institutional role, quality, demand, quality of efficiency, and potential for change. The overall effect is to create a reporting mechanism that acts as a programme evaluation. Managerial criteria frame the evaluation. Essentially COSMIC shifts the context and appraisal of professorial work. One important implication of this is that normal tenure and promotion practices that have been an important dimension of professorial control can be left in place, but are rendered irrelevant in terms of financial and programme planning.

The character of the shift becomes clearer through further examination of the management reporting criteria. In the reporting framework, each criterion is defined, elaborated, scaled. The criteria measure performance and institutional relevance. The criterion "institutional role" offers an illustration. It is defined as "compliance of the 'program' to the mission of the university, contribution to and effect on the university, and regional and national contribution." Here we see then that the work of research, teaching, and service is relevant, valuable, mandated, and recognizable in so far as it contributes to the "institutional role," which is not defined in terms of the creation and dissemination of knowledge, but in terms of institutionally defined boundaries. This plan accommodates both the requirements for planning and externalized decision making by university managers. It provides the basis on which to value the work of professors in view of managerial priorities.

The "criteria matrix" (as it is referred to in the COSMIC proposal) is both "a self study document and part of a process of external evaluation and review." To use the criteria matrix for external evaluation and review, however, faculty must adopt this particular conception and reporting of their work. The report recognizes a barrier to the implementation of the programme evaluation plan:

> In general, these programs (service, teaching and faculty workload measures) are two of the most difficult pieces of information to construct for programs at Dalhousie. They have a direct relationship in the determination of current and future program capacities. Faculty workload should be available from Faculty/Department offices. However, no consistent definition exists for measurement purposes (COSMIC, 1989).

These reporting practices present the work of the professoriate in view of the priorities of accountability. But to implement COSMIC programme evaluation, reporting practices must be uniform. It is here that the issue of annual reports arises.

From the point of view of COSMIC, annual reports by faculty are hopelessly idiosyncratic affairs. Each faculty has devised its own form and some truly maverick departments have insisted upon their own versions. Most reports are qualitative. These are, of course, of no use in a system that is not interested in the material forms of the work.

One report stands out as an instructive example of a managerially outlined approach, the Faculty of Health Professions. This report gathers information on the type of appointment, teaching responsibilities, hours taught, and number of students enrolled. It goes on to elaborate teaching, research, professional activities, administrative duties, and honours and research awards received. This report is designed to make it possible for university administrators to "know" and make decisions about the work reported without interacting with the people doing the work. This offers a view of what reporting will begin to look like to meet the requirements of COSMIC.

The reactions of faculty to these initiatives are interesting. Of course, faculty were involved in designing COSMIC. But the study's recommendations have been largely ignored. One unit head pointed out that while COSMIC does not take sufficient account of the work of professors, its precisely defined criteria eliminate the flexibility essential to and inherent in academic freedom:

> No longer will it be possible for individuals and units to justify broadly accepted—but not necessarily favoured—activities on the basis of a vaguely expressed mission statement. Instead, the university will categorically be endorsing some activities and discouraging others. Faculty will act accordingly, often to the benefit of the university; but at times to the detriment of both the programs in which they work and to the relationship of the university to the community.

In her work, Dorothy Smith has identified the way in which power is organized and conducted in conceptual practices (1990a). The instances of COSMIC and annual reports offer "moments" of a shift in power taking place in the university in which professorial work is being brought under the control of new goals and definitions of knowledge creation and dissemination. The objectification of work through reporting practices is a key dimension of the shift in power.

Conclusion

We have discussed some of the changes taking place at our university. These changes in the academy are directly consequential for the work of the professoriate. At the same time the changes are in part made possible by the orientations and practices of the professoriate in relation to administration and the academy. Placed in the context of accountability and the accompanying development of management as the mode of organization of the academy, the issues that are arising at our university suggest a broader shift in the social location and internal organization of the university.

The forms of accountability and management arise in and are part of the general form of institutional organization in business and government. They create and rely upon a division of labour and form of control in which the execution of work is separated from its planning and design. In addition, specification of the activities of labour is a principled basis of organization, a division between management and the work process is presupposed, and management and the interests defined by management form the authoritative basis for decision making.[14] These are prescriptive forms that create uniformity and compliance.[15] It must be recognized that various disciplines represented within the university have contributed and do contribute to the creation and maintenance of such forms as part of their scholarship.

The professoriate have been slow to respond to these developments. General indifference to administration and increased workloads have tended to encourage many professors to be prepared to "leave it to administrators." But tacitly what is assumed is that nothing much will change, that administrators will proceed in much the same fashion as they would themselves. This is of course not the case, as we have discussed. Faculty unions have been responding to this by attempting to develop and strengthen collective agreements.

There is no doubt that university administrators are inventing internal forms of managerial control within a changing context for universities. Many see themselves as responding to a set of external demands. At the same time universities and university administrators have as a prerogative the creation, and presumably the critique of knowledge, including such practices. Universities are not institutions which must unquestioningly accept external forms of control. There is a broad social interest in knowledge creation, which is being threatened by the processes described above. At the very least, alternative forms of governance and reporting practices need to be developed and proposed.

NOTES

1   The names of the authors of this essay are listed alphabetically. Their order does not reflect priority of contribution.

2   Quoted in Vesey (1965:389).

3   For developments in higher education in the United States in this respect, see, for example, Johnson and Marcus (1986), Olswang and Lee (1984). In the field of health care, see Campbell (1984).

4   Canadian community colleges and the CEGEP system, however, are analyzed in the recent collection edited by Muller (1990).

5   A brief but rich compilation of relevant anecdotes is to be found in Locke (1990:8-16).

6   Quoted in *The NSCUFA Bulletin/de la CAPUNE* (1989:6).

7   At Dalhousie the most authoritative level of this cadre has taken to calling itself the "Senior Officers." The group consists of the upper-level administrators and presidential advisers. It includes the academic deans but these are outnumbered by the non-academic senior administrators. The President presides.

The phrase "senior officers" of course has a military ring to it: the university president who aspires to act as a commanding general is another trend that might bear investigation.

[8] University presidents get rewarded these days primarily for having successfully steered their vessels through shoals of turbulent financial waters. An example is afforded by the resignation announcement of the President of Mount Allison University:

> Mr. Crawford (Chair of Mount Allison's board of regents) praised the outgoing president for exhibiting strong leadership...The chairman [sic] said Mr. Wells helped to ensure the university's future by strengthening budgetary controls and by introducing new management information systems." *The Halifax Chronicle-Herald*, (1989:2)

[9] Including those of four vice-presidents and their staffs, an Associate Vice-President, administrative assistants, secretaries, the legal counsel and his assistant (also a lawyer), presidential advisors, institutional planners, policy planners and, of course, the President himself with his own immediate entourage. This growing ensemble of administrators and their staffs is co-ordinated by an office manager.

[10] It is worth noting that the assumptions and style of this orientation are distinctly male in character. Most of the influential players are, of course, men. They bring to their tasks an aura of domination and control in action and in language. A matter for separate investigation, therefore, would be the way in which this masculinity is being embedded in the governance of the university in its managerial manifestation. For an historical perspective on male dominance within academe see Dorothy Smith's "Whistling Women: Reflections on Rage and Rationality" in this volume.

[11] This promotion of the products of the academic milieu as marketable has become widespread as a goal of university administrators. The venerable British institution, the University of Oxford, has entered the arena in its appointment of an "Industrial Liaison Officer." This officer delivered a paper to a conference in Belgium (the conference being "The Economics of the Transfer of Technology") entitled "A Strategy for Higher Education: the Oxford Experience." Despite its grand title this paper confined itself to the matter of how Oxford was getting along in its technology transfer policy. For a brief report see the Oxford alumni magazine *Oxford Today* (1990:46).

[12] That such scrutiny is now new is established by Vesey's information and comment that

> at...Columbia in 1909 there was a printed form on which chairmen of departments were asked to rate all their subordinates according to a coded system resembling a student's report card. This kind of administrative bureaucracy obviously affronted the self-respect of all who were forced to submit to it (Vesey, 1965:387).

What is new is the embeddedness of such practices within an articulated discourse of management.

[13] This tendency is apparent in the managerially approved notion of "excellence"—a hierarchized idea of value is obviously inherent in this latest buzzword. A headline in a recent alumni publication left no doubt about this:

"Centres of excellence involve the best and brightest on campus" it pro-
claimed, thus relegating to dronehood those who were not part of them (see
Dalhousie Alumni Magazine, 1990:4).

[14] There is a large literature on this now which begins with Braverman's innovative and influential contribution (Braverman, 1974). A view of managerial
technologies and their generalized social form is offered in Cassin (1990).

[15] Ursula Franklin offers an interesting discussion and perspective on this (1990).

LIBERATING THE UNIVERSITY: A CRITIQUE OF THE PROJECT OF RADICAL EDUCATION IN NORTH AMERICAN POST-SECONDARY INSTITUTIONS

Claire Polster

Introduction

Radical educational wisdom has it that the relationship between liberatory education[1] and social organization is such that the former is the catalyst to progressive change in the latter. While this relationship has been verified historically—or perhaps precisely because it has been borne out in practice—radical educators tend to over-emphasize it at the expense of the other half of the dialectic, namely, the constraints that a form of social organization imposes on liberatory education. In my initial conception of this paper, my aim was to correct for this oversight by examining ways in which changes in the organization of public universities in Canada and the United States that have taken place over the last twenty years limit the ability of radical academics to practise liberatory education within these institutions.[2] The larger goal of this analysis was to develop strategies to alter this situation and to secure conditions favourable to liberatory educational practice within the university.

In the course of writing this paper, however, it became clear to me that it was not enough to focus on the material limitations on the *practice* of radical education. For the university imposes material limitations on the *project* of radical education as well. Recognition of this additional set of constraints necessitated the development of a different kind of strategy than I had originally anticipated, the beginnings of which are traced in the final section of this paper. As well as creating the conditions to overcome the material limitations on the practice and project of radical education, this strategy also attempts to transcend the *conceptual limitations* in the project that impede the realization of its aims.

The nature of my argument requires that a significant amount of background material be provided at the start. I will begin by briefly outlining what I mean by the project of radical education and the practice or implementation of this project. Following this, I will discuss some changes in university organization that have taken place in the last twenty years and show how these changes are limiting the practice of radical education in North American universities. The stage having been set, I will argue against my original contention that radical academics should combat these changes in order to secure their ability to practise liberatory education. Instead, I will make the case that in order to achieve the aims to which they are committed, these academics must fight to change the university in more fundamental ways and towards more radical ends.

The Project of Radical Education

A project is not some clearly defined political programme that is written down and followed by a united group. Rather, it is a theoretical abstraction that can be derived from the writings and actions of numerous individuals and collectives. All those whose theory and practice comprise a project share a general understanding of a problem as well as a desired solution to that problem. However, between this general understanding and desired solution there can be great variety in terms of people's specific analyses of the problem and the particular strategies they adopt in order to resolve it.

The project of radical education in North American universities aims to reverse what many critical educators[3] see as the main problem with traditional higher education, namely, that it reproduces the patriarchal capitalist status quo. Radical educators try to do this by teaching counter-cultural content (i.e., socialist, feminist, and other kinds of oppositional knowledge) so as to enlighten and empower students to become active in the struggle for fundamental social change (Wright, 1978; Castles and Wustenberg, 1979; Weiler, 1988). In addition to teaching alternative material, radical educators believe they must teach it in a different way. In contrast to traditional "banking" methods of education,[4] they advocate problem-posing education, which takes as its starting point the needs and interests of students and then critically explores them through a dialogical process in an atmosphere of community and trust (Shor, 1980). According to Freire, this active engagement of students in the process of creating knowledge leads them first to critical consciousness and then to action for change (Freire, 1970).

The Development of Space for Radical Education in the University

From the late 1950s to the early 1970s, there was considerable space to teach counter-cultural ideas with non-traditional methods in North American public universities. This space—which has both structural and discursive dimensions—was the product of a confluence of various favourable conditions inside of the university as well as in the wider society.[5] Prime among the conditions that opened up structural space for the practice of radical education were the state-sponsored programmes of university expansion that created a high demand for university professors. This demand, coupled with relatively undeveloped university administrations, afforded academics a considerable degree of power to shape departmental and university policy and to determine what and how they would teach. Financial resources available in the university further facilitated the practice of liberatory education. In addition to making available various resources that permitted experimentation with alternative pedagogical methods, financial resources also made possible the creation and expansion of alternative courses and programmes in areas such as black studies and women's studies. In terms of the wider society, adequate funding for higher education enabled the university to preserve its relative independence from external forces traditionally hostile to radical education. Indeed, until well into the 1960s, most corporate donations to Canadian universities came with few strings attached and were justified as means to help the universities preserve their autonomy *vis-à-vis* government (Axelrod, 1982; Newson and Buchbinder, 1988:11-23; Shor, 1986:1-29).

Although these structural changes were an important condition for the practice of radical higher education, changes in the space open to radical discourse were perhaps of even more significance. Beginning in the early 1960s, radical discourses that were previously censored, marginalized, or underdeveloped began to gain both currency and legitimacy within the university. Much of the impetus behind this development came from students who were concerned with the lack of democracy and equality within institutions of higher learning and with these institutions' involvement in the military industrial complex. Aided and abetted by sympathetic professors, these students pushed for the development of new courses and programmes as well as alternative educational forms (such as interdisciplinary study, independent study, and community action projects) that were more relevant to and compatible with their new questions and concerns. These changes opened up space for the discussion of fresh ideas and perspectives inside (and outside) of university classrooms. Perhaps more importantly, they also helped produce an expansion of radical scholarship, which further established radical discourse and its respectability in the university. In addition to forces within the university, forces outside it including the growing Canadian women's movement, the Quebec nationalist movement, and the New Left also helped to sustain and legitimate radical academic discourse. International social movements such as the anti-war and student movements in the U.S. and several western European countries had a similar impact on liberatory education in Canadian and other universities (McGuigan, 1968; Reid and Reid, 1969).

Organizational and Ideological Transformation

The early 1970s brought a reversal in the structural conditions that were favourable to the practice of liberatory education. Within the university the main cause of this turn-around was the drastic cut in funding that began in the early 1970s, which led to hiring freezes, tuition and work-load increases, reductions in course offerings, and eventually to the closing of programmes and to the firing of professors (Axelrod, 1986:54; Shor, 1986:20). In order to deal with these and other results of the funding crisis, such as the growth of faculty unions, university administrations were significantly expanded and charged with the task of reorganizing academic work.[6] According to Newson and Buchbinder, this reorganization has set in motion a process through which faculty members are increasingly fragmented and marginalized within their workplace. Simultaneously, the power of administrations to circumscribe decision-making processes is expanding (Newson and Buchbinder, 1988: 23-33; see also Newson's chapter in this volume).

These organizational changes inside the university have been accompanied by an intensification of the links between universities and big business. The origin of this change lies in the general crisis of capitalism that began in the 1970s and worsened in the 1980s. In Canada, the United States, and many other industrialized countries in the Western world, this crisis brought to power several conservative governments whose agenda includes the goal of dismantling the welfare state. The desire of these governments to "get public institutions off their backs" has provided big business with the opportunity to expand into the so-called "nonproductive" sectors of the economy in an effort to increase productivity (Beverly, 1978: 76). And one prime target of corporate expansion, especially in the last ten years, has been the university. As Maxwell and Currie imply, investment in higher education is attractive to corporations because the university can supply them with the technological know-how they need to be internationally competitive at a fraction of what it would cost them to do the research themselves (Maxwell and Currie, 1984). Corporate investment in higher education is also attractive to university administrators (and to some academics) because it promises to restore to the university both quality of education and social respectability and prestige. Although some opposition to the proposed "partnership for growth" has recently been voiced, for the most part this criticism has been drowned in a sea of praise and public relations work by government, third-party bodies, some members of the university community, and big business.[7] Criticism of this partnership is also becoming irrelevant to administrators who feel compelled to jump on the corporate bandwagon, lest they give other universities a competitive edge in the market for students and faculty.

The 1980s also brought changes to discursive relations that had favoured radical higher education. Within the university, growing numbers of administrators, academics, and even some students expressed concern that excessive democracy in the university as well as the proliferation of alternative courses and programmes (such as socialist studies, ethnic studies, etc.) were damaging the quality of North American higher education. Laments such as Bercuson's et al. *The Great Brain Robbery* and Bloom's equally conservative but more sophisticated *The Closing of the American Mind* are typical expressions of this point of view. At the same time, many radical academics also experienced (and continue to experience) less polite and more direct attempts to silence them. Sheila McIntyre's ordeal at the Queen's University law school is a striking but far from isolated example of the increasingly bold harassment of radical educators on North American university campuses (CAUT Bulletin, 1987:7-11). According to Shor, the assault on radical discourse within the university should be seen as only one aspect of the ideological war being waged by the Right as part of its strategy for a conservative restoration. He claims that nationwide calls for the return to educational basics and classics are aimed not at producing academic excellence, but at delegitimating critical discourses and restoring hierarchy and elitism to the university and to society at large. He further argues that the attribution of economic slowdown to alleged low-quality education is nothing more than an ideological buttress for the corporate agenda for the university mentioned above (Shor, 1986).

Material Limitations on the Practice of Radical Higher Education

The organizational and ideological changes that have taken place in the last twenty years combine to limit, in two ways, the ability of radical academics to practise liberatory education in the university. On the one hand, these changes are *closing down spaces* in which radical professors are able to engage in liberatory education (and they are making it more difficult for these academics to do anything about the situation). On the other hand, these changes are *opening up new spaces* that allow those opposed to the practice of liberatory education to undermine it and to prevent it from taking place. Below, I provide two examples that illustrate both "that" and "how" radical educational practice is being limited in North American universities. The first focuses in a theoretical way on an issue that affects professors individually. The second is based on an account of an assault launched by the administration of an American university on a radical educational programme.

The issue of class size illustrates how the changes discussed above are closing down the spaces available to radical academics to practise liberatory education. Since the mid-1970s, class sizes—particularly those of under-graduate classes—have been steadily increasing in North American universities. From 1970-71 to 1985-86, the student/faculty ratio at Ontario's universities rose from 12.9 to 16.3. This represents an increase of 26 per cent (Ontario Federation of Students, 1988:59-60). This trend is similar in other Canadian provinces and in the United States. One reason for these increases is the desire of administrations to make their institutions more cost effective. The intensification of university-corporate links may also be partially responsible for the greater numbers of students per class.[8] These increases in class sizes put serious constraints on the practice of radical education in the university. For example, the greater the number of students there are in a class, the more difficult it is for a professor to include them in decisions about what they will learn or how they will be evaluated. The possibilities of creating community among students and of engaging in dialogical educational process are also reduced in proportion to increases in class size.[9]

The actual increase in the number of students per class is not, however, the only problematic aspect of the class size issue. Changes in the way that decisions about class sizes are made also impose constraints on radical educational practice. According to Newson, prior to the expansion of university administrations, decisions about class sizes were made collectively within many university departments, primarily on the basis of academic criteria. Today, however, class sizes are generally negotiated between deans and department heads, increasingly on the basis of administrative criteria (J. Newson, personal communication, Sept. 9, 1989). It should be noted that radical (as other) academics still have some say on the issue, for example, through the collective bargaining process of their unions. However, the parameters that circumscribe their say are substantially reduced relative to what they once were.[10]

Finally, the growing inability of radical academics to mitigate the negative effects of increasing class sizes also indicates that the space in which to practise radical education is shrinking in the university. Changes in the organization of academic work have often led to increased work loads, particularly for part-time faculty. Consequently, professors have less time to spend with a growing number of students and less time to devise innovative strategies to overcome the barriers to radical education. Those professors who take the time by neglecting their own research risk jeopardizing their promotions if they are tenured and possibly their careers if they are not. For as administrative and business values and priorities have infiltrated into the tenure and promotion process, the importance of an academic's publication record as a criterion for advancement has substantially increased relative to the importance of one's teaching and service records.[11]

At the same time that it is becoming increasingly difficult for radical professors to practise liberatory education, it is becoming easier for those opposed to radical education to subvert and/or to prevent it. One very effective method that administrations have used to attack radical educational programmes is to manipulate various bureaucratic mechanisms in order to change programme policies and personnel in such a way that these programmes' liberatory goals are undermined (Pollack, 1985:19). In her account of the assault on the women's studies programme at the SUNY College at New Paltz,[12] Schniedewind states that the administration attempted to undermine the programme by challenging its faculty and governance process. In terms of the former, the administration argued that women's studies fell within liberal arts and challenged the faculty status of people who taught in arts, education, and physical education. In terms of the latter, the administration refused to accept decisions of the programme's steering committee (comprised of faculty, students, a community representative, and a staff person) and only accepted decisions made by full-time faculty members. The administration also attempted to subvert the programme by removing its decision-making power on personnel and curriculum issues. In 1984, the administration effectively removed the programme's power to choose its own co-ordinator. The administration also attempted to change the qualifications necessary to be a women's studies faculty member in order to allow anti-feminist instructors into the programme and to bar certain feminist teachers who did not meet the new criteria. One final strategy employed by the administration was to reconceptualize and redefine women's studies. By defining women's studies as the study of women that was based in standard academic disciplines, administrators rendered interdisciplinary work "insignificant at best and sometimes invalid." Feminist or experiential pedagogical approaches also came under attack. They were defined as soft and therefore illegitimate (Pollack, 1985:20).[13]

According to Schniedewind, this "1980s style of attack" is quite effective for several reasons. First, the very nature of this kind of assault makes it difficult for those against whom it is directed to perceive that they are actually under attack.

> The administrative and bureaucratic nature of the effort to "transform" women's studies made it difficult for us to pinpoint what was happening. Only in the course of this process did we become able to name and analyze the nature of the attack (Pollack, 1985:19).

Second, this form of attack is also difficult to challenge. The energy it takes to respond to each bureaucratic incursion takes its toll on people so that they become progressively more willing to let issues slide. Dealing with a constant barrage of memos and the tangle of bureaucratic rules also keeps people so busy that they have neither time nor energy to identify the larger administrative strategies that underlie each bureaucratic move. Thus, in the course of winning isolated battles, those under attack may set themselves up to lose the war (Pollack, 1985:21-2). Finally, the general disempowerment of the professoriate in North American universities also works to the advantage of administrations as many academics become intimidated and are less willing to take up an assertive stance. "An increasingly repressive atmosphere brought out in some faculty members a more liberal tendency...they became more willing both to pick for crumbs rather than see, and fight for, the whole loaf, and to accept the changed rules of the game, even though those rules were unjust" (Pollack,

1985:22). On a more positive note, Schniedewind's account of how her programme fought back proves that this kind of attack does not preclude successful resistance. However, each administrative victory renders the next such victory that much easier and increases the time and energy that must be expended if resistance is to succeed.

The above are only two of many possible examples that illustrate that changes taking place within the university and between the university and the wider society are limiting the ability of radical academics to practise liberatory education. Again I emphasize that these limitations do not make the practice of radical education in the university impossible. They do, however, mean that the efforts expended by radical professors are continually yielding diminishing returns. The initial conclusion that I drew from this analysis was that rather than spending more and more energy trying to manoeuvre in a space that is growing smaller all the time, radical academics would do better to fight the changes underway in the university and to secure their ability to teach for change. I have since come to realize that fighting these changes would not be enough to achieve the ends desired by radical academics. For in addition to imposing limitations on the practice of radical education, the university imposes limitations on the project of radical education as well.

Material Limitations on the Project of Radical Education

Even were they free to teach counter-cultural ideas with non-traditional methods, I would argue that radical academics would not be likely to achieve the ends to which they are committed. This is so because the way education is organized in most North American universities makes it difficult for these professors to bring about either much ideological change in students or much collective action by students aimed at fundamental social change.[14] First, radical academics, who do not comprise the majority of the professoriate, do not have access to all the students in the academy. In the course of their years at university, many students will simply not be exposed to radical content, much less have the opportunity to be taught with problem-posing methods. Those students who do get exposure to radical ideas seldom have the continuity that is necessary for these ideas to mature into a coherent world-view. At the same time that they take radical courses, these students are also likely to be taking other mainstream courses. As a result, the radical perspective tends to become just another way of seeing, a different professor's perspective that they must master in order to do well in a course. Lack of temporal continuity in university education further contributes to the marginalization of radical perspectives. As course offerings are seldom organized to permit students to continue studying in one tradition or with one professor, any ideological change initiated in one course often fails to develop as it is not sustained in courses chosen (or simply available) the next year.

At the same time that the organization of university education puts up obstacles to ideological change in students, it also puts up obstacles to collective action by students aimed at fundamental social change. One way it does this is by reinforcing individualistic values that are incompatible with those that motivate this kind of collective action. Forcing students to compete for grades is the most obvious way in which university education reinforces individualistic values. The massification of students in the university is a more subtle way in which individualism in students is reproduced. As there is no collective project shared by students, indeed as there seems to be little connecting them to one another at all, the only way apparent to students to make it in the university (as in a massified society) is to rely on themselves and to stand out as individuals. Massification of students also militates against collective action for change in that the anonymity of people inside the university makes it difficult for those who would like to get involved to find like-minded people. In the absence of an outlet in which they can find expression and develop, the motivation and initiative of these students tend to dissipate rapidly.[15]

Finally, the organization of higher education impedes the realization of radical academics' aims by keeping liberatory education separate from larger processes of social transformation that occur outside of the university. Put differently, the university institutionalizes a separation between theory and practice, the unity of which is essential both to ideological change and to practical change. In most radical courses, students do not learn about social problems or social movements through direct involvement with them, but through texts and lectures in which they are objectified. Coursework also generally entails writing about some social issue or movement as opposed to getting directly involved in it. Just as students are not encouraged to make contact with those working for change outside of the university, the nature of the institution makes it difficult for the latter to get inside the university in order to connect with students. For example, representatives of various social sectors (such as welfare recipients) are often unwelcome in the academy because they lack the expert qualifications that legitimate their addressing a university class. Taking on some community project as the practical work of a course is also generally discouraged, both because mechanisms to evaluate such practical activities are not readily available and because these activities are often deemed to be political and thus inappropriate for the university to become involved with. The result of this separation of theory from practice is that the radical content students learn tends to remain abstract and foreign to them. As it is difficult for students to make a connection between much of this content and their own lives, significant changes in their thinking and practice seldom occur.

It should be noted that these material limitations on the radical academic project are being and will continue to be exacerbated by changes presently underway in the university. For example, the implementation of the corporate agenda in the university will entrench the separation between those inside of the academy and those fighting for change outside of it. However, as changes taking place in the university do not produce but simply reinforce the material limitations on the project of radical education, combatting these changes is a *necessary but insufficient condition* for the realization of the ends to which radical academics are committed. In order to achieve these ends, a strategy that overcomes the limitations imposed by the university on both the practice and project of radical education will have to be devised. The development of this strategy is a collective task that must be worked out by radical educators in coalition with others, and in practice. I would argue, however, that in order to create the conditions under which such a strategy might take shape, radical academics should initiate the struggle for university autonomy.

Towards a New Project for Radical Education: University Autonomy as the Means to this End

In the modern liberal discourse on higher education, university autonomy is generally taken to mean freedom from external intervention in the university, particularly on the part of government. The university's independence or isolation from society is defended in the interest of protecting academic freedom and ensuring the production of disinterested scientific research (Polin, 1983:39-45). In contrast, my conception draws on the Latin American tradition of university autonomy that has grown out of the university reform movements of the twentieth century.[16] This conception also involves freedom from external intervention in the university. Indeed, in many Latin American countries, governments are constitutionally prohibited from intervening in university affairs (other than providing them with full funding). However, this conception differs from that of modern liberal discourse in two important respects. First, university autonomy involves a far greater degree of democracy within the university than exists in industrialized Western societies. Democratization consists of a broad policy of accessibility as well as the election of university administrators (who also set university research policy) by students and faculty. Second, autonomy involves the university's explicit commitment to solving national social, economic, and political problems. This commitment is at the core of the university's mission. It is also written into many Latin American constitutions (Mariategui, 1963; Gonzalez, 1985; Walter, 1968:39-63).

These two aspects of university autonomy provide different conditions and a different meaning for academic freedom than those that exist in industrialized Western societies. Full university funding, broad accessibility, and the election of its administrative officers allow the university far more room to develop its research and academic policy free from undue external influence on the part of government, industry, or other interest groups. On the other hand, decisions about the use of university resources are not left up to the particular whims of individual researchers, but are constrained by the general priorities (laid out in the platforms of administrators running for office) that have been voted on by students and faculty.[17] In the national universities of Latin America, academics are still afforded considerable freedom in terms of determining what and how they research. However, this freedom exists in and is defined by a context of social responsibility and accountability as opposed to one in which the rights of individual academics (that are highly susceptible to particular interests) take precedence over larger collective needs.[18]

For various historical, political, and economic reasons, the process of achieving university autonomy (as I have used the term here) cannot be the same in North American countries as it was in Latin American countries. Nevertheless, in order to achieve university autonomy in Canada and the United States, some of the same conditions will have to be satisfied. As Gonzalez notes, one vital pre-condition for university autonomy is financial self-sufficiency (Gonzalez, 1985:256). And given present historical conditions in North American society, the best way to get it is to fight for full, sustained, and unconditional government funding for public higher education.[19] One necessary condition for success in this struggle is the support of faculty, students, and other workers in the academy. In educating and mobilizing the university community around the struggle for full funding (and the larger project of university autonomy), radical academics can play a central role, most obviously through their faculty unions but through their departments, learned societies, interest area networks, and/or research agencies as well.[20] However, even if all university workers and students united around this cause (which is unlikely, as many are satisfied with the status quo), they would not be able to muster enough lobby power to get the government to concede to their wishes. As such, those working for change inside the university should also enlist the help of progressive groups fighting for change outside of the university, such as women's groups, native groups, and organized labour.[21]

As Beverly rightly points out, it is unlikely that progressive (or any other) groups outside of the university will support the call for greater funding for the university if they have nothing to gain from it. Thus, in order to win the backing of these groups, demands that link their interests to the interests of the academic community will have to be articulated and integrated into the project of university autonomy (Beverly, 1978:87). In building links that will allow those inside and outside the university to identify and work towards common interests and goals, radical academics can again play a central role. They can help bring the two together through projects such as community outreach programmes or through more ambitious efforts such as broad-based coalitions designed to respond to issues of common concern.[22] Radical academics can also build support for university autonomy through ongoing consultation with progressive groups outside the university through institutions like the European science shops (Dickson, 1984:1158-60) and through joint conferences such as that recently held by the Ontario Federation of Labor (for the proceedings of this conference that brought together academics, education activists, and trade unionists see *Ourschools/Ourselves* 1[8]). The specific demands that will emerge from the negotiation and co-operation between progressive forces inside and outside of the university are likely to include calls for tuition roll-backs and open admissions as well as a strengthened commitment to affirmative action by defending and expanding courses and programmes in women's studies, black studies, and Third World studies. They might also include challenging the way the university is run by fighting, among other things, for greater participation on boards of trustees of representatives of labor, community, and minority groups as well as students and faculty (Beverly, 1978:87-88). In promoting university autonomy inside the academy, it is particularly important that radical academics build support for the demands of their external allies. Meeting these demands is an important condition for winning autonomy for the university. It will also open up many promising possibilities for change once university autonomy is achieved.

Were these demands to be met and autonomy for the university to be achieved (which is no small task), conditions would be created to reverse changes inside the university and between the university and the wider society that are limiting the practice of radical education. The redistribution of power inside the academy would give greater voice to those whose vision of the university conflicts with that of corporations, administrations, and academic entrepreneurs. As well, the availability of adequate financial resources would eliminate one of the main factors that has made corporate infiltration into the university difficult to resist. Note that the achievement of university autonomy guarantees neither an automatic reversal in changes internal and external to the university nor the establishment of an environment more favourable to liberatory educational practice. It will, however, make it easier for those who support these developments to fight for them.

In addition to creating the conditions to transcend the limitations on the practice of radical education, the process of achieving autonomy for the university would also create the conditions to overcome some of the limitations on the project of radical education. As the struggle for autonomy has the potential to unite students around issues of common concern, such as tuition rates and quality of education, it could break down some of the individualism that is reproduced in the university and create some basis for student unity and organization. Further, as the fight for financial self-sufficiency might get students personally involved in action for change, the gap in their education between theory and practice could also be partially bridged. Perhaps most importantly, however, the fight for autonomy would create contact between those inside the university and those struggling for change outside of it. Such contact could help to break down the objectification of radical content inside the academy and enable students to make the connection between their interests and those of people struggling for change outside the university. This contact could also allow the university to become more intimately connected to processes of social transformation that are occurring in the wider society. For example, changes in the makers and the making of university policy that would result from the struggle for university autonomy might lead to the establishment of different mechanisms for evaluating and rewarding student activity so that they could become practically involved in social movements or social issues as opposed to being restricted to doing research about them.

The value of the struggle for university autonomy, however, lies not simply in creating the conditions for liberatory education to be more easily practised in the university and to have more of an effect on students' thought and action, but in creating the conditions for radical academics to struggle to transform the very nature of the university so that it serves popular needs and interests as opposed to those of patriarchal capital. With university autonomy radical educators could become more than dissidents within an institution designed to meet ends to which they are opposed. They could begin to act transformatively to make the university itself play a more socially progressive role. In so doing, radical academics will not only coach or prepare others to make change. They too will become players in the process as they fight to make their own workplace one in which and from which progressive social change is made.

Paradoxically, then, the attempt to overcome the material limitations on the project of radical education suggests qualitative changes in the project itself. This qualitatively transformed project is superior to the original for several reasons, not least of which is that it transcends the conceptual limitations of the original project that militate against progressive social transformation. The original project is flawed by a mechanistic conception of social change in which the university is conceived as a tool that, if properly used, can bring fundamental change to the whole of society. Missing from this instrumentalist conception is a notion of social totality and the dialectical conception of change that follows from it. These notions are, however, implicit in the alternative project sketched above. For the *condition and result* of transforming the university so that it serves popular need is an alliance of those inside the university with other forces for social change outside of it. In addition to linking the university up with other forces for social change, the confluence of forces inside the university that would result from the process of achieving autonomy could establish it as an institutional platform that opens political space for even greater possibilities and action for social change.

It is worth noting that the same kind of mechanistic thinking that limits the project of radical education can also weaken the response to the mounting threat to radical education within the university. This kind of thinking may lead radical academics to the conclusion that it is enough for them to attempt to turn the clock back in the university—to re-establish the favourable conditions of the 1960s. This strategy overlooks the extent to which conditions in the university are inextricably linked to conditions in the wider society. For conditions inside the university to change, changes in the wider society must occur at the same time. This is not to say that all efforts to resist the assault on radical education in the university should be abandoned. Rather, resistance needs to be placed in a new context in which it is not regarded as sufficient unto itself, but as one part of a larger strategy that integrates the efforts of a variety of groups and aims at a fundamental transformation of the university. This new context will alter the criteria by which battles inside the university are chosen as well as the manner in which these battles are approached. Though it will likely complicate an already difficult process of resistance, such a contextual shift will, in both the short and the long term, enhance the effectiveness of this resistance and enlarge the political space it opens up.

NOTES

1   Liberatory education refers to that kind of education that aims to challenge dominant social ideologies that are oppressive to various social groups such as women, people of colour, homosexuals, and workers. In addition to helping students to develop critical self-consciousness, liberatory education also promotes action aimed at fundamental social change. The longer range goal of libratory education is the creation of fully developed human beings who have the ability to collectively identify and meet their needs. In this paper, the term "radical education" will be used synonymously with liberatory education.

2   The following discussion focuses on public universities particularly in Canada but in the United States as well. Many of the observations are also relevant to private universities and to universities in other industrialized Western countries.

3   In addition to the authors mentioned below, Henry Giroux, Michael Apple, Peter McLaren, and the two collections on feminist pedagogy, *Gendered Subjects* and *Learning Our Way*, have made significant contributions to the project of radical education in North America. The journal, *Our schools/Ourselves* is also making an important contribution to radical educational theory and practice, particularly in Canada.

4   These methods consist of all-knowing teachers filling up ignorant students with fragments of knowledge that are often irrelevant to the latter's realities and needs. The job of students is to passively receive and memorize this knowledge and then to spit it back in essays and exams. In addition to preventing critical thinking, banking methods also tend to pacify learners (Freire, 1970).

5   Constraints of space preclude a more detailed discussion of the various conditions that favoured the development of radical education in the university as well as thorough exploration of the relation between the structural and discursive dimensions of the space afforded to radical academics. It is possible that such an exploration would reveal that the distinction between these two dimensions of space is more problematic and ambiguous than is that presented here.

6   Significant aspects of this reorganization of academic work include a renewed attack on tenure, an increasing reliance on part-time and contractually limited instructors, and an increasing separation of the three academic functions so that teaching can become the primary responsibility of untenured faculty, research can be the most important activity of tenured professors, and service, once the means by which academics could exercise collegial control in the university, can be taken over primarily by management and management committees (Newson and Buchbinder, 1988:23-33).

7   See, for example, recent publications of the Corporate–Higher Education Forum, the Canadian Manufacturer's Association, the Science Council of Canada, and the Economic Council of Canada.

8   In 1984, the President of the University of Waterloo suggested that closer ties to the corporate sector may force the university to pull faculty from undergraduate teaching so that they can concentrate on graduates and research (Shore, 1984:2-5). The less professors there are to teach a stable or expanding student body, the larger class sizes are likely to be. Moves by various administrations to cut the budgets of arts programmes in order to finance high-tech research facilities (as was done at the University of Michigan in 1984 [Shor, 1986:129]) are also likely to exacerbate the class size problem. For one way that these programmes can cope with the situation is to intensify the use of their human resources.

9   Note that I am not arguing that small-size classes guarantee the practice of liberatory education or that they are a sufficient condition for it. My point is that smaller classes provide more material conditions that are favourable to this kind of educational practice than do large classes. (For a more detailed discussion of these conditions, see York University's 1983 *Report of the Joint Committee on Class Size*).

10 For example, part-time faculty at York University can request teaching assistance if class sizes exceed a certain number of students. They cannot, however, control the number of students in their classes.

11 It should also be mentioned that the infiltration of business and administrative values into the university may increase the risks associated with practising radical education even if it does not detract from an academic's publication record. If the attitude expressed by a Vice-President of Waterloo becomes generalized, that attitude being that the development of university-corporate

links is the responsibility of all faculty members (Shore, 1984:2-5), then
colleagues and administrators are bound to look even less favourably upon
radical academics who not only disagree with this principle, but insist both in
the form and content of their teaching on biting the corporate hand that feeds.

12   Schniedewind's description of the women's studies programme portrays it as
a model of liberatory education. She writes that the programme

...developed interdisciplinary teaching and research...synthesized
cognitive and affective learning, utilized feminist teaching processes, represented heterogeneous groups of women, and put
into practice feminist processes in programme governance. Such
a women's studies programme helps students to be critical,
active, and feel empowered (Pollack, 1985:20).

13   Although they are not nearly as detailed as the account provided by
Schiedewind, there are accounts that suggest that similar kinds of assaults on
women's studies programmes are taking place in Canada. For example, in
1984, the Women's Studies Programme at Simon Fraser University was
transferred from the Faculty of Interdisciplinary Studies into the Faculty of
Arts, described by Kimball as "less supportive of interdisciplinary studies in
general and of women's studies in particular" (Kimball, 1985:16). This placed
the programme in "a more conservative and problematic setting" and forced
the programme into new battles such as the fight for individual representation
on various university committees.

14   The following remarks are largely confined to undergraduate education,
although many points apply to graduate education as well.

15   Whereas their associations would seem a logical place to promote student
unity and organization, at present most of these associations negate as opposed
to fulfilling this role. Their primary objective is to help individual students
survive in the academic jungle, and not to organize them into a self-conscious
collective that would fundamentally change either the university or the wider
society.

16   Note that this tradition of university autonomy applies only to the national
(public) universities in Latin America. I am indebted to Marco Fonseca for
introducing me to this conception of university autonomy.

17   Due to the policy of broad accessibility to higher education, these people are
a relatively representative sample of the population. Thus, university policy
and research is (at least in theory) responsive and accountable to the needs of
the wider society.

18   It seems to me that the almost complete lack of attention to the Latin American
conception of university autonomy seriously weakens the debate on higher
education in Canada and the United States. The vast majority of these
countries' literature on higher education in the 1980s turns on the antagonism
between the two supposedly opposite ideals of university as bastion of
disinterested research and university as corporate handmaiden. As a result,
discursive space in which to propose the alternative of a democratic university
committed to social (as opposed to simply corporate) development is all but
eclipsed.

19   Note that the attainment of such funding is not unprecedented in contemporary
Western history. Indeed, in several Latin American countries such as Guatemala,

students won the right to have the budgets of the national universities guaranteed in their countries' constitutions. In principle, these funds are also unconditional; that is, they are to be administered solely at the discretion of the universities' elected officials.

[20] Depending on the leadership and the strength of particular academic unions, they may not be the best location from which to work to mobilize faculty and other members of the university community around the struggle for full funding and the project of university autonomy. In fact, in these "postmodern" times, it might be best for radical educators to work from a multiplicity of organizational sites.

[21] I advocate uniting with such groups because they are more likely to favour university autonomy than is the business community and because they are more organized and conscientized than is the general public. The prime advantage of joining with them, however, is the potential result (to be examined below) of meeting the demands they would put forth as a condition of lending their support to the struggle for university autonomy.

[22] Two examples from the past that can inform and guide future action are the bridging programme initiated between York University's Atkinson College and women of the surrounding, low-income Jane-Finch corridor (see Wilkinson and Heyworth in *Canadian Women's Studies*, 6[3]:70-73) and the attempt initiated by the York University Faculty Association to build a coalition among various university and non-university unions to combat government cutbacks in the early 1980s (see YUFA bulletins from 1981-84).

Part Four
Sociology, Anthropology and Social Change

ANTHROPOLOGISTS AND SOCIOLOGISTS, AND THEIR CONTRIBUTIONS TO POLICY IN CANADA

Bruce A. McFarlane[1]

Anthropology and Sociology in Canada are vigorous disciplines that have come of age in Canada during the adulthood of many of their practitioners. What anthropologists and sociologists do in Canada would not necessarily be tolerated in some countries, in pre-Gorbachev Soviet Union, for example, primarily because of the critical nature of some of their output. Much of the teaching and research of sociologists and anthropologists does not rock the boat, but some of it does, challenging the complacent with interpretations of our way of life that run counter to mainstream interpretations.

The intention here is not to produce an overall evaluation of the role of the practitioners of these two disciplines in our society. Rather it is to document the usefulness of their work in the search for alternative ways of doing something about issues that bear on social relations. The sets of issues that confront the state pertain more than ever to social relations, whatever the sphere—family, community, ethnicity, gender, health, the work place, the school, the prison, the Indian reserve.

One of the major problems faced by social scientists in general is that the more successful they are in their social analyses, the more likely it is that their concepts of analysis and findings will find their way into the intelligent lay person's general vocabulary and thought processes and their social scientific origins be forgotten. It all soon becomes "common sense," that is, much as the physical science concept of *gravity* is now deemed to be "common sense" or as brightness is expressed in watts, such as a 40-watt or 60-watt light bulb, rather than as the work of one joule per second. John Trent recently cited twenty-four examples of this phenomenon in the social sciences (Abu-Laban and Rule, 1988:78). Perhaps I may add to Trent's list at this time. One is derived from the title of John Porter's classic study *The Vertical Mosaic* (Porter, 1965). While Porter may or may not have been the first to use the phrase, it came into wide usage after his acute analysis of Canadian society. A discussion of Canada and its population seldom takes place today without "the mosaic" being introduced as the distinguishing difference between Canadian society and the American "melting-pot" society. The origin of the concept in this comparative context is frequently forgotten or, more likely, unknown. In addition, the term "Citizen-Plus" to describe the status of Canada's indigenous peoples was introduced in *The Hawthorn-Tremblay Report* (1966:13). In similar vein the concept "welfare colonialism" was introduced into general language after Robert Paine's usage of it in his study *The White Arctic* (Paine, 1977). These and many other social science concepts may be found in non-academic work with no signal as to their origins.

What is the kind and the scope of the contribution that anthropologists and sociologists make to issues that exercise the wits of policy makers and the interested publics? This is the question to try to answer. When it is said that a scholar's work or a research programme makes a contribution to policy, it is not meant that the findings are deemed to be directly applicable or the recommendations endorsed by the sponsors. No; what is meant is that the findings and recommendations are fed into the stream of public discourse, to be fought over, ignored, acted upon.

Perhaps most visible of sociology's and anthropology's contribution to knowledge about Canadian society since the end of World War II has been the contribution of anthropologists and sociologists to research carried out under the auspices of royal commissions and other commissions of inquiry whose recommendations frequently became the bases for policy. A few cases have been selected to illustrate contributions in the post-1945 period. In some instances the researchers noted will be primarily anthropologists, in others mostly sociologists, and in some cases both groups will be represented. It must be pointed out, however, that in each of the cases chosen members of social science disciplines other than anthropology and sociology were also actively engaged in the interdisciplinary enterprise. The cases chosen all fall in the 1960s and early 1970s (i.e., in the early days of the CSAA) and have been selected primarily because sufficient time has elapsed so that their impact on policy may be more easily teased out.

The cases selected for illustration are the following:

- Royal Commission on Health Services (Hall Commission) 1961-64
- Royal Commission on Bilingualism and Biculturalism (Dunton-Laurendeau Commission) 1963-67
- A Survey of Contemporary Indians of Canada: Economic, Political, Educational Needs and Policies (Hawthorn-Tremblay Report) 1964-66
- Commission royale d'enquête sur l'enseignment au Québec (Parent Commission) 1961-64
- Royal Commission on the Status of Women in Canada (Bird Commission) 1967-70

In addition to these cases two books will be singled out for a brief special mention because of their undoubted impact on many facets of social science and policy in Canada. These are *The Vertical Mosaic* (Porter, 1965) and *The Double Ghetto* (Armstrong and Armstrong, 1978). (The latter book published in 1978 actually falls slightly beyond the early 1970s but in the sense in which it will be treated here it cannot be overlooked.)

When assessing the contributions of the members of these two disciplines to policy in Canada it is often difficult to attribute a *direct* contribution of any one study, book, individual, or piece of research, but much of what is noted in the cases treated below resulted in some public as well as academic discussion and, on occasion, considerable controversy. In addition, many of the research findings for the royal commissions, study groups, et cetera, have resulted in recommendations that eventually found their way into public policy, albeit in modified form. Hence, we may assume that in the limited sample of cases noted below the research findings contributed to our understanding of social relations and culture in Canadian society and so to public policy. It is interesting to note, as we did above, that research findings in these two disciplines as often as not run in the face of conventional wisdom. To this extent practitioners in these disciplines are often viewed as "negative" critics of society and recommendations that follow from their findings frequently upset those who would uphold and maintain the status quo. This is not likely to endear either the disciplines nor their practitioners to anyone, especially to those in power. While this is true, it is also true that many of the academics and others whose work is noted below were, and still are, being used as consultants by federal and provincial government departments and agencies, research councils, other public bodies, and increasingly by private industry and private organizations. Hence, their contributions, although not always easily visible, extend far beyond the completion and publication of a study no matter how interesting and/or non-controversial it may be.

While the case study approach has been selected for this presentation, we would be remiss not to note some whose work in the period covered has made important contributions to policy but who, for one reason or another, were not associated with the particular cases chosen. We will do so in a *brief* summary paragraph following the case studies and the two books.

Sociology and anthropology as distinct disciplines, when compared to economics and political science, had rather late beginnings in anglophone Canada, really only coming of age in the mid-1960s, which was somewhat later than in francophone Canada and some decades after the other social sciences. This is not to say that no anthropologists or sociologists were carrying out research or teaching their subjects in Canadian universities before this time (Shore, 1987:72-8). They were; indeed, some of the major influences on post-1945 anthropology and sociology in Canada had their beginning in the research carried out in the pre-World War II period (Shore, 1987:195-261). For example, the work of Marius Barbeau, Carl Dawson, Léon Gérin, Diamond Jenness, and Everett Hughes on the conditions of Canada's indigenous peoples, the human ecological approach to urban growth and planning, the study of ethnic groups in the west, education and Quebec's rural population, and ethnic relations, particularly anglophone-francophone relations, all carried out from the late 1880s to the late 1930s, have had a lasting influence. It is not without interest that the research problems that taxed this group—ethnicity, work relations, education, rural-urban movement, social problems in urban areas, and Canada's native peoples—were also at the forefront of research in the 1960s.

Some scholars who bridged these two periods were Jean-Charles Falardeau, Thomas McIlwraith, Oswald Hall, Leonard Marsh, and S.D. Clark, all of whom began their research careers in the 1930s and were important and influential figures during the period of rapid growth in these disciplines in the 1960s (in the 1950s in Quebec). Everett Hughes, albeit a scholar who began his work in the 1920s, was also important in this sense because of both his own research and that of his students, francophone and anglophone, throughout the 1940s, 1950s, and 1960s. In a similar vein Diamond Jenness' work as a consultant to government departments on Canada's north, the circumpolar region, and on Canada's native peoples had considerable influence as late as the 1960s.

This growth from humble beginnings was also reflected in institutional growth, and while Dawson was appointed to teach sociology at McGill as early as 1921, McIlwraith began to teach anthropology at Toronto in 1925, and Edward Sapir headed the Anthropology Division (later the Museum of Man) of the Canadian Geological Survey as early as 1910, the numbers engaged in these activities remained small. Even during the 1930s, the few university departments and other employing agencies were, in effect, two- and three-person enterprises as far as these disciplines were concerned. Following World War II there was slow but steady growth until the 1960s, when the growth was dramatic. In 1956 the body of sociologists and anthropologists had grown to sixty-nine, forty two of whom were teaching at the universities. In 1961 there were fewer than one hundred sociologists and anthropologists but by 1974 the number had shot up to more than nine hundred! Kathleen Herman's *1986-87 Guide to Departments of Sociology, Anthropology and Archaeology in Universities and Museums in Canada* lists 1,629 scholars of whom 1,134 are in sociology, 440 in anthropology, and 55 in archaeology.

We will now examine the research and other roles played by anthropologists and sociologists in some royal commissions and other inquiries in Canada in the 1960-1975 period. Concentration on these two disciplines does not mean that the role of the other social sciences is being minimized. The case for the other social sciences and their practitioners has been very well made elsewhere by others. For example, the reader may refer to John Trent's very interesting and illustrative chapter entitled "Contributions of Social Science Research in Canadian Society: in the Eye of the Beholder" in *The Human Sciences* (Abu-Laban and Rule, 1988:77-126), and to Margrit Eichler, Donald Savage and David Smith, in *University Research and the Future of Canada* (Abu-Laban, 1989).

Royal Commission on Health Services (Hall Commission)

This royal commission, set up under the Chairmanship of Chief Justice Emmett Hall of Saskatchewan following Order in Council P.C. 1961-83 was charged with, among other things, inquiring into and reporting existing facilities, present and future needs for health services for Canadians, and recommending measures (in keeping with the division of legislative powers) that would ensure that the best possible health care was available to all Canadians.

In order to carry out their mandate the Commissioners appointed a sociologist, Bernard R. Blishen, as Director of Research. The research he initiated was of an interdisciplinary nature and included research by political scientists, economists, physicians, nurses, dentists, pharmacists, and sociologists, among others. A large number of studies were undertaken and among the twenty-six research studies published by the Commission four were by sociologists (Oswald Hall, 1964; Bruce McFarlane, 1964; Donald Mills, 1964; and Reg Robson, 1967).

Based on the research and other evidence put before it, the Commission put forward two hundred recommendations in its final *Report*. A sizeable number of these recommendations found their way into public policy and, in fact, in 1968 Parliament introduced the legislation that helped to create the structure for the present-day health care delivery system in Canada. That is, the recommendations, many of them directly related to the research findings of the social scientists including sociologists, had a direct impact on social policy: wide sweeping changes were made in the organization, structure, and provision of health care services in Canada. These changes have affected the lives of all Canadians, whether in their roles as patients, health care professionals, health educators and researchers, hospital employees, or through access to and the provision of services through the auspices of provincial government health and hospital insurance schemes.

Royal Commission on Bilingualism & Biculturalism (Dunton-Laurendeau Commission)

Canada, like most countries, is a mélange of cultural, linguistic, and racial groups and so is not special in this respect. It is, however, regarded as special in that it gives *de jure* recognition to diversity and has provided through legislation the machinery to foster this diversity.

The development of this machinery and the values that support it was due in no small measure to the Royal Commission on Bilingualism and Biculturalism, an important component included in whose work was social scientific research. There are not many large-scale research undertakings in the world that can match the scope and quality of the output provided by the social scientists involved in this Commission and its work.

A sizeable proportion of the researchers engaged in this large-scale enterprise were members of the groups under discussion and represented among other things the two charter language groups, francophone and anglophone. Of the thirteen-member Supervisors' and Consultants' Staff, four were sociologists: Oswald Hall, responsible for Social Studies, and three sociologists expert in survey research—Soucy Gagné, John Johnstone, and Tony Boisvert.

A large array of studies were carried out under the auspices of the Commission. Many were published, and those not published were all available for public scrutiny and are frequently cited. At least eighteen of these studies were carried out by sociologists and anthropologists and had considerable impact on the Commission's recommendations, hence on public policy. The following sociologists and anthropologists were among the many who prepared studies, all of which had *considerable* input into the recommendations, hence on subsequent policies: Jacques Brazeau, Colette Carisse, S.D. Clark, Pierre Coulombe, L. Courcelles, Roger de la Garde, Jacques Dofny, Soucy Gagné, Charles Hobart, Everett Hughes, John Johnstone, Monique Mosseau, Peter Pineo, John Porter, Marcel Rioux, and Frank Vallee. Of singular importance in the work of this Commission was the role played by Jean Burnet. John Trent has noted, "On the Ottawa scene, the York sociologist, Jean Brunet has often been credited with being the proponent of Multicultural research on Bilingualism and Biculturalism and Beyond." (Abu-Laban and Rule, 1988:106). Her recent (1990) Order of Canada award was a reflection of her important contribution in this area.

The policies that resulted from the government's acceptance of some of the Commission's recommendations has had a profound and lasting effect on the lives of Canadians either directly or indirectly. This impact may be appreciated when we mention a few of the policy areas that reflected the government's acceptance of some of the recommendations: the establishment of a Commissioner of Official Languages to monitor the use of Canada's two official languages in the public service and Crown corporations; Canada's multiculturalism policies; support granted to the provinces for second official language immersion programmes at elementary and secondary school levels; hiring policies in areas of federal jurisdiction; the designation of posts as "bilingual" posts and a heavy concentration on second-language training within the federal public service itself; and so on. Also of importance is the fact that the social sciences in general played a very important role in the deliberations and research activities of the Commission. It was, in fact, a very good example of an interdisciplinary undertaking. This is best reflected in the composition of the thirteen-member *Consultative Committee—Research* wherein were located three historians, four sociologists, four political scientists and two economists, among whom were Jacques Parizeau, S.D. Clark, Pierre-Elliott Trudeau, Jacques Brazeau, Myer Brownstone, Aileen Ross, William Morton, and Paul Fox.

A Survey of the Contemporary Indians of Canada: Economic, Political, Educational Needs and Policies (The Hawthorne-Tremblay Report)

At roughly the same time as the Royal Commission on Bilingualism and Biculturalism was launched, the federal Department of Citizenship and Immigration, through its Indian Affairs Branch, commissioned a national survey on the situation of Indians in Canada. Two prominent Canadian anthropologists headed the study: Harry Hawthorn as Director and Marc-Adélard Tremblay as Associate Director assisted by, among others, Frank Vallee and Joan Ryan.

In the approximately two-year research period (1964-66) more than fifty persons were involved either as part of the main research team as consultants or as independent researchers whose projects were funded by the study. The large majority were anthropologists or graduate students in anthropology, which is hardly surprising considering the traditional role of anthropologists in cross-cultural research among indigenous people. Notable among this group were Bernard Bernier, Gordon Inglis, Eric Schwimmer, Paul Charest, Tom McFeat, and Lucien Laforest. There also was, however, substantial involvement of scholars from education, economics, law, political science, and psychology.

Field work was carried out in scores of reserves and other communities across the country. On the basis of this field work and politico-legal analyses a *Report* was published in two volumes (1966 and 1967). No fewer than 150 recommendations were made in the *Report*, covering almost the whole spectrum of issues confronting Indians and the state. The most important general thrust of these recommendations was the recognition of collective rights of Indians and not simply their individual rights as citizens—the term *Citizen Plus* was coined to convey this idea: the continuation of a federal role as guarantor of these rights, even though the Indians would benefit from more provincial government services in the future than they had in the past, and a broadening of the mandate of federal responsibility to include Indians off the reserve, especially in the cities.

Some of the minor proposals of the *Report* dealing with community development and local government were implemented, but none of its major recommendations were acted upon by the federal government. Instead, a set of proposals were presented in the White Paper of June 1969 (Department of Indian Affairs and Northern Development, 1969) that, if implemented, would have terminated the special responsibility of the federal government and the Indian Affairs Branch and would have shifted to the provinces the onus of responsibility for services to Indian people. What was envisaged in the White Paper was the ultimate abolition of special status or collective rights.

An important point to make is that the research-based recommendations, while not accepted by government in the short run, still had a
significant impact on the policy process. This impact was made through the
responses to the White Paper by native organizations, expressed most
forcibly in their Red Paper (Citizens Plus, 1970), and by other associations,
such as the Indian-Eskimo Association. The gist of the counter-arguments
to the White Paper were: the rejection of the proposed termination policy
and of the shifting of responsibilities to the provincial level; the demand for
Citizen Plus status; and the demand that priority be given to the just
settlement of land and other claims. To a certain extent, then, the recommendations of the Report formed the basis not only for the government's position
but also for the counter-arguments put forward by the indigenous peoples
themselves (Weaver, 1980).

In the long run, many of the policies that have been put into place
conformed to the most important recommendations of the Hawthorn-
Tremblay Report which, in most cases, were based on social science research. The consequences of not implementing many of the other recommendations were highly visible at Oka and elsewhere in Canada in the
summer of 1990.

Commission royale d'enquéte sur l'enseignement au Québec (Parent Commission)

Perhaps one of the most important inquiries ever made into education
in Canada was that undertaken by the Commission royale d'enquête sur
l'enseignement au Quebec under the chairmanship of the Rt. Rev. Alphonse
Marie Parent (Québec, 1963-65). The Parent Commission examined all
aspects of education in Quebec, public and private (including collèges
classiques), Protestant and Roman Catholic, French and English, and from
kindergarten to professional and post-graduate education in the universities of Quebec.

The five-volume report of the Commission contained 650 recommendations based on extensive research carried out by sociologists, anthropologists, other social scientists, and experts in the humanities and law, plus
over three hundred briefs presented by interested parties at the public
hearings. The educational reforms that followed the acceptance of the
Commission's recommendations changed the whole course of public and
private education for Quebec's 1.5 million pupils and students, the 50,000
teachers, and the 6 universities (three French and Roman Catholic and three
English and secular).

Perhaps the most far-reaching recommendations (other than those
concerned with administration) were those contained in Volume 2, Recommendations 82-109, concerned with a new stage in the educational

process intermediate to the traditional secondary school and the tertiary or university level, that is, the introduction of a new institution, the CEGEP (collège d'enseignement general et professionnel). The introduction of the CEGEP as a compulsory stage in the journey from high school to university or as a vocational training stage for those who do not plan to go to university and the virtual elimination of the collèges classiques has had a profound impact on the education of Quebec youth. In addition to opening up the possibility of higher education to a much wider audience than heretofore it also made this possible by distributing these institutions on a regional basis throughout the province. It also opened up through the CEGEPs the possibility for a much larger proportion of girls to continue their education beyond high school than was the case before in Quebec (Denis and Lipkin, 1972; Denis, 1975).

Guy Rocher, at the time Head of the Département de sociologie at l'Université de Montréal, was one of the Commissioners, and because of his long-standing interest in research on education, undoubtedly had a hand in the framing of the recommendations. In addition, the research carried out for the Commission under the direction of the distinguished sociologist-demographer Jacques Henrepin and the forecasts that followed from their analysis have played an important role in educational planning in Quebec. A number of other sociologists and anthropologists such as Marcel Rioux, Rev. Norbert Lacoste, Jacques Brazeau, and Gérard Malo were also involved in research for the Commission. The changed social composition of the francophone students at universities today in Quebec as compared to some twenty years ago is probably the best single indicator of the impact that the social science research for the Commission, and its subsequent recommendations as put into practice by the provincial government, has had on public policy in education.

Royal Commission on the Status of Women in Canada (Bird Commission)

This Royal Commission was set up on 16 February 1967 under the chairmanship of Florence Bird and was among other things to "inquire into...the status of women in Canada...to ensure equal opportunities with men in all aspects of Canadian society." Just as did the other commissions noted above, this one also called upon experts in the social sciences, including sociologists and anthropologists, to assist them in their deliberations either as consultants or as researchers.[2] Jacques Henripin was named as one of the Commissioners, sociologist Monique Bégin was appointed the Executive Secretary and sociologist David Kirk was named the first Research Director. In addition, a large number of sociologists and anthropologists (including graduate students) were employed in the Secretariat or as consultants. Among them were Colette Carisse, Charles Hobart, Ron Lambert, Jim Lotz, and Reg Robson. Thirty-four original background studies were prepared for the Commission, of which seven were prepared by anthropologists and sociologists. The 167 recommendations of the Commission were based on an analysis of these original reports, on the 469 formal briefs that they received, and on the information gathered at the public hearings.

Just as in the case of the other inquiries under discussion, not all of the Commission's recommendations were accepted or, if accepted by the government, did not necessarily find their way immediately to policy. It is true, however, that the government of the day did take action and slowly but surely the recommendations based among other things on the sociological and other social science and legal research are gradually finding their way into public policy either through legislation or administrative regulations (Canadian Advisory Council on the Status of Women, 1983). Noteworthy, of course, was the federal government's establishment in 1973 of the Canadian Advisory Council on the Status of Women and the naming of a cabinet minister responsible for the Council. Also worthy of note following the recommendations has been the enlistment of women to full duties in the RCMP, and into most if not all occupations in the Canadian Armed Forces, the admission of women to the military colleges, amendments in the federal Income Tax Act, and the institution of "status of women" offices (as monitoring agencies) in all government departments and Crown corporations. This latter pattern has been followed by many provincial government departments, universities, and private corporations.

Among the studies that contributed to the Commissioners' understanding of the problems under study were those carried out by sociologists and anthropologists. I will cite a few of these: Colette Carisse's study of the portrayal of women in the mass media, Reg Robson's study of men's and women's salaries in the academic profession, Jim Lotz's study of the role of Indian women, and Charles Hobart's study of young Canadians and changing orientations to marriage. All of these had a direct bearing on the recommendations, hence had some impact on subsequent policy.

After this brief examination of some royal commissions and the Hawthorne-Tremblay Report, let us now consider the two books mentioned earlier, *The Vertical Mosaic* and *The Double Ghetto*.

Setting the Environment

The late John Porter's now-classic book *The Vertical Mosaic: An Analysis of Social Class and Power in Canada* (1965) is a landmark study in the sociology of Canadian society. Its influence has been considerable and felt throughout the social sciences, the humanities, and society at large. To a great extent it marked for anglophone Canada "the coming of age" of sociology—people in anglophone Canada now began to take sociology as a discipline and sociologists as a group seriously. This, of course, had been true in francophone Canada for some time, and individual sociologists from both language groups had long had the respect of their peers in other disciplines in Canada; some of these were Marius Barbeau, Carl Dawson, Jean-Charles Falardeau, Oswald Hall, S.D. Clark, David Solomon, Léon Gérin, Tom McIlwraith, and Diamond Jenness among others.

In like manner *The Double Ghetto* (1978) by Pat and Hugh Armstrong reached a wide audience far beyond the confines and devotees of our two disciplines. Following the publication of each of these two books no public discussion of any import on the social issues with which they were concerned could disregard the documentation and acute analyses of the inequities in Canada that existed because of the accident of one's birth, language, gender, religion, social class, or ethnicity—inequities that were perpetuated by the educational and occupational opportunity structures in Canada. To this extent Porter and the Armstrongs have had considerable influence on policy by setting the environment within which discussions and policy deliberations could take place. Like Everett Hughes in an earlier period, Porter's influence is still felt today through his students, for example, Wallace Clement and Dennis Olsen, who are now making their own contributions; and the Armstrongs, through their important research and publications and through the important roles they play with others who work within a political economy analytical framework.

As noted earlier, it would be remiss not to note some anthropologists and sociologists whose work in the 1960s and early 1970s has made important contributions to policy but who, for one reason or another, were not directly associated with the particular cases chosen as illustrations. Needless to say, it would be impossible to cite all sociologists and anthropologists in Canada who have made contributions via their research and consultancies in a paper of this type; hence, I will be very selective and, perhaps even somewhat idiosyncratic.

Among this group must be mentioned Tony Richmond, whose studies of immigration and immigrants in Canada have had considerable input in any consideration of Canada's Immigration policy; Hubert Guindon, whose studies and knowledge of the "new middle classes" in Quebec have placed him in great demand as a Consultant to most of the royal commissions noted above; the sociologists and anthropologists of the Institute of Social and Economic Research (ISER) of Memorial University, Newfoundland, whose studies of the province's outports among other things have had a direct input into educational, health, and other provincial development policies (see Bibliography); Victor Valentine and the crucial role he played in policy-oriented research at the Department of Northern and Indian Affairs; Gérard

Fortin and his studies of rural development, social change and industrialization which contributed immeasurably to the ten-volume *Report of the
B.A.E.Q., Plan du développement du Bas-Saint-Laurent, de la Gaspésie et des Iles-
de-la-Madeleine for ARDA-Québec* (1966); Raymond Breton, a consultant for
many royal commissions, whose national study of the factors involved in
career decisions of Canadian youth has had impact in most provincial
education jurisdictions (Breton, 1972); Frank Jones, Jacques Brazeau, and
the late David Solomon, whose sociological studies with the Department of
National Defence during the 1950s and 1960s contributed to the establishment of a permanent social research unit within the Canadian Armed
Forces.

At this point I will draw this study to a close, fully cognizant that whole
areas of research by anthropologists and sociologists that have contributed
to policy in the period under discussion have not been treated. Some areas
have received short shrift and some have received no mention whatsoever.
If one were to try to assess every contribution to policy by anthropologists
and sociologists during the short lifetime of our Association it would
require a great deal more time than most of us have at our disposal. It is a
task that I, in moments of wild fantasy, am thinking of attempting. Each day,
however, the task looms larger and larger, even if one were to look only at
royal commissions and other commissions of inquiry: for example, the
Abella Commission, the Badgley Report, the Ouimet Report, the Goldenberg
Report on Parole, the Berger Report on the MacKenzie Valley Pipeline, the
Report of the Special Senate Committee on Youth, the eight-volume report
"Aspirations scolaires et orientations professionnelles des étudiants
(l'ASOPE)" by Pierre Belanger and Guy Rocher, etc. Even in the limited
period selected for this study (1960 to mid-1970) there were, of course, *many*
other important commissions and inquiries in which sociologists and
anthropologists in Canada were involved and which we could have examined: Commission d'enquête sur la santé et le bien-être social, in which
Nicholas Zay, Joy Wolfrey, Marc-Adélard Tremblay, and Gérard Fortin
were involved; The Commission on Post-Secondary Education in Ontario,
in which, among others, sociologists Ron D'Costa and Edward Harvey
participated; and the Commission d'enquête sur l'enseignement des arts au
Quebec, which was chaired by Marcel Rioux and in which Marc Laplante
played a role.

It was pointed out recently by Professor Lars Osberg that major three-
or four-year royal commissions, such as those we have examined above, are
no longer the norm. More recent inquiries have been of much more modest
scope, have carried out very little basic research, and have been of shorter
duration. This comment was made at the time of this author's presentation
of a brief, "The Contributions of the Social Sciences to Social Policy in
Canada With Particular Respect to Sociologists and Anthropologists," to

the University Research Committee of The Royal Society of Canada, April 1990 (McFarlane, 1991). Professor Osberg's observation is an extremely important one and this scaling down of public inquiries has also seen the rise in the number of government inquiries in the form of task forces. It would appear that governments now prefer internally handled task forces because they are not bound to make the task forces' findings public, as in the case of royal commissions. This effectively removes task force findings and recommendations from public discourse, except in the case of "leaked" reports.

William Carroll has pointed out to me that this change is not surprising.[3] He notes,

> ...1960-74 was precisely the era in which the welfare state was consolidated. Also a distinctive approach to the Quebec question was adopted which partially acknowledged language claims but denied national rights. One could argue that in this period sociologists and anthropologists could play an especially influential part in contributing to expansive social reform because their own professional emphasis on social relations and culture which you noted earlier "corresponded" with the state's agenda for nation-building. This was the period of post-war economic boom, prior to the recession of 1974-75 and the fiscal crisis, and at the early stages of the rise of Quebec nationalism as a mass movement.... The later 1970s and 1980s took a different turn. Perhaps the shift from royal commissions to task forces is a reflection of the neo-conservative drift in the last fifteen years, a drift which has actually marginalized many of the sociological and anthropological perspectives which informed public policy in the period under consideration. One example would be the 1985 MacDonald Commission, whose vision was almost purely shaped by the perspective of neo-classical economics.

While all of the foregoing, including Professor Osberg's observation, certainly fits the present-day pattern of government inquiries, there are notable exceptions. At least two royal commissions, in which social scientists including sociologists and anthropologists have and are playing major roles, have been established recently. These are the recently completed Royal Commission on Employment and Unemployment in Newfoundland and the ongoing federal Royal Commission on New Reproductive Technology. A sociologist, Professor Douglas House of the Memorial University of Newfoundland, was the Chairman of the former and Maura Hanrahan, a sociologist, was one of the major researchers; and Professor Louise Vandelac, a sociologist, of l'Université de Québec à Montréal is one of the Commissioners on the latter. In the case of the Newfoundland royal commission it is not without interest that shortly after the tabling of the Report, Professor House was named Chairman of the Economic Recovery Commission of Newfoundland. It would be hard to find a more direct contribution to policy. In the case of the ongoing Royal Commission, Margrit Eichler, a sociologist, played an active and important role in helping to get this commission established.

This brief study has been an attempt to indicate the contributions to policy made by anthropologists and sociologists most of whom were or are members of the Canadian Sociology and Anthropology Association. A fifteen-year period ending fifteen years ago was selected for study, since it was felt that was long enough ago for the social scientific research and subsequent recommendations of royal commissions and other public inquiries to be reflected in policy. Such was indeed the case, and the contributions by the anthropologists and sociologists to policy have been even more extensive than their most enthusiastic supporters would have predicted.

NOTES

[1]   This paper grew out of a report Frank Vallee and I prepared for the Social Science Federation of Canada (McFarlane–Vallee, 1982 SSFC Report) at the request of the Canadian Sociology and Anthropology Association. The SSFC hoped to use the contributions of its various constituent members to convince the federal Cabinet that the government should contribute more money to the Social Sciences and the Humanities. For a number of reasons the larger project fell through.

At the outset let me say that this is not a social history of the CSAA nor of the development of sociology and anthropology in Canada. Nor is it a history of the contributions of the CSAA to social and public policy in the sense that Douglas Verney's 1974 study of the SSFC's contribution to Science Policy in Canada was, or Jean-Charles Falardeau's *The Rise of the Social Sciences in French Canada* (1964), or Stephen Brooks' and Alain Gagnon's more recent study, *Social Scientists and Politics in Canada: Between Clerisy and Vanguard* (1988), or Don Whyte's recent piece, "Sociology and the Constitution of Society: Canadian Experiences" (1989). What it is, I hope, will become clearer as I progress.

[2]   Before the secretariat was established and the Research Director appointed I was asked by the Chairperson to assist her by preparing a short research agenda for the Commission.

[3]   Personal correspondence from the editors of this volume.

THE IDEOLOGICAL AND STRUCTURAL ROOTS OF THE FAILURE OF SOCIOLOGY AS A FOUNDATION FOR ENGLISH CANADIAN SOCIAL POLICY

Jim Harding

Sociology and Social Policy

In this essay I will explore some of the historical, political, and philosophical roots and antecedents to the problematic relationship of sociology and social policy. Hopefully, this general treatment can provide a basis for others to undertake more concrete analyses, perhaps along regional lines.

My starting point is the apparent minimal involvement of anglophone sociologists in social policy research and processes. The papers at the 25th Annual Conference are a case in point. On the basis of titles in the index for the meetings of the CSAA I found less than ten of one hundred and fifty papers that explicitly addressed social policy matters. I realize that many others have implications for social policy, including some of those in sessions reporting on feminist research or women's studies. But the question remains why the relationship to social policy is so rarely explicitly conceptualized in English Canadian sociological discourse.

One Characteristic example is the distinct lack of sociologists among the authors of a recent, re-issued textbook on social policy (Shankar, 1987). Of the twenty-two contributors to this book, only one was affiliated with a sociology department. In contrast, nine of the contributors were from social work programmes. And while this in part may have resulted from the book being compiled and edited from within a social work programme, it is used as a text in some sociology courses on social policy. Furthermore, the explanation for the lack of involvement of sociologists in this case was not that social policy was defined narrowly as social welfare, which is often the case within social work. The editor clearly states that social welfare was but "one facet of social policy" (1987:3), and the list of major issues analyzed in the book reflected a broad range of social policy matters.

A recently published book on unemployment and social policy (Riches and Ternowetsky, 1990) has only two sociologists among the sixteen contributors, none affiliated with sociology departments, with the vast majority of contributors having a background in social work. In my own experience editing a forthcoming book of essays on social policy under the Blakeney NDP in Saskatchewan (1971-82), I was only able to obtain one other person formally educated in sociology as a contributor. The bulk of the authors that finally agreed to work on the project had academic backgrounds in social work, law, or other applied and human services fields.

I am not going to undertake an anglophone profile of sociologists' involvement or lack of involvement in social policy processes and problems. Rather, I am going to explore some of the underlying theoretical and historical questions that shape how we see the relationship of social science, including sociology, to social policy. However, one can only hope that out of this kind of discussion we will, collectively, become more aware of our intellectual roots. In particular, in Canada we must face up to the influence of the metropole and periphery upon sociology and its relation to social policy. As David Nock discusses elsewhere in this volume, much of what gets noted as being a significant sociological influence on social policy focuses on sociology at the centre. While central Canadian sociology may relate more directly to Canada-wide policy-making, peripheral sociologists are confronted with the impact of central policy within the regions. This study is no less important.

The Need for Regional Analyses

I acknowledge that various regional traditions, which link sociological and social science practice to social policy, exist. These, however, don't necessarily find themselves translated into "national" publications or discussions. In the case of Saskatchewan one cannot ignore the ambivalent relationship that social policy researchers have had to both the CCF and NDP political traditions. Critical social policy in Saskatchewan has been as much rooted in the agendas of socio-political protest movements as in government processes themselves (Harding, forthcoming). In Saskatchewan the role of the bygone Centre for Community Studies at the University of Saskatchewan in the shaping of policy-related research would need scrutiny. The Centre exposed an up-and-coming generation of social scientists, including myself, to people like American-trained sociologist Arthur Davis and British social anthropologist Peter Worseley, who were involved in direct research on the North and rural Saskatchewan. Jim McCrorie, past editor of the CSAA Journal and now Director of the Canadian Plains Research Centre at the University of Regina, was also influenced by this Centre. Another person influenced by the Centre was Paul Phillips, who has researched Canadian labour history.

The added fact that Saskatchewan was the home of Canadian Medicare has also shaped the nature of social policy research. Though bio-medical research dominates health-related research in Saskatchewan as elsewhere, there is a respectable tradition of socio-health, community health, and health policy–related research, including that undertaken by sociologists within the Applied Psychiatric Research Unit in Saskatoon. Contemporary university research units like Sample Survey, the Social Administration Research Unit (SARU), and Prairie Justice Research (PJR) in the School of

Human Justice—all at the University of Regina—and the Social Research Unit and defunct Institute of Northern Studies at the University of Saskatchewan have all, in their own way, built up a policy-related applied knowledge base in the province. Furthermore, as aboriginal groups gain more control of post-secondary education, their research capacity in the social policy area has developed. The Saskatchewan Indian Federated College (SIFC) and Gabriel Dumont Institute (GDI) have both linked Indian and Native studies to matters of social policy, including aboriginal self-government.

The products of research from these Saskatchewan units would certainly be a starting place for any direct research on the make-up and impact of social policy research in the Prairie region. Manitoba and Alberta, of course, have their own rich regional history of social research. Elsewhere in this volume, Barbara Neis discusses some of the sociological research that has been relevant to social policy in another hinterland region—Newfoundland and Labrador.

That having been said, these various research milieus in Saskatchewan do not have any underlying common policy research mission and greatly reflect the fragmentation of social knowledge within universities at large. Furthermore, it is safe to assume that knowledge of work of this kind, whether in Saskatchewan or other hinterland provinces and regions, remains less influential within Canadian sociology than that work done at the centre (i.e., southern Ontario), which has had more direct ties to national governmental policy processes. (In the preceding essay in this volume Bruce McFarlane explores the role of sociologists in royal commissions). Certainly the field is largely open to those interested and willing to see if and how the links between sociology and social policy differ among regions and between these and central(ized) Canada.

Competing Schools of Sociology: Implications for Social Policy

It isn't possible to disentangle the matter of sociology and social policy here or anywhere without looking at the conflicting definitions of the sociological project that developed along with the field of study. In this regard, it is important to break totally with the fallacy that only the radical tendency within sociology has roots in a political perspective on, and commitment to, reforming society. This is the persisting fallacy of the end of ideology.

August Comte, who along with Émile Durkheim, was the precursor of the dominant functionalist sociology, was a clear advocate of the industrial technocratic society that functionalist sociology has served so well. As

Raymond Aron wrote about Comte:

> Comte was the serene herald of the new order. The sociologist is a sort of peace-loving prophet who trains our minds, rallies our souls, and secondarily is himself the high priest of the sociological (or Sociographical) religion (1965:99).

The problems of leadership, intervention, and even vanguardism, are not peculiar to radical and Marxian sociology.

Obviously this creator of the term "sociology" saw a primary role for his exhaustive discipline (which was to be the synthesis of all scientific knowledge) in directly shaping society. One could argue that Comte's instrumental vision of positivist (and scientistic) sociology, as the motor of social reform in the service of social order, was reflected in the U.S. government's short-lived Project Camelot in the 1960s. This multi-million dollar research project, funded by the U.S. military, was to try to provide the knowledge of social systems needed to help avert social revolutions, particularly in South America. About this controversial "social policy" project Horowitz commented:

> The identification of revolution and radical social change with a social pathology is the final proof, if such were necessary, that a functionalist credo of order, stability, pattern maintenance, stress management and so forth does indeed reveal strong conservative drives (1967:44).

One could say that, even for the capitalists and their neo-liberal supporters, sociology always had a mission to inform social policy. Rather than a commitment to social policy aimed at social change, its commitment was to social policy aimed at social control. This form of sociology repeatedly attempts to achieve hegemony through a perversion of Max Weber's value-free doctrine. During the Cold War and prior to the 1960s revolts in North America, the discipline was highly integrated into the ideology and practices of the dominant society. As a corollary to this, as sociology became more critical in its stance, largely through the 1960s and 1970s, it also became more alienated and removed from the social policy-making processes.

This is not to suggest that sociologists should not have been critical, but only to indicate that the relationship of sociology to government policy-making processes depends upon some complementarity between the two. As Canadian politics moved towards neo-liberal (neo-conservative) policies in the 1980s, one would not expect sociologists critical of structural inequality to have any openings into social policy-making processes. I will address these Canadian realities in more detail below.

It is both possible and instructive to categorize competing schools of sociology in terms of how they see the relationships of the social, political, and economic. Political sociology sees political events as fairly autonomous in relation to social or economic forces. Political economy (and Marxian and conflict sociology) tends to see social and political events as being over-determined by economic interests. And functionalist sociology tends to see social behaviour and organization as relatively autonomous in relation to politics and economics and worthy of being studied in their own regard.

Aron has argued that theorists such as Tocqueville, Marx, and Durkheim helped consolidate these three major thrusts in sociology. Their specific analyses, not surprisingly, did not always fit neatly into these three schools or tendencies of thought:

> In theory, Marx tried to reduce politics and its conflicts to the relations between social classes and their conflicts. But on several points, his insight as an observer prevailed over his dogmatism as a theorist, and he recognized involuntarily, as it were, the strictly political factors in such conflicts and the autonomy of the state itself in relation to various groups. But to the extent that there is state autonomy in relation to classes and class conflicts, one element in the evolution of societies is not reducible to the struggle of social classes. What decisions are made depends on who takes possession of the state (Aron, 1965:258).

It is largely because of this sort of "contradiction" that sociology is, I think inherently, involved in social policy disputes, even if from a variety of perspectives and interests.

It is, of course, vital to know what tendencies in society and history are ignored or missing in these dominant schools of sociology. Where, for example, are the interests of women and of feminism, or those of the wretched of the earth (most of whom are women and children), or for that matter, the interests that counter the domination of the earth itself?

Exploring these questions, and the dispute over whether the socio-political theories out of which sociology has been institutionalized and professionalized ever contained these new interests of historical change, has set the stage for much of today's sociological agenda. Not surprisingly, this challenge to the sociological order of today comes from ascending social movements and the kinds of social policy controversies that result from this (Smith: 1990).

All these classical and emerging tendencies have direct implications for the involvement of sociology with social policy. According to the political sociologists, direct involvement in social policy would be essential to influence the concrete nature of society. Sociologists with liberal and social democratic commitments in Quebec and English Canada alike would be more inclined to this view of the necessity of intervention in the state. Sociologists who are more rooted in political economy, especially with a deterministic, Marxist bent, would more likely focus on "class struggle" and see social policy processes and disputes as being trivial and/or simply a reflection of this more fundamental conflict. If they become involved it is usually to advance the interests of workers (as they see these) or of the oppressed groups seen to be allied with the exploited classes.

Finally, sociologists of the functionalist perspective would see themselves engaging in social policy to help make policy makers more aware of the nature and workings of institutions, organizations, communities, and groups so as to be able to plan more scientifically (technologically). This latter group remains the dominant tendency within sociology, in spite of the failure of mega-projects like Project Camelot.

It is of course, quite possible that all these dominant classical tendencies are sufficiently short-sighted to be wrong. Without going to a deeper paradigmatic and historical level of analysis and criticism it is not possible to really confront or consider this possibility.

Various feminist critiques of these dominant tendencies in sociology certainly would argue both for new problems, new constituencies, and new processes of theory construction. Their approaches to policy interventions, and the dilemmas about reform and structure posed by these, are so far strikingly similar to those confronted by liberals, social democrats, and Marxists. Without the conditions and pressure for social transformation, the choices facing sociologists involved in social policy reform have remained some version of pragmatism, macrostructuralism, or piecemeal functionalism.

The Trappings of Scientism and Historicism

It is itself a political ploy to try to stereotype and dismiss the more political or economic approaches to sociology (and social policy) as being more ideological than those that tend to study social relations and organization as though they are largely independent of political and economic forces and structures. Furthermore, it is important to recognize how approaches to sociology that tend to reify the social out of history have created and/or reinforced basic confusion about the ways sociology applies to both social problems, undoubtedly having economic characteristics, and to social policies, which arise within the political process. I believe this confusion stems in large part from attempts to reduce sociological inquiries to a science—whether of the positivist or the crude Marxist version (Harding, 1970).

The very definition often given to sociology as a discipline exhibits this problem. In trying to define sociology, first in the 1920s and again in the 1950s, Sorokin wrote:

> Sociology has been, is and either will be a science of the general characteristics of all classes of social phenomena, with the relationships

and correlations between them; *or there will be no sociology* [my emphasis] (1956:761).

I think it is clear, according to this definition and view, that there never will be a sociological science. To try to treat the "social" as though it were a factual basis of observation, generalization and prediction, in the sense done in pre-quantum physics is to hide not only one's historical but also one's philosophical assumptions. (It also hides one's misunderstandings about the nature and philosophy of physical and natural science).

The very way in which the history of sociology as a scientific discipline has been depicted in many of the major texts continues to perpetuate these confusions and misunderstandings. What Martindale wrote many years ago is still widely believed in sociological circles:

Sociology is part of that great evolution in thought in Western civilization which passes from religion through philosophy to science.... The formula for the construction of science out of philosophy was in considerable measure fixed by the physical sciences, which pioneered the movement, and this fact has left a deep imprint on all the social sciences, including sociology (1960:4).

This ideology of scientism has left a deep imprint on sociology. But it hasn't helped deepen the understanding of the interrelations of the social, political, and economic within society. As Winch showed convincingly over thirty years ago:

...the central concepts which belong to our understanding of social life are incompatible with concepts central to the activity of scientific prediction (1958:94).

The inappropriate treatment of sociology as a science (and especially an inductive science) has fuelled a mostly unenlightening debate about sociological verifications, which has influenced whether and how social policy research and intervention has been valued. Much of this debate has been about the role of human practice in testing and correcting sociological theory. (The most politically influential version of this has been in Marxian sociology). This view can lead to a variety of ways of linking sociological studies to social policy interventions. In practice it has mostly led to a dismissal of the need to work in the area of social policy.

The major flaw in this approach is that it assumes lawful relations and hence the possibilities of both prediction and control. Though the focus of the "left" view of the unity of theory and practice has been on the macro and societal level, whereas that of the "right" has been on the micro and organizational level, this underlying naive scientism remains. Linked to beliefs in determinism, political vanguardism, and statism, this view can become as authoritarian as the view of sociology espoused by Sorokin and his contemporaries.

Another approach to this problem rejects the possibility of prediction but still holds to the test of theory. Harris's handling of this problem within anthropological theory is pertinent to sociology:

> In the historical sciences, the doctrine of the unity of theory and practice is rendered superfluous by the possibility of subjecting one's predictions to the test not of future, but of past events. That is, there is no reason why the social sciences cannot accept retrodiction as the test of theory (1968:220).

What this means is that the test of theory and explanation in sociology will and should be limited to being both retrospective and historically specific. To the extent that there is historical continuity in interrelated social, political, and economic systems, one can make some predictive claims. But changes in these systems and relations within them will, inevitably, undermine such predictive validity. I believe C. Wright Mills made a major contribution in advancing our understanding of the need for historical specificity. Were more contemporary "left" sociologists more astute in this regard, fewer would have been shocked by events in eastern Europe in the early 1990s.

This view clearly challenges sociologists, whether involved in social policy or not, to face some inherently ideological questions. Social policy can be motivated to try to maintain the apparent stability among social, political, and economic systems and relations. Or it can be motivated to try to alter these relationships, or the systems themselves. Commitments to particular views and values of justice, equality, and the like will remain at the centre of one's intellectual praxis. There are neither historical nor scientific criteria for judging which direction to take; nor for that matter, whether the direction taken will have the desired effect. Having one's studies solidly grounded in problems of social policy, however, will make inconsistencies more apparent and contradictions less easy to dismiss or rationalize. This may be one reason why so many sociologists steer clear of the whole area.

The discussion of scientistic dead-ends in conceiving the relations of sociology and social policy implies many questions about the relationship of sociology to other fields of study. As Winch pointed out some years ago:

> As is well known, there has always been some dispute about the role which sociology ought to play *vis-à-vis* the other social studies. Some have thought that sociology should be the social science par excellence, synthesizing the results of special social studies, like economic and political theory, into a unified theory of society in general. Others, however, have wanted to regard sociology simply as one science on the

same level as all the others, confined to a restructured subject matter of its own (1958:40).

Clearly the followers of both Comte and Marx in sociology see sociology in the former sense, as providing a unifying theory about social order and/or social change. Most of those seeing sociology in the latter way, as a singular social science, still hold to an inadequate functional and scientistic approach.

One way to avoid the pitfalls of both approaches may be to see sociology as a singular but not unifying discipline, within a multidisciplinary approach to social science. I would argue that such an approach has far more potential as a way to address problems of social policy. In fact, I would argue that the inability of most sociologists to engage directly in social policy research is, in part, shaped by the result of the field's polarization between those, including the structural Marxists, who see it as a unifying discipline, and those who have accepted the fragmented, overly specialized depiction of the discipline.

In saying this I do not want to advance a traditional view about the distinction between pure and applied science. There is clearly some value in seeing anthropology, political science, economics, psychology, and sociology as being more basic than other fields, in the sense that they should ask more basic questions than those posed in policy circles. At the same time, functionalist approaches in these so-called basic social sciences have contributed to multidisciplinary policy studies that tend to serve the dominant interests. Conversely, critical approaches in these so-called basic social sciences could also be combined in multidisciplinary ways to undertake relevant, rigorous, and accessible research committed to basic reforms and transformation.

It is sometimes helpful to consider administration, education, law, planning, criminology, and social work as applied fields of study. Yet anyone working reflectively in these areas knows that the approaches in these fields most often mirror dominant interests. Rarely does applied, professional research get grounded in the interests of victims, clients, or any group of people repressed, oppressed, and/or exploited by the dominant structures and systems. Furthermore, these applied fields often ignore the very knowledge in the so-called basic social sciences that could provide direction for more effective policy and programme planning intervention and service delivery in the interests of the disadvantaged and under-class. The fact that this knowledge would raise critical questions about the political and economic system and its managers usually means it is largely ignored.

It is in this sense that the distinction between so-called basic and applied studies (often seen as distinguishing academic and professional studies) is not particularly enlightening. It is more accurate to speak of multidisciplinary and inter-professional problem-oriented studies, which could be committed to reform and human betterment, in contrast to interrelated functionalist disciplines and training-oriented professions.

There are very different ways of conceptualizing and combining social studies. It is, of course, always possible to have critical macro, structural studies, largely disinterested in or incapable of broaching issues of policy or practice. This has, unfortunately, been a major tendency among most sociologists and social scientists, including some who remain, in some fashion, committed to social change.

Seeing sociology as inherently historical offers a rationale for its involvement in social policy (as part of social change), and yet this also presents philosophical and methodological problems. Crysdale and Beattie supportively quoted Guy Rocher that

> ... historicism poses a greater problem in the case of sociology than the other social sciences because our science studies in a more immediate way even the world of values. Sociology cannot, like economics, put the world of values between brackets, or, like psychology, accept it as an external given fact (1973:293).

It is true that, as presently constituted, these other disciplines are more likely to bypass the direct study of values. It is this imperative for sociology to directly encounter values that probably makes sociologists more self-conscious about the effect of their own value preferences on the selection of problems and approaches to study and the effect of social values on social policies themselves.

This is likely equally true whether sociologists see their main pursuit as the study of meaningful behaviour, symbolized interaction, or the structural determinants of behaviour. However, some more scientistic versions of sociology, including structuralist and Marxian varieties, can also try to bypass the study of values and by implication downplay social policy. Once historically specific generalizations become treated as laws of history, historicism can actually become a reason not to dwell on problems and processes of social policy. In this sense sociology can be like, not unlike, economics and psychology as conceived in narrow positivistic terms.

To the extent that sociology is better grounded in cultural awareness, this historicism and scientism is less likely to develop. But this only serves to point out the limits of sociology conceived in disciplinary rather than multidisciplinary terms. It is my contention that all science is inherently multidisciplinary and that the notion of identities of disciplines has more to do with the institutionalization, professionalization, and bureaucratization of knowledge (including in the universities) than with substantive matters. (This is as true for physics and other so-called "hard sciences" as it is for sociology). It follows from this that to the extent that sociology is relegated to being a single discipline—for example, neither studying the problems of labour and capital, markets and planning (in the case of economics), nor those of perception, motivation, and learning (in the case of psychology)— it will become less conscious of values and hence less self-critical even if it engages in social policy research.

The Canadian Debate

Since the early 1970s, sociologists like Crysdale and Beattie argued in introductions to the field for a very direct involvement of Canadian sociologists in social policy processes. They stated that

> Sociology cannot escape its interaction with history. Neither can it avoid being involved in the formation as well as the investigation of social policy (1973:293).

However, their attempt to distinguish sociology from other disciplines regarding its interest in values, and hence social policy, ignores a deeper problem of history—that of ideology and paradigms. Sociology's very historical roots—for example, in conflicting reflections on the French revolution as an archetype for the development of "modern" industrial capitalist society—are now limiting its ability to engage in research or theory with any profound implications for redirecting and transforming society. The same forces of historical change that made "sociology" ascend as a field of study can also make the field descend in importance.

Crysdale and Beattie were fairly typical in preferring to explore the complexities of sociology's impact on social policy in more pragmatic terms. The lesser role of sociologists in social policy formation than either psychologists or economists was explained by them as a result of the discipline coming later to Canada. This is seen to be changing with the greater involvement of sociologists in government commissions. According to these authors, writing in the seventies, sociologists and the CSAA itself were becoming more involved in matters of social policy such as those pertaining to social and environmental impact studies, particularly upon aboriginal communities.

There is no disputing that this has been one main route of entry of many sociologists (and anthropologists) into matters of social policy. In my case, it was the route into not only social policy, but also health, criminal justice, and resource policy. I think it should be noted, however, that much of the involvement of sociologists in government policy, including commissions, has not had to do with social policy so much as with national policy. It is not so much sociology in the service of societal change to improve the general quality of life, as sociology in the service of the stability of the crisis-ridden nation-state.

Crysdale and Beattie also asserted that the lack of Canadian graduates in sociology, which relates to the late arrival of the field of study, has contributed to the field's "meagre" influence on social policy. Quoting Coburn (1970) they pointed out that from 1957 to 1964 only one Ph.D. in sociology was awarded in Canada. (From 1965 to 1968 only another 5 or 6 were awarded). This compared to 165 in psychology and 60 in economics, political science, and political economy (combined) from 1957 to 1964. Or, more telling, it compared to 968 in the physical sciences and 543 in the biological sciences from 1957 to 1964. From 1957 to 1968, when university teachers went from 4,342 to 16,000 people, sociology teachers went from a measly 32 to a still meagre 274 people.

Sociology—and anthropology as well—has clearly been a minority group within a minority group. The physical and biological sciences, and then—though much less so—the more pragmatic social sciences (psychology and economics), have clearly been emphasized and favoured within Canadian universities.

A related matter was the "colonization" of Canadian sociology by British and United States professors and perspectives. Most of my own sociology professors—both conservative and critical—were U.S.-born and/or educated. A sizeable majority of non-Canadian faculty members did no research of any sort (much less social policy related research) in Canada. Their reference point was still publishing in the United States. They, as well as many of our early Canadian sociologists, were consequently not good role models for social policy research. Furthermore, by the time some Canadians were getting the opportunity to study sociology, opportunities to work directly in the field had already shrunk.

The supply side explanation of sociology's minimal involvement in social policy remains superficial. It is quite unlikely that the influence of sociology and sociologists upon social policy has increased in proportion to the growth in the number of graduates in sociology, relative to other fields. Though more students are now studying and graduating from sociology, for the most part most English Canadian sociologists remain quite uninvolved in social policy research and practice. Clearly, a more empirical study would help enlighten us all on this matter.

Comparisons with Francophone Sociology

Crysdale and Beattie articulated the view, still widely held, that

French Canadian sociologists show greater concern than their English speaking compatriots for the bearing of their efforts on knowledge in general and on social policy (1973:294).

I think there were, however, some fairly clear-cut political reasons for this. With the rise of French Canadian nationalism, and the crisis of federalism, francophone sociologists could more easily link their social and political studies to a policy context. It was not so much that social policy was more vital to them as that social and national policies were more clearly intertwined. (See both Whyte and Rocher, in this volume.) The very nationalism in the Quebec universities clearly helped shape a generation of sociologists more inclined to see links between social science and political policy.

In English Canada, which was on the other side of this crisis of federalism, sociologists were more likely to be drawn into reform policies like biculturalism and bilingualism which were aimed at preserving, not transforming, political relationships. Both involvements had to do explicitly with the bi-national political context, which differed greatly in the two parts of Canada.

Ideally we would have a direct study of social policy involvement among English Canadian sociologists to compare to a recent one done on Quebec sociologists (Renaud, Doré and White, 1989), to assist with this discussion. Perhaps the essays in this book will encourage such research. Lacking that, I am left with my general knowledge of English Canadian sociology, and my own years of direct work in social policy–related research (Harding, forthcoming).

Unlike some observers of francophone sociology, I neither romanticize nor envy the apparent greater role of sociologists in social policy processes in Quebec since the Quiet Revolution. To some extent I agree that this was a "twenty-year experiment in social engineering" (Renaud et al., 1989:427), with many unintended consequences, in part due to the commitment of many Quebec sociologists to a macrostructuralist perspective. In this regard Quebec sociology has not been that different from anglophone sociology, except, as stated already, that the latter lacked the nationalist political context within which to participate in politics and social policy processes.

Renaud et al. actually found that the bulk of the research on social reform in Quebec was

...not concerned directly with policies, but with the process of policy development. Social policy is examined as an indicator of the evolution of the state, its relation to civil society, its class base, party structure and the government bureaucracy.

They therefore concluded that

...the theme of the state...has been the dominant theme of Quebec sociology over the last 20 years...social policy is significant only as the exclusive instrument of the state and the social classes that it serves. Social policies and their outcomes are secondary (1989:429).

The same tendency to focus on the state and class has been ascendent in anglophone sociology since the 1960s. The main difference is that in English Canada there was not the same close relationship with political parties and government that existed with the Parti Québécois in Quebec. The only thing that came close to this was with the Waffle in the NDP. But even if the Waffle had survived either inside or outside of the NDP, and provided a policy "practice" for Marxist and structuralist sociologists, it was clearly never destined to have any major relationship to power as was the case with the P.Q. in Quebec. The rising popularity of the provincial and federal NDP may yet provide the opportunity for left liberal, social democratic, and feminist-leaning sociologists to influence social policy.

When Quebec's left nationalism was in decline, Quebec's own neo-liberal economic realism was on the rise. Quebec sociologists found themselves without a mooring in the state. With few exceptions Quebec sociologists were as unable as anglophone sociologists, facing similar political and structural shifts, to make the transition from ideological criticism to the concrete analysis of concrete conditions.

In this sense all of the social sciences in the Western capitalist world have been faced with the same historical juncture that has faced the more statist-oriented political regimes. The crisis facing both socialist and social democratic politics is the same underlying historical crisis facing sociology and all social sciences that grew up assuming welfare capitalism was a base line for social research or social policy advocacy and intervention.

It would be naive not to recognize that, in addition to the opportunity to engage in relevant but critical theory, Quebec sociologists' employment and status needs were also met by this past link to government. As Renaud et al. say

> When the State was their main, perhaps their only vehicle for status attainment, social-policy was the direct or, more often, indirect focus of a majority of sociologists' works (1989:432).

Furthermore, shifts in the make-up and ideological function of the university have reinforced what might be called the re-marginalization of Quebec sociology from the mainstream political and social policy processes, and this made it more like anglophone sociology. Also, as in English Canada since the 1970s, Quebec has seen the growth of applied social science based on more positivist and functionalist methods and approaches—everything from administration to social work. Renaud et al. comment, "In the process, Sociology departments have often lost their nascent applied side" (1989:432).

I think it would be at least as accurate to say that, in the process of these structural and ideological shifts, the lack of a concrete, applied, critical sociology to challenge the emerging technocratic applied social sciences has become more apparent. A particular convergence of critical but macroscopic structuralist sociology, social dislocations, and the political ferment in Quebec during the period of industrial modernization allowed sociology to be relevant, even if not directly related, to social policy. It, of course, remains to be seen what opportunity and role sociologists in Quebec will have in the post-Meech era—whether in a restructured Canada or a sovereign Quebec.

Clearly a more concrete analysis of clusters and trends among anglophone sociologists would be required to fully assess similarities and differences with Quebec. It might be helpful to follow the approaches used by Renaud et al., looking at both the evolution of influential sociology departments, and generations of sociologists shaped by these (e.g., Universities of Laval, Montreal, Quebec). I doubt, however, that it would be quite as self-evident, although there are some universities (e.g., Simon Fraser University) that have clearly had a significant impact on the development of western Canadian sociology and social science after the 1960s, and could probably be analyzed as such.

Renaud et al. list four "generations" of such agendas in Quebec:
1. The shift from traditional to modern society
2. The rise in the independence movement
3. The debate and splitting over the national question, including the role of the state and welfare state
4. The present shift to a sociological pragmatism

There are some interesting parallels between the theoretical and political agendas within both Quebec and anglophone sociology. It would, however, be more accurate to see the expansion of corporate capitalism and industrialism into agriculture and resource extraction—especially in the west and north—as an underlying historical and structural set of forces raising questions about social policies in relation to "modernization," continentalism, the welfare state, and environmental impact. There remains the need for critical, and much more concrete, applied social studies in these areas. Furthermore, the development of resistance and alternatives to this overbearing and unecological "developmental" trend constitutes an intellectual project for an emerging "generation" of sociologists. I am not at all proposing that sociology must acquiesce to the confusion and contradiction of "sustainable development," but rather begin to seriously and systematically help with the understanding necessary for the transformation to ecologically sustainable societies.

In this sense, though in different contexts, Quebec and anglophone critical sociology both confront the same challenge. This common challenge requires being able to make a transition from macrostructuralism to concrete socio-historical analysis. Part of this will involve moving towards participatory, action research that encourages and helps provide an intellectual basis for fundamental social alternatives, and ultimately social transformation.

This, of course, raises issues of historical and societal analysis, to which sociology should always refer in shaping its projects.

The Future of Sociology

Scientism has formed an underlying commonality between conservative and radical tendencies within sociology. Though the functionalist approach has stressed inductive methods, and the structuralist approach has stressed more deductive methods, they both have tried in vain to apply outmoded natural science philosophies about causality, determinism, and prediction to legitimize their methods and theories. This has greatly limited the ability of both tendencies in sociology to be conceptualized in such a way that social policy research and intervention can creatively interrelate with both theoretical and methodological problem-solving and advancements.

This underlying scientism itself reflects an historically rooted, increasingly problematic paradigm that complemented the rise and ascendancy of capitalist industrialization. Furthermore, it reflects the dominance of the very ideologies and structures that are now threatening to undermine ecological sustainability on this planet.

In retrospect, it is quite revealing that when Sorokin tried to define sociology as an inductive science of social phenomena he used a biological metaphor, referring to the need of the "scientific gardener" to get "sterile flowers" and "weeds" out of sociological theory (1956:760). One implication of this comparison with monoculture was that for sociology to become a predictive science, society itself had to become standardized so that a few "laws" could in fact "explain" social phenomena.

From a critical ecological perspective, the standardization of society also standardizes nature. We now realize that the reduction of cultural and ecological diversity—largely through the globalization of capitalist accumulation, colonization, and imperialism—go hand in hand. We must also come to realize that the organization of the human sciences can contribute to this spread of planetary monoculture.

The global ecological crisis is at once a social, political, economic, and ideological crisis. To help overcome this evolutionary crisis, theory and method will require some deep rethinking of our assumptions in all of the social sciences, including sociology.

Sociology itself developed along with the changes in society that emerged from the European industrial and democratic revolutions of the eighteenth century. Most sociological tendencies can be traced directly back to attempts to comprehend the breakdown of the feudal order in France, Germany, and England. As Nisbet has written:

> The intellectual elements of sociology are refractions of exactly the same forces and tensions that also produced the outlines of modern liberalism, conservatism and radicalism (1966:21).

Whereas politics tries to "reconsolidate" these elements in practical ways, Nesbit argues that sociology has tried to reconsolidate them in theoretical ways. This dialectical relationship between politics and sociology will continue to re-create the feasibility and challenge for sociology to concretely address problems of social policy intervention.

For both sociology rooted in the statics and dynamics of Comte, and sociology rooted in the class struggle over the state in Marx, the quest is directed, as Nisbet says, "at conceptualizations of elements crucially involved in the two revolutions" (1966:317) of industrialization and democratization. Though we are celebrating the 25th anniversary of the CSAA, it is more relevant to understanding the sociological heritage and the vital relationship of the field to social policy that we have just passed the 200th anniversary of the French Revolution. If the models, theories, and hypotheses stemming from the classical theorists are still revealing, it is because we are still living within the same historical forces, contradictions, possibilities, and impossibilities. Certainly many of the same kinds of patterns (whether social, political, or economic) that stimulated such vociferous theoretical debate and creativity in Europe—especially around events between 1848 and 1851 in France—can still be seen in unfolding events today, whether in the Third World, in Eastern Europe, or in the capitalist heartland itself (Amin, 1991).

Towards an Ecological Sociology

Sociology has now reached an historical juncture. Will sociologists continue to dot the i's and cross the t's of the theories rooted in the great dislocations from feudalism to the emerging industrial, democratic state? To do so will inevitably reinforce a kind of scientism, and a highly functionalist or pragmatic approach to social policy. This road remains one, whether from a more liberal or a social democratic stance, that accepts sociology within a perspective of modernization and the end of ideology. In fact, as macro-structuralism proves its irrelevance to political struggles and social policy, pragmatism will be the only choice left. For, from within this historically rooted sociological paradigm,

> ...like it or not, the two revolutions, in any concrete sense of the word, have been accomplished. We are urban, democratic, industrial, bureaucratic, rationalized, large-scale, formal, secular and technological (Nesbit, 1966:317).

The other choice and path is for sociology to embrace the problems of the planetary evolutionary (ecological) crisis brought on by the forces of industrialization and colonization and decolonization unleashed over the last two hundred years, and especially since the Second World War, with the same breadth and depth with which the classical theorists tackled their historical challenge. This means that rather than being drawn into more pragmatism and fragmentation (and with it professional institutionalization), sociology will have to work with critical philosophy, history, and economics, in the same way that the classical sociologists worked across these perspectives, to jointly redefine the sociological project.

Not only were all the great sociological theorists inherently multidisciplinary but, unlike many of today's sociologists, they were personally, politically, and intellectually in touch with the great epochal transformations facing them in their times. Our post-nuclear generations stand on the threshold of an epochal global challenge, which goes to the very root of society. This must, as always, confront the social, political, and economic, but it must also now critically confront the technological and cultural, and most importantly, the ecological.

If we look closely at most contemporary social policy controversies they all imply this challenge. Meeting this challenge will likely lead to a transformation of the organization of human knowledge itself. But should it really surprise anyone with any historical perspective that a "discipline" reified out of past great historical changes should itself become problematic, once the unsustainability of the evolutionary direction brought on by these historical changes is itself becoming clearer?

SOCIOLOGY AND THE CONSTITUTION OF SOCIETY: CANADIAN EXPERIENCES

Donald Whyte

Introduction

I have examined elsewhere how the current images of Canadian society developed by sociologists have reflected a nationalist preoccupation and a simultaneous distancing of societal understanding from United States models. I have shown that more than one image of society has held sway, reflecting the particularities of Quebec, and to a lesser extent, of geo-socio-economic regions in anglophone Canada (Whyte, 1985).

I contend that the task of "constituting society," of creating knowledge about, and articulating a wholist account of, the total society, is no longer central to current concerns of sociologists in Canada. As the discipline of sociology has grown it has become internally differentiated into specialist sub-fields, precluding the kind of wholist account needed to constitute a conception of Canada. Simultaneously, the political and economic circumstances of Canadians during the past two decades have resulted in the devaluation of sociological knowledge on the part of those whose function it is to articulate an image of Canada. Constitutional issues invite legal expertise; economic issues invite economic expertise; trade relations in a the world economy invite specialist knowledge in trade relations, and so on. Within sociology, issues of race and ethnicity invite specialists in that field, as is the case with other sub-fields. Consequently, specific issues come to be explained without reference to a conception of their immediate societal context. Sociologists, it seems, have little to say at this time about the subject of Canadian society. This paper is a look at the historical context of the situation and an inquiry into why the age-old project of constituting society, once briefly embraced as a definitive practice of sociology in Canada, seems to have been abandoned.

Periodization: Society and Societies

The project of a Quebec sociology has been intimately tied to the project of building a society in Quebec, which is distinct from that of the larger Anglo-American context of North America. Initially, this project was dedicated to the preservation of the unique values and institutions of French Canada; later, during the 1960s, criticism of the clerisy and of conservative values generally was expressed in the project of *rattrapage*, catching up, or modernization. This Quiet Revolution, as it came to be called, was signalled by the call to become *maîtres chez-nous*. By the 1970s, the Quiet Revolution had evolved into an *indépendentiste* movement, harkening to the call of sovereign national status for Quebec.

In each of these periods, sociologists played key roles both in articulating an image of society for Quebec, and as agents for the realization of that image. During the early conservative period, the image that prevailed was that of the "folk-urban" community within which the forces of modernity were perceived with apprehension and as a threat to authentic values and the culture of francophone *Canadiens*. The second period, coinciding with that of the Quiet Revolution, was dominated by an image of Quebec as a dependent society, truncated in its modernizing impulse by its secondary status *vis-à-vis* British North America. The folk-urban continuum was recast in terms of modernization, and French Canada became Quebec Society. This image was again recast in the third period, signalling a shift from an ethnic dynamic to a class dynamic and to an image of a society that was incomplete because it lacked an indigenous dominant class. These interpretations of Quebec society reflected the social, economic, and political events of the times as well as the institutional vantage point of the sociologists/intellectuals who formulated them. These "social science intellectuals," as Brooks and Gagnon point out, were "both a product and expression of the transformation of Quebec Society" (Brooks and Gagnon, 1988:24).

Anglophone sociology in Canada also shows three periods with distinctive images of Canadian society. Relative to Quebec, little sociological activity occurred in anglophone Canada prior to the 1960s, a consequence of the intellectual imperialism of disciplines already established in British academic circles and imported to Canada from the mother country. "In the majority of universities, what sociology was taught was reformist in orientation and associated with social work" (Whyte, 1985:108). Early research among English-language sociologists focused on immigrant communities, settlement patterns in the west, the rise of political movements, and the role of the church and the clergy in social reform. No explicit image of Canada as a society is evident in this early period; the sociological project of constituting society in Canada began in earnest in the 1960s.

That decade saw a phenomenal growth in numbers of students studying the discipline, in numbers of professionals working inside academia, in numbers of academic departments in universities, and in productivity as measured in research projects, scholarly papers, and professional journals (Whyte, 1985:111ff).

The majority of professors and technocrats who filled these roles in Anglo-Canadian universities and governments were products of doctoral programmes in the United States, programmes that were framed in the context of cold-war McCarthyism. These value-neutral social scientists brought to Canada the hegemonic model of U.S. export sociology which was, during the same period, being carried to Third World countries as the exemplar of the modern national society. In Canada, this model was expressed in the standard American academic curriculum of the new sociology departments. American textbooks and the internal differentiation of sociology into conventional specialties were quickly instituted in academic departments. Insofar as an image of Canadian society was articulated at all, it was as a variant of American society, constituted in the techno-functionalist mode, grounded in a voluntaristic premise of value consensus. One of the earliest and most influential images of Canada as a "modern national society" was expressed in the following terms in the 1960s:

> ...power—the positive principle of coherence—involves the elaboration of a range of cultural accomplishments...such accomplishments proceed within a consensus.... A general consensus of a society—its dominant value system—in turn is recognized through the accomplishments that can be attributed to the members of that society (Naegele, 1968:17-18).

The principal differences between Canada and the United States were presented as deviations from the liberal-pluralist model epitomized by "the first new nation," and were explained by the fact that Canada had not made a radical break from its European political origins (Lipset, 1963). A methodological preoccupation with abstracted empiricism and the theoretical orthodoxy of systemic functionalism combined, in Canada, to dissociate sociology from its social welfare and reform associations of an earlier time. As S.D. Clark observed of the time, "much of the work going forward in sociology within Canadian universities had little to contribute to public policy" (Clark, 1979:397).

The legacy of the 1960s export model continues in Anglo-Canadian sociology to the present, reflecting the entrenchment of a generation of academics and the continuation of their practice by graduate students trained in the U.S. post-war tradition. The model has been truncated somewhat, having retreated from the voluntaristic, imperialistic image of the modern rational society, but remains fundamentally empiricist, atheoretical, and technicist. The retreat from grand theorizing was effected by counter-developments within Canadian sociology, but was a response to the more widespread criticism that theory was but a reification of American society. The narrow, but in its time contextually correct, understanding of the part that U.S. export sociology was playing in rationalizing the Western world order was perceived in Canada as a pernicious example of technocratic rationality being applied in the realm of social control (Grant, 1969).

A third period in Anglo-Canadian sociology was signalled by the publication, in 1965, of John Porter's *The Vertical Mosaic*. As an analysis of the structure of power in Canada, Porter's work challenged both the conventional view of Canada as a democratic and egalitarian society and the export model of a functionally integrated social system.

...Porter's analysis, while undertaken from a macrostructural perspective, refuted the conception of Canada as a society based on a consensus of values, and showed how culture, history, and geography had combined in Canada to create a configuration of regional sub-societies subordinated to dominant economic interests and maintained by institutions which ensure a monopoly of power to the central Anglophone elites. For the first time, social scientists in Canada and abroad were offered a conception of Canada as a whole, a macro-structural perspective on the society which distinguished it from the prevalent conception of the United States (Whyte, 1985:114).

What Porter's book provided to a new generation of sociologists was a uniquely "Canadian" perspective on Canada, one that addressed issues of concern to both language communities, and that served to distinguish the image of society in Canada from the hegemonic modern rational society image.

Porter's work also gave room in sociological practice to the political economy paradigm pioneered by Harold Innis. It offered a society-centred perspective for a revitalized political economy "made in Canada." Class analysis and a focus on the structure of power (also pursued by Third World dependency detractors within the sociological community, and ideological and political nationalists in both Quebec and Canada) was a fruitful paradigm. An image of class conflict as the dynamic underlying structured inequalities in Canada was augmented by the analysis of regional inequalities, cultural confrontations, and national aspirations as sources of ideological formation. A holistic image of Canada emerged in anglophone sociology comparable to that which prevailed in the francophone sociology of Quebec. The agenda in Quebec, however, continued to be that of society-building, or more particularly, nation-building. Anglophone political economy sought to reclaim Canada from U.S. economic and cultural hegemony and to effect reforms towards greater social equality, by focusing on the reformation of the political process and the reconstitution of the national state system.

Convergence and Disengagement

The attainment of a holistic perspective in the new political economy represented a convergence between anglophone and francophone sociologists. Conceptually, both communities distanced themselves from the export model of American sociology and adapted the structuralist paradigms of European theorists to their respective analyses. The class dynamic of society was central to each, and the history of Canada and Quebec took on greater empirical significance in their respective research agendas.

Despite their conceptual and empirical convergences, sociologists played fundamentally different and even contradictory roles in the two contexts. Brooks and Gagnon point out that "the Quebec acquisition of a distinctive orientation was helped by the growth of the Quebec state as a funding agent and by the participation of social scientists in the fields of planning, party politics, and extra-parliamentary social movements, all of which lent an *engagé* flavour to their intellectual discourse" (Brooks and Gagnon, 1988:52). Jean-Jacques Simard, they point out, "has gone so far as to call this generation of social scientists Quebec's own version of the Comtean Priests of Humanity" (Brooks and Gagnon, 1988:48).

Two factors combined in the 1970s to foster a disengagement in anglophone sociology: a long tradition of colonized intellectual life, and a dependency perspective that reinforced a critical stance devoid of significant intellectual dissent. Anglophone sociologists were increasingly being co-opted into the, by now official, ethno-linguistic conception of a multicultural nation. Critical sociologists, unable to motivate public opposition, adopted symbolic stances and distancing arguments. Brooks and Gagnon conclude:

> ...the influence of the political economy approach within sociology and political science during the 1960s should not be exaggerated. With an electoral system that discouraged class alignments, and in the absence of politically significant supportive constituencies—a working class capable of being mobilized, or an ascendant middle class as in Quebec—the political impact of these left-wing social scientists was insubstantial in English Canada (Brooks and Gagnon, 1988:105).

The leftist critique became involuted. Links to the earlier political economy school of Harold Innis, the incorporation of Marxist concepts, the establishment of a distinctive professional journal, an internal discourse on national issues—all of these had little impact in Canada beyond the confines of academic treatises and intellectual criticism. Where the two roles of the sociologist as intellectual and as expert were fused in Quebec through an alliance of nationalist social science and the rise of a new middle class, in anglophone Canada the two roles remained separate. The expert in policy matters entered into the technocratic corps in the service of the powers that be; the intellectual, as social critic, organized around limited oppositional publics, or, lacking such publics, devolved in theoretical abstractionism or ideological reductionism. Anglophone sociology succeeded in differentiating itself from the export model of the early 1960s by articulating an alternative conception of society, but it failed to situate that conception in a broad field of practice.

Conclusions

The establishment of a strong state system in Quebec has been accompanied by a growing market nationalism and a decline in the hegemony of the social science and literary intelligentsia. The rise of a new business-oriented bourgeoisie is correlated with the shift from social science studies to business-related programmes in universities. New forms of intellectual capital are valued, and Quebec's intellectuals "have re-discovered the virtues and comfort of withdrawal and of the qualified statement" (Brooks and Gagnon, 1988:74). The roles of sociologist and expert have not converged in anglophone sociology in Canada for reasons already noted. Consequently, the devolution of sociology is less apparent than in Quebec, where the two roles were fused. What appears evident, however, is that sociologists in anglophone Canada have been profoundly silent on critical social issues. National debates over the proposed constitutional revisions and the free-trade agenda have elicited no collective responses from sociologists. The effect of a mass of unused and unusable workers in the context of an eroding welfare cushion is a matter of profound significance to the way society is constituted, as Britain's experience has shown. The surfacing of linguistic resentment between francophone and anglophone, diffused and activated by resentments between nation and nation, region and region, ideological enclave and ideological enclave: this is historically seminal, *and* publicly disclosed. So too, increased evidence of racial bigotry and violence as non-Caucasion immigration increases, a detachment of conceptions of disease and health practices from the human community, the potential for massive growth in environmentally conscious publics: these signify important, and to date relatively unexamined, areas where a sociological perspective is necessary.

But the perspectives offered by sociology in Canada do not address these issues. The devolution of the state is not central to contemporary theorizing. Cultural, linguistic, racial, national, and ethnic cleavages are not reducible to class formations and economic relations in the way that regional cleavages have been. Conceptions of power that centre on elite linkages and state systems overlook the formation of oppositional publics and their impact. The Citizen as subject, whether of state practice, medical science, or environmental degradation, has been ignored. Indeed, a reversion to satellite interpretations *vis-à-vis* the U.S., or more generally, the world economy, seems all too convenient an explanation for what is happening in Canada today.

The issues facing Canadians, the oppositional publics emerging around those issues, and the devolution of the national state present new challenges to sociologists studying Canada. The methodological and theoretical advances realized over the past quarter-century need to be directed to the project of engaging in and interpreting emergent discourses. We need to be asking not just how the system dominates and controls, but what kinds of subjects we are. In what ways are we empowered or disempowered as Citizens?

The most significant advances in Canadian sociology during the past quarter-century came from the challenge posed by accepted interpretations. The new paradigms that developed reflected the issues of the times, and appealed to diverse and broadly based publics: students, political activists inside and outside establishment parties, organic intellectuals within the state system, media opinion leaders, and detached intellectuals of all sorts. These paradigms have now become the accepted interpretations. They address the concerns of students and colleagues, rarely those of the educated, non-academic publics outside the profession of sociology. The answers they prefer have become professional capital, detached from wider societal and cultural imperatives. Outside the classroom and the professional consortium, who in Canada is listening to the sociologists?

THE UNEASY MARRIAGE OF ACADEMIC AND POLICY WORK: REFLECTIONS ON THE NEWFOUNDLAND AND LABRADOR EXPERIENCE[1]

Barbara Neis

> Too seldom do we teach our students about the realities of anthropology, especially concerning fieldwork and the decisions that must be made from personal, ethical and professional viewpoints.... Part of the reality is that many conflicts are *inherent* in the anthropological experience itself. Regrettably, we are still inclined to deny this truth so that when there are difficulties in connection with an active engagement in advocacy, the all-too-likely response of academia is to deny the validity of such activity and to dissociate from it...(Ryan, 1985:208).

The history of policy work carried out by anthropologists and sociologists in Canada reveals some important differences between regions, between English Canada and Quebec, and between different subsections of the disciplines. Throughout that history, policy work has taken many different forms and has been directed towards a broad range of audiences. It has included work within universities in the form of teaching practices and efforts to influence the development of universities and our professions. In addition, it has included work, often sponsored by policy makers, that is designed to reinforce or change policy. Finally, policy work has included research, the initial audience for which is specific interest groups or even the general public.

As argued elsewhere in this book, policy work is by no means either relevant or irreverent (Armstrong and Armstrong; Reiter). Unfortunately, if it is reverent, it is more likely to be identified as relevant by those in positions of power. In addition, as marginal groups often recognize, if this work is irreverent, support for it within university and government will be limited and tenuous.

This paper uses a partial case study of the history of policy work within anthropology and sociology in Newfoundland and Labrador to explore different types of policy work and historical changes in assumptions regarding the relationship between policy work and the disciplines.[2] This history has been constructed from interviews with some anthropologists and sociologists whose policy work has focused primarily on issues relevant to Newfoundland and Labrador, and on a partial review of reports and publications.

The case study reveals a rich and multi-faceted thirty-year history of different approaches to policy work organized through a variety of institutional structures. Some of these structures have been university-based, others have not. During the early years, the relationship between the work of anthropologists and sociologists and that of the policy makers was viewed as unproblematic. This changed during the 1960s and 1970s. The discussion will begin with an examination of policy work carried out through institutions at Memorial University as base research for policy makers. It will then examine some more radical, critical institutions within and outside the university through which anthropologists and sociologists attempted to influence policy. The final section examines some of the dilemmas experienced by two anthropologists who work as advocate/researcher and paid consultant, outside of the university and somewhat separate from the professions.

In Newfoundland and Labrador, some policy work has been the result of government initiatives and some has resulted from critical responses to government policy. Policy work has often been prompted by the ethical and other dilemmas that Joan Ryan defines as an *"inherent* part of the anthropological [and sociological] experience."* Changes in universities, the professions, and in wider society are contributing to the separation of policy work and academic work within anthropology and sociology. As Joan Ryan argues, this separation cannot be justified on the basis of any absolute distinctions between policy and academic work. In addition, the divorce of policy and academic work threatens to impoverish the critical insights anthropology and sociology can provide policy makers while it undermines the contribution of policy work to academic research and theorizing. The concluding section of the paper addresses these issues.

The Case Study

The history of sociology and anthropology at Memorial University does not seem to be typical of that of other departments in English Canada. It begins with a joint department, and with anthropologists and sociologists who were trained in Britain, Norway, the United States, and elsewhere in Canada. It is a relatively short history in comparison to other universities in Canada because it was not until the late 1950s that there were any anthropologists or sociologists at Memorial (MacLeod, 1990). The history is also anomalous in that, during the early years, anthropology seems to have been a more powerful presence within the joint department than sociology.

From the department's inception, some anthropologists and sociologists have been involved with policy work but the nature of this involvement has varied over time. As in the case of Don Wilmott, the first sociologist to join the department, this involvement has partly reflected the fluctuating interest of governments in availing themselves of the expertise anthropologists and sociologists had to offer.

Wilmott came to Newfoundland in 1956 in a joint appointment with the Department of Social Studies at Memorial and the provincial government's

Department of Welfare. During his stay, he taught for part of the year and spent the remainder touring the province, writing reports for the Department of Welfare. According to Wilmott, this was part of a short-lived period during which the Smallwood government came to the university looking for the expertise of "outsiders" like himself. This interest in the university faculty soon evaporated. Wilmott says:

> We were all eventually fired or quit when [Smallwood] didn't like what we had to say. He replaced us with people with no qualifications, "yes" men, when he wanted to secure his support in Newfoundland. He got rid of the mainlanders and distanced himself from the "eggheads" at the university. (Personal interview)

Before he left the province, Wilmott helped establish the Institute of Social and Economic Research (ISER). ISER has played a key role in facilitating and shaping the relationship between anthropology, sociology, and policy work in Newfoundland and Labrador over the past thirty years.[3] It is one of the oldest social scientific research institutes in Canada.

ISER and Basic Research for Policy Makers

During the early 1960s, ISER and its researchers seem to have limited their policy work to the provision of empirical studies to be used by government policy makers. According to anthropologist Robert Paine who has been involved with ISER since the 1960s, the Institute's involvement with policy research was encouraged by the federal government's interest in carrying out its own research, independent of the Smallwood government.

ISER's primary mandate was to promote research on Newfoundland and Labrador. The main ISER-funded projects in the 1960s included a succession of community studies, primarily ethnographies, conducted by doctoral fellows from American universities (see Faris, 1966; Philbrook, 1966; Firestone, 1967).[4] Other early research projects were funded by the federal Department of Fisheries, Agricultural Rehabilitation and Development Act (ARDA), and federal Departments of Agriculture and Northern Affairs and Resources. The purpose of the ARDA studies was to "provide basic material for the ARDA policy makers," by collecting information in areas selected by the administrators. This approach was similar to that associated with ARDA-funded studies in Quebec during the same period (Salisbury, 1977:60).

At this time, research for government was considered to be secondary to ISER's primary mandate, basic research. It was justified by the major social and economic changes taking place in Newfoundland and Labrador, and the dearth of basic information required for "the rational formulation of long term policies. It [was] hoped that the background and other data collected by the Institute [would] be of value to policy makers." (ISER Report, 1961-1963:3).

ISER's directors believed that the relationship between social science and policy-making involved a clear-cut division of labour between researchers and policy makers; social scientific research would inform policy-making, but social scientists would not confine their research to the needs of policy makers nor formulate the policy recommendations they felt were implied by their research. ISER's founders did not identify any possible contradictions between the frameworks and goals of policy makers and those of social scientists. They also operated with a pluralist model of government in that they did not identify contradictions between the interests of policy makers and those groups they were studying. This relationship between anthropological and sociological research and the policy makers changed, somewhat, as a consequence of the so-called "resettlement debate."

Basic Research: Some Unintended Consequences

During the 1960s, several researchers got involved in studies related to the federal and provincial governments' programme to stimulate economic development by resettling small outport communities into "growth centres." Some of these studies were designed to help policy makers understand the roots of opposition to the programme. According to Ralph Matthews, one of these researchers, the original studies were not dissimilar to those that had been carried out through ISER in the past (Iverson and Matthews, 1979). This is supported by Robert DeWitt's statement about the goals of his study *Public Policy and Community Protest: the Fogo Case.*

> I consider that social scientists can become involved with political questions—such as are dealt with here—and still produce work which is faithful to scientific objectivity. Involvement with normative questions, nevertheless, often produces bias. The lines between the sociologically significant and the insignificant can become blurred when sociological analysis is used for political purposes. It is emphasized that this report is "applied sociology;" attitudes and social structures on Fogo Island have been studied to aid Government planners.

> My knowledge has been applied to this setting to demonstrate (a) whether certain goals are attainable, (b) if so, how they can be efficiently attained and, (c) what the consequences of attaining—or not attaining—them may be. I have no interest in prescribing goals but I hope that the findings will be used to benefit the people of Fogo Island (1969:vii).

This value-neutral stance was eroded somewhat when the results of this research were picked up by the media, and used to help crystallize mounting opposition to resettlement. Public opposition was further encouraged by an ISER-sponsored colloquium on resettlement and by the research of two ISER-associated Norwegian scholars, Ottar Brox and Cato Wadel. Brox's (1972) study *Newfoundland Fishermen in the Age of Industry* challenged the modernization approach that had informed both previous research and government policy in relation to rural Newfoundland. This critique and the movement against resettlement created a theoretical and policy-formation vacuum into which development models, informed by models of rural revitalization based on Schumacher's "small is beautiful" approach, were introduced. In his detailed critical analysis of this approach and its prevalence in Newfoundland and Labrador studies of this period, Jim Overton, a local sociologist argues:

> What started out as a mainly intellectual, university-based movement for alternative development on the part of those who took up the problems of the rural poor, began in the 1970s to become something of a popular movement of rural revitalization (1990:31).

A key element in this movement was a concerted campaign to oust the Smallwood regime. Brox and Wadel worked with the Conservatives to bring this about. According to Robert Paine:

> The membership of the opposition Conservative Party was all new. They had ideas, or they didn't have ideas but they came to us and acquired ideas.... They took to Cato Wadel and he actually spoke at their annual meeting. They knew about Brox too. I started colloquia,...we had one on resettlement. We were batting around the actual problems that faced the community at large. At the same time, we were doing academic work like Faris' *Cat Harbour* (1966). (Personal interview).

Elliott Leyton, who joined the joint department during this period, recalls:

> These were pretty exciting times.... We were just beginning to develop a critical and sometimes adversarial role, especially around the resettlement program. The department saw itself as an objective critic of the Smallwood dictatorship. (Personal interview).

Leyton says that the debates fuelled by this new, critical role contributed to his own interest in doing socially relevant work on Newfoundland and Labrador. This interest, concern generated by conversations with one of his students from the community of St. Lawrence, and financial support from ISER were key ingredients in his decision to research and write *Dying Hard*, an important and widely read study of industrial disease. Exposure to suffering and corruption he had not known existed were also important:

> The idea of how much suffering there was didn't really hit me until St. Lawrence.... I'm a rich doctor's son. I'm married to the daughter of a rich businessman, and I grew up entirely in upper middle class Vancouver.... [I believed] professionals were people who all did their jobs, and doctors were good people. So, it wasn't until this revelation in St. Lawrence, where the medical people entered with the civil servants into a conspiracy to fuck these people.... I couldn't believe it. (Personal interview).

These revelations prompted Leyton to follow up *Dying Hard* with a study of the Workers' Compensation Commission and other policy work, copies of which he submitted to the provincial government. The government's lack of response convinced Leyton that he should focus his efforts to achieve social change by writing books in a form that "grip the public by the entrails" and using the media to get his message out to the public. He has worked hard to make himself attractive to the media and is regularly consulted for his opinions. Leyton does these interviews because he feels it is his "civic responsibility as a professor who has thought about a subject. I feel I am paid to interpret this civilization. Whatever you may think of my analysis, I don't think you can argue with my doing it. I think we should all be doing it..." (Personal interview). Although enormously successful as a writer, and widely quoted as an expert, he is only marginally involved with his own department and the university as a whole. This combination of success and professional marginality raises some important issues about, at the very least, the public and private identities of anthropology.

During the 1970s, ISER's research mandate expanded from Newfoundland and Labrador to the northern North Atlantic. A large Killam grant generated important policy-related research on the Inuit of the Arctic and Northern Labrador (see Paine, 1977). Jean Briggs, an ISER fellow and social anthropologist at Memorial University, was part of this expansion. She carried out research on the Inuit during this period. Briggs has not been involved in extensive public criticism of public policy related to the Inuit nor in trying to carry out research for policy makers. This position reflects her belief that there are basic contradictions between the worlds of policy makers and social scientists. She remembers hearing these contradictions articulated at a national conference in the 1970s:

> The goals and time frame and everything about the worlds that social policy makers and social scientists live in are different. The social policy makers have to please an electorate or they get booted out. They have to work fast to do that and so they are not interested in complex understanding of the phenomena they are trying to deal with. They are interested in band-aid solutions which will be popular, rather than somehow true or profound solutions.... Fundamentally, their bottom line is always economics because they always have to deal with money and also because the electorate thinks largely in terms of money, their income, where is the

bread coming from rather than what is going to happen to the planet. Social scientists are the opposite in all these respects. They think in the very long term, if they are intelligent and wise, and they are interested in links and ramifications. The policy makers cannot afford to deal with these. (Personal interview).

Policy makers made similar arguments at this conference. Briggs recalls them saying they "found it very difficult to communicate with us because we always wanted longer studies, we always raised objections to their solutions. We said, `yes, but what if,' and they said `we can't afford to think in "what if" terms.'" (Personal interview).

In this account, Briggs equates policy makers with politicians. She also draws hard lines between narrow definitions of policy making as politically determined and the making of non-political social science.

Although she identifies fundamental inconsistencies between academic and policy-related work, Briggs is supportive of much of the social policy work of her colleagues. She has also used her field work among the Inuit as the basis for talks to Arctic medical researchers and professionals in several countries in an attempt to influence their involvement with the Inuit (Briggs, 1974, 1975, 1983, 1985, 1990). During her field work, she developed a strong commitment to helping the Inuit. The Inuit, she says, "became an important part of my world, a part I love and cherish. I feel defensive on their behalf."

The Centre for the Development of Community Initiatives: Research for the Community

At the same time as ISER researchers were raising important policy questions about the impact of white society on the Inuit, industrial disease, and resettlement, some anthropologists and sociologists were becoming involved with other institutions related to policy work. One such institution was the newly created Centre for the Development of Community Initiatives, also at Memorial University. In many cases, the initiatives for the policy work carried out through the Centre came from the community rather than government or the professional literature of anthropology and sociology. The Centre was also quite separate from both ISER and the departments of sociology and anthropology at Memorial.

Gordon Inglis, an anthropologist, was the head of the Centre for Community Initiatives. His account of this experience provides some interesting insights into this type of policy work. One of Inglis's early goals for the Centre was to use it as a way to facilitate access by members of the community to university services and to academics with expertise that could help them meet their goals. The Centre provided an opportunity for a different level of integration of anthropology and social policy than Inglis had experienced through his involvement with the Hawthorn research on native peoples prior to coming to Newfoundland. Through the Centre he participated in a wide range of activities including a research project on alcohol abuse in Nain, Labrador, that contributed to the construction of a women's shelter there, and an abortive project designed to put humus toilets into an area of St. John's without water and sewerage.[5]

A key area of focus for members of the Centre for Community Initiatives was the possibility of oil-related development in Newfoundland. In the days prior to the requirement for an Environmental Assessment Review Process (EARP), they lobbied government to carry out socio-economic impact assessment research and introduce policies designed to limit the negative impacts of oil-related development. Inglis also sat as a Commissioner on the People's Commission on Unemployment in 1978, a study sponsored by the Federation of Labour as an alternative to the royal commissions dominated by representatives of industry and government.

In 1977, Inglis published a discussion paper on applied anthropology in Canada in which he examined a range of different applied anthropology roles from data collector and analyst, to evaluator of a programme, public educator, interpreter and spokesperson, to social critic and political activist. He outlined the ethical dilemmas associated with efforts to make anthropology more socially relevant, but argued that

> we cannot retreat from them. We must become *engaged* in our society, and while we must not let our moral concerns lead us into doing bad science, we must equally not let our concern for scientific objectivity lead us into being bad citizens (1977:185).

Inglis also expressed concern that "applied anthropology" would become equated with short-term contract work in which the anthropologist was little more than a "general-purpose social engineer, applying bits and pieces of theory and technique from anywhere and everywhere, his or her major asset being a nodding acquaintance with a variety of concepts and methods" (1977:181). I heard echoes of this concern when I interviewed him in 1990. In reflecting back over his career as an anthropologist, he said,

> I guess I feel this all sort of happened. I've ended up without any body of expertise. By my time in an academic career, one ends up either dead or some sort of expert in a field, and I am neither dead nor an expert. I haven't carved out a field for myself. In some sense, I feel a lack.... If I was a different person, I would have set out to educate myself on labour, broadly on the fishery, etc. That's the sort of thing I mean. Maybe that's also what I mean about being a little bit lazy. Part of the reason is I wouldn't have been able to do other things that I've found much more interesting and fun.

Inglis has far more than a "nodding acquaintance with a variety of concepts and methods" but the comment points to a possible dilemma for those people whose career is based on policy work. One risk associated with responding to initiatives from the community is the failure to acquire the kind of knowledge that is recognized as expertise within the professions of anthropology and sociology.

Inglis's assessment of his own career, however, leaves unchallenged the definition of "expertise." For example, the expertise he acquired to facilitate dialogues between academics and the wider community is overlooked in this definition. He also leaves unexplored the possibility that it is the preoccupation of anthropologists and sociologists with acquiring "expertise" and "expert" status, and not simply our "concern for scientific objectivity," that leads us into being "bad citizens." This preoccupation can result in the failure to carry out research of critical concern to the citizenry because such research does not fit with the research agendas of the anthropology and sociology disciplines.

Support Groups and Greater Separation of Policy and Academic Work

Community-based support groups were another important vehicle through which anthropologists and sociologists in Newfoundland and Labrador engaged in policy work in the 1970s and 1980s. For example, anthropologist Adrian Tanner helped found the "Indian and Inuit Support Group" (IISG), one of several such groups involving anthropologists and sociologists in St. John's in the 1970s and 1980s. Members of these groups engaged in public education and public criticism of government policy.[6]

Tanner decided to establish the IISG when he became disenchanted with the provincial government's approach to native issues. His exposure to the "wrong-headed and unjust government policies for native peoples" at both levels of government through his involvement in public hearings for the federal government's *White Paper* on changes to the Indian Act, and work with the James Bay Cree and Micmac and Innu in Newfoundland and Labrador convinced him of the need to influence policy makers. He felt a support group was necessary in order to make governments listen to native demands and to provide a forum and legitimacy for the expression of anthropological concerns about native people. He comments:

I've had a schizophrenic life. No one from government comes to you. As an academic, I've never once been asked for my advice by either the federal or provincial government, despite valuable publicly-funded research that I've carried out....The prime motivation for me in all of this has been the native groups. They start an organization and you support them; they start a court case and you support them. Your legitimacy as an intervenor comes from those groups.... I have to wait for a native group to come forward, to present its interest in a white competitive model. Until such a situation arises, it is difficult for someone who is neither part of industry, nor part of groups. There is no place for such a person to contribute mainly because government does not ask us.

Many of these support groups were short-lived. According to Jim Overton, who has written about the history of the Newfoundland Association of Full Employment (NAFE), a group he helped establish, there are some important shortcomings to this approach to policy work (Overton, 1981). Groups have their own requirements, including the need to achieve short-term gains. In the case of NAFE, these gains were partially blocked by suspicion within the leadership of key organizations essential for the group's success, such as the Federation of Labour.

Advocacy Research and Consultancy: The Threatened Divorce of Policy and Academic Work

In the 1980s, new institutions for policy work including environmental impact assessment, native land claims negotiations, and women's organizations were created. These institutions were a response to public protests and lobbying and organizing work to which anthropological and sociological research contributed, and in which anthropologists and sociologists participated. These institutions have provided new opportunities for policy work for anthropologists and sociologists within universities. They have also enhanced employment opportunities for these and other professional groups outside in the form of consultancy work and paid advocacy-research. In some cases, these anthropologists and sociologists and their work are quite marginal to the professions. This section explores the separation of policy and academic work through the experiences of an advocate researcher and a paid consultant.

As a result of the land claims process and the Environmental Assessment Review Process, some native groups now employ anthropologists to conduct research and promote their land claims and other matters. Peter Armitage, a local anthropologist, is an advocate researcher employed by the Naskapi-Montagnais Innu Association (NMIA) in Labrador. Armitage identifies his work with the NMIA as an extreme form of advocacy:

> I've had a very activist style of advocacy. Instead of just acting as a spokesperson or a researcher I've played a variety of roles as an advocate, organizing, networking, doing public relations, public speaking, all in a public campaign.

Armitage attributes this intense, multi-faceted participation to the fact that, unlike most anthropologists, he is not a full-time teacher. In addition, he has been "forced into it because of the absence of others willing to do these kinds of work." He has been extensively involved in the campaign to stop low-level military flight training in Labrador. Armitage describes his involvement in the campaign in the following way:

> There's a sociologist called Gusfield [1981] who has written about the sociology of public problems. He defines a public problem as having two components: a "cognitive" component and a "moral" component. The cognitive component of the public problem is its factual basis, the actual data, the facticity behind the problem. The moral part is that which makes its resolution important, which makes it repugnant. My job in this has been to develop the cognitive side of the public problem. That's where all of the research comes in. I play a major role in pumping out arguments and data to support groups across the country on different aspects of the issue—whether it be cultural survival, environmental, or peace aspects. The Innu have been responsible for the moral aspect.

> At times, we've worked at odds with one another in that the Innu have been sloppy with their facts. Certainly the environmental and peace movements are sloppy with their facts, and that's been a big problem. When the facts get too garbled the people that you're up against, your opponents, accuse you of spreading misinformation. I've played a real role in trying to gather the facts in the first place, make the arguments, and keep the arguments straight, as close to the truth as possible. My role has been a complementary one to the Innu. I supplement what they have been doing. There is a need for experts when you are presenting any public problem, and I've been one of the main so-called experts talking about this issue.

In his role as expert, Armitage has had to develop a comprehensive understanding of a wide range of subjects beyond the confines of traditional anthropology (see Armitage, 1990; 1991). In environmental impact assessment, one of his areas, the technological, political, economic, social, and scientific are interconnected. The person responsible for organizing and synthesizing a comprehensive critique of an Environmental Impact Statement (EIS) has to have some knowledge in all of these areas.[7] In addition, advocacy research requires a broad range of organizational skills, as well as a coherent media strategy.

There are some obvious risks associated with the need to develop broader knowledge of an issue (usually with limited resources) and to combine advocacy and expert roles. These risks are greater when the pool of sympathetic experts is small and costly to access. Armitage's comments reflect these dilemmas:

I wish there were more experts around. When you mix roles like this, advocacy roles and social science roles, you are running a big risk you're going to have your credibility as a social scientist challenged.

For the advocate researcher, evidence of self-censorship is one way credibility can be undermined. Self-censorship, the deliberate exclusion of some information, a failure to "tell it [entirely] like it is," is an integral part of advocacy research. But self-censorship is also integral to most ethnographic work (Dyck, 1989). Peer review of advocacy research could be used to protect credibility and remind non–social scientists that some degree of self-censorship is part of all ethnography, often essential in ethical research.

Another risk associated with advocacy research stems from the application of "professional" criteria for expert status to those who do it. The absence of a doctoral degree and limited numbers of publications in professional journals can be used to challenge the arguments of advocacy researchers, however valid they might be. The products of advocacy work are not, however, easily turned into professional publications, and reports generated in advocacy work are not necessarily recognized in academic doctoral programmes. To the extent that the professions do not examine their criteria for professionalism nor establish mechanisms for effective and fair review of the products of advocacy research, the work and credentials of the anthropologists and sociologists who do advocacy research will be in jeopardy. Their research will be subject to rejection in the face of alternative research carried out by those with less understanding but with formal professional credentials.

Another feature of social policy work in the 1980s has been an increase in policy-related work carried out by paid consultants. The practice of contracting out work to consultants that would formerly have been carried out by permanent employees or by university academics has contributed to this trend.[8] Anthropologists and sociologists working as paid consultants are included in this new group of often marginal workers.

"Eileen" is a former academic anthropologist who now works as a paid consultant for local firms and the government. In contrast to paid advocates like Armitage, who are employed by relatively marginalized and disempowered groups, Eileen says that

being a consultant is to be open to the charge that you have been co-opted by the power structures. You find yourself in ethically very difficult situations...working for X is definitely not the same as working for a band council. Accepting this employment means accepting a situation in which you cannot claim to be "pure." Anthropologists, you may have noticed, have this kind of, arrogance isn't exactly the word I want, but anthropologists are, let's face it, just so much more pure than anyone else.... Anthropologists in theory, although not always in practice, identify with underdogs, study them. On the one hand they live off underdogs, but on the other hand, the trade-off is that you are their advocate, their mediator, their channel to the power structure. And you do that partly by not being co-opted by the power structure, and you do it largely as a volunteer effort, sometimes entirely.... That's part of being an anthropologist; it's purity and consultants aren't pure.

As Eileen points out, and as illustrated by the above discussion of advocacy research, neither academic nor advocacy anthropology and sociology are all that pure. There are some differences, however.[9] According to Eileen, in contrast to academic work and, to a lesser extent, to advocacy,

in the consulting world, they set the parameters starting with the time frame, how many days they will pay you, when it has to be done. They define the project. Sometimes they tell you in very explicit terms exactly how they want it done, how they want the product to look, other times it can be more open-ended, although clearly this can get one into trouble. Anyway, they set out what it is they want, and to a greater or lesser degree how they want it done and the time frame within which they want it done. So, within those constraints you can do work which you are more or less pleased with and you can tell them things you think are more or less important, and present them in a way you hope will be compelling, and people will see the sense of and act on them. But it is very difficult in that context to define the problem yourself, to do it your own way, to introduce things you know they will consider extraneous.

In addition, the resulting consultant's report belongs to the sponsoring agency and not the consultant. This means the consultant lacks control over use and distribution of her work.

Despite the very real problems she identifies with consultancy work, Eileen feels that it is important work. Furthermore, she says there are some freedoms and possibilities associated with it that are less available in academic life. For example, affiliation with government gives her easier access to places and individuals than she might have as an academic field worker.

In addition, working with non academics means she has to learn to say things simply and clearly. The absence of a shared community and shared agreement on the "importance" of her work, a feature she identifies with academic life, means that no one assumes that what she has to say is important. She has to "sell" her audience on its relevance. This contributes, she says, to greater clarity of thought and argument.

Eileen also maintains that there is more opportunity to influence policy decisions if you are working inside the bureaucracy. She finds:

one of the gratifying things is that, if you are inside that power structure, they are listening to you anyway. You can sometimes get them to do things and actually get things to happen.

She has found ways to increase her influence by applying her anthropological scrutiny to the organization, searching for ways to operate within its constraints. When possibilities emerge for a more consultative and critical approach to her work, she takes advantage of them.[10] Eileen is irritated by the failure of the Canadian Anthropology Society and the Canadian Sociology and Anthropology Association to address issues that confront paid consultants. She often finds that Association meetings make her angry because

> nobody seems to be aware of, take into account, or even imagine the existence of people who do the thing I do, consulting. So, it is not in any way part of the consciousness, knowledge or concern of the membership.

She attributes this neglect partly to the fact that most of those who do consultancy work are not in universities, and are not members of the professional associations. However, one of the reasons why they are not in the associations, she maintains, is the associations' preoccupation with academic, and to a lesser extent advocacy, concerns.

Conclusion

The history presented in this paper documents varied and changing involvements in policy work among anthropologists and sociologists in Newfoundland and Labrador. It touches on some of the institutions that have contributed to involvement in this kind of work and the practices that have influenced the form it has taken. The institutions have included ISER, the Centre for Community Initiatives, support groups, and more recently, women's institutions and the land claims and Environmental Impact Assessment process. The practices that have affected the extent and goals of policy work among anthropologists and sociologists include fluctuating interest in social scientific research within the provincial and federal governments, social movements like the anti-resettlement, women's and native peoples' movements, and understandings and commitments linked to the field work experience.[11] The structure of the professions of anthropology and sociology in the 1960s and 1970s, an era of expansion, seems to have encouraged the involvement of academics in these disciplines in policy work. Elliot Leyton pinpointed early tenure as an important factor and Gordon Inglis pointed to the absence of clearly defined boundaries for anthropology and for subdisciplines within anthropology. For those whose research focus was Newfoundland and Labrador, the presence in their classrooms of students from the communities they studied may also have contributed to this involvement in social policy work. Inevitably, the subjects of their research were also their audience in a way that is not typical of anthropology and sociology elsewhere.

Universities have changed considerably in the past ten years. Opportunities for younger, untenured academics to combine policy and academic work have declined. Limited employment opportunities have heightened the competition for academic jobs in anthropology and sociology. In addition, these limited opportunities have contributed to an increase in, and tightening of, the requirements for access to those jobs. Unlike the past, it is now almost impossible to get an academic job without a doctoral degree.

In most cases, those academic anthropologists and sociologists who have engaged extensively in policy work share with their more academic colleagues assumptions that priorize "academic" over policy work in the hiring process. As a result, even in departments with a strong history of policy work, the ability of new recruits to continue this tradition without jeopardizing their access to university employment has been substantially eroded. At the same time, academic anthropologists and sociologists continue to dominate the professions and their associations. Many of the new institutional bases for policy work are outside of universities, and those who do this work have a marginal relationship to the professions. Whatever their relationship to the professions (some may be tenured professors who have become actively involved in consultancy), their work is often not subject to professional scrutiny.[12]

The combined forces of professionalization, cutbacks to the social sciences, and related changes in the definition of the university (Buchbinder and Newson, 1988), as well as the expansion of consultancy and advocacy research, are undermining the already uneasy marriage of academic and policy work. Its dissolution could divide us into academic professionals (members of inward-looking churches, struggling to hold on to institutional privileges on the basis of traditional rights and adopting a disconnected relationship to our students and to those we study), and consultants and advocates (excluded from the professional protections associated with the university and immune from professional ethics).[13]

As argued by Joan Ryan in the quote that opened this paper, responding to the inevitable scrutiny and criticism of the policy work of consultants and advocate researchers by drawing firm boundaries between "pure" and "applied" work means ignoring the ethical and political questions that permeate our "pure" work and that have, in the past, provided the impetus for our involvement in policy work. As exemplified by the contrast between ISER's initial model for policy work and later models, the experience and knowledge acquired through policy work has often challenged researchers' assumptions about the relationship between government and society. The section on the resettlement debate suggests that, on occasion, involvement with social movements can contribute to paradigm shifts in anthropological and sociological thinking.

As anthropologists and sociologists inside and outside the academy we should not turn our backs on the ethical dilemmas that permeate all of our work, the important insights policy work can provide, and the significance of changes within universities and the wider society. This is important for the future of our disciplines and those we study. Instead, we need to identify and struggle for new institutions and practices that will encourage critical, self-reflexive thinking that is responsive to social realities and can broaden tolerance for difference and innovation within anthropology and sociology and within different cultural contexts.

NOTES

[1]   I would like to acknowledge the kind co-operation of friends and colleagues at Memorial University who put up with my invasive interviews, most often on very short notice. I would particularly like to thank Peter Armitage, Ann-Louise Brookes, Raoul Andersen, Peter Baehr, Raymond Currie and the other editors of this book, Elliott Leyton, Rosemary Ommer, and Robert Paine for comments on earlier drafts. Of course, all mistakes and misconceptions are my own.

[2]   This paper is a small portion of a comparative study of the history of anthropology, sociology, and policy work in Newfoundland and Labrador and Quebec.

[3]   Although interdisciplinary, the organization of the Institute was heavily influenced by anthropologists and sociologists. This was particularly true during the early years.

[4]   There is still no Ph.D. programme in anthropology at Memorial University. Sociology's Ph.D. programme began in 1991.

[5]   According to Inglis, Canada Mortgage and Housing Corporation (CMHC) had agreed to pay for the toilets when John Evans, his partner in the project, discovered that they did not work. Evans went to Montreal and found a huge warehouse filled with returned, defective humus toilets.

[6]   The other groups included the Newfoundland Association for Full Employment (NAFE) and the Labour Support Group. Jim Overton and I were involved in these groups (see Overton, 1981).

[7]   The need for more people with the skills and knowledge to bridge the social science and "pure" science divide was emphasized in a recent assessment of the difficulties associated with predicting environmental impacts (see Berkes, 1988). In my own work on the social impact of technological change and occupational safety and health, I have encountered the same requirement to develop expertise in a broad range of areas, from medicine to engineering and technology. Like Armitage, I have also experienced the problems and dilemmas that can result from the absence of "experts" in other areas who are not committed to the status quo, and have a sociological understanding. This has forced me to be silent or run the risk of commenting in areas outside my own immediate realm of expertise and thereby having my credibility challenged (Fishery Research Group, 1986; Williams and Neis, 1990).

[8]   In his comments on an earlier draft of this paper, Raymond Currie pointed out that government policy has contributed to this trend. Academics often cannot apply for work of this kind through the university but only as self-employed individuals. As a result, they take on contracts with private companies, as in the case of some federal contracts relating to the Solicitor General's Office.

[9]   It is not insignificant that this is the one person I interviewed whose identity and the identity of the organization for which she works need to be disguised.

[10]   Doug House, a local sociologist and former Chair of the Newfoundland government's Royal Commission on Employment and Unemployment was recently appointed head of the provincial government's Economic Recovery Commission (ERC). The mandate of the ERC is to look for ways to implement the recommendations of the Royal Commission. It is certainly unusual for a social scientist to have the opportunity to participate in the implementation of recommendations he helped draft. House also maintains that occupying a position within the civil service has contributed to his understanding of the way the civil service works. He feels that the previous government's limited response to the recommendations of the Royal Commission on Employment and Unemployment was partly a consequence of the autonomy of the Commission from those in charge of implementing policy.

[11]   During field work, researchers are inevitably "faced with complex ethical issues as a result of being personally and professionally involved with the lives of people," problems that pervade all forms of advocacy work (Van Esterik, 1983:61).

[12]   This contributes to their marginality. The publications that count within the professions are those that have been through a referee process. Social policy work may be like teaching, in that it involves organization and administration rather than pure research. Like teaching, this aspect of social policy work can be dismissed in the hiring process because it has not been "overseen" by members of the profession. The publications that result from social policy work are not always suitable for professional journals and are often not written in "academic" language. This means that they are not refereed, and hence, tend not to count in the academic hiring, promotion, and tenure.

[13]   By highlighting the dangers associated with divorcing "pure" and "applied" anthropology and sociology, I do not mean to suggest that there are no problems with policy work. As suggested by Jean Briggs, there are inconsistencies between the policy-making process and the requirements and goals of good anthropological and sociological research. The best way to deal with these inconsistencies is to look for ways to resolve them. For example, how can we effectively deal with the media? Most of the anthropologists and sociologists I interviewed for this paper did not have an understanding of the media. Those that did had acquired it in the course of doing policy work, often after painful experiences. There are fundamental problems with using the mass media to get our message out. But despite important constraints, the media is like any other institution. There are those within it who are more committed to investigative journalism and to challenging common sense understandings. There are some formats, such as commentaries, where there is more opportunity than in others to pose problems in our own terms. Similarly, there are opportunities within government to work for change.

BETTER IRREVERENT THAN IRRELEVANT

Pat Armstrong and Hugh Armstrong

In that great Canadian classic, *The Vertical Mosaic*, John Porter (1965:492) argued that

> A view of intellectuals as a class opposed to the social order is, of course, wrong. As many trained and brilliant minds have helped to shore up social orders as have helped to tear them down.

But not all intellectuals are neatly lined up vigorously supporting or undermining things as they are. Indeed, Porter (1965:500) went on to suggest that Canadian intellectuals have not so much been irreverent as they have been irrelevant.

> It may be argued that the impact of these sages on the ideological structure is weak. Very few of them write, as do so many academics in the United States, books which become widely read interpretations of social life. Very little of what they write could be considered social criticism. With few exceptions their attitudes and values are conventional. Their contribution therefore to a dynamic dialogue is minimal.

What would constitute relevant intellectual work, particularly of the kind that would help shape social policy? While the answers are far from simple, it is clear that at a minimum such work must be critical, accessible, and rigorous.

Critical intellectual work implies a refusal to accept conventional assumptions and explanations without investigation, a refusal merely to take things as they are or to make alternatives unthinkable. It implies situating human behaviour and interaction within the context of history, economy, and politics and recognizing that people come in different sexes and races, from different cultural communities and age groups. It implies reflection on how we know as well as on how we find out what we want to know. It implies establishing links and developing explanations. As Justice Bertha Wilson (1990) made clear in writing the recent Supreme Court decision on the battered wife syndrome, social scientists can provide the expertise necessary in moving beyond everyday understandings to provide different interpretations and to expose the underlying pressures on individual behaviour.

But critical intellectual work, no matter how unconventional, can have little impact on social policy, or to individuals outside academe, if it is accessible only to the initiated or to the well-placed. Such work generally needs to inform, and be informed by, the efforts of popular movements if its impact is to be substantial. To be relevant for movement activists, and not solely for a few widely read intellectuals, students in graduate classes, or high-level bureaucrats, intellectual work must be accessible in terms of both readability and availability. This does not imply the abandonment either of theory or of rigorous and sophisticated research. Indeed, relevance implies that intellectual work is theoretically informed and based on systematic investigation. Without an explicit and clear theoretical grounding, intellectual work provides description rather than analysis, still pictures rather than moving critique, convention rather than challenge to tradition. Without an explicit and clear scientific base, intellectual work remains unconvincing and speculative commentary rather than exposition. Furthermore, it can have little impact on social policy.

To be relevant to social policy, critical intellectual work cannot be confined to the classroom, although certainly we must always bring our critical skills to bear on what happens within our academic institutions. Indeed, critical intellectual work implies reflection on what is taught, on how it is taught, and on how work is organized within these workplaces. It also implies reflection on our professional organizations, on what these organizations do and how they do it. Finally, it implies involvement in the world outside academe, not only through the examination of what goes on out there but also through the investigation of how we both influence and are influenced by that other world.

Have we, in the quarter-century since Porter wrote *The Vertical Mosaic* and the Canadian Sociology and Anthropology Association (CSAA) began, managed to develop such relevant and unconventional intellectual work? In this paper, we address this question in terms of the intellectual work that is related to women. We have chosen to look at this issue because it has been perhaps the most prominent issue of the last two decades, because it provides an exemplar of both the limits and possibilities of intellectual work, and because it is the area we know best.

Moreover, feminist intellectuals have been by definition committed to the unconventional and committed to changing social policy. Feminist sociologists and anthropologists have been pioneers in exposing and challenging the structure and methods of teaching, the organization and publications of their professional organization, and the social policies outside academic institutions that serve to keep women in their place. But their efforts have not always been successful and they are in constant danger of becoming conventional, of losing the irreverence that keeps their critical edge.

Social Policy within Academic Institutions

Educational institutions have a social responsibility to transmit knowledge and to create knowledge. Feminist intellectuals have brought their critical view to bear on both areas and much of their work would fit into Porter's definition of social criticism. Unlike the sages Porter describes, they have had an impact on the ideological structure of these institutions.

Feminists have challenged both the male standard and the standard male as the basis of research and analysis (Armstrong and Armstrong, 1978; Luxton, 1984; Smith, 1975). They have exploded the myths of the happy family, complementary roles, and passive female sexuality (Eichler, 1980; Guberman and Wolfe, 1985; Valverde, 1985). They have attacked the notion that work is defined by what is done for pay in the market and have exposed the problems with class analysis based exclusively on male market relations (Connelly, 1978; Connelly and MacDonald, 1989; Fox, 1980; Hamilton, 1978; O'Brien, 1981). They have revealed the fundamental inequities in the market, in the home, and in academic institutions. As well, they have explored many of the mechanisms that serve to keep women in their place. Rejecting positivism and the idea of objectivity, they have critiqued traditional methodologies and ways of presenting social science in the classroom and in publications (Armstrong and Armstrong, 1983; Eichler, 1987; McCormack, 1981; Tomm, 1989). In short, they have opposed the entire order of sociology and anthropology, re-examining our theory, our research, and our practice in the classroom and in academic institutions as a whole.

Feminists have not only attacked the basic assumptions of our disciplines; they have offered alternatives to current assumptions and policies. Feminists have been explicitly committed to making the personal political, to making private troubles public issues, and to demonstrating how the public invades the private and is in turn shaped by the private. This has meant an increasing emphasis, in both research and teaching, on letting women "speak for themselves" about their "everyday and everynight" experiences, on participative approaches to how we know and how we learn (Smith, 1989).

What is emerging is what many call a feminist methodology and a feminist pedagogy. Both are designed to increase access to feminist work while maintaining a scientific basis for their claims. The material that is produced by these feminists and used in their courses is often published in unconventional places and takes unconventional forms. It is frequently directed at policy change.

Feminist intellectual work has also meant an interdisciplinary approach as feminists seek to locate women's subordination within the historical context of a particular political economy. In the process, the concepts of patriarchy, of capitalism, and of reproduction in particular have been revised by feminists seeking to link various aspects of women's lives in order to explain the continuing subordination of women and the fundamental changes they are experiencing.

In large part because feminists have been committed to change, much of their research and teaching has had an explicit theoretical component that attempts to link investigation to explanation so that strategy can be based on an understanding of the pressures that serve to keep women in their place. Although in the 1960s feminists placed the emphasis on what women shared, there has been an increasing interest in exploring the differences among women. This has had a significant impact on their theory and research as feminists struggle to address, in theoretical and strategic terms, the tension between similarities and differences in women's condition.

Within their workplaces, feminists have struggled to put research into practice and to develop research for practice. This has frequently brought them into direct conflict with the structure and policies of their academic institutions. They have used their research demonstrating the inequities within these institutions to alter hiring and promotion policies. Part of this struggle has been the demand that research that is policy-directed, that appears in accessible, unconventional publications, that is based on alternative methodologies, and that has an explicit commitment to change be counted as legitimate academic work for the purposes of hiring, promotion, and tenure. Feminists have also used their research both as the basis of their women's studies courses and as a way of demonstrating the needs for such courses.

Feminists have, in many ways, succeeded in changing policies within academic institutions. But victory has its own contradictions, and a great deal of unfinished business remains. While women's studies has become a legitimate part of the curriculum at most post-secondary institutions, the content and critiques that have been central to their development have not been integrated into other courses throughout these institutions. In too many cases, feminists have not been able to sustain a dynamic dialogue with those supporting the old social order and have instead been segregated into acceptable ghettos.

Moreover, women's studies courses themselves may have lost their critical edge as they have become increasingly legitimate and are increasingly taught by those who do not define themselves as feminists. We do not know if the students leave with the habit of critical thinking or whether they have simply adopted a new orthodoxy and a revised view of the existing social order. Nor do we know whether the hiring and promotion of women has made a significant difference in terms of women's concerns.

But we do know that an increasing number of feminists have been drawn into the bureaucratic structures of their institutions, a process that consumes their energy, diverting them from other pursuits, and that often serves to blunt their critiques. Although we know of no research to support the claim, there seems to be an increasing tendency for the material used in the classroom and written about women to become less accessible to the uninitiated and less directed at social policy change. Feminists are by definition critical thinkers, but their success in claiming legitimacy has made women's issues more conventional, opening the door to those without the necessary irreverence.

Social Policy within the CSAA

Our primary professional organization is involved in publishing, in organizing annual conferences and meetings, in lobbying inside and outside the university and in appointing members to a variety of public and para-public committees. Feminists have sought to influence policies in all these areas. They have organized a Women's Caucus and achieved official sanction for a Status of Women Sub-committee, both of which have a continuing impact on the structures and practices of the CSAA.

In part at least as a result of research demonstrating women's exclusions and of demands for policy changes, women have become increasingly prominent in the various committees of the organization. We have had a succession of female presidents as well as a female editor of *The Canadian Review of Sociology and Anthropology (CRSA)*. Women have been more frequently named as representatives to sit on committees outside the organization. And women's concerns are routinely included on the agenda of CSAA Annual Meetings.

Very soon after the CSAA was founded, some women members began to question the publishing policies of the organization's journal and suggested that a special issue be devoted to papers on "the role and status of women" (Henry, 1975:352). But it was not until International Women's Year and until "women members of the Executive with the able support of their more liberated colleagues put the case in strong terms" (Henry, 1975:352) that the Executive supported the project. Volume 12, issue 4, part 1 of *The Canadian Review of Sociology and Anthropology* contained a host of path-breaking articles. These articles, according to Francis Henry's (1975:352) introduction, indicated scholars "are seriously engaging the subject matter of women in society and testing their premises and assertions according to the dictates of scientific method." Although another issue devoted to such questions was not to appear for more than a decade (*The Canadian Review of Sociology and Anthropology*, 1988), the Editorial Board has responded to demands from feminists and has gradually increased the number of articles by and about women. The other publication of the CSAA, *Society/Société*, also now regularly publishes articles by and about women, many of which address policy issues.

Feminists' concerns have made their way into CSAA sessions at the Learned Societies meetings as well. Over the last fifteen years, there has been a significant increase in the number of sessions organized by women, in the number of sessions devoted to women's issues, and in the number of sessions that include papers by women. The increase reflects both responses to feminist demands for policy changes and women's growing involvement in the discipline.

As is the case within academic institutions, there is a double edge in these victories over the established CSAA order, and some of the changes have failed to penetrate into all aspects of that order. Although there are more articles and sessions by and about women, the articles or sessions that are not explicitly about women often fail to take into account the feminist critiques. For example, the special issue of the CRSA (1985) on the state of the art of sociology in English Canada had one article on women but women were virtually absent from the rest of the volume. The special issue on Canadian political economy (CRSA, 1989) had articles by women but there was little evidence throughout the volume of feminist concerns.

Moreover, many of the articles that are about women do not challenge the existing order, do not have a critical concern. To be acceptable for publication, articles have usually had to follow traditional forms. As work on women has become more acceptable, the values and attitudes have become even more conventional. Although we have no data to support the claim, it also seems to be the case that many such articles do not have a policy concern and are less than accessible to the uninitiated.

As is the case within academic institutions, there has been little attempt to examine the impact on women, or on the organization, of women's increasing involvement. Work for the CSAA is voluntary and often exhausting. Men may well have ceded places because they had other things to do. The CSAA has done little lobbying either within universities or outside them in recent years, and the organization has low visibility on policy issues. Perhaps this voluntary work has been left to women primarily because it has little influence on social policy.

Social Policy in the World outside Academe

Senator and sociologist Lorna Marsden (1988:3) has argued in Society/ Société that:

> In the universities it is not respectable to be politically involved and in political life it is not deemed important to have carefully thought through one's ideas or carefully documented one's facts or logic.

Although, as Marsden's argument suggests, feminist scholars have received little respect for their political involvement and although there is not a great deal of evidence to show that politicians base their decisions primarily on facts or logic, it is clear that feminist sociologists and anthropologists have been active, and sometimes successful, in shaping public policy.

Feminist research has been widely used by a variety of politically active organizations to substantiate their demands. This is particularly evident in demands for pay and employment equity; in demands for policies on sexual harassment and violence against women; in demands for marital property rights and day care; in demands related to labour standards, pensions, and reproductive rights. A simple glance at the bibliographies in submissions to and by governments, far too numerous to list here, indicates the importance of feminist research in demonstrating the occupational segregation and unequal pay of women in general and of visible minority women and immigrant women in particular; in demonstrating that large numbers of women are the victims of violence and harassment; in demonstrating that women make a critical contribution to family maintenance through their household labour, that their responsibility for child care prevents their equal participation in the labour force and often sentences them to poverty, especially when they parent alone and when they reach old age; that minimum standards apply primarily to women and that restrictions on reproductive rights apply exclusively to women.

We now have legislation or at least some policy in all these areas. While the contribution of feminist research to this process cannot easily be measured, it seems clear that it played an integral and not insignificant role. It also seems clear that the research was useful because it was based on rigorous scientific investigation, making it more difficult for politicians to dismiss. At the same time, much of it was accessible to a wide audience because it was written in a manner that made it comprehensible and meaningful to large numbers and thus easier to use in organizing for change.

Feminists have also had an impact on public policy related to research. They successfully pressured the Social Sciences and Humanities Research Council of Canada (SSHRCC) to devote one of its strategic grant areas to women and work. Research exposing the absence of women from the bodies that make decisions about research helped back up demands for greater participation by women. State organizations responded to pressure by appointing more women to various committees and by establishing advisory boards within the state. Although here too it is difficult to measure the precise impact of these developments, it is clear that the state has been funding more research on women and that more of the research directly produced by state organizations looks at women. [See, for example, Statistics Canada's *Women in Canada* (1990a) and *Nursing in Canada* (1990b); Connelly and MacDonald, *Women in the Labour Force* (1990)]. Moreover, feminists have been successful in pressuring many state organizations to adopt guidelines on non-sexist research.

Feminists have also had an impact on public policy through their work as advisors and experts. Increasingly, human rights cases, labour relations board cases, federal and provincial court cases in a variety of areas and tribunal hearings are allowing expert witnesses to express their views on the issues at stake. Sociologists or anthropologists have, for example, testified about the division of labour in the home and the worth of women's domestic work, about gender bias in job evaluation schemes, about the consequences for women of Sunday shopping, about how the structures of an organization can discriminate against women in terms of hiring or promotion and about how housing regulations can serve to deny women a place to live. The decisions from such cases do more than help individual women win; they set precedents for all cases involving women and thus have an impact on public policy. Justice Bertha Wilson's statement about the important contribution that can be made by expert witnesses to Supreme Court decisions suggests that this work will become increasingly important in the future.

Many feminist sociologists and anthropologists have been active in a wide variety of organizations and groups devoted to political change related to their areas of study. Senator Marsden herself offers an excellent example of a sociologist who has drawn on her sociological expertise to preside over Canada's largest feminist lobby group, the National Action Committee on the Status of Women. The then-incoming President of the CSAA, Margrit Eichler (1989), used the pages of *Society/Société* to call for sociologists to become active in the debate around new reproductive technologies. She has not hesitated to take political initiative in this area either. She was a central member of the Canadian Coalition for a Royal Commission on New Reproductive Technology and it was this work, combined with her research on family social policy, that was the basis for her being named a Woman of Distinction by the Toronto YWCA. These feminist sociologists are not simply exceptions. There are many more who are active in unions, in community groups, and in political parties. And they are clearly identified as social scientists when they undertake this work.

They are also clearly identified as social scientists when they establish publications and organize conferences. Journals such as *Atlantis, Canadian Woman Studies, Broadside, Resources for Feminist Research,* and *Healthsharing* continually address social policy issues that fall outside academe. Many of the conferences, such as those on pay and employment equity or on racism and pedagogy, do as well. Although it is mainly academics who read these journals and attend these conferences, this is not exclusively the case. With sensitive planning, many journals and conferences have been successful in reaching a wider audience.

This political activity is not without its problems and contradictions, however. As Marsden indicated, political work is not respectable. Political activity may be used against feminists when they apply for jobs or promotion. At best, it does not count to their credit when they are considered for jobs or merit pay. Yet this work can consume enormous amounts of time and energy, diverting feminists from accumulating more respectable items on their curriculum vitaes.

At the same time, the more research on women becomes respectable, the greater the pressures to become conventional. Although women have been successful in altering somewhat the criteria for support, it is still the case that grants are largely allocated on the basis of traditional ideas about evidence, legitimacy, and expertise. Precisely because some money is available, feminists may feel the pressure to tailor their projects to fit the grants, especially given that the availability of money draws more conventional scholars into the competition. The pressure is reinforced by the declining financial support within the university, which increasingly means that there is no access to photocopying and computers without a grant. It is also reinforced by the fact that a growing number of women have been hired in academic institutions and need acceptable research in order to keep these jobs. Moreover, doing research for the state not only means pressure to conform and avoid explicit criticism; it may also mean that the research disappears or at least becomes quite inaccessible.

But critical research has clearly not become respectable enough. The federal government has just withdrawn support from a number of women's journals and the women and work strategic grant allocation is under threat. This means less money for research, fewer places to publish, and greater pressure to be conventional in our work. Moreover, the new guidelines from various funding agencies encourage co-operation with corporate sponsors, a policy that is unlikely to promote critical feminist research aimed at social change.

Conclusion

The call for papers on Sociology and Social Policy that gave rise to this section of this volume began:

> As a general statement, it would be hard to argue that sociologists and anthropologists in Anglophone Canada have been in the forefront of major social issues, either in formulating social policy or addressing existing social policy (Currie, 1989:28).

John Porter said something very similar a quarter-century ago. This paper argues that this is not the case when we look at intellectual work on women. Sociologists and anthropologists have been active in formulating and addressing existing social policy related to women. They have had a profound impact on the ideological structure and have produced widely read interpretations of social life that could clearly be considered social criticism.

This area of sociology and anthropology offers an important example of what we as scholars can do. Our disciplines are well placed to address the most critical social issues of the day. We have the tools to provide rigorous research to back our claims. We have a perspective that allows us to place these issues within a broader context that exposes the social construction of current conditions as well as the social processes and structures that maintain or change them. Engagement with social policy both requires and encourages the critical skills so central to sociological and anthropological work.

But it also offers an indication of the risks involved in doing this kind of work. Not only does engagement with social policy not count as respectable academic work; it also may count against academics and certainly limits their ability to do other kinds of work. Those who do social policy work for a living outside academe may find it difficult to undertake the more rigorous, theoretical, and committed research work. As the research becomes more acceptable, it may also be in danger of losing its critical component, of becoming irrelevant to social policy change. This is particularly the case as funded research becomes increasingly important to survival and as conservative politics pervade every aspect of Canadian social life. Moreover, as the social policy area becomes more respectable it may become more inaccessible. Theoretical and empirical work in this area may become more sophisticated and complex at the same time as the scholars undertaking it become less committed to social change.

John Porter criticized the conventional and called for scholars to contribute to a dynamic dialogue. Feminist scholars have done just that. However, it is perhaps an indication of the rest of the discipline that no feminist book received the award designed to commemorate his name until 1990, when the CSAA took up Marilyn Porter's (1989) suggestion by selecting Dorothy Smith's *The Everyday World as Problematic* (1987).

THE PRICE OF LEGITIMACY:
ACADEMICS AND THE LABOUR MOVEMENT

Ester Reiter

Gil Levine, retired research director of CUPE, noted in *Labour/Le Travail* the lack of connection between left academics and labour. Most research on labour relations, he maintains is
1. not done at the request of labour
2. practically unread by labour
3. not useful to labour in Canada (Levine, 1988:191).

In this paper I will argue that the price of "legitimacy," or recognition within the labour movement and within the academic community as experts on the labour movement, often makes useful research difficult, if not impossible. The way we academics work with the trade union movement and readily pronounce on what they should be doing is not only inappropriate, but supports the kind of unionism that is not the activist, democratic trade unionism we theoretically support.

I am not suggesting that there are not other dimensions to the story. Wilensky, for example, describes the difficult position of university-educated unions' staff experts. He concludes that one of the recipes for survival as a union staffer is best described as "know your place and stay in it," accepting at all times the superiority of the *real* workers. An exaggerated humility and vigorous expressions of anti-intellectualism are necessary to live down a college degree (Wilensky, 1956:273).

Certainly, how the trade union movement views academics and uses our skills and resources is not above criticism. However, that discussion would be better left to those who work within the trade union movement to address. In this paper, I will look into the views held about academics and locate the chasm between academics and labour, described by Levine, within debates about the nature of scientific knowledge, and the tension between theoretical and practical knowledge. I will note how the structure of our collective bargaining system, as well as the nature of the academic milieu, enters into this discussion, and I will review some of the criticisms made of us. Academics, trade unionists maintain, are arrogant, use inaccessible language, and have neither an adequate understanding of the labour movement, nor the necessary humility to learn. The structural constraints under which academics operate, when combined with the bureaucratic nature of unions, mitigate against doing useful research. Some of the consequences for our work as academics will be noted in the changing nature of our workplace, the university.

My sources for this paper vary in their location in the labour movement. Most are rank and file activists in public sector unions; a few hold staff positions. The information was gathered in part in unstructured interviews, in part in informal conversations and interactions over several years with trade unionists who have more formal education and more experience with academics than most of their co-workers.[1] There were six formal interviews, and approximately two dozen informal interviews. All the interviews were with people living and working in Ontario.

My own experience also contributed to the information relayed here. I held a staff position as researcher with the United Electrical Workers in 1983-84. I was also active in Organized Working Women, an organization of unionized working women who have promoted women's interests within the organized trade union movement in Ontario. I did an evaluation of the Toronto Labour Council's Labour Education Program for its accreditation by George Brown College. Finally, I am related to the trade union movement in my personal life—as the partner of an activist, I have come to know a number of rank and file activists as the "spouse" rather than as an academic.

The Opposition between Science and Practical Knowledge

Scientific method as understood in the West, Ursula Franklin maintains, is a way of "separating knowledge from experience" (1990:38). Scientific constructs have become the dominant model in describing reality, reducing the reliance of people on their own experience. Feminists have amply demonstrated, both theoretically and empirically, why reciprocity is necessary, why we need to respect what our objects of study have to say in order to assess what passes for scientific knowledge.[2]

In an exchange between Eric Olin Wright and Michael Burawoy in the *Berkeley Journal of Sociology* on Marxism and science, Wright affirms the necessity for a sceptical approach in which science (truth) and revolution (politics) are antithetical. Burawoy maintains that this is a false dichotomy. The theory of knowledge he proposes suggests that knowledge is a "function of engagement with the world. The more thorough going, the more radical that engagement, other things being equal, the more profound our understanding" (1987:59). Political struggles are an integral part of the pursuit of truth, because that is how we learn what the truth is.

In a response to Burawoy, Edna Bonacich takes his argument one step further. She maintains that the problem lies in the contradiction between being an academic in a capitalist society and striving for social change. The belief that academic research can somehow further the revolution requires "considerable self-delusion" (1989:67). She argues for a reflexive knowledge that will make us aware of our role in perpetuating an unjust social system, as knowledge creators. This is different from academic knowledge, which she maintains is a game. "As an academic, one pursues knowledge to keep one's job, to get publications, to earn a merit increase, to gain status, to look clever, to win grants, to make more money, to be famous and admired" (1989:72). Academics who want to align themselves with the struggles of others have to do so with humility, given the limitations of our own class position.

Hegemony in knowledge—conceptions, values, language, relations, and interests—are translated into daily practices in ways that most of us simply take for granted. Fasheh, a Palestinian mathematician, reflects in the *Harvard Educational Review* (February 1990) upon his knowledge of math, which is based on the manipulations of abstract symbols and theories linked, he says, to technological advancement and control. He compares it with the richness and complexity of his mother's math. His mother was an illiterate seamstress, who earned her livelihood by creating beautifully fitting clothes from rectangles of cloth without the help of patterns. After the six-day war, he began to look at things differently, to question the assumed superiority of his knowledge of math over that of his mother. Both embodied order, pattern, relations and measurement, and breaking a whole into smaller parts and reconstructing a new whole from the pieces. The difference was that mistakes in her math entailed practical consequences.

Fasheh argues that the belief in the inherent superiority of one way of thinking—when one believes that this way of doing things transcends class, gender, and culture—actually demonstrates hegemony at its most successful (Fasheh, 1990). What Fasheh discusses perhaps needs to be considered in the trade unionist activist critiques of academic research. A conception of learning, of finding out about the world as oscillating between life and the mental construction of it, means that practice and context are both necessary parts of the learning and research process.

Unions, the Collective Bargaining System, and the Rank and File

The context for trade union activities first needs to be briefly considered. The working class in Canada, male and female, varied in ethnic mix and racial background, has been a major driving force for progressive political and social change (Heron, 1989). Unions, because they are valuable vehicles in advancing the interests of working people, need to be supported. For the most part, both progressive academics and union activists share this starting point.

As we enter the last decade of this century, these common commitments to progressive social change and a strong trade union movement acquire particular urgency. Our unions in Canada face an onslaught on their memberships and their gains, aided and abetted by the free trade agreement, the globalization of production, and the escalating tendencies we have seen in recent years towards a "level playing field" in social programmes. Privatization, contracting out, and deregulation are major challenges the Canadian labour movement faces (Pro Canada Network, 1991). Unions vary greatly in the kind of positions they publicly support, and in their encouragement of the democratic participation of their membership towards achieving their goals. The role of progressive academics is to use our skills in such a way as to encourage resistance to the rule of the "bottom line" in everything from transportation, social services, and working conditions to knowledge itself.[3]

Trade unions, as the route to improving the position of workers in this society however, are not unproblematic. Trade unions, like universities, are full of contradictions. Organized labour is part of a bureaucratic structure that also includes the employer and the state. Unions operate within a collective bargaining system, established and refereed by the state, that is both a protection and a way of managing and diffusing class conflict.

Critics such as Harry Glasbeek have written about the conservatizing effect of the collective bargaining process itself (Glasbeek, 1986:81). Once a union is certified, it has a fair amount of security. However, a union certified as a bargaining agent for workers is then obligated to ensure that its workers remain peaceful, and obey the rules. Glasbeek notes that it is the union, not the workers represented by the union, that is the party to the collective agreement. Within this system, grievance arbitration can become a substitution for the exercise of political power. The union is then put in a position of ensuring that its workers abide by the collective agreement, which is based upon the basic inequality in the organization of work (Glasbeek, 1986:81).

Given the structure of the collective bargaining system, there is a tension between the leadership representing the union and its rank and file. In some unions, activists feel that two struggles need to be waged simultaneously—against the bureaucracy as well as the employer. Sometimes they also need to challenge those who hold power in their union to make it responsive to members' needs. The established leadership in some unions can sometimes feel quite threatened by independent rank and file activities they can't completely control. This will vary, not only from union to union, but from local to local within a union. One member of a local where the same clique has been in charge for years comments:

> Most people in my workplace don't see the distinction between the union and the boss. They see both as different sides of the same coin, and that the union plays the game of being bureaucratic, keeping workers depoliticized, making deals with management.

However, unions can also offer very positive experiences (Moody, 1989:2). Unions can function as schools for workers' democracy where workers, through their participation in rank and file decision-making, can learn to oppose the strict authority of the capitalist bosses and prepare for a different kind of society (Moody, 1989). Examples abound of the empowering experience of speaking out (Reiter, 1989).

Structure of the Academic Milieu

The working conditions of academics locate us in a rather unique situation. We are privileged in the flexibility of our jobs, our pay, and the lack of physical exertion required. These conditions separate us from many other workers. Teaching as a profession usually offers some measure of intrinsic interest and satisfaction, the chance to use our minds, to operate responsibly but with a great deal of autonomy. "In a job," in contrast, as a factory worker described it, "we are not paid to think" (1990). One works for money. Thus for many in the labour movement, academic work is not work as they know it.

In *Fear of Falling* (1989), Barbara Ehrenreich discusses the attempts of the professional middle class to protect an occupational niche through professionalism. Those who wish to contribute to the disciplines of sociology, political science, psychology must have the appropriate credentials. Holding on to the "capital" of knowledge or expertise, only sociologists are qualified to decide what should be dignified as sociology (Ehrenreich, 1989: 81). Popular views presented in the media of the working class are distorted; workers are depicted as crude ignorant people, with sexist, racist views, prone to authoritarian personalities, and interested only in defending their access to the appurtenances of the consumer culture (Ehrenreich, 1989:143).

Of course, "labour friendly" academics see themselves as exceptions, free from the dominant stereotypes described above. As in the attempt to understand the all–pervasive sexism and racism in this society, perhaps we underestimate the force of the prevailing culture, and also the effect of the institutional structure in which we operate.

Arrogance

One of the themes common to the view of academics held by all the trade unionists I spoke with was the sense that many academics felt themselves "better" than workers—more intelligent and more knowledgeable. Academics appeared to feel that they had nothing to learn from workers, even when it came to the terrain on which workers operated. Academics and other professionals, such as lawyers, are always ready to jump in as "experts." Thus, the expert's role is to provide difficult-to-understand technical solutions to what are really political problems.

Intellectuals assume that they can explain workers' experience to workers. They assume they can direct trade unions, defend organizations of the working class, but ultimately what happens is that they carve a reality of trade unions that is merely an image of themselves. Workers feel estranged from their own organization (Technician).

Another respondent, now in university, who had worked in an auto parts factory for fifteen years, felt insulted that her professors in university courses that were labour-related insisted on treating her as an exception, because she knew how to do well in school. She maintained that professors disregarded workers' knowledge. It was invisible, disqualified and dismissed as naive.

> Until an academic says it's true, it's not true. Unless they prove it, it's just intuition, not knowledge. That academic arrogance pisses off the labour movement. The respect doesn't go both ways. Academics look at workers as skilled, not as intelligent, or having valuable knowledge. I can't be representative of union people, of the people I worked with in the factory. I have to be seen as an exception because I do well in school. That's not accurate. There is so much that I knew before I came back to school—now I know what it is called.

> Working class people know the system doesn't work—that if they work hard they will be rich some day. They know it's not intelligence and skill that will make that happen. A lot of it is where you are and who you are. If you come from a working class background you are streamed. A lot of the people active in the labour movement see the wall, share this knowledge (Factory worker–student).

Indeed the experience of many prominent labour leaders at the hands of our educational system has been almost uniformly negative. Gord Wilson, the President of the Ontario Federation of Labour, who left school at sixteen after an insulting incident remarks, "I was far more compromised in school than I ever have been by any manager or government official" (Toronto, 1989).

Inaccessibility

The language used by academics makes information inaccessible to workers. Thus, even when useful things are said, the implied audience is a university trained group, rather than workers. We use a specialized language that those outside a particular discipline cannot understand.

> Language is a major barrier. Most rank and file shop stewards can't understand what is being said. Academics have learned the art of inventing their own language which makes them unintelligible even to most of the intelligentsia (Technician).

If you take and distill the information out of that literature [academic writings on the labour movement], it doesn't come down to much more than that the labour movement is bureaucratic, and that the real needs of the working class have been distorted and that there is collusion. So what? Who doesn't know that? It's only when it's put in that framework with impressively stylized language that it looks impressive. Everyone who has ever worked in a job in a union environment knows that (Computer programmer).

The flip side of this arrogance and an equally limiting view is what is termed "workerism." Workerism is the resolution to be the humble servant of workers, the attempt to accept uncritically any view expressed by workers. The working class is noble, and larger than life.

The Demands of Academic Life and How We Do Research

There is a literature on the conservatizing influences of academic life and the role of intellectuals in defending the status quo. (See for example Jacoby, 1987, Ehrenreich, 1989, Chomsky, 1988.) Universities, as Newson and Buchbinder (1988) document, are changing in structure, and consequently academic workers are losing control of their work. Academics must show themselves to be "professionals," and display appropriate entrepreneurial energy in order to get and hold onto secure employment. Only a chosen few of Ph.D. graduates will enter the first tier of workers with secure jobs. Writing for a general audience or periodical is to risk being thought insufficiently serious (Jacoby, 1987:153). A union staff person commented:

If you think of the similarities between the nature of the work of an academic and an owner-operated clothing store, there are a lot of parallels. If you don't promote yourself, nobody else promotes you. You are in competition with others. Your competition is stronger at certain times than at other times. Somebody else's gain is your loss in the job market, so if the fellow down the street starts selling more stuff you are in trouble. The shape of it is very much an individual competitive world. And that's got to affect them—everybody's world affects them.

Once having sold our wares, we are still not free of the entrepreneurial considerations of producing what is saleable, rather than useful research projects. This affects the kind of research that will be done relating to workers' concerns.

Where do intellectuals get the time, the resources, the capability, to do research, to reflect and write about workers' experiences? Somebody has to pay for that. Not the workers. How is it possible for someone to perform that function without responding to the demands of people paying for it?

There is tremendous pressure on intellectuals to defend their professional position: their jobs, their tenure, which places very narrow restrictions on the work they do. One has to apply for grants, and apply within a certain framework. The working class has very little pressure on these people, very little input (Technician 1).

Worthwhile labour research can place the researcher in conflictual situations. It will invariably rock the boat—not just of the employer but of the union as well. Few academics, given the pressure upon them to be good funding entrepreneurs, are willing to take these kinds of risks. In one account of an exception, a research project that a respondent considered useful, here's what happened.

The local requested a job classification data base. The funding proposal was written in such a way as to say something about new technology and its effect on market positions in the industry. In this case, the actual research turned out to be so useful that the national union office freaked out and threatened the researchers. The button that triggers the internal politics of the union was pushed—the relationships between the local versus the national official, the national office and the international. The company influencing the situation behind the scenes didn't want this either. A violent situation was produced simply by trying to solve a problem because there are lots of vested interests in leaving the problem unsolved. The research could have been structured in such a way that didn't happen, but then it wouldn't have been useful (Technician 2).

Thus, "safe" research is generally irrelevant research. Not stepping on any toes is a good indication of the uselessness of the research and few academics are willing to operate differently. What we want to do may not coincide with providing the kind of information activists will find most useful.

Real useful working class research is not going to promote careers. Very few intellectuals are open to sitting down with trade unionists and being told by them what they want done. Academics figure out a project they want to do—for either their careers, or whimsy, or some theoretical line they have developed—and they will never leave it (Technician 2).

Relationship of Academics to the Trade Union Structures

When researchers come in from the outside, we often seem oblivious to the web of bureaucratic intrigue at which some unions seem to excel. If an intellectual's career is riding on his/her performance, then we have to play the game as well—we have to align ourselves with the winners. Given the confines within which academics operate, the connections with the labour movement are usually with the top, the elected national leadership of a union, or staff persons, rather than the rank and file. Thus academics have come to equate relating to the working class with talking to union presidents. Giving a keynote speech at a conference is considered labour activism.

> Primarily intellectuals receive their legitimacy, their right to speak about anything, from the universities and the state. When they make pronouncements about the working class, and working class organizations, they have a vested interest in continuing the lie that trade union bureaucrats necessarily serve to protect the working class...it is a bit self-deluding that way. Who else can arrange for them to get grants through the state? (Technician 1)

Academics walk in and talk to the union leadership who have the resources and the expertise to give whatever impression of themselves they wish to. "Politically they know how to do that—they know what the academics want and that's what they give them" (Factory worker–student).

> They end up supporting the powers that be inside trade unions. It's an unenviable position. Let's not deceive ourselves. There is not much that intellectuals can do for the labour movement in this country unless they can carve out for themselves an independent relationship which so far none has managed to do (Technician 2).

The example of the Greater London Council (GLC) from 1981 to 1985 when it was controlled by the Labour Party, under the leadership of Ken Livingstone, confirms the importance of developing this kind of relationship. The GLC saw the organized labour movement as their natural allies, and indeed it was very important to develop and maintain effective working relations with trade union officials. But they also learned that the input from shop floor trade unionists was crucial. They found that "it is only at the workplace level that the unions have the detailed knowledge and power necessary to a strategy for intervening in production in the interests of working people" (Mackintosh and Wainright, 1987:409).

In the aftermath of the 1990 Ontario provincial election, a group of left academics organized a one-day workshop on democratic administration. The participants consisted primarily of academics and some elected ministers from the Ontario government. The organizers failed to involve the public sector union in the planning process. Without the necessary development of mutual confidence and trust, the result was minimal public sector union representation. The experience from the Greater London Council would indicate that this failure to develop a good working relationship with the union, with input from shop floor trade unionists, renders the initiative a meaningless exercise.

Without these working relations, a local authority, however well intentioned, will end up relying on management, accepting management arguments and propping up the status quo. Moreover it is at the workplace that much of the power lies to implement changes resisted by the employers, whether in the public or private sector (Mackintosh and Wainright, 1987:410).

These working relationships do not develop overnight. Some of the necessary qualities involve experience, having something to offer as well as to learn, honesty about what is on offer, and deliberate attempts to strengthen trade union autonomy (Mackintosh and Wainright, 1987).

Academics' Understanding of the Labour Movement

I am struck by how out of touch most labour friendly academics are with the labour movement. Whenever I go talk to friends who are academics, I am amazed at how off-the-wall their conceptions of the labour movement are (Union staff person).

The volatile, constantly changing, and challenging environment of union politics is something that outsiders have difficulty understanding. Academics approach unions oblivious to the complexity of internal union politics.

The union culture is evolving and changing all the time—which is why it is such a politically charged atmosphere. The pace is fast and the ability to survive and flourish in this environment requires being able to read and respond to a situation quickly, not study something for years at a time.

For many activists their union work is a way of life, with very demanding hours.[4]

For a lot of people in factories, the union is a real life line. Not so much for what they can do for the union, but what the union gives them in return— by opening up these possibilities. It allows them to use their intelligence for something they believe in. Most people don't realize what a commitment it is—it's more than paying your dues and going to the meeting. It is a whole way of life, and a whole way of living, and I don't think academics understand this (Factory worker–student).

Thus despite the good intentions of academics, the world of rank and file union people is very foreign. Even union leaders have difficulty staying in touch with their rank and file.

The reason that it's hard for leaders to be very useful to the rank and file in their day-to-day struggles in their workplace is because they are not in the workplace. It's hard for outsiders to have a real feeling for what is going on. It's harder for academics who are outside the labour movement entirely (Union staff person).

Many trade unionists would maintain that labour friendly academics, like many leaders, are not in a position to know what workers' concerns really are. They are limited by the constraints under which they operate and their virtual inability to be plugged into the daily life of people.

The Academic as Expert: Irrelevant or Downright Destructive?

Thus, I was told, what academics do is quite irrelevant to the process of building a strong trade union movement. Academics are simply not listened to very much. The only real training for work in the labour movement is activism or organizing. Sitting around thinking great thoughts or figuring out what everyone else should be doing was not seen as helpful.

> Academics can have a bad effect, because they walk in as experts. Building a strong trade union movement involves getting rid of the experts—the high-priced lawyers and consultants. It means getting people to have the self-confidence that they can do it themselves and help provide them with the skills they need to do that.

> Let's take the case of women feeling harassed by a man, which occurs in our workplace occasionally. A discussion of the nature of sexism is not what they want—they need the courage to complain about that harassment and somebody to go to the man and say "stop it." That is what is appreciated. That's the difference between intellectuals and non-intellectuals. You either make something happen, or you talk about it. There is a big difference. The union should reflect and help workers understand their own experiences so they don't feel intimidated (Technician 1).

Knowledge, from an activist's point of view, is for something—it is to be used to enhance activism, and a broad understanding of the political and social dimensions of unionism.

Unions find a limited function for using academics as policy makers in government or, as corporations often do, to legitimate positions that have already been arrived at. Thus academics with positions that reflect those held in the labour movement will be used as allies. Some recent examples are economists documenting the effects of free trade, or academics who have sophisticated criticisms of the GST. The criteria for constructive involvement are very clear for the activists—helping to build a strong union movement at the base. The point is to provide information to empower workers, not for one's own self-aggrandizement.

The Academic Worker

Intellectuals need to enter the labour movement, not as experts, or as servants, but as colleagues, helping trade unionists articulate their views in a working partnership.

I bring some kinds of experiences, you have other kinds of experiences. Maybe working together we can really do something. Academics can't help but feel remote. Once they stop worrying about it, that's a sure sign that they are not doing okay. There's a contradiction there—the fact that the relationship is troubling will make for a better relationship (Union staff person).

The only way to do this is to approach the trade union movement as fellow workers. Rather than looking to other people's workplace as "real," activists maintain that one's own backyard might be a useful and worthwhile training ground. This means recognizing academic employers as different tentacles of the same monster.

In the academic world people refer to those in the non-academic world as the "real world." It tells you something about the terms of reference. Intellectuals don't think of what they are doing as real. So they study the labour movement and that is what they define as real. In a way this can be thought of as flattering, but it's condescending really. Similarly, it is a step down from being a labour bureaucrat to being a worker. There is no distinction to be made between academia and the "real world." The struggle as trade unionists and progressives is everywhere (Technician).

One academic, active in his faculty union, remarked upon a range of changes that are transforming the nature of academic work. When the academic is responsible, not to the collegium, but to the organization, academics need to be very concerned. The Centres of Excellence are examples of this trend. They are groupings that are funded through the Province of Ontario with their own boards not under the jurisdiction of the university. Their charge is to develop marketable products, and successful professors can reduce their teaching load by buying out courses. A new graduate can then be hired to teach the course on a piecework basis without any fringe benefits or job security for less than one-fourth the cost of the salaried professor.

Although many of us don't see ourselves as academic workers who need to concern ourselves with our workplace, the shift in emphasis from research to collaboration with industry will have an effect on our jobs. The freeze on tenure stream appointments and the burgeoning part-time, poorly paid course directors are but the beginning. Universities face increasing pressures to operate as businesses concerned with the "bottom line," rather than public institutions concerned with teaching students and developing a critical position towards society. Administration increasingly becomes ruled by "management" principles, and decision-making is becoming more centralized[5] (Newson and Buchbinder, 1988).

The problem in the university is no different than that in any other workplace: how do you mobilize people and build a base? Trade unionists maintain that few academics will do any actual organizing in support of the labour solidarity they in theory defend, if it won't show up on their curriculum vitae. This inaction is limiting in two ways. Our heads are in the sand when in comes to our own academic future. Also, perhaps it is only through these kinds of activities that we can have something to say to the trade union movement.[6]

> The real training for work in the labour movement is activism—organizing. That's what puts people in touch with the world and provides a base for being in touch with the labour movement. One of the most useful things academics can do is be trade unionists in their own workplace. Instead of figuring out what Gord Wilson or the OFL should be doing, why not organize your own university? Make it more militant, in the same way that anyone in the CAW is struggling with a largely disinterested, passive membership.

> The problem is that kind of struggle isn't very dramatic, it's slogging, tedious, unrewarding as opposed to offering great thoughts to leadership. That's precisely what every local president [is concerned with]—how to get people to meetings, how to get them involved with the union, et cetera. If you don't live in that world, why do you think you can give advice to people who do live in that world? (Union staff person)

Conclusion

As I indicated at the beginning, the views recounted here are one half of the argument, the half that pertains to who we are. I find these views disconcerting, because despite arguing in real life against the views described above (defending myself and what I do), I think there is a great deal of truth to them.

A number of the people I spoke with held the view that the only good academic is an ex-academic. I don't agree. There are no "pure" jobs. In this paper, I dwell on the problems of process that we face in making contributions as academics to ends that we support. If we look beyond Canada to intellectuals working in countries such as Nicaragua, El Salvador, China, we can find inspiring examples of how there need be no rift between scholarship and citizenship.

NOTES

1   The respondents spoke freely with the understanding that they will not be identified.

2   See, for example, the work of Dorothy Smith, Sandra Harding, and Joan Kelly Gadol.

3   A good example is the recent University of Toronto library workers' strike. Despite the importance of that facility for medical, academic research, and for the ongoing work of any number of students, the university found it more convenient (and economical) to not negotiate. When union demands were reduced to a request for binding arbitration, the university still balked at reaching any settlement.

4   One woman activist commented, "If it's a male activist and he has to choose between the union and the family, the union wins." Although there are far more women activists than twenty years ago, most of these women are either not married, or don't have children. This is a digression, but worth noting.

5   The University of Toronto library workers at the time of writing (June 1991) have been on strike for over three months, and the largest research institution in Canada is a mess. The university won't agree to compulsory arbitration to settle the strike. It seems a clear example of the rule of bottom line over commitment to research, students, staff, and the community.

6   This chasm that exists in North America does not exist everywhere. In many Third World countries, academics have been on the front lines of attack and they themselves have been very vulnerable.

Part Five
Selected Bibliography

THE DEVELOPMENT OF CANADIAN SOCIOLOGY AND ANTHROPOLOGY: A BIBLIOGRAPHY

Gale Moore

Objective

The primary purpose of this chapter is to provide a bibliography on the development of the disciplines of sociology and anthropology in Canada.[1] Both sociology and anthropology have been taught in Canadian universities since the early decades of this century, but the institutionalization of these disciplines, both as departments in universities and in terms of professional organization, did not occur on a large scale until the 1960s. In addition, the disciplines have developed in separate and quite distinct ways in French and English Canada.

The project was originally conceived as a bibliography to the literature published since the 1960s, with an emphasis on sources concerned with the question of the existence and/or development of a national sociology/anthropology. However, as the project developed it became clear that the usefulness of the bibliography would be enhanced by including some material from the earlier period and including a brief summary of the major changes that have occurred as the disciplines developed in Canada. This is, however, not an easy task, given both the differences in the developments of the disciplines in the anglophone and francophone communities and the differences between the disciplines. The task is further complicated by the fact that the development of the disciplines in terms of the sociology of knowledge remains, as yet, largely unwritten.[2] The summary essay that follows focuses specifically on developments that have taken place in sociology, while in the bibliography I attempt to bring together the literature that addresses the question of the development of sociology and anthropology in French and English Canada.[3]

Organization of the Bibliography

The bibliography is arranged very simply in two major sections: *Developments Prior to the 1960s* and *Developments Since the 1960s*. A periodization of Canadian sociology/anthropology would permit materials to be organized systematically and in the context of the major events of each period, but there is at present no single scheme suitable for the task.[4]

The bibliography is organized as follows:

Developments Prior to the 1960s

- General Studies—Sociology and Anthropology
- Institutionalization
- Pioneers

Developments Since the 1960s

- General Studies—Sociology and Anthropology
- Anglophone Sociology
- Francophone Sociology
- Anglophone Anthropology
- Francophone Anthropology

Special Topics

- The Canadianization Issue
- National Sociology in the Context of Canadian Nationalism
- Political Economy
- Feminist Studies

The majority of the items included in the bibliography deal with the development of the disciplines in general terms, but the question of the development of a national sociology/anthropology is a topic to which specific attention has been paid. A special section has been included on the Canadianization debate of the 1970s, a debate in which both anthropologists and sociologists played a significant role. Brief sections on nationalism and political economy have been included, as these provide a context for this issue and a guide to the theoretical perspective that informed much of the debate. Finally, a special section has been included on feminist studies. While this literature only began to appear in the late 1960s, research in this area has had an impact on the development of the disciplines as a whole. The items included are a judgemental sample of works that have had an impact on the disciplines, in particular sociology, and to some extent represent the first Canadian works in the field.[5]

The Development of Sociology as a Discipline in Canada

The recognition of sociology as an autonomous discipline was a relatively late development in Canada. While courses were taught in a number of universities in the early part of the century, and an honours course offered at the University of Toronto in the 1930s, the Department of Sociology at McGill University, formed in 1923, was still the only autonomous department of sociology in a Canadian university at the beginning of the 1960s (Clark, 1979:397). But this was to change and to change rapidly. In 1960-61 there were sixty-one faculty members in sociology in Canada. Less than half of the faculty had a Ph.D., and of those with doctorates, 72 per cent had received them in the United States. In the decade of the 1960s, Canada produced only nineteen doctorates in sociology, and with the enormous expansion of the university system that was beginning to take place in the early 1960s, fifty to sixty new faculty members in sociology were required annually (Hiller, 1979:129). In English Canada, the American style of sociology had already come to dominate anglophone sociology, and this trend was reinforced through the appointment of large numbers of American sociologists and American-trained Canadians to the new posts available. In addition, given the marginal nature of the discipline in Canada until the 1960s, the majority of materials for teaching were also either American or American in orientation.

In French Canada the situation was different. To some extent the linguistic barrier militated against a direct and unconscious adoption of American theories and models, but more importantly the discipline as practised by francophones sociologists in Quebec was grounded in Quebec society and culture. As Clark points out, sociological practice in French Canada had always been intimately connected to a concern for the fate of that society (Clark, 1975:230).

By the end of the 1960s a national consciousness was developing in Canada around the issue of foreign, that is, primarily American, dominance over Canadian economic, social, and cultural institutions. In the universities, in addition to concerns about the high percentage of foreign nationals, there was growing concern that scholarship was so American-oriented that it no longer served the interests of the country (Clark, 1975). Many anglophone sociologists argued that there was the need for a distinctly Canadian theoretical orientation, that is, a national sociology. As Stolzman and Gamberg note, there was an increasing need to defeat the sociology-knows-no-national-boundaries thesis (Stolzman and Gamberg, 1975:98-9), and a recognition that what appeared to be universal theories and methods were, in fact, American products (Clark, 1973:212-4). The Canadianization issue was the major issue within sociology in the 1970s and according to Hiller, the end result of the debate within the discipline of sociology was an identifiable Canadian Sociology Movement (Hiller, 1979:125).

By 1978-79 the Canadianization issue had come to an end, and in the years that followed a Canadian sociology emerged hand-in-hand with a new and less self-conscious sociology of Canada (Jackson, 1985:615). The discipline of sociology in English Canada today is far more eclectic than in the past—the political economy paradigm continues to be relevant; American theories and methods remain; and there is increasing interest in European models and methods. At the present time, developments in French and English Canada are not as distinct as in the past. As Marcel Fournier has noted, "... if one were to compare the theoretical streams and authors which interest English and French-language sociologists today, there would no longer seem to be major differences between intellectual communities— political economy, critical theory, phenomenology, and the introduction of a feminist perspective" (Fournier, 1985:798).

NOTES

1   There is now a considerable literature on this topic and while the sources are, in general, not obscure, they are scattered.

2   This is especially true in the case of anthropology. The literature on.the development of anthropology in Canada is sparse. One may speculate on the reasons why this is the case. It may be that the struggle for recognition as a separate discipline was less intense in anthropology and therefore the need to define and defend the discipline less urgent—for example, the first chair in anthropology was created at St. Michael's College in 1919, and by 1925 a full-time lectureship had been established at the University of Toronto (Barker, 1987:253). A department of sociology, on the other hand, was not established at the University of Toronto until 1963. This may also reflect the differences between the disciplines in terms of the type of questions considered of interest and the paradigms used. The sociology of knowledge, for example, is concerned precisely with questions of this nature.

3   The secondary sources used in the compilation of the bibliography are primarily in English, and so no claim for comprehensiveness can be made for the coverage of developments in francophone sociology and anthropology. I hope that the developments in French Canada have been adequately represented by the items selected.

4   Some work has been done on the periodization of Canadian sociology. For example, Hiller (1980) has developed a periodization that includes both anglophone and francophone sociology, and notes that one other periodization of anglophone sociology has been attempted, and that two periodizations of francophone sociology have appeared (Hiller, 1982:169-70).

5   Some of the earliest Canadian feminist studies in sociology and anthropology appeared in the interdisciplinary journal *Atlantis,* and in newsletters of the associations that were forming. These include:

Atlantis: A Women's Studies Journal, which first appeared in 1975 and was published at Acadia University in Wolfville, Nova Scotia. The journal is now located at the Institute for the Study of Women, Mount Saint Vincent University, Halifax. The proceedings of the first two general meetings of CRIAW: Canadian Research Institute for the Advancement of Women were published in Atlantis in volumes 3(2:2):1978 and 4(2:2):1979.

Canadian Newsletter of Research on Women which began in 1972. The first editors were Marylee Stephenson and Margrit Eichler. The newsletter was distributed first from Windsor, Ontario and then from Waterloo, Ontario. In 1979 (with vol. 8) the title was changed to *Resources for Feminist Research / Documentation sur la recherche feministe* and was published out of the Ontario Institute for Studies in Education at the University of Toronto.

CRIAW: Canadian Research Institute for the Advancement of Women. This organization was formed in April of 1976. The organization publishes a series of working papers and conference proceedings, and has published a newsletter since 1981.

BIBLIOGRAPHY

Developments Prior to the 1960s

General Studies—Sociology and Anthropology

Anand, A.
1973   *A Sociological History of French-Canadian Sociology: 1900-1920.* Ottawa: Carlton University. [MA thesis]

Avrith, Gale
1986   *Science at the Margins: The British Association and the Foundations of Canadian Anthropology, 1884-1910.* Philadelphia: University of Pennsylvania. [Doctoral dissertation]

Campbell, Douglas F.
1983   *Beginnings: Essays on the History of Canadian Sociology.* Port Credit, Ont.: Scribblers' Press.

Christiansen-Ruffman, Linda and Raymond F. Currie, eds.
1990   *Celebrating our History:* Special edition, 25th anniversary, Canadian Sociology and Anthropology Association/*Célébrons nôtre héritage,* Édition spéciale, 25ième anniversaire, La Société canadienne de sociologie et d'anthropologie. *Society/Société* 14(3):1-45.

Clark, S.D.
1939   "Sociology and Canadian social history." *Canadian Journal of Economics and Political Science* 5(3):348-57.

Cole, Douglas
1973   "The origins of canadian anthropology, 1850-1910," *Journal of Canadian Studies* 8(Feb.):33-45.

Corbett, David
1959   "The social sciences in Canada: an appraisal and a program." *Queen's Quarterly* 66(1):56-72.

Falardeau, Jean-Charles
1944   "Problems and first experiments of social research in Quebec." *Canadian Journal of Economics and Political Science* 10(3):365-71.

Falardeau, Jean-Charles and Jones, Frank E.
1956   "La sociologie au Canada." *Transactions of the Third World Congress of Sociology* 7:14-22.

Helmes-Hayes, Richard C.
1986   *Images of Inequality in Early Canadian Sociology, 1922-1965.* Toronto: University of Toronto. [Dissertation]

Keirstead, B.S. and Clark, S.D.
1951   "Social sciences." Pp. 179-89 in *Royal Commission Studies: A Selection of Essays Prepared for the Royal Commission on National Development in the Arts, Letters and Sciences.* Ottawa: Queen's Printer.

McFeat, Tom
1980   *Three Hundred Years of Anthropology in Canada.* Halifax: Dept. of Anthropology, Saint Mary's University. (Occasional Papers in Anthropology, No. 7)

McIlwraith, T.F.
1930   "The progress of anthropology in Canada." *Canadian Historical Review* 11(2):132-50.
1949   "Anthropological trends in Canada." *Canadian Journal of Economics and Political Science* 15(4):533-39.

Tremblay, Maurice and Faucher, Albert
1951   "L'enseignement des sciences sociales au Canada de langue française." Pp. 191-203 in *Royal Commission Studies: A Selection of Essays Prepared for the Royal Commission on National Development in the Arts, Letters and Sciences.* Ottawa: Queen's Printer.

Institutionalization

Campbell, Douglas F. and Hall, Oswald
1989   "Review Symposium: Sociologists examine an historian's account of the development of social research at McGill." *Canadian Review of Sociology and Anthropology* 26(2):333-37.

Card, B.Y.
1973   *The Expanding Relations: Sociology in Prairie Universities.* Regina: Canadian Plains Studies. (Canadian Plains Studies Paper, No. 1)

Fournier, Marcel
1982   "Un intellectuel à la recontre de deux mondes: Jean-Charles
         Falardeau et le développement de la sociologie universitaire au
         Québec." *Recherches sociographiques* 23(3):361-85.

Helmes-Hayes, Richard C., ed.
1988   *A Quarter-Century of Sociology at the University of Toronto, 1963-1988:
         A Commemorative Volume.* Toronto: Canadian Scholars' Press.

Levesque, Georges-Henri
1984   "La premiere décennie de la faculté des sciences sociales à l'université
         Laval." Pp. 51-63 in G.H. Levesque et al., eds., *Continuité et rupture:
         les sciences sociales au Québec: colloque du Mont-Gabriel, 1981.* Montréal:
         Les Presses de l'Université de Montréal.

Palantzas, Thomas.
s.d.   *A Chicago Reprise in the "Champagne Years" of Canadian Sociology,
         1935-1964.* Thunder Bay: Lakehead University. [M.A. thesis]
1991   "A search for 'autonomy' at Canada's first sociology department."
         Society/Société 15(2):10-18.

Ross, Aileen D.
1984   "Sociology at McGill in the 1940s." *Society/Société* 8(1):4-5.

Shore, Marlene G.
1987   *The Science of Social Redemption: McGill, the Chicago School and the
         Origins of Social Research in Canada.* Toronto: University of Toronto
         Press.

Tomovic, V.A.
1975   *Sociology in Canada: An Analysis of its Growth in English Language
         Universities, 1908-1972.* Waterloo: University of Waterloo. [Doc-
         toral dissertation]

Tremblay, Marc-Adélard and Gold, Gerald
1976   "L'anthropologie dans les universites du Québec: l'emergence
         d'une discipline." Pp. 7-49 in Jim Freedman, ed., *The History of Ca-
         nadian Anthropology.* Ottawa: Canadian Ethnology Society. (Its Pro-
         ceedings, No. 3)

Pioneers

Barker, John
1987   "T.F. McIlwraith and anthropology at the University of Toronto, 1925-1963." *Canadian Review of Sociology and Anthropology* 24(2):252-68.

Carrier, Hervé
1960   *Le sociologue canadien Léon Gérin 1863-1951.* Montreal: Les Éditions Bellarmin.

Clark, S.D.
1964   "Thomas Forsyth McIlwraith, 1899-1964." *Proceedings of the Royal Society of Canada.* Series 4, 2(pt. 2):125-26. [Obituary]

Clement, Wallace
1981   "John Porter and the development of sociology in Canada." *Canadian Review of Sociology and Anthropology* 18(5):583-94.

Clement, Wallace, ed.
1981   Special Issue in Memory of John Porter, 1921-1979. *Canadian Review of Sociology and Anthropology* 18(5):583-673.

Epp, Henry T. and Sponsel, L.E.
1980   "Major personalities and developments in Canadian anthropology, 1860-1949." *Na Pao* 10:7-13.

Falardeau, Jean-Charles
1963   "Le sens de l'oeuvre sociologique de Léon Gérin." *Recherches sociographiques* 4(3):265-89.

Forcese, Dennis P.
1981   "The macro-sociology of John Porter." *Canadian Review of Sociology and Anthropology* 18(5):651-56.

Hall, Oswald
1964   "Carl A. Dawson, 1887-1964." *Canadian Review of Sociology and Anthropology* 1(2):115-17.

Hamel, Jacques
1985   "Bibliographie de Marcel Rioux." *Sociologie et sociétés* 17(2):133-44.

Hatfield, Leonard F.
1990   *Sammy the Prince:The Story of Samuel Henry Prince.* Hantsport, N.S.: Lancelot Press.

Helmes-Hayes, Richard C.
1990   "Hobhouse twice removed: John Porter and the LSE years." *Canadian Review of Sociology and Anthropology* 27(3):357-89.

Hoecker-Drysdale, Susan
1990   "Women sociologists in Canada: the careers of Helen MacGill Hughes, Aileen Dansken Ross, and Jean Robertson Burnet." Pp. 152-76 in Marianne Gosztonyi Ainley, ed., *Despite The Odds: Essays on Canadian Women and Science.* Montreal: Véhicule Press.

Hofley, John R.
1981.   "John Porter: his analysis of class and his contributions to Canadian sociology." *Canadian Review of Sociology and Anthropology* 18(5):595-606.

Levin, Michael, Avrith, Gale and Barrett, Wanda
1984   *An Historical Sketch, Showing the Contribution of Sir Daniel Wilson and Many Others to the Teaching of Anthropology at the University of Toronto.* Toronto: The Department.

Magill, Dennis W. and Helmes-Hayes, Richard C.
1986   "Leonard Charles Marsh: A Canadian social reformer." *Journal of Canadian Studies* 21(2):49-66.

McCardle, B.
1980   *The Life and Anthropological Works of Daniel Wilson, 1816-1892.* Toronto: University of Toronto. [M.A. thesis]

N.A.
1982   "Bibliographie de Jean-Charles Falardeau." *Recherches sociographiques* 23(3):429-37.

Nock, David A.
1983   "S.D. Clark in the context of canadian sociology." *Canadian Journal of Sociology* 8(1):79-97.
1988   "John Porter: the unknown functionalist." *Society/Société* 12(3):12-22.

Olsen, Dennis
1981   "Power, elites and society." *Canadian Review of Sociology and Anthropology* 18(5):607-14.

Ostow, Robin
1984   "Everett Hughes: the McGill years." *Society/Société* 8(3):12-16.
1985   "Everett Hughes: from Chicago to Boston." *Society/Société* 9(1):8-12.

Pineo, Peter
1981   "Prestige and mobility: the two national surveys." *Canadian Review of Sociology and Anthropology* 18(5):615-26.

Porter, Marion
1981   "John Porter and education: technical functionalist or conflict theorist." *Canadian Review of Sociology and Anthropology* 18(5):627-38.
1988   "John Porter." *Society/Société* 12(2):1-5.

Preston, Richard
1980   "Reflections on Sapir's anthropology in Canada." *Canadian Review of Sociology and Anthropology* 17(4):367-75.

Reisman, David
1983   "The legacy of Everett Hughes." *Contemporary Sociology* 12(5):477-81.

Ross, Aileen D.
1964   "Carl Addington Dawson, 1887-1964." *Proceedings of the Royal Society of Canada*. Series 4, 2(pt.2):93-94. [Obituary]

Trigger, Bruce G.
1966   "Sir Daniel Wilson: Canada's first anthropologist." *Anthropologica* 8:3-28.
1966   "Sir John Dawson: A faithful anthropologist." *Anthropologica* 8:351-59.

Vallee, Frank G.
1979   "John Porter, 1921-1979." *Proceedings of the Royal Society of Canada*. Series 4, 17(pt 2):91-96. [Obituary]
1979   "Obituary: John Porter (1921-1979)." *Society/Société* 4(1):14.
1981   "The sociology of John Porter: ethnicity as anachronism." *Canadian Review of Sociology and Anthropology* 18(5):639-50.

Van West, John J.
1976   "George Mercer Dawson: An early Canadian Anthropologist."
        Anthropological Journal of Canada 14(4):8-12.

Developments Since the 1960s

General Studies—Sociology and Anthropology

Anderson, Alan B. et al.
1975   "Sociology in Canada: a developmental overview." Pp. 159-71 in
        Raj P. Mohan and Don Martindale, eds., *Handbook of Contemporary
        Developments in World Sociology*. Westport, CT: Greenwood Press.
        (Contributions in Sociology, No. 17)

Breton, Raymond
1975   "The review and the growth of sociology and anthropology in
        Canada." *Canadian Review of Sociology and Anthropology* 12(1):1-5.

Bruce, Erika V. C. and Fox, Alan F.
1987   "The social sciences in Canada." *International Social Science Journal*
        39(1):127-34.

Clarkson, Stephen
1976   "Socking it to the scholars: The First National Conference of the
        Social Sciences and Humanities Research Council of Canada."
        Queen's Quarterly 83(4):547-55.

Curtis, James E., Connor, Desmond M. and Harp, John
1970   "An emergent professional community: French and English soci-
        ologists and anthropologists in Canada." *Social Science Information*
        9(4):113-36.

Dandurand, Renée B.
1989   "Fortunes and misfortunes of culture: sociology and anthropology
        of culture in francophone Quebec, 1965-1985." *Canadian Review of
        Sociology and Anthropology* 26(3):485-532.

Dumont, Fernand and Yves Martin, eds.
1962   *Situation de la recherche sur le Canada français: premier colloque de la
        revue* Recherches sociographiques *du département de sociologie et
        d'anthropologie de l'Université Laval*. Québec: Les Presses de
        l'Université Laval. (*Recherches sociographiques* 3(1-2): 1962)

Falardeau, Jean-Charles
1964   *L'essor des sciences sociales au Canada français.* Québec: Ministère des affaires culturelles. (Collection art, vie et sciences au Canada français, 6)
1967   *The Rise of Social Sciences in French Canada.* Quebec City: Department of Cultural Affairs. (Series on the Arts, Humanities and Sciences in French Canada, 6) [Translation of preceding work]

Forcese, Dennis and Richer, S.
1975   "Social issues and sociology in Canada." Pp. 449-66 in D. Forcese and S. Richer, *Issues in Canadian Society: An Introduction to Sociology.* Scarborough, Ont.: Prentice-Hall.

Fournier, Marcel
1973   "L'institutionnalisation des sciences sociales au Québec." *Sociologie et sociétés* 5(1):27-57.

Hiller, Harry H.
1980   "Paradigmatic shifts, indigenization, and the development of sociology in Canada." *Journal of the History of the Behavioral Sciences* 16(3):263-74.

Jones, Frank E.
1990   "Establishing the Canadian Sociology and Anthropology Association (CSAA)." *Society/Société* 14(3):30-37.

Levesque, G.H. et al., eds.
1981   *Continuité et rupture: les sciences sociales au Québec: colloque du Mont-Gabriel.* Montréal: Les Presses de l'Université de Montréal. 2 vols.

Morrow, Raymond A.
1991   "Introduction: the challenge of cultural studies to Canadian sociology and anthropology." *Canadian Review of Sociology and Anthropology* 28(2):153-72.

Rocher, Guy
1990   "The two solitudes among Canadian sociologists." *Society/Société* 14(3):3-4.

Rush, G.B., Christensen, E. and Malcolmson, J.
1981   "Lament for a notion: The development of social science in Canada." *Canadian Review of Sociology and Anthropology* 18(4):519-44.

Spray, S. Lee
1976   "Some observations on the social organization of Canadian sociology." *Sociological Focus* 9(2):209-15.

Timlin, Mabel Frances and Faucher, Albert
1968   *The Social Sciences in Canada: Two Studies/Les sciences sociales au Canada: deux études.* Ottawa: Social Science Research Council of Canada.

Anglophone Sociology

Brym, Robert J.
1979   "Introduction: new directions in anglo-Canadian historical sociology." *Canadian Journal of Sociology* 4(3):vii-xi.
1986   Trend report: anglo-Canadian sociology. *Current Sociology* 34(1):1-152.

Brym, Robert J. with Fox, Bonnie
1989   *From Culture to Power: The Sociology of English Canada.* Toronto: Oxford University Press.

Carroll, William K.
1990   "Reconstructuring capital, reorganizing consent: Gramsci, political economy and Canada." *Canadian Review of Sociology and Anthropology* 27(3):390-416.

Fournier, M.
1985   "Sociological theory in English Canada: A view from Quebec." *Canadian Review of Sociology and Anthropology* 22(5):794-803.

Harp, John.
1991   "Political economy/cultural studies: exploring points of convergence." *Canadian Review of Sociology and Anthropology* 28(2):206-24.

Harrison, Deborah
1981   *The Limits of Liberalism: The Making of Canadian Sociology.* Montreal: Black Rose Books.
1983   "The limits of liberalism in Canadian sociology: some notes on S.D. Clark." *Canadian Review of Sociology and Anthropology* 20(2):150-66.

Hiller, Harry H.
1980-81 "Research biography and disciplinary development: S.D. Clark and Canadian sociology." *Journal of the History of Sociology* 3(1):67-86.

1982 *Society and Change: S.D. Clark and the Development of Canadian Sociology.* Toronto: University of Toronto Press.

Hunter, Alfred A.
1985 "Doing it with numbers." *Canadian Review of Sociology and Anthropology* 22(5):645-72.

Jackson, John D., ed.
1985 Special Issue on the State of the Art and New Directions. Vol. 1: Sociology in Anglophone Canada. *Canadian Review of Sociology and Anthropology* 22(5):615-803.

Jones, Frank E.
1977 "Current sociological research in Canada: views of a journal editor." *Journal of the History of the Behavioral Sciences* 13(2):160-72.

Magill, Dennis W.
1983 "Paradigms and social science in English Canada." Pp. 1-34 in J. Paul Grayson, ed., *Introduction to Sociology: An Alternate Approach.* Toronto: Gage.

Marchak, M. Patricia
1985 "Canadian political economy." *Canadian Review of Sociology and Anthropology* 22(5):673-709.

Matthews, Ralph
1980 "Significance and explanation of regional divisions in Canada: toward a Canadian sociology." *Journal of Canadian Studies* 15(2):43-61.

Millett, David
1989 "Canadian sociology on the world scene." Pp. 38-54 in Nikolai Genov, ed., *National Traditions in Sociology.* London: Sage. (Sage Studies in International Sociology, 36)

Morrow, Raymond A.
1985 "Critical theory and critical sociology." *Canadian Review of Sociology and Anthropology* 22(5):710-47.

Nielsen, Greg M. and Morrow, Raymond A., eds.
1991 Special Issue on Cultural Studies in Canada. *Canadian Review of Sociology and Anthropology* 28(2):153-298.

O'Neill, John
1985   "Phenomenological sociology." *Canadian Review of Sociology and Anthropology* 22(5):748-70.

Rich, H.
1976.   "The Vertical Mosaic revisited: toward a macrosociology of Canada." *Journal of Canadian Studies* 11(1):14-31.

Richardson, R. Jack and Wellman, Barry.
1985   "Structural analysis." *Canadian Review of Sociology and Anthropology* 22(5):771-93.

Tepperman, Lorne
1978   "Sociology in English-speaking Canada: The last five years." *Canadian Historical Review* 59(4):435-46.

Francophone Sociology

Béland, François and Blais, André
1989   "Quantitative methods and contemporary sociology in francophone Quebec." *Canadian Review of Sociology and Anthropology* 26(3):533-56.

Bibeau, Roch and Maheu, Louis
1980   "Discipline sociologique, milieu institutionnel et itinéraires d'apprentissage: quelques problèmes d'arrimage." *Sociologie et sociétés* 12(2):107-41.

Bourque, Gilles
1989   "Traditional society, political society and Quebec sociology: 1945-1980." *Canadian Review of Sociology and Anthropology* 26(3):394-425.

Breton, Raymond
1989   "Quebec sociology: agendas from society or from sociologists?" *Canadian Review of Sociology and Anthropology* 26(3):557-70.

Dumas, Brigitte
1987   "Philosophy and sociology in Quebec: a socio-epistemic inversion." *Canadian Journal of Sociology* 12(1-2):111-33.

Falardeau, Jean-Charles
1974   "Antécédents, débuts et croissance de la sociologie au Québec." *Recherches sociographiques* 15(2-3):135-65.

Fournier, Marcel
1972   "De l'influence de la sociologie française au Québec." *Revue française de sociologie* 13(Supplement):630-65.
1974   "La sociologie québécoise contemporaine." *Recherches sociographiques* 15(2-3):167-99.

Fournier, Marcel and Houle, Gilles
1980   "La sociologie québécoise et son objet: problématiques et débats." *Sociologie et sociétés* 12(2):21-43.

Garigue, Philippe
1964   "French Canada: a case-study in sociological analysis." *Canadian Review of Sociology and Anthropology* 1(4):186-92.

Houle, Gilles, ed.
1987   Special Issue on Quebec. *Canadian Journal of Sociology* 12(1-2):1-149.

Juteau, Danielle and Maheu, Louis
1989   "Sociology and sociologists in francophone Quebec: science and politics." *Canadian Review of Sociology and Anthropology* 26(3):363-93.

Juteau, Danielle and Maheu, Louis
1989   State of the Art Issue: Francophone Quebecois Sociology. *Canadian Review of Sociology and Anthropology* 26(3):363-570.

Laurin-Frenette, Nicole
1989   "The Sociology of social classes." *Canadian Review of Sociology and Anthropology* 26(3):457-84.

N.A.
1980   "Réflexions sur la sociologie." *Sociologie et sociétés* 12(2):3-201.

Nock, David
1974   "History and evolution of French Canadian sociology." *Insurgent sociologist* 4(4):15-29.

Renaud, Marc, Doré, Suzanne and White, Deena
1989   "Sociology and social policy: from a love-hate relationship with the state to cynicism and pragmatism." *Canadian Review of Sociology and Anthropology* 26(3):426-56.

Anglophone Anthropology

Ames, M.M.
1976   "Introduction." Pp. 2-6 in Jim Freedman, ed., *The History of Canadian Anthropology*. Ottawa: Canadian Ethnology Society. (Its Proceedings, No. 3)

Ames, Michael and Preston, Richard, eds.
1975   Special Issue: Symposium on the History of Canadian Anthropology. *Canadian Review of Sociology and Anthropology* 12(3):243-315.

Burridge, Kenelm
1983   "An ethnology of Canadian ethnology." Pp. 306-20 in Fred Manning, ed., *Consciousness and Inquiry: Ethnology and Canadian Realities*. Ottawa: National Museum of Man. (Canadian Ethnology Service Paper, No. 89E)

Corrigan, Samuel W.
1978   "Sweet's Canadian anthropology." *American Anthropologist* 80(2):372-74.

Darnell, Regna
1975   "The uniqueness of Canadian anthropology: issues and problems." Pp. 399-416 in Jim Freedman and Jerome H. Barkow, eds., *Proceedings of the second Congress, Canadian Ethnology Society*. Ottawa: Canadian Ethnology Society. (Canadian Ethnology Service Paper, No. 28)
1976   "The Sapir years at the National Museum, Ottawa." Pp. 98-121 in Jim Freedman, ed., *The History of Canadian Anthropology*. Ottawa: Canadian Ethnology Society. (Its Proceedings, No. 3)

Freedman, Jim, ed.
1976   The History of Canadian Anthropology. *Proceedings of the Canadian Society of Ethnology* No. 3, 2-200.

Inglis, Gordon
1977   "Applied anthropology in Canada: a discussion." Pp. 177-87 in Jim Freedman, ed., *Applied Anthropology in Canada*. Ottawa: Canadian Ethnology Society. (Its Proceedings, No. 4)
1978   "Anthropology and Canada." *American Anthropologist* 80(2):374-75.
1982   "In bed with the elephant: anthropology in anglophone Canada." *Ethnos* 47(1-2):82-102.

Manning, Frank, ed.
1983   *Consciousness and Inquiry: Ethnology and Canadian Realities.* Ottawa:
        National Museum of Man. (Canadian Ethnology Service Paper, No.
        89E)

McFeat, Tom
1976   "The National Museum and Canadian anthropology." Pp. 148-174
        in Jim Freedman, *The History of Canadian Anthropology.* Ottawa:
        Canadian Ethnology Society. (Its Proceedings, No. 3)

Preston, Richard J.
1983   "The social structure of an unorganized society: beyond intentions
        and peripheral Boasians." Pp. 286-305 in Fred Manning, ed., *Con-
        sciousness and Inquiry: Ethnology and Canadian Realities.* Ottawa:
        National Museum of Man. (Canadian Ethnology Service Paper, No.
        89E)

Price, John A.
1982   "Recent changes in Canadian anthropology." *Society/Société* 6(1):5-
        8.

Salisbury, Richard F.
1976   "Anthropology in anglophone Canada." Pp. 136-47 in Jim Freed-
        man, ed., *The History of Canadian Anthropology.* Ottawa: Canadian
        Ethnology Society. (Its Proceedings, No. 3)

Sweet, Louise E.
1976   "What is Canadian anthropology?" *American Anthropologist*
        78(4):844-50.
1978   "Response to Inglis and Corrigan: Canadian anthropology."
        American Anthropologist 80(2):375-77.

Francophone Anthropology

Gold, Gerald L. and Tremblay, Marc-Adélard
1982   "After the Quiet Revolution: Quebec anthropology and the study of
        Quebec." in *Ethnos* 47(1-2):103-32.
1983   "Steps toward an anthropology of Quebec 1960-1980." Pp. 47-83 in
        Fred Manning, ed., *Consciousness and Inquiry: Ethnology and Cana-
        dian Realities.* Ottawa: National Museum of Man. (Canadian Eth-
        nology Service Paper, No. 89E)

Tremblay, Marc-Adélard, ed.
1983   *Conscience et enqûete: l'ethnologie des réalités canadiennes.* Ottawa: Musées nationaux du Canada. (Dossier service canadien d'ethnologie, no. 89F)

Special Topics

The Canadianization Issue

Baldus, B., Berkowitz, S., Craven, P., Felt, L. and Wayne, J.
1974   *Manifesto for a Relevant Canadian Sociology.* Toronto: Department of Sociology, University of Toronto. [mimeo]

Butler, Michael and Shugarman, David
1970   "Americanization and scholarly values." *Journal of Canadian Studies* 5(3):12-28.

Clark, S.D.
1973   "The American takeover of Canadian sociology: myth or reality." *Dalhousie Review* 53(2):205-18.
1975   "Sociology in Canada: an historical overview." *Canadian Journal of Sociology* 1(2):225-34.
1979   "The changing image of sociology in English-speaking Canada." *Canadian Journal of Sociology* 4(4):393-403.

Coburn, David
1970   "Sociology and sociologists in Canada: problems and prospects." Pp. 36-59 in J. Loubser, ed., *The Future of Sociology in Canada/L'Avenir de la sociologie au Canada.* Montreal: Canadian Sociology and Anthropology Association.

Connor, Desmond M. and Curtis, James E.
1970   *Sociology and Anthropology in Canada: Some Characteristics of the Disciplines and Their Current University Programs.* Montreal: Canadian Sociology and Anthropology Association.

Davis, Arthur K.
1970   "Some failings of anglophone academic sociology in Canada." Pp. 31-35 in J. Loubser, ed., *The Future of Sociology in Canada/L'Avenir de la sociologie au Canada.* Montreal: Canadian Sociology and Anthropology Association.

1978   "The failure of American import sociology in anglophone Canada."
        Pp. 212-30 in Randle W. Nelsen and David Nock, eds., *Reading,
        Writing and Riches: Education and the Socio-Economic Order in North
        America*. Kitchener, Ont.: Between the Lines Publishers.

Felt, Lawrence F.
1975   "Nationalism and the possibility of a relevant Anglo-Canadian
        sociology." *Canadian Journal of Sociology* 1(3):377-85.

Gousse, Claude
1970   "Réflexions sur l'avenir de la sociologie au Québec." Pp. 4-12 in J.
        Loubser ed., *The Future of Sociology in Canada/L'Avenir de la sociologie
        au Canada*. Montreal: Canadian Sociology and Anthropology As-
        sociation.

Grayson, Paul. J. and Magill, Dennis W.
1981   *One Step Forward, Two Steps Sideways: Sociology and Anthropology in
        Canada*. Montreal: Canadian Sociology and Anthropology Associa-
        tion.

Gurstein, Michael
1972   "Towards the nationalization of Canadian sociology." *Journal of
        Canadian Studies* 7(3):50-58.

Hedley, Alan R. and Warburton, T. Rennie
1973   "The role of national courses in the teaching and development of
        sociology: The Canadian case." *Sociological Review* n.s. 21(2):299-319.

Herman, Kathleen
1974   "CSAA statement on the Canadianization issue." *CAUT Bulletin*
        22(3):32-33.

Hiller, Harry H.
1979   "The Canadian Sociology Movement: analysis and assessment."
        Canadian Journal of Sociology 4(2):125-50.
1979   "Universality of Science and the Question of National Sociologies."
        The American Sociologist 14(3):124-35.

Jarvie, I.C.
1975   "Nationalism and the social sciences." *Canadian Journal of Sociology*
        1(4):515-28.

Keyfitz, Nathan
1974   "Sociology and Canadian society." Pp. 10-14 in T.N. Guinsburg and G.L. Reuber, eds., *Perspectives on the Social Sciences in Canada*. Toronto: University of Toronto Press.

Kornberg, Allan and Tharp, Alan
1972   "The American impact on Canadian political science and sociology." Pp. 55-98 in Richard A. Preston, ed., *The Influence of the United States on Canadian Development: Eleven Case Studies*. Durham, NC: Duke University Press.

Lambert, Ronald D. and Curtis, James E.
1973   "Nationality and professional activity correlates among social scientists: data bearing on conventional wisdoms." *Canadian Review of Sociology and Anthropology* 10(1):62-80.

Lamy, Paul
1976   "The globalization of American sociology: excellence or imperialism?" *The American Sociologist* 11(2):104-14.

Loubser, Jan J., ed.
1970   *Future of Sociology in Canada/L'Avenir de la sociologie au Canada*. Montreal: Canadian Sociology and Anthropology Association.

Mangalam, J.J.
1970   "Toward an international perspective for the growth and development of sociology in Canada." Pp. 60-69 in J. Loubser, ed., *The Future of Sociology in Canada/L'Avenir de la sociologie au Canada*. Montreal: Canadian Sociology and Anthropology Association.

N.A.
1972   "Canadian academics concerned over U.S. faculty members." *The American Sociologist* 7(3):1,4.

O'Neill, John
1975   "Facts, myths and the nationalist platitude." *Canadian Journal of Sociology* 1(1):107-24.

Ramu, G.N. and Johnson, Stuart D.
1976   "Toward a Canadian sociology." Pp. 479-94 in G.N. Ramu, and Stuart D. Johnson, eds., *Introduction to Canadian Society: Sociological Analysis*. Toronto: Macmillan.

Rex, John
1975   "Nations, nationalism and the social scientist." *Canadian Journal of Sociology* 1(4):501-14.

Rocher, Guy
1970   "L'avenir de la sociologie au Canada." Pp. 13-20 in J. Loubser, ed., *The Future of Sociology in Canada/L'Avenir de la sociologie au Canada*. Montreal: Canadian Sociology and Anthropology Association.
1973   "L'influence de la sociologie américaine sur la sociologie québécoise." *Transactions of the Royal Society of Canada*. Series 4, 11(sec. 1):75-79.

Smith, Dorothy E.
1975   "What it might mean to do a Canadian sociology: the everyday world as problematic." *Canadian Journal of Sociology* 1(3):363-76.

N.A.
1975   Socio-National Factors and the Development of Sociology: Special Section. *Canadian Journal of Sociology* (1):91-124, 225-34, 345-85, 501-28.

Stolzman, James and Gamberg, Herbert
1975   "The National Question and Canadian sociology." *Canadian Journal of Sociology* 1(1):91-106.

Vallee, Frank G. and Whyte, Donald R.
1968   "Canadian society: trends and perspectives." Pp. 833-52 in Bernard R. Blishen et al. eds., *Canadian Society: Sociological Perspectives*. 3rd ed. Toronto: Macmillan of Canada.

Watson, G. Llewellyn
1975   "The poverty of sociology in a changing Canadian society." *Canadian Journal of Sociology* 1(3):345-62.

Whyte, Donald
1985   "Sociology and the nationalist challenge in Canada." *Journal of Canadian Studies* 19(4):106-29.

National Sociology in the Context of Canadian Nationalism

Laxer, Robert M., ed.
1973   *(Canada) Ltd.: The Political Economy of Dependency*. Toronto: McClelland and Stewart.

Lumsden, Ian, ed.
1970   *Close the 49th Parallel, etc.: The Americanization of Canada.* The University League for Social Reform. Toronto: University of Toronto Press.

Symons, Thomas H.B.
1975   *To Know Ourselves: The Report of the Commission on Canadian Studies.* Ottawa: Association of Universities and Colleges of Canada. 2 vols. 1984.

Symons, Thomas H.B. and Page, James E.
1984   *Some Question of Balance: Human Resources, Higher Education and Canadian Studies.* Ottawa: Association of Universities and Colleges of Canada. (*To Know Ourselves: The Report of the Commission on Canadian Studies,* vol. 3)

Grant, George
1965   *Lament for a Nation: The Defeat of Canadian Nationalism.* Toronto: McClelland and Stewart.

Laxer, James and Laxer, Robert
1977   *The Liberal Idea of Canada: Pierre Trudeau and the Question of Canada's Survival.* Toronto: Lorimer.

Levitt, Kari
1970   *Silent Surrender: The Multinational Corporation in Canada.* Toronto: Macmillan.

Mathews, Robin and Steele, James
1969   *The Struggle for Canadian Universities.* Toronto: New Press.

Rotstein, Abraham and Lax, Gary, eds.
1974   *Getting it Back: A Program for Canadian Independence.* The Committee for an Independent Canada. Toronto: Clarke, Irwin.

Political Economy

Drache, Daniel
1976   "Rediscovering Canadian political economy." *Journal of Canadian Studies* 11(3):3-18.

Drache, Daniel and Clement, Wallace, eds.
1985   *The New Practical Guide to Canadian Political Economy.* Toronto: Lorimer.

Mallory, J.R.
1976 "Commentary: the political economy tradition in Canada." *Journal of Canadian Studies* 11(3):18-20.

McCrorie, James N., ed.
1980 Special Issue on Dependency, Underdevelopment and Regionalism. *Canadian Review of Sociology and Anthropology* 17(3):195-297.

Myles, John, ed.
1989 Special Issue: Comparative Political Economy. *Canadian Review of Sociology and Anthropology* 26(1):1-192.

N.A.
1981 Special Issue: Rethinking Canadian Political Economy. *Studies in Political Economy* 6:3-182.

Watkins, Melville H.
1963 "A staple theory of economic growth." *Canadian Journal of Economics and Political Science* 29(2):141-58.
1977 "The staple theory revisited." *Journal of Canadian Studies* 12(5):83-95.

Feminist Studies

Armstrong, Pat and Armstrong, Hugh
1978 *The Double Ghetto: Canadian Women and Their Segregated Work.* Toronto: McClelland and Stewart. [Rev. ed.:1984]

Armstrong, Pat and Connelly, Pat, eds.
1989 "Feminism and political economy." *Studies in Political Economy* 30:5-196.

Armstrong, Pat and Hamilton, Roberta, eds.
1988 25th Anniversary Issue: Feminist Scholarship. *Canadian Review of Sociology and Anthropology* 25(2):157-308.

Benston, Margaret
1969 "The political economy of women's liberation." *Monthly Review* 21(4):13-27.

Connelly, Mary Patricia
1978 *Last Hired, First Fired: Women and the Canadian Work Force.* Toronto: Women's Press.

Currie, Dawn
1988   "Re-thinking what we do and how we do it: A study of reproductive decisions." *Canadian Review of Sociology and Anthropology* 25(2):231-53.

Eichler, Margrit
1980   *The Double Standard: A Feminist Critique of Feminist Social Science.* London: Croom Helm.
1983   *The Relationship Between Sexist, Non-Sexist, Woman-Centered and Feminist Research.* Toronto: Ontario Institute for Studies in Education.
1985   "And the work never ends: feminist contributions." *Canadian Review of Sociology and Anthropology* 22(5):619-44.

Eichler, Margrit et al.
1990   "Reports of the Canadian Women's Studies Project." *Atlantis* 16(1):3-118.

Fox, Bonnie
1988   "Conceptualizing 'patriarchy.'" *Canadian Review of Sociology and Anthropology* 25(2):163-82.
1989   "The feminist challenge: a reconsideration of social inequality and economic development." Pp. 120-67 in Robert J. Brym with Bonnie Fox, *From Culture to Power: The Sociology of English Canada.* Toronto: Oxford University Press.

Fox, Bonnie, ed.
1980   *Hidden in the Household: Women's Domestic Labour Under Capitalism.* Toronto: Women's Press.

Henry, Frances and Smith, Dorothy E., eds.
1975   "Women in the Canadian social structure." *Canadian Review of Sociology and Anthropology* 12(4:1), 352-481.

Juteau, Danielle and Laurin, Nicole
1988   "L'évolution des formes de l'appropriation des femmes: des religieuses aux 'meres porteuses.'" *Canadian Review of Sociology and Anthropology* 25(2):183-207.

Laurin-Frenette, Nicole, ed.
1981   "Les femmes dans la sociologie." *Sociologie et sociétés* 13(2):3-157.

Luxton, Meg
1980   *More Than a Labour of Love: Three Generations of Women's Work in the Home.* Toronto: Women's Press. (Women's Press Domestic Labour Series, vol. 2)

Maroney, Heather-Jo and Luxton, Meg, eds.
1987   *Feminism and Political Economy: Women's Work, Women's Struggles.* Toronto: Methuen.

Marshall, Barbara L.
1988   "Feminist theory and critical theory." *Canadian Review of Sociology and Anthropology* 25(2):208-30.

Miles, Angela R. and Finn, Geraldine, eds.
1982   *Feminism in Canada: From Pressure to Politics.* Montreal: Black Rose Books. [2nd ed., 1989, entitled *Feminism: From Pressure to Politics*]

O'Brien, Mary
1981   *The Politics of Reproduction.* London: Routledge & Kegan Paul.

Seccombe, Wally
1974   "The housewife and her labour under capitalism." *New Left Review* 83:3-24.

Smith, Dorothy E.
1987   *The Everyday World as Problematic: A Feminist Sociology.* Toronto: University of Toronto Press.

Stephenson, Marylee, ed.
1973   *Women in Canada.* Toronto: New Press. [Rev. ed. General Publishing, 1977]

Vorst, Jesse et al., eds.
1989   *Race, Class, Gender: Bonds and Barriers.* Toronto: Between the Lines in cooperation with the Society for Socialist Studies. (Socialist Studies, 5)

Part Six
References

REFERENCES

Abu-Laban, Baha and Rule, Gail Brendan, eds.
1988   *The Human Sciences: Their Contribution to Society and Future Research Needs*. Edmonton: The University of Alberta Press.

Abu-Laban, Baha
1989   *University Research and the Future of Canada*. Ottawa: University of Ottawa Press.

Adamson, N., Briskin, L. McPhail, M.
1988   *Feminist Organizing For Change: The Contemporary Women's Movement in Canada*. Toronto: Oxford University Press.

Agger, Ben
1989   "Do Books Write Authors? A Study of Disciplinary Hegemony," in *Teaching Sociology* 17 (July): 356-59.

Agonito, Rosemary
1977   *A History of Ideas on Women*. New York: Putnam.

Ainsworth, Lynne
1990   "'Favoritism' Urged in Funding of Universities," in *Toronto Star* 31 January.

Ambert, Anne-Marie and Hitchman, Gladys Symons
1976   "A Case Study of Status Differential: Women in Academia," in Anne-Marie Ambert, *Sex Structure*. 2nd rev. Don Mills: Longman Canada, 113-46.

Ambert (Henshel), Anne-Marie
1973   *Sex Structure*. Don Mills: Longman Canada.
1975   "Letter," in *Women in Canadian Sociology and Anthropology Newsletter* 2(1):8-9.
1976a   "Report on Women's Studies in Graduate Departments of Anthropology and Sociology," in *The Canadian Sociology and Anthropology Association Bulletin* 39:4-5.
1976b   "Personal Addendum to the Report on the Status of Women's Studies at the Graduate Level," in *The Canadian Sociology and Anthropology Association Bulletin* 39:3-4.
1977   "Academic Women: On the Fringe?" in *Society/Société* 1(1):6-8, 11-13.

American Sociological Association
1989   *Guide to Graduate Departments of Sociology.* Washington, D.C.: ASA.

Amin, S
1991   "The Real Stakes in the Gulf War," in *Monthly Review.* July-August,
        14-24.

Annama, Joy
1984   "Sexism in Research: Anthropological Perspectives," in Jill McCalla
        Vickers, ed., *Taking Sex into Acount: Policy Consequences of Sexist
        Research.* Canadian Research Institute for the Advancement of
        Women. Ottawa: Carleton University Press, 101-15.

Armitage, Peter
1989   *Homeland or Wasteland.* Submission on behalf of the NMIA to the
        Federal Environmental Review Panel.
1990   *Compendium of Critiques of The Goose Bay EIS, compiled for Naskapi
        Montagnais Innu Association, Sheshatshit Nitassinan.* Submitted
        to the Federal Environmental Assessment Panel Reviewing Military
        Flying Activities in Nitassinan.
1991   "Indigenous Homelands and the Security Requirements of Western
        Nation States: The Case of Innu Opposition to Military Flight
        Training in Eastern Quebec and Labrador," in *The Pentagon and the
        Cities,* Andrew Kirby, ed., Beverly Hills: Sage Publications Inc.

Armstrong, Pat and Armstrong, Hugh
1978   *The Double Ghetto: Canadian Women and Their Segregated Work.*
        Toronto: McClelland and Stewart.
1983   "Beyond Numbers: Problems with Quantitative Analysis," in
        Alternate Routes 6:1-40.

Armstrong Pat and Hamilton, Roberta, eds.
1988   *The Canadian Review of Sociology and Anthropology.* 25th Anniversary
        Issue, 25(2).

Aron, R.
1965   *Main Currents in Sociological Thought I.* London: Basic Books, Inc.

Aronowitz, Stanley
1988   *Science as Power: Discourse and Ideology in Modern Society.* Minneapolis:
        University of Minnesota Press.

Asheton-Smith, Marilyn
1979   "John Porter's Sociology: A Theoretical Basis for Canadian Education," in *Canadian Journal of Education* 4(2):43-54.

Association of Commonwealth Universities
1988   *Commonwealth Universities Yearbook* 1988. Vol. 2. London, U.K.: A.C.U.

Association of Universities and Colleges of Canada
1990   *Trends: The Canadian University in Profile.* Ottawa.

Atwood, Margaret
1973   *Surfacing.* Markham: Distican Inc.

Axelrod, Paul
1982   *Scholars and Dollars: Politics, Economics, and the Universities of Ontario 1945-1980.* Toronto: University of Toronto Press.
1986   "Service or Captivity? Business-University Relations in the Twentieth Century," in William Neilson and Chad Gaffield, eds., *Universities in Crisis.* Montreal: The Institute for Research on Public Policy, 45-69.

Backhouse, Constance B., Harris, Roma, Michel, Gillian and Wylie, Alison
1989   *The Chilly Climate for Faculty Women at UWO: Postscript to the Backhouse Report.* University of Western Ontario.

Bailey, Alfred G.
1937   *The Conflict of European and Eastern Algonquin Cultures 1504-1770: A Study in Canadian Civilization.* Saint John: Saint John New Brunswick Museum.

Bain, Read
1926-27 "Trends in American Sociology," in *Social Forces* 5:413-22.

Baker, M.
1988   "Teacher or Scholar? the Part-Time Academic," in *Society/Société* 9(1):3-7.

Bannister, Robert C.
1987   *Sociology and Scientism: The American Quest for Objectivity.* Chapel Hill and London: University of North Carolina Press.

Barker, John
1987   "T.F. McIlwraith and Anthropology at the University of Toronto, 1925-1963," in *The Canadian Review of Sociology and Anthropology* 24(2):252-68.

Barnes, Barry
1977   *Interests and the Growth of Knowledge.* London: Routledge and Kegan Paul.

Bass, Alan
1990   "Fewer to be Admitted to Popular Programs," in *London Free Press* 13 April.

Baum, Gregory
1977   *Truth Beyond Relativism: Karl Mannheim's Sociology of Knowledge.* Milwaukee: Marquette University Press.

Bercuson, David, et al.
1984   *The Great Brain Robbery.* Toronto: McClelland and Stewart.

Berger, Carl
1976   *The Writing of Canadian History.* Toronto: Oxford University Press.

Berkes, Fikret
1988   "The Intrinsic Difficulty of Predicting Impact: Lessons from the James Bay Hydro Project." Environmental Impact Assessment Review. Vol. 8, 201-220.

Berkowitz, S.D.
1984   "Models, Myths and Social Realities: A Brief Introduction to Sociology in Canada," in S.D. Berkowitz, ed., *Models and Myths in Canadian Sociology.* Toronto: Butterworths, 5-28.

Berland, Alwyn
1970   "Report on the Simon Fraser Dispute," *CAUT Bulletin,* 18-(2):42-50.

Bernard, Jessie
1964   *Academic Women.* New York: New American Library.

Beverly, John
1978   "Higher Education and the Capitalist Crisis," in *Socialist Review* 8(6):67-91.

Bird Commission
1970   *Report of the Royal Commission on the Status of Women.* Ottawa: Queen's Printer.

Bittner, E.
1965   "The Concept of Organization," in *Social Research* 32(4):239-255.

Black, Edwin
1975   *Divided Loyalties: Canadian Concepts of Federalism.* Montreal: McGill-Queen's University Press.

Bladen, V.W.
1960   "A Journal Is Born: 1935," in *Canadian Journal of Economics and Political Science*, 26:1-5.

Blishen, Bernard, et al., eds.
1961   *Canadian Society.* New York: The Free Press of Glencoe.

Bloom, Allan
1987   *The Closing of the American Mind.* New York: Simon and Schuster.

Bock, Philip
1980   *Continuities in Psychological Anthropology.* San Francisco: W.H. Freeman.

Boddy, Janice
1989   *Wombs and Alien Spirits: Women, Men, and the Zar Cult in Northern Sudan.* Madison: University of Wisconsin Press.

Bonacich, Edna
1989   "Marxism in the University: A Search for Consciousness," in *Berkeley Journal of Sociology*, Vol. 34, 65-79.

Braverman, Harry
1974   *Labor and Monopoly Capital.* New York: Monthly Review Press.

Breton, Raymond
1972   *Social and Academic Factors in the Career Decisions of Canadian Youth: A Study of Secondary School Students.* Ottawa: Manpower and Immigration.

Briggs, Jean
1974   "Eskimo Women: Makers of Men," in Carolyn Matthiasson, ed., *How Bold Her Face.* New York: Free Press.
1975   "Health-Related Aspects of Traditional Inuit Life," in *University of Manitoba Medical Journal*, 91-98.

1983   "Expecting the Unexpected: Inuit Attitudes toward the Unfamiliar," in *Recherches amerindiennes au Québec*, 13(1).

1985   "Socialization, Family Conflicts and Responses to Culture Change Among Canadian Inuit," in *Arctic Medical Research* 40:40-52.

1990   "Playwork as a Tool in the Socialization of an Inuit Child," in *Arctic Medical Research* 49:34-38.

Briskin, Linda

1989   "A Feminist Politic for the University: Beyond Individual Victimization and Toward a Transformed Academy," in *CAUT Bulletin*, 36(3).

Brooks, Stephen and Gagnon, Alain G.

1988   *Social Scientists and Politics in Canada: Between Clerisy and Vanguard.* Kingston and Montreal: McGill-Queen's University Press.

Brox, Ottar

1972   *Newfoundland Fishermen in the Age of Industry: A Sociology of Economic Dualism.* St. John's: Institute of Social and Economic Research.

Brym, Robert J.

1984   "Social Movements and Third Parties," in S.D. Berkowitz, ed., *Models and Myths in Canadian Sociology.* Toronto: Butterworths, 29-49.

1986   *Regionalism in Canada.* Toronto: Irwin Publishing.

1986   "Anglo-Canadian Sociology," in *Current Sociology* 34(1):1-152.

1987   *Report of the Sociology Editor to the Annual Meeting of the CRSA Editorial Board*, Hamilton, 1 June (mimeo).

1988   *Report of the Sociology Editor to the Annual Meeting of the CRSA Editorial Board*, Windsor, 3 June (mimeo).

1989   *Report of the Sociology Editor to the Annual Meeting of the CRSA Editorial Board*, Quebec, 2 June (mimeo).

1989   "Class and Power in Anglo-Canadian Sociology." San Francisco, ASA meetings.

Brym, Robert J. and Myles, John

1989   "Social Science Intellectuals and Public Issues in English Canada," in *University of Toronto Quarterly* 58(4):442-51.

Brym, Robert J. and Sacouman, R. James

1979   *Underdevelopment and Social Movements in Atlantic Canada.* Toronto: New Hogtown Press.

Brym, Robert J., with Fox, Bonnie
1989   *From Culture to Power: The Sociology of English Canada.* Toronto: Oxford University Press.

Buchbinder, Howard and Newson, Janice
1988   "Managerial Consequences of Recent Changes in University Funding Policies: a Preliminary View," in *European Journal of Education* 23:151-65.
1990   "Corporate-University Linkages in Canada: Transforming a Public Institution," in *Higher Education* 20:355-79.

Burawoy, Michael
1987   "The Limits of Wright's Analytical Marxism and an Alternative," in *Berkeley Journal of Sociology,* (VI):51-72.

Burns, Janet M.C.
1990   *Technical and Physical Conditions, Work Organizations, and Culture: The Case of Pacific Coast Canadian Commercial Fishermen.* Unpublished Ph.D. Thesis. Burnaby: Simon Fraser University.

Burridge, Kenelm
1983   "An Ethnology of Canadian Ethnology," in F. Manning, ed., *Consciousness and Inquiry: Ethnology and Canadian Realities.* Ottawa: National Museum of Man.

Campbell, Douglas F.
1983   *Beginnings: Essays on the History of Canadian Sociology.* Port Credit, Ont.: Scribbler's Press.

Campbell, Marie
1984   *Information Systems and Management of Hospital Nursing: A Study in the Social Organization of Knowledge.* Toronto: Unpublished doctoral dissertation, OISE.

Canadian Sociology and Anthropology Association
        Minutes of Executive Meetings and Annual General Meetings, 1968-75, 1979-84.

Canadian Sociology and Anthropology Association Annual General Meetings.
        Minutes of Meetings on file at offices of CSAA in Montreal.

Canadian Advisory Council on the Status of Women
1983   *As Things Stand: Ten Years of Recommendations.* Ottawa.

Candian Journal of Sociology
1989   *The Canadian Journal of Sociology Index,* 1974-1988.

Canadian Review of Sociology and Anthropology
1986   *The Canadian Review of Sociology and Anthropology Index, 1964-1984.*
        Toronto: University of Toronto Press.

Canadian Sociology and Anthropology Association Executive
        Committee.
        Minutes of meetings on file at offices of CSAA in Montreal.

Canadian Sociology and Anthropology Association Board
        Minutes of meetings on file at offices of CSAA in Montreal.

Cantor, Nathaniel
1949   "The Teaching and Learning of Sociology," in *American Journal of
        Sociology* 55:18-24.

Card, B.Y.
1973   *The Expanding Relations: Sociology in Prairie Universities.* Regina:
        Canadian Plains Studies.

Carden, Maren Lockwood
1990   "Authors and Networks: Gender in Sociological Journal Articles,"
        in *Footnotes* 18(1):11-12.

Cassin, A. Marguerite
1980   *The Routine Production of Inequality: Implications for Affirmative Action.*
        Unpublished Paper. Ontario Institute for Studies in Education.
1990   *The Routine Production of Inequality: A Study of the Social Organization
        of Knowledge.* Ph.D. dissertation, University of Toronto.

Castles, Stephen and Wustenberg, Wiebke
1979   *The Education of the Future.* London: Pluto Press.

Cheal, David
1990   "Authority and Incredulity: Sociology Between Modernism and
        Post-modernism." *Canadian Journal of Sociology,* 15 (2)129-147.

Chomsky, Noam
1988   *Language and Politics.* Montreal: Black Rose.

Christiansen-Ruffman, Linda
1979   "Positions For Women in Canadian Sociology and Anthropology,"
        in *Society/Société* 3(3):9-12.
1981   "Social Policy Report," in *Society/Société* 5(1):10-11.
1986   "Report on Task Force on Elimination of Sexist Bias in Research,"
        in Social Science Federation of Canada.
1989   "Inherited Biases Within Feminism: The 'Patricentric Syndrome'
        and the 'Either/Or Syndrome' in Sociology," in A. Miles and G.
        Finn, eds., *Feminism: From Pressure to Politics.* Montreal: Black Rose,
        123-46.
1990   "Looking Back Toward the Future: Twenty-five Years of the Atlantic
        Association of Sociologists and Anthropologists and its
        Communities," in Janet Burns, Gail Pool and Chris McCormick,
        eds., *From the Margin to the Center.* Saint John: University of New
        Brunswick, 9-29.

Christiansen-Ruffman, Linda, Murphy, Alleyne, Stark-Adamec, Cannie,
        Davidson, Robert, et al.
1986   "Sex Bias in Research: Current Awareness and Strategies to Eliminate
        Bias within Canadian Social Science." *Report of the Task Force on the
        Elimination of Sexist Bias in Research to the Social Science Federation of
        Canada (SSFC).* Ottawa.

Citizens Plus
1970   (The Red Paper) *Indian Chiefs of Alberta.* Ottawa, 4 June.

Clark, S.D.
1973   "The American Takeover of Canadian Sociology: Myth or Reality?"
        in *Dalhousie Review* 53(2): 205-18.
1975   "Sociology in Canada: An Historical Overview," in *Canadian Journal
        of Sociology* 1(2):225-34.
1979   "The Changing Image of Sociology in English-Speaking Canada,"
        in *Canadian Journal of Sociology* 4(4):393-403.

Clifford, James and Marcus, George, eds.
1986   *Writing Culture.* Berkeley: University of California Press.

Coburn, David
1970   "Sociology and Sociologists in Canada: Problems and Prospects,"
        in J. Loubser, ed., *The Future of Sociology in Canada = L'Avenir de la
        sociologie au Canada.* Montreal: Canadian Sociology and
        Anthropology Association, 36-59.

Cole, Jonathan and Cole, Stephen
1971   "Measuring the Quality of Sociological Research: Problems in the
        Use of the Science Citation Index," in *The American Sociologist* 6(1).
1973   *Social Stratification in Science*. Chicago: The University of Chicago
        Press.

Connelly, M. Patricia
1978   *Last Hired, First Fired*. Toronto: Women's Press.

Connelly, M. Patricia and MacDonald, Martha
1989   "Class and Gender in Fishing Communities in Nova Scotia," in
        Studies in Political Economy 30(Autumn):61-86.
1990   *Women and the Labour Force*. 1986 Census of Canada. Ottawa: Supply
        and Services Canada.

Conway, J.F.
1978   "Populism in the U.S., Russia and Canada: Explaining the Roots of
        Canada's Third Parties," in *The Canadian Journal of Political Science*
        11:99-124.
1979   "The Prairie Populist Resistance to the Nationalist Policy: Some
        Reconsiderations," in *The Journal of Canadian Studies* 14:77-91.
1983   *The West*. Toronto: James Lorimer.

Coombe, Rosemary
1991   "Encountering the Postmodern: New Directions in Cultural
        Anthropology," in *The Canadian Review of Sociology and Anthropology*
        28(2):188-205.

Crane, Diana
1965   "Scientists at Major and Minor Universities: A Study of Production
        and Recognition," in *American Sociological Review* 30(5):699-714.
1967   "The Gatekeepers of Science: Some Factors Affecting the Selection
        of Articles for Scientific Journals," in *The American Sociologist*
        12(4):194-201.

Crook, Rodney
1975   "Teaching and Learning Sociology," in Dennis Forcese and Stephen
        Richer, eds., *Issues in Canadian Society*. Scarborough: Prentice-Hall,
        467-98.

Crothers, Charles
1984   "Patterns of Regional Social Differences in New Zealand," in *The
        Australian and New Zealand Journal of Sociology* 20(3):365-76.

Crysdale, S. and Beattie, C.
1973 *Sociology Canada: An Introductory Text.* Toronto: Butterworths.

Currie, Raymond F.
1989 "Sociology and Social Policy," in *Society/Société* 13(1 February):28.

Curtis, James and Teppermen, Lorne
1990 *Images of Canada: The Sociological Tradition.* Scarborough, Ont.: Prentice-Hall.

Dagenais, Huguette
1981 "Quand la sociologie devient action: l'impact du féminisme sur le pratique sociologique," *Sociologie et Société* 13(2):49-66.

Dagg, Anne I. and Thompson, Patricia J.
1988 *Mis-education: Women and Canadian Universities.* Toronto: OISE Press.

Daniels, Arlene Kaplan
1975 "Feminist Perspectives in Sociological Research," in Marcia Millman and Rosabeth Moss Kanter, eds., *Another Voice.* Garden City, N.Y.: Anchor Books, 340-80.

Davis, Arthur K.
1971 "Canadian Society and History as Hinterland versus Metropolis," in Richard J. Ossenberg, ed., *Canadian Society: Pluralism, Change and Conflict.* Scarborough, Ont.: Prentice-Hall, 6-32.

de Beauvoir, Simone
1949 *Le Deuxième Sexe.* 2 Vols. Paris: Librairie Gallimard.
1954 *The Second Sex.* London: Jonathan Cape.

Denis, Ann B.
1975 "Some Social Characteristics of CEGEP Graduates," in *The Canadian Journal of Higher Education* 2:39-56.

Denis, Ann B. and Lipkin, John
1972 "Quebec's CEGEP: Promise and Reality," in *McGill Journal of Education* VII(2:Fall).

Denis, Claude
1990 "Discussant's Notes," in *Session on the Sociology of Knowledge.* CSAA Meetings, University of Victoria.

Department of Indian Affairs and Northern Development
1969   (The White Paper). *Statement of the Government of Canada on Indian Policy*. Ottawa: Queen's Printer.

Department of Housing, Family and Social Statistics Division, Statistics Canada
1990a   *Women in Canada*. 2d ed. Ottawa: Supply and Services Canada.

Department of Sociology
1984   *Graduate Program in Sociology*, The University of Alberta.

Dewdney, A. K.
1984   *The Planiverse: Computer Contact with a Two-Dimensional World*. Toronto: McClelland & Stewart.

Dewdney, Selwyn H.
1970   "Ecological Notes on the Ojibway Shaman-artist," in *Arts Canada* (August).
1975   *Sacred Scrolls of the Southern Ojibway*. Toronto: University of Toronto Press.

Dewdney, Selwyn H. and Kidd, Kenneth
1967   *Indian Rock Paintings of the Great Lakes*. 2d ed. Toronto: University of Toronto Press.

DeWitt, Robert L.
1969   *Public Policy and Community Protest: The Fogo Case*. Institute for Social and Economic Research, Memorial University, St. John's, Nfld.

Dickson, David
1984   "'Science Shops' Flourish in Europe," *Science* 223:1158-60.

Dixon, M.
1975   "The Sisterhood Rip-Off: the Destruction of the Left in the Professional Women's Caucuses," in *Women in Canadian Sociology and Anthropology Newsletter* 2(2):3-7.

Douglas, J.
1967   *The Social Meaning of Suicide*. Princeton: Princeton University Press.

Douglas, Mary
1966   *Purity and Danger*. Harmondsworth: Penguin Books.

Drakich, Janice and Maticka-Tyndale, Eleanor
1991   "Feminist Organizing in the Academic Disciplines: The Canadian
        Sociology and Anthropology Association," in Jeri Wine and Janice
        Ristock, ed., *Social Change, Feminist Women and Activism in Canada.*
        Toronto: James Lorimer, 283-98.

Drummond, Lee
1986   "The Story of Bond," in H. Varenne, ed., *Symbolizing America.*
        Lincoln: University of Nebraska Press.

Dunning, R.W.
1959   *Social and Economic Change Among the Northern Ojibway.* Toronto:
        University of Toronto Press.

Dunton-Laurendeau Commission
1968-70 *Report of the Royal Commission on Bilingualism and Biculturalism.* 5 vols.
        Ottawa: Queen's Printer.

Durkheim, Émile
1987   *Suicide.* Glencoe: Free Press.

Durkheim, Émile and Mauss, Marcel
1970   *Primitive Classification.* Trans. R. Needham. London: Routledge &
        Kegan Paul.

Dyck, Noel
1989   "'Telling it Like it Is:' Some Dilemmas of Fourth World Ethnography
        and Advocacy," Department of Sociology and Anthropology, Simon
        Fraser University, Vancouver.

Ehrenreich, Barbara
1989   *Fear of Falling.* New York: Pantheon Books.

Eichler, Margrit
1975   "Sociological Research on Women in Canada," in *Canadian Review
        of Sociology and Anthropology* 12(4):474-81.
1980   *The Double Standard: A Feminist Critique of Feminist Social Science.*
        London: Croom Helm.
1985   "And the Work Never Ends: Feminist Contributions," in *Canadian
        Review of Sociology and Anthropology* 22(5):619-44.
1987   "The Relationship Between Sexist, Non-sexist, Woman-centred
        and Feminist Research in the Social Sciences," in Greta Hofmann
        Nemiroff, ed., *Women and Men: Interdisciplinary Readings on Gender.*
        Toronto: Fitzhenry & Whiteside, 3-20.

1988   *Nonsexist Research Methods.* Winchester, Mass.: Allen and Unwin.
1989   "Reflections on Motherhood, Apple Pie, the New Reproductive Technologies and the Role of Sociologists in Society," *Society/Société* 13(1):1-5.
1990a "On Doing the Splits Collectively: Introduction to the Canadian Women's Studies Project," *Atlantis* 16(1):3-5.
1990b "What's in a Name: Women's Studies or Feminist Studies?" in *Atlantis* 16(1):40-56.
       Forthcoming "Not Always An Easy Alliance: The Relationship between Women's Studies and the Women's Movement in Canada," in C. Backhouse and D.H. Flaherty, eds., *The Contemporary Women's Movement in Canada and the United States.*

Eichler, Margrit and Lapointe, J.
1985   *On the Treatment of the Sexes in Research.* Ottawa: Social Science and Humanities Research Council of Canada.

Eichler, Margrit, with the assistance of Louise Vandelac.
1990   "An Awkward Situation—Men in Women's Studies—Part I," *Atlantis* 16(1):69-91.

Eichler, Margrit, with the assistance of Rosonna Tite.
1990   "Women's Studies Professors in Canada: Collective Self-Portrait," *Atlantis* 16(1):6-24.

Eliade, Mircea
1984   "Cosmogonic Myth and `Sacred History,'" in Alan Dundes, ed., *Sacred Narrative.* Berkeley: University of California Press, 137-51.

Falardeau, Jean-Charles
1967   *The Rise of the Social Sciences in French Canada.* Quebec: Department of Cultural Affairs. (French Version, 1964).

Faris, James
1966   *Cat Harbour: A Newfoundland Fishing Settlement.* St. John's: Institute of Social and Economic Research.

Fasheh
1990   "Community Education: To Reclaim and Transform What Has Been Made Invisible," in *Harvard Educational Review* 60(1):19–35.

Felt, Lawrence F.
1975 "Nationalism and the Possibility of a Relevant Anglo-Canadian Sociology," in *Canadian Journal of Sociology* 1(3):377-86.

Feyerabend, Paul K.
1970 "How to be a Good Empiricist—A Plea For Tolerance in Matters Epistemological," in B.A., Brody, ed., *Readings in the Philosophy of Science*. Englewood Cliffs: Prentice-Hall, 319-39.
1975 *Against Method: Outline of an anarchistic theory of knowledge*. London: Verso.

Firestone, Melvin
1967 *Brothers and Rivals: Patrilocality in Savage Cove*. St. John's: Institute of Social and Economic Research.

Fishery Research Group
1986 *The Social Impact of Technological Change in the Newfoundland Deepsea Fishery*. Labour Canada–funded study administered by Institute for Social and Economic Research (ISER) and available from ISER, St. John's.

Fleck, L.
1979 *Genesis and Development of a Scientific Fact*. Chicago: University of Chicago Press.

Forcese, Dennis and Richer, Stephen
1975 "Social Issues and Sociology in Canada," in *Issues in Canadian Society*. Scarborough, Ont.: Prentice-Hall of Canada.

Foucault, M.
1985 *The Use of Pleasure. The History of Sexuality*. Vol. 2. New York: Vintage Books.

Fournier, M.
1985 "Sociological Theory in English Canada: A View from Quebec," in *Canadian Review of Sociology and Anthropology* 22(5):794-803.

Fox, Bonnie, ed.
1980 *Hidden in the Household*. Toronto: Women's Press.

Franklin, Ursula
1990 *The Real World of Technology*. CBC Massey Lecture Series. Toronto: CBC Enterprises.

Frazer, Sir James George
1918   *Folklore in the Old Testament,* Vol. 1. London: Macmillan.

Freire, Paulo
1970   *Pedagogy of the Oppressed.* New York: Continuum.

French, Orland
1990   "Engineering Students Discuss Gun Laws," in *The Globe and Mail,*
        January 12:A10.

Frye, Northrop
1981   *The Great Code.* Toronto: Academic Press.
1982   *Divisions on a Ground: Essays on Canadian Culture.* Toronto: Anansi.

Gailey, Christine Ward
1987   "Evolutionary Perspectives on Gender Hierarchy," in Beth B.
        Hess and Myra Marx Ferree, eds., *Analyzing Gender. A Handbook of
        Social Science Research.* Newbury Park, 32-67.

Gans, Herbert J.
1980   *Deciding What's News: The Study of CBS* Evening News, *NBC* Nightly
        News, Newsweek and Time. New York: Vintage Books.

Garfinkel, H., Lynch, M. and Livingstone, E.
1981   "The Work of Discovering Science Construed with Materials from
        the Optically Discovered Pulsar," in *Philosophy of the Social Sciences*
        1:131-58.

Garigue, Phillipe
1956   "St. Justin: a Case Study in Rural French-Canadian Social
        Organization," in *Canadian Journal of Economics and Political Science*
        22:301-18.
1958   *Études sur le Canada français.* Montréal: Faculté des sciences sociales,
        économiques et politiques, Université de Montréal.

Geertz, Clifford
1983   *Local Knowledge.* New York: Basic Books.
1988   *Works and Lives: The Anthropologist as Author.* Stanford: Stanford
        University Press.

Genov, Nikolai, ed.
1989   *National Traditions in Sociology.* International Sociological
        Association, SAGE Studies in International Sociology, 36.

Giddens, Anthony
1977   *Studies in Social and Political Theory*. London: Hutchinson.
1982   *Sociology*. New York: Harcourt Brace Jovanovich.

Giddings, Franklin H.
1901   *Inductive Sociology*. New York: Macmillan.

Gittings, Gary, ed.
1980   *Paradigms and Revolutions: Appraisals and Applications of Thomas Kuhn's Philosophy of Science*. Notre Dame and London: University of Notre Dame Press.

Glasbeek, Harry
1986   "Voluntarism, Liberalism, and Grievance Arbitration: Holy Grail, Romance and Real Life," in *Essays in Labour Relations Law*. Don Mills: CCH Canadian, 57-102.

Gold, Gerald, and Tremblay, Marc-Adélard
1983   "Steps Toward an Anthropology of Quebec 1960-80," in F. Manning, ed., *Consciousness and Inquiry: Ethnology and Canadian Realities*. Ottawa: National Museum of Man.

Golde, Peggy
1986   *Women in the Field*. 2d ed. Berkeley: University of California Press.

Gonzalez, Paulino
1985   "Las Luchas Estudiantiles en Centro America," in Daniel Camacho and Rafael Menjivar, eds., *Movimientos Populares en Centro America*. San Jose: EDUCA, 38-90.

Gordon, Jane and Breslauer, Helen
1990   "Violence and the University," in *Society/Société* 14(2):5-7.

Government of Canada
1970   *Royal Commission on the Status of Women*. Report. Ottawa.

Graham, Bill
1989   "Premier's Council Has a Narrow View of Education," in *The OCUFA Forum*, November.

Grant, George
1965   *Technology and Empire*. Toronto: House of Anansi.
1985   *Lament for a Nation: The Defeat of Canadian Nationalism*. Macmillan of Canada.

Grayson, Paul J. and Magill, Dennis W.
1981   *One Step Forward, Two Steps Sideways: Sociology and Anthropology in Canada* Montreal: Canadian Sociology and Anthropology Association.

Guberman, Connie and Wolfe, Margie, eds.
1985   *No Safe Place.* Toronto: Women's Press.

Guindon, Hubert
1960   "The Social Evolution of Quebec Reconsidered," in *Canadian Journal of Economics and Political Science* 26:533-51.

Guinsburg, T.N. and Reuber, G.L., eds.
1974   *Perspectives on the Social Sciences in Canada.* Toronto: University of Toronto Press.

Guppy, Neil
1989   "Rank, Age, and Salary in Anthropology and Sociology," *Society/ Société* 13(2):14-17.

Gurney, J.N.
1985   "Not One of the Guys: The Female Researcher in a Male-Dominated Setting," in *Qualitative Sociology* 8:42-62.

Gusfield, Joseph R.
1981   *The Culture of Public Problems: Drinking-Driving and the Symbolic Order.* Chicago: University of Minnesota Press.

Haas, Adelaide and Haas, K.
1990   *Understanding Sexuality.* Toronto: Times, Mirror/Mosby.

Hacker, Sally
1990   *Doing It the Hard Way: Investigations of Gender and Technology,* ed. Dorothy E. Smith and Susan Turner. Boston: Unwin Hyman.

Hagedorn, R.
1983   "What is Sociology," in R.Hagedorn, ed., *Sociology.* 2d ed. Toronto: Holt, Rinehart and Winston, 3-25.
1990   *Controversies in Sociology. A Canadian Introduction.* Toronto: Copp Clark Pitman.

Hagedorn, R. and Hedley, R.A.
1983   "Social Research," in R. Hagedorn, ed., *Sociology.* 2d ed. Toronto: Holt, Rinehart and Winston, 535-61.

Hall Commission
1964-65 *Report of the Royal Commission on Health Services.* Vols. I and II. Ottawa: Queen's Printer.

Hall, Oswald
1964 *Utilization of Dentists in Canada.* Ottawa: Queen's Printer.

Hamilton, Roberta
1978 *The Liberation of Women.* London: George Allen & Unwin.

Hammer, Heather-Jo
1983-84 *Mature Dependency: The Effects of American Direct Investment on Canadian Economic Growth.* Ph.D. dissertation, University of Alberta.

Hammer, Heather-Jo and Gartrell, John W.
1986 "American Penetration and Canadian Development: A Case Study of Mature Development," in *American Sociological Review* 51:201-13.

Handelman, Don and Leyton, Elliott
1978 *Bureaucracy and World View: Studies in the Logic of Official Interpretation.* St. John's: Institute of Social and Economic Research.

Handler, Richard
1988 *Nationalism and the Politics of Culture in Quebec.* Madison: University of Wisconsin Press.

Hanrahan, Maura
1988 *Living on the Dead: Fishermen's Licensing and Unemployment Insurance Programs in Newfoundland.* Institute for Social and Economic Research, Memorial University, St. John's, Nfld.

Harding, J.
1970 *The Ideology and Logic of Scientism.* Doctoral Thesis, Simon Fraser University.
Forthcoming *The Politics of Social Policy: The Blakeney Years in Saskatchewan.*

Harris, M.
1968 *The Rise of Anthropological Theory: A History of Theories of Culture.* New York: Thomas Y. Crowell Co.

Harrison, Deborah
1981 *The Limits of Liberalism: The Making of Canadian Sociology.* Montreal: Black Rose Books.

Hattiangadi, J.N.
1977   "The Crisis in Methodology: Feyerabend," in *Philosophy of Social Sciences* 7:289-302.

Hawthorn, H.B., with Cairns, H.A.C., Jamieson S.M., and Lysyk, K.
1966   *A Survey of the Contemporary Indians of Canada*. Vol. I. Ottawa: Queen's Printer.

Hawthorn, H.B. with Tremblay, M.A., Vallee, Frank G., and Ryan, Joan
1967   *A Survey of the Contemporary Indians of Canada*. Vol. II. Ottawa: Queen's Printer.

Helmes-Hayes, R., ed.
1988   *A Quarter-Century of Sociology at the University of Toronto, 1963-1988*. Toronto: Canadian Scholars' Press.

Henry, Frances
1975   "Introduction," in *The Canadian Review of Sociology and Anthropology* 12(November 4):352.

Heritage, J.
1984   *Garfinkel and Ethnomethodology*. Oxford: Polity Press.

Herman, Kathleen and Peter Carstens, eds.
1978-79 *Guide to Departments: Sociology, Anthropology, Archaeology in Universities and Museums in Canada*. n.p.: Canadian Sociology and Anthropology Association and Canadian Ethnology Society. Ottawa.
1986-87 *Guide to Departments/Annuaire des départements, Sociology, Anthropology, Archaeology in Universities and Museums in Canada*. Montréal: Canadian Sociology and Anthropology Association and Canadian Ethnology Society.

Heron, Craig
1989   *The Canadian Labour Movement*. Toronto: Lorimer.

Hiller, Harry H.
1977   "Internal Party Resolution and Third Party Emergence," in *Canadian Journal of Sociology* 2:55-75.
1979   "The Canadian Sociology Movement: Analysis and Assessment," in *Canadian Journal of Sociology* 4(2):125-50.
1980   "Paradigmatic Shifts, Indigenization, and the Development of Sociology in Canada," in *Journal of the History of the Behavioral Sciences* 16(3):263-74.

1982   *Society and Change: S.D. Clark and the Development of Canadian Sociology.* Toronto: University of Toronto Press.
1986   *Canadian Society: A Macroanalysis.* Scarborough, Ont.: Prentice-Hall.

Hitchman, Gladys Symons
1974   "A Report on the Reports: The Status of Women in Canadian Universities," in *Canadian Sociology and Anthropology Association Bulletin* 34:11-13.

Hite, Shere
1976   *The Hite Report.* New York: Alfred Knopf.
1985   *Working Offshore: The Other Price of Newfoundland's Soil.* Institute for Social and Economic Research, Memorial University, St. John's, Nfld.

Horowitz, I.L., ed.
1967   *The Rise and Fall of Project Camelot: Studies in the Relationship Between Social Science and Practical Politics.* Cambridge: The M.I.T. Press.

House Commission
1990   *Report of the Royal Commission on Employment and Unemployment in Newfoundland.* St. John's.

House, Douglas
1990   "Management: Textually Mediated Social Organization," in *School of Public Administration,* Dalhousie University, unpublished paper.

Howes, David
1988   "We, the Other People," in *The Canadian Forum* (January 1988):8-10.
1990a   "Controlling Textuality: A Call for a Return to the Senses," in *Anthropologica* 32(1):55-72.
1990b   "We Are The World and Its Counterparts: Popular Song as Constitutional Discourse," in *International Journal of Politics, Culture and Society* 3(3):315-39.
1991a   "In the Balance: The Art of Norman Rockwell and Alex Colville as Discourses on the Constitutions of the United States and Canada," in *Alberta Law Review* 29(2):475-97.
1991b   "Sensorial Anthropology," in D. Howes, ed., *The Varieties of Sensory Experience: A Source book in the Anthropology of the Senses.* Toronto: University of Toronto Press.

Huber, Joan
1976   "Review Essay, Sociology" in *Signs* 1(3), Part 1: 685-97.

Hull, David L.
1988   *Science as a Process: An Evolutionary Account of the Social and Conceptual Development of Science*. Chicago: University of Chicago Press.

Hunt, Jennifer
1984   "The Development of Rapport Through the Negotiation of Gender in Fieldwork Among Police," in *Human Organization* 43:283-96.

Inglis, Gordon
1972   "A Discourse on Married Life with Sociology: Or, Life Among the Savages," in *CSAA Bulletin* No. 30, April.
1977   "Applied Anthropology in Canada: A Discussion," in *Applied Anthropology in Canada*. Proceedings No. 4, Canadian Ethnology Society, 177-87.
1987   "A More Solid Base for Pursuing Goals on Unemployment Problems," in *Social Perspectives* 5(1): March.

Institute of Social and Economic Research. Reports, 1961-1989.

Irigaray, Luce
1989   "Is the Subject of Science Sexed?" Transl. Carol Mastrangelo Bové, in Nancy Tuana, ed., *Feminism and Science*. Bloomington: Indiana University Press, 58-68.

Iverson, Noel and Matthews, D. Ralph
1979   *Communities in Decline: An Examination of Household Resettlement in Newfoundland*. St. John's: Institute of Social and Economic Research, Studies, No. 6.

Jackson, John D.
1985   "Introduction to Special Issue on the State of the Art and New Directions: Sociology in Anglophone Canada," in *Canadian Review of Sociology and Anthropology* 22(5):615-18.

Jackson, John D., ed.
1985   *Canadian Review of Sociology and Anthropology. Special Issue on The State of the Art and New Directions (CRSA)*. Vol. 1: Sociology in Anglophone Canada. 22(5).

Jacoby, Russell
1987   *The Last Intellectuals*. New York: Basic Books.

Jaques Cattell Press
1978   *American Men and Women of Science: Social and Behavioral Sciences,*
        13th edition. New York: R.R. Bowker Company.

Jarvie, I.C.
1976   "Nationalism and the Social Sciences," in *Canadian Journal of Sociology*
        1(4):515-28.

Johnson, Janet and Marcus, L.R.
1986   *Blue Ribbon Commission on Higher Education: Changing Higher*
        Education from the Outside. Washington, D.C.: Higher Education
        Reports.

Jones, Frank E.
1977   "Current Sociological Research in Canada: Views of a Journal
        Editor," in *Journal of the History of the Behavioral Sciences* 13(2):160-72.

Juteau, Danielle, and Maheu, Louis
1989a   "Sociology and Sociologists in Francophone Quebec: Science and
        Politics," in *Canadian Review of Sociology and Anthropology* 26(3):363-
        93.

Juteau, Danielle, and Maheu, Louis eds.
1989b   "State of the Art Issue: Francophone Quèbecois Sociology." *Canadian*
        Review of Sociology and Anthropology 26(3).

Kant, Immanuel
1977   "The Interrelations of the Two Sexes," from *Kant's Observations on*
        the Feeling of the Beautiful and Sublime, trans. John Goldthwait.
        Berkeley: University of California Press, 1960. Excerpted by
        Rosemary Agonito, *A History of Ideas on Women: A Source Book,* New
        York: G.P. Putnam.

Kaplan, Ilene M.
1988   "Women Who Go to Sea: Working in the Commercial Fishing
        Industry," in *Journal of Contemporary Ethnography* 16(4):491-514.

Keller, Evelyn Fox
1985   *Reflections on Science and Gender.* New Haven, CT: Yale University
        Press.
1989   "The Gender/Science System: Or, Is Sex to Gender as Nature Is to
        Science?" in Nancy Tuana, ed., *Feminism and Science.* Bloomington:
        Indiana University Press, 33-44.

Keller, George
1983   *Academic Strategy: The management revolution in American higher education.* Baltimore: Johns Hopkins University Press.

Kelly, Alison, Whyte, Judith and Smail, Barbara
1984   *Girls into Science and Technology.* Final Report. Manchester: GIST, Department of Sociology, University of Manchester.

Kimball, Meredith
1985   "Women's Studies at Simon Fraser University," in *Canadian Woman Studies* 6(3):15-16.

Kopinak, Kathryn and Tannenbaum, Deborah
1975   "Letter," in *Women in Canadian Sociology Newsletter* 2(1).

Kuhn, Thomas S.
1962   *The Structure of Scientific Revolutions.* Chicago: University of Chicago Press.
1970   "The Function of Dogma in Scientific Research," in Brody, B.A., ed., *Readings in the Philosophy of Science.* Englewood Cliffs: Prentice-Hall, 356-73.

Lambek, Michael
1981   *Human Spirits: A Cultural Account of Trance in Mayotte.* Cambridge: Cambridge University Press.

Lambert, Ronald D. and Curtis, James
1973   "Nationality and Professional Activity Correlates Among Social Scientists: Data Bearing on Conventional Wisdoms," in *Canadian Review of Sociology and Anthropology* 10(1):62-80.

Larkin Committee
1991   *Realizing the Potential: A Strategy for University Research in Canada.* Report Submitted by the University Research Committee of the Royal Society of Canada. Ottawa: The Royal Society of Canada.

Lenton, Rhonda
1990a   "Academic Feminists and the Women's Movement in Canada: Continuity or Discontinuity," in *Atlantis* 16(1):57-68.
1990b   "Influential Feminist Thinkers for Academics in Canadian Women's Studies," *Atlantis* 16(1): 92-118.

Lerner, Harriett Goldhor
1985   *The Dance of Anger.* New York: Harper and Row.

Lévi-Strauss, Claude
1963   *Structural Anthropology*. Trans. C. Jacobson and B. Grundfest Schoepf. New York: Basic Books.

Levine, Gilbert
1988   "Relations Between Unions and Universities in Research and Teaching: Union Expectations," in *Labour/Le Travail* 21:191-97.

Leyton, Elliott
1977a   *Dying Hard: The Ravages of Industrial Carnage*. Toronto: McClelland & Stewart.
1977b   "Public Consciousness and Public Policy," in J. Freedman, ed., *Applied Anthropology in Canada*. Ottawa: Ethnology Society.
1979   *The Myth of Delinquency*. Toronto: McClelland & Stewart.
1984   "Universities' Positions on the Employment of Canadian Women," in *Society/Société* 8(2):7-8.

Lipset, S.M.
1963   "Value Differences, Absolute or Relative: the English-Speaking Democracies," in *The First New Nation: United States in Historical Perspective*. New York: Basic Books, 248-73.

Lloyd, Genevieve
1984   *The Man of Reason: Male and Female in Western Philosophy*. Minneapolis: University of Minnesota Press.

Locke, Michael
1990   "The Decline of Universities and the Rise of Edubis," *Society/Société* 14(2):8-16.

Lorber, Judith
1975   "Women and Medical Sociology: Invisible Professionals and Ubiquitous Patients," in Marcia Millman and Rosabeth Moss Kanter, eds., *Another Voice*. Garden City, N.Y.: Anchor Books, 75-105.

Luxton, Meg
1984   "Conceptualizing Women in Anthropology and Sociology," in CRIAW, eds., *Knowledge Reconsidered: A Feminist Overview*. Ottawa: CRIAW, 59-76.

Macdonald Commission
1985   *Report of the Royal Commission on Economic Union and Development Prospects for Canada*. Ottawa: Supply and Services Canada.

MacIntyre, Alasdair
1988   *Whose Justice? Which Rationality?* Notre Dame: University of Notre Dame Press.

Mackie, Marlene
1986   "Women in the Profession: Collegiality and Productivity," *Society/Société* 10(3).

MacKintosh, Maureen and Wainright, Hilary, eds.
1987   *A Taste of Power: The Politics of Local Economics.* London: Verso.

Macklem, Patrick
1991   "Of Texts and Democratic Narratives," in *University of Toronto Law Journal* 41:114-45.

MacLeod, Malcolm
1990   *A Bridge Built Halfway: History of Memorial University College 1925-50.* Montreal: McGill-Queen's University Press.

Macpherson, C.B.
1973   *Democratic Theory: Essays in Retrieval.* Oxford: Clarendon Press.

Magill, Dennis W.
1981   "Sociology and Anthropology in the 1975 Symons Report: Re-examination of the Canadianization Issue," in *Society/Société* 5(1):4-9.

Mann, W.E.
1968   *Canada: A Sociological Profile.* Toronto: Copp Clark.

Marchak, M. Patricia
1985   "Canadian Political Economy," in *Canadian Review of Sociology and Anthropology* 22(5):673-709.
1986   "The Rise and Fall of the Peripheral State: The Case of British Columbia," in Robert J. Brym, ed., *Regionalism in Canada.* Toronto: Irwin Publishing, 133-59.

Marchak, M. Patricia, Breton, Raymond, Inglis, Gordon, and Peters, Suzanne
1988   *CSAA Task Force Report on Priorities and Reform.* Unpublished. On file at CSAA Offices in Montreal.

Marchand, Philip
1989   *McLuhan: The Medium and the Messenger.* Toronto: RandomHouse.

Marcus, George and Cushman, Dick
1982   "Ethnographies as Texts," in *Annual Review of Anthropology* 11:25-69.

Marcus, George and Fischer, Michael
1986   *Anthropology as Cultural Critique.* Chicago: University of Chicago Press.

Mariategui, José Carlos
1963   *Siete Ensayos de Interpretacion de la Realidad Peruana.* La Habana: Casa de las Americas.

Marsden, Lorna
1988   "Intellectuals and Public Policy: The Case for Open Borders," in *Society/Société* 12(3):3-11.

Martin, Jane Roland
1985   "Rousseau's Sophie," in *Reclaiming a Conversation: The Ideal of the Educated Woman.* New Haven: Yale University Press.

Martindale, D.
1960   *The Nature and Types of Sociological Theory.* Boston: Houghton Mifflin Co.

Mascia-Lees, Frances E., Sharpe, Patricia and Cohen, Colleen Ballerino
1989   "The Postmodern Turn in Anthropology: Cautions from a Feminist Perspective," *Signs* 15(1): 7-33.

Mathews, Robin and James Steele, eds.
1969   *The Struggle for Canadian Universities.* Toronto: New Press.

Maticka-Tyndale, Eleanor
1981   "Women in Canadian Colleges," in *Society/Société* 5(2):11-13.
1987   "Status of Women Committee and Women's Caucus," in *Society/Société* 11(3):29-30.

Maxwell, Judith and Currie, Stephanie
1984   *Partnership for Growth.* Montreal: The Corporate–Higher Education Forum.

Maxwell, M.P.
1981   "Report on Survey of Progress Toward the Elimination of Sexist Language in Printed Materials of Departments of Sociology and Anthropology," in *Society/Société* 5(3):9-11.

McCormack, Thelma
1981   "Good Theory or Just Theory? Toward a Feminist Philosophy of Science," in *Women's Studies International Quarterly* 4(1):1-12.

McCrorie, James N.
1971   "Change and Paradox in Agrarian Social Movements," in Richard J. Ossenberg, ed., *Canadian Society*, 36-51.

McDermott, John
1986   "Pragmatic Sensibility: The Morality of Experience," in J. de Marco and R. Fox, eds., *New Directions in Ethics*. London: Routledge and Kegan Paul.

McFarlane, Bruce A.
1964   *Dental Manpower in Canada*. Ottawa: Queen's Printer.
1965   *Preliminary Report of the Committee to Consider the Problems of an Autonomous Association*. Unpublished.
1991   "The Contributions of the Social Sciences to Social Policy in Canada with Particular Respect to Sociologists and Anthropologists," in *Realizing the Potential: A Strategy for University Research in Canada*. Ottawa: the Royal Society of Canada.

McFeat, Tom
1976   "The National Museum and Canadian Anthropology," in J. Freedman, ed., *The History of Canadian Anthropology*. Ottawa: Canadian Ethnology Society.

McGuigan, Gerald, ed.
1968   *Student Protest*. Toronto: Methuen Publications.

McIntyre, Sheila
1987   "Gender Bias Within a Canadian Law School," in *CAUT Bulletin* 34(1):7-11.

McKillop, A.B.
1987   *Contours of Canadian Thought*. Toronto: University of Toronto Press.

McMurtry, John
1989   "Education for Sale," in *The OCUFA Forum*. November issue:3.

Merchant, Carolyn
1980   *The Death of Nature: Women, Ecology and the Scientific Revolution.*

New York: Harper & Row.

Merton, Robert K.
1967   *Social Theory and Social Structure.* New York: Free Press.

Millett, David
1989   "Canadian Sociology on the World Scene," in Nikolai Genov, ed., *National Traditions in Sociology.* London: Sage Studies in International Sociology 36, 38-54.

Millman, Marcia
1975   "She Did It All For Love: A Feminist View of the Sociology of Deviance," in Marcia Millman and Rosabeth Moss Kanter, eds., *Another Voice.* Garden City, N.Y.: Anchor Books, 251-79.

Mills, Donald
1964   *Study of Chiropractors, Osteopaths and Naturopaths in Canada.* Ottawa: Queen's Printer.

Moody, Kim
1989   *An Injury to All.* Detroit: Labor Notes.

Morrow, Lance
1987   "The Ark of America," *Time* 130(1), July.

Morton, Nelle
1985   *The Journey is Home.* Boston: Beacon Press.

Moulton, Janice
1983   "A paradigm of philosophy: The adversary method," in Sandra Harding and Merrill B. Hintikka, eds., *Discovering Reality.* Dordrecht: Reidel, 149-64.

Muller, Jacob, ed.
1990   *Education for Work. Education as Work. Canada's Changing Community Colleges.* Toronto: Garamond Press.

Mullins, Nicholas C.
1973   *Theories and Theory Groups in Contemporary American Sociology.* New York: Harper and Row.

Murphy, John W.
1988   "Making Sense of Post-Modern Sociology," in *The British Journal of Sociology* 39(4):600-614.

Murray, Janet Horowitz
1982   *Strong-Minded Women and Other Lost Voices from 19th Century England.*
        New York: Pantheon Books.

Myles, John, ed.
1989   *Canadian Review of Sociology and Anthropology (CRSA).* Special Issue:
        Comparative Political Economy 26(1).

N.A.
1971   *Towards 2000.* Report for the Committee of Presidents of Universities
        of Ontario. Toronto: McClelland and Stewart.

N.A.
1973   *Bricoleur,* Newsletter of the Founding Committee of the Canadian
        Ethnological Society/Bulletin du Comité de la Fondation de la
        Societé Canadienne d'Ethnologie, No. 2, September.

N. A.
1974   "Reorganization of Sub-Committee Structure within the CSAA,"
        Canadian Sociology and Anthropology Association Bulletin, July:7.

N. A.
1989a   "Financial Accountability,"*Nova Scotia Confederation of University
        Faculty Association Bulletin (NSCUFA)/de la Confèderation des
        Associations de Professeurs des Universités de la Nouvelle-Ecosse/
        CAPUNE,* October, 9(2):6.

N. A.
1989b   "University Head Resigns," in *The Chronicle-Herald,* Halifax:
        December 11, 41(293):B3.

N. A.
1990a   "Centres of Excellence Involve the Best and Brightest on Campus,"
        in *Dalhousie Alumni Magazine,* 7(1):4. (Winter)

N. A.
1990b   "Making Money From Research," in *Oxford Today,* 2(2):46.

Naegele, Kaspar D.
1968   "Modern National Societies," in B. Blishen et al., eds., *Canadian
        Society,* 3d ed.; Macmillan of Canada, 1-18.

Needham, Rodney
1970   "Introduction," in É. Durkheim and M. Mauss, *Primitive Classification*. London: Routledge and Kegan Paul.

Nettler, Gwynn
1970   *Explanations*. New York and Toronto: McGraw-Hill.

Newson, Janice and Buchbinder, Howard
1988   *The University Means Business*. Toronto: Garamond.

Nisbet, Robert
1966   *The Sociological Tradition*. New York: Basic Books Inc., 1966.
1976   *Sociology as an Art Form*. New York: Oxford University Press.

O'Brien, Mary
1981   *The Politics of Reproduction*. London: Routledge & Kegan Paul.
1983   "Feminism and Education: A Critical Review Essay," *Resources for Feminist Research* 12(3): 3-16.

O'Brien, Peter
1985   "An Interview with Christopher Dewdney," in *Rubicon* 5:88-117.

O'Neill, John
1975   "Facts, Myths and the Nationalist Platitude," Canadian Journal of Sociology 1 (1):107-24.

O'Rand, Angela M.
1989   "Scientific Thought Style and the Construction of Gender Inequality," in Jean F. O'Barr, ed., *Women and a New Academy: Gender and Cultural Contexts*. Madison: University of Wisconsin Press, 103-21.

Oakley, Ann
1981   "Interviewing Women: A Contradiction in Terms," in H. Roberts, ed., *Doing Feminist Research*. Boston: Routledge & Kegan Paul, 30-61.

Ohnuki-Tierney, Emiko
1981   *Illness and Healing Among the Sakhalin Ainu*. Cambridge: Cambridge University Press.

Okin, Susan Moller
1981   "Women and the Making of the Sentimental Family," in *Philosophy and Public Affairs* 11(1): 65-88.

Oliver, M.
1961   *Social Purpose for Canada*. Toronto: University of Toronto Press.

Olswang, Steven G. and Lee, Barbara A.
1984   "Faculty Freedoms and Institutional Accountability: Interactions
        and Conflicts," in *ASHE-ERIC Higher Education Research Report No.
        5*. Washington, D.C.: Association for the Study of Higher Education.

Ontario Federation of Students
1988   *Cut to the Bone (May)*. Toronto: OFS Research Department.

Ostow, Robin
1984   "Everett Hughes: The McGill Years," in *Society/Société* 8:12-16.

Overton, Jim
1981   "Politics and Unemployment: the Activities of the Newfoundland
        Association for Full Employment," paper prepared for the meetings
        of the Committee on Socialist Studies, The Learned Societies,
        Halifax.
1985   "Unemployment in Newfoundland: A Proposal."
1990   "The Crisis and the `Small is Beautiful' Model of Development." A
        shortened version of this manuscript is forthcoming in *Restructuring
        and Resistance in Atlantic Canada*, ed. Bryant Fairley, Colin Leys and
        James Sacouman. Toronto: Garamond.

Paine, Robert, ed.
1977   *The White Arctic: Anthropological Essays on Tutelage and Ethnicity*. St.
        John's: Institute for Social and Economic Research (ISER).
1985   *Advocacy and Anthropology, First Encounters*. St. John's: Institute for
        Social and Economic Research (ISER).

Panabaker, John
1987   *From Patrons to Partners*. Montreal: The Corporate–Higher Education
        Forum.

Passmore, John
1970   *The Perfectibility of Man*. London: Duckworth, 1-28.People's
        Commission on Employment and Unemployment
1978   *Now That We've Burned Our Boats....* Ottawa: Mutual Press.

Philbrook, Tom
1966   *Fishermen, Logger, Merchant, Miner: Social Change and Industrialization
        in More Newfoundland Communities*. Institute for Social and Economic
        Research, Memorial University, St. John's, Nfld.

Polin, Raymond
1983   "Freedom of Mind and University Autonomy," in J. Chapman, ed., *The Western University on Trial.* Berkeley: University of California Press, 39-45.

Pollack, Sandra
1985   "Exposing the Conservative Agenda: Women's Studies Minus Feminism," in *Radical Teacher* 29:19-23.

Porter, John
1965   *The Vertical Mosaic: An Analysis of Social Class and Power in Canada.* Toronto: University of Toronto Press.
1975   "Foreword," in W. Clement, *The Canadian Corporate Elite.* Toronto: McClelland and Stewart.

Porter, Marilyn
1989   "Porter Prize Committee Report," in *Society/Société* 13 (3, October): 14-5.

Preston, Richard
1983   "The Social Structure of an Unorganized Society: Beyond Intentions and Peripheral Boasians," in F. Manning, ed., *Consciousness and Inquiry: Ethnology and Canadian Realities.* Ottawa: National Museum of Man.

Pro Canada Network
1991   "Inside Fortress North America," in *Pro Canada Dossier #29.*

Québec, B.A.E.Q.
1966   *Plan du développement dans Bas-Saint-Laurent, de la Gaspésie et des Iles-de-la-Madeleine.* Mont Joli; ARDA-Québec, 10 cahiers.

Radcliffe-Brown, A.R.
1952   *Structure and Function in Primitive Societies.* New York: The Free Press.

Reid, Tim and Reid, Julyan
1969   *Student Power and the Canadian Campus.* Toronto: Peter Martin Associates Limited.

Reimer, M.A.
1987   *The Social Organization of the Labour Process: A Case Study of the Documentary Management of Clerical Labour in the Public Service.* Ph.D. thesis, Ontario Institute for Studies in Education.

Reiter, Ester
1989   *Education for Trade Unionists: An Evaluation of the Labour Studies Program of the Metro Labour Education and Skills Training Centre.* Mimeographed.

Renaud, M., Doré, S., and White, D.
1989   "Sociology and Social Policy: From a Love-Hate Relationship with the State to Cynicism and Pragmatism," in *Canadian Review of Sociology and Anthropology* 26(3):426-56. (May)

Rex, John
1975   "Nations, Nationalism and the Social Scientist," *Canadian Journal of Sociology* 1(4):501-14.

Riches, G. and Ternowetsky, G., eds.
1990   *Unemployment and Welfare: Social Policy and the Work of Social Work.* Toronto: Garamond.

Richmond, Anthony H.
1967   *Post War Immigrants in Canada.* Toronto: University of Toronto Press.

Robertson, Claire, Dyer, Constance E. and Campbell, D'Ann
1988   "Campus Harassment: Sexual Harassment Policies and Procedures at Institutions of Higher Learning," in *Signs: Journal of Women in Culture and Society* 13(4):792-812.

Robson, R.A.H.
1964   *Sociological Factors Affecting Recruitment into the Nursing Profession.* Ottawa: Queen's Printer.

Rocher, Guy
1968   *Introduction à la sociologie générale.* Montréal: Éditions HMH Ltèe.
1974   "La sociologie canadienne et québécoise."
1990   "Les deux solitudes chez les sociologues canadiens." Paper presented at Learned Societies Conference, Victoria, B.C., May 28, 1990.

Rooney, Phyllis
1991   "Gendered Reason: Sex Metaphor and Conceptions of Reason," in *Hypatia* 6(2):76-103.

Ross, Aileen
1984   "Sociology at McGill in the 1940s," in *Society/Société* 8(1):4-5.

Rossides, D.W.
1968   *Society as a Functional Process: An Introduction to Sociology.* Toronto: McGraw-Hill.

Rousseau, Jean-Jacques
1979   *Émile or on Education,* introduction and translation by Alan Bloom. New York: Basic Books.

Rush, G.B., Christensen E. and Malcomson, J.
1981   "Lament for a Notion: The Development of Social Science in Canada," in *Canadian Review of Sociology and Anthropology* 18(4):519-44.

Ryan, Joan
1985   "Decolonializing Anthropology," in Robert Paine. ed., *Advocacy and Anthropology: First Encounters.* St. John's: Institute for Social and Economic Research (ISER).

Said, Edward
1983   "The Music Itself: Glenn Gould's Contrapuntal Vision," in J. McGreevy, ed., *Glenn Gould Variations.* Toronto: Macmillan of Canada.

Salisbury, R.
1977   "Training Applied Anthropologists—the McGill Program in the Anthropology of Development 1964-1976," in *Applied Anthropology in Canada, Proceedings No. 4.* Canadian Ethnology Society.

Sandler, Bernice R.
1988   "The Classroom Climate: Chilly for Women?" in Deneef A. Leigh, Crawford D. Goodwin and Elen Stern McCrate, eds.,*The Academic's Handbook.* Durham: Duke University Press, 146-52.

Schiebinger, Londa
1989   *The Mind Has No Sex? Women in the Origins of Modern Science.* Cambridge: Harvard University Press.

Schwendinger, Julia and Herman Schwendinger
1971   "Sociology's Founding Fathers: Sexists to a Man," in *Journal of Marriage and the Family* 33(4):783-99.

Shankar, A. Yelaja, ed.
1987   *Canadian Social Policy.* Waterloo: Wilfrid Laurier University Press. (Revised edition)

Sherwin, Susan
1988   "Philosophical Methodology and Feminist Methodology: Are They Compatible?" in Lorraine Code, Sheila Mullett, and Christine Overall, eds., *Feminist Perspectives: Philosophical Essays on Method and Morals*. Toronto: University of Toronto Press, 13-28.

Shevelow, Kathryn
1989   *Women and Print Culture: The Constitution of Feminity in the Early Periodical*. London: Routledge.

Shor, Ira
1980   *Critical Teaching and Everyday Life*. Montreal: Black Rose Books.
1986   *Culture Wars*. Boston: Routledge and Kegan Paul.

Shore, Marlene
1987   *The Science of Social Redemption*. Toronto: University of Toronto Press.

Shore, Valerie
1984   "Waterloo... More in Touch With The Real World," in *University Affairs*, August–September:2-5.

Sinclair, Peter
1985   *The State Goes Fishing: The Emergence of Public Ownership in the Newfoundland Fishing Industry*. Institute for Social and Economic Research. Memorial University, St. John's, Nfld.

Smith, Dorothy E.
1974a   "The Ideological Practice of Sociology," in *Catalyst* 8 (Winter):39-54.
1974b   "The Social Construction of Documentary Reality," in *Sociological Inquiry* 44(4):257-68.
1975   "What it Might Mean to Do a Canadian Sociology: The Everyday World as Problematic," *Canadian Journal of Sociology* 1(3):363-76.
1975   "Ideological Structures and How Women Are Excluded," in *The Canadian Review of Sociology and Anthropology* 12(4, November):353-69.
1975   "An Analysis of Ideological Structures and How Women Are Excluded: Considerations for Academic Women," in *Canadian Review of Sociology and Anthropology* 12(4):353-69.
1979   "A Sociology for Women," in Julia A. Sherman and Evelyn Torotn Beck, eds., *The Prism of Sex*. Madison, Wis.: University of Wisconsin Press, 135-88.
1979   "Using the Oppressor's Language," in *Resources for Feminist Research*, Special Publication no. 5 (Spring):10-18.

1983　"No One Commits Suicide: Textual Analysis of Ideological Practices," in *Human Studies* 6: 309-59.

1987　*The Everyday World as Problematic: A Feminist Sociology*. Toronto: University of Toronto Press.

1989　"Gender, Power and Peace," in Janice Williamson and Deborah Graham, eds., *Up and Doing: Canadian Women and Peace*. Toronto: Women's Press.

1990a　*The Conceptual Practices of Power: A Feminist Sociology of Knowledge*. Toronto: The University of Toronto Press.

1990b　*Texts, Facts, and Femininity: Exploring the Relations of Ruling*. London and New York: Routledge.

Solomon, David N.
1954　*Sociological Research in a Military Organization*. CJEPS 20:531-41.

Solway, Jacqueline, and Richard Lee
1990　"Foragers, Genuine or Spurious: Situating the Kalahari San in History," *Current Anthropology* 31:109-46.

Somerville, Mary
1982　"Education of a Woman of Science," in Janet Horowitz Murray, *Strong-minded Women and Other Lost Voices from 19th Century England*. New York: Pantheon Books.

Sorokin, P.A.
1956　*Contemporary Sociology Theories: Through the First Quarter of the Twentieth Century*. New York: Harper Torchbooks, 1956.

Spradley, James P. and Mann, B.J.
1975　*The Cocktail Waitress: Women's Work in a Man's World*. New York: John Wiley and Sons, Inc.

Statistics Canada
1990　*Nursing in Canada*. Cat. 82-003522

Statistics Canada
1990　*Women in Canada*. Second Edition. Cat. 89-503E

Stebbins, Robert A.
1990　*Sociology: The Study of Society*, 2nd edition. New York: Harper and Row.

Stephenson, Marylee, ed.
1973   *Women in Canada*. Toronto: New Press [Rev. ed.: 1977].

Stolzman, James and Gamberg, Herbert
1975   "The National Question and Canadian Sociology," in *Canadian Journal of Sociology* 1(1):91-106.

Straus, Murray A. and Radel, David J.
1969   "Eminence, Productivity, and Power of Sociologists in Various Regions," in *The American Sociologist* 4(1):1-4.

Sydie, R.A.
1987   *Natural Women, Cultured Men*. Toronto: Methuen.

Symons, Thomas H. B.
1975   *To Know Ourselves:* The Report of the Commission on Canadian Studies. Ottawa: Association of Universities and Colleges in Canada.

Symons, Thomas H.B. and Page, James E.
1984   *Some Questions of Balance:* Human Resources, Higher Education and Canadian Studies. Ottawa: Association of Universities and Colleges in Canada.

Tancred-Sheriff, Peta and de Vries, Peter J.
1986   *Report of the Sociology and Anthropology Editors to the Annual Meeting of the CRSA Editorial Board*, Winnipeg, June 3, 1986 (mimeo).

Teevan, J.J., ed.
1989   *Introduction to Sociology: A Canadian Focus*. 3d ed. Scarborough, Ont.: Prentice-Hall of Canada.

Tepperman, Lorne and Richardson, R. Jack, eds.
1986   *The Social World: An Introduction to Sociology*. Toronto: McGraw-Hill Ryerson.

Tibbets, P.
1977   "Feyerabend's `Against Method': The Case for Methodological Pluralism," in *Philosophy of Social Sciences* 7:265-75.

Tite, Rosonna with the assistance of Margaret Malone
1990   "Our Universities' Best Kept Secret: Women's Studies in Canada," in *Atlantis*, 16(1):25-39.

Tomm, Winnie, ed.
1987   *The Effects of Feminist Approaches on Research Methodologies.* Waterloo: Wilfrid Laurier University Press.

Trigger, Bruce
1985   *Natives and Newcomers: Canada's 'Heroic Age' Reconsidered.* Montreal: McGill-Queen's University Press.

Turner, D.H.
1985   *Life Before Genesis.* New York: Peter Lang.

Valverde, Mariana
1985   *Sex, Power and Pleasure.* Toronto: Women's Press.

Van Esterik, Penny
1983   "Confronting Advocacy Confronting Anthropology," in Robert Paine, ed., *Advocacy and Anthropology,* St. John's: Institute for Social and Economic Research (ISER).

Vandelac, Louise
1990   "Le profil des professeurs-es d'études féministes dans les universités canadiennes—ou au choix... Études feministes: le secret le mieux gardé des universités canadiennes," *Interface,* 1990.

Verney, Douglas V.
1975   "The Role of the Private Social Science Research Council of Canada in the Formation of Public Science Policy 1968-1974," *Canadian Public Policy / Analyse de Politiques* 1(1:Winter): 107-17.

Vesey, Laurence R.
1965   *The Emergence of the American University.* Chicago and London: University of Chicago Press.

von Zur Meulen, Max
1982   *A Profile of Full-Time University Teachers at Canadian Universities: A Statistical Review for the Eighties.* Statistics Canada.

Wadel, Cato
1969   *Marginal Adaptations and Modernization in Newfoundland: A Study of Strategies and Implications of Resettlement and Redevelopment of Outport Fishing Communities.* Institute for Social and Economic Research, Memorial University, St. John's, Nfld.

Walter, Richard
1968   *Student Politics in Argentina.* New York: Basic Books.

Warren, Carol
1988   *Gender Issues in Field Research.* Newbury Park: Sage.

Weaver, Sally M.
1972   "A Canadian Federation of Anthropological Sciences," in *CSAA Bulletin* No. 30, April.
1980   *Making Canadian Indian Policy: The Hidden Agenda, 1968-70.* Toronto: University of Toronto Press.

Weiler, Kathleen
1988   *Women Teaching For Change.* Massachusetts: Bergin and Garvey Publishers, Inc.

Weinstein, Michael A.
1985   *Culture Critique: Fernand Dumont and New Quebec Sociology.* Montreal: New World Perspectives.

Westhues, Kenneth, ed.
1987   *Basic Principles for Social Science in Our Time.* Waterloo: University of St. Jerome's College Press.

White, Hayden
1973   *Metahistory: The Historical Imagination in Nineteenth-Century Europe.* Baltimore: The Johns Hopkins University Press.

White, James D.
1984   *When Words Lose Their Meaning: Constitutions and Reconstitutions of Language, Character and Community.* Chicago: University of Chicago Press.

Whitehead, Tony L. and Conaway, Mary E.
1986   *Self, Sex and Gender in Cross-Cultural Fieldwork.* Chicago: University of Illinois.

Whyte, Donald R.
1982   "Sociology and the Nationalist Challenge in Canada," Carleton University, Department Working Paper 82-2.
1984   "Sociology and the Nationalist Challenge in Canada," *Journal of Canadian Studies*, 19(4): 106-29.

1989   *Sociology and the Constitution of Society: Canadian Experiences.* Working Paper, Department of Sociology / Anthropology. Ottawa: Carleton University.

Wilensky, Harold L.
1956   *Intellectuals in Labor Unions: Organizational Pressures on Professional Roles.* Glencoe: The Free Press.

Williams, Raymond
1981   *Culture.* Glasgow: Fontana.
1980   *Problems in Materialism and Culture.* London: Verso.

Williams, Susan and Neis, Barbara
1990   *Occupational Health in Newfoundland's Deepsea Fishing Industry: Stress and Repetitive Strain Injuries among Plantworkers; Accidents on Board Trawlers, Final Report.* St. John's: Institute for Social and Economic Research (ISER).

Wilson, Bertha
1990   "Battered Wife Syndrome Ruled Justified Defence," in *Toronto Star* (May 4).

Winch, P.
1958   *The Idea of Social Science and its Relation to Philosophy.* London: Routledge and Kegan Paul.

Women's Caucus. Minutes of meetings on file at offices of CSAA in Montreal.

Woodcock, George
1988   *A Social History of Canada.* Markham Penguin Books.

Woolf, Virginia
1929   *A Room of One's Own.* New York: Harcourt Brace.

Wright, Eric Olin
1978   "Intellectuals and the Class Structure of Capitalist Society," in Pat Walker, ed., *Between Labor and Capital.* Montreal: Black Rose Books, 191-213.

Yawney, Carole
1982   "To Grow a Daughter: Cultural Liberation and the Dynamics of Oppression in Jamaica," in Angela Miles and Geraldine Finn, eds., *Feminism in Canada. From Pressure to Politics.* Montreal: Black Rose Books, 1982, 119-44.

Contributors

HUGH ARMSTRONG is Associate Dean, School of Communication and General Studies, Centennial College.

PAT ARMSTRONG teaches in the Department of Sociology at York University.

JANET M.C. BURNS teaches in the Department of Sociology at the University of New Brunswick in Saint John.

A. MARGUERITE CASSIN teaches in the School of Public Administration at Dalhousie University in Halifax.

JANICE DRAKICH teaches in the Department of Sociology and Anthropology at the University of Windsor.

MARGRIT EICHLER teaches in the Department of Sociology in Education at the Ontario Institute for Studies in Education.

SYLVIA HALE teaches in the Department of Sociology, St. Thomas University in Fredericton.

JIM HARDING teaches at the School of Human Justice, University of Regina.

JOHN R. HOFLEY is Associate Dean of Arts and Professor of Sociology at the University of Winnipeg.

DAVID HOWES teaches in the Department of Anthropology at Concordia University in Montreal.

GORDON INGLIS teaches in the Department of Anthropology at Memorial University of Newfoundland.

FRANK E. JONES is Professor Emeritus of Sociology at McMaster University in Hamilton.

ELEANOR MATICKA-TYNDALE teaches in the Department of Psychiatry at the University of Calgary.

BRUCE McFARLANE teaches in the Department of Sociology and Anthropology at Carleton University in Ottawa.

J. GRAHAM MORGAN teaches in the Department of Sociology and Social Anthropology at Dalhousie University.

GALE MOORE holds a doctorate in sociology and is Book Selector at the Robarts Library, University of Toronto.

BARBARA NEIS teaches in the Department of Sociology at Memorial University of Newfoundland.

JANICE NEWSON teaches in the Department of Sociology at York University.

DAVID NOCK teaches in the Department of Sociology at Lakehead University in Thunder Bay.

CLAIRE POLSTER is a graduate student in the Department of Sociology at York University.

ESTER REITER teaches in the Department of Sociology at Brock University in St. Catharines.

GUY ROCHER teaches in the Faculté de droit at l'Université de Montréal.

DOROTHY E. SMITH teaches in the Department of Sociology in Education at and the Ontario Institute for Studies in Education.

DONALD WHYTE teaches in the Department of Sociology and Anthropology at Carleton University in Ottawa.

9067

BESU

Printed in Canada